Hadoop® FOR DUMMIES®

A Wiley Brand

by Dirk deRoos, Paul C. Zikopoulos, Bruce Brown,
Rafael Coss, and Roman B. Melnyk

FOR DUMMIES®

A Wiley Brand

Hadoop® For Dummies®

Published by: **John Wiley & Sons, Inc.,** 111 River Street, Hoboken, NJ 07030-5774, www.wiley.com

Copyright © 2014 by John Wiley & Sons, Inc., Hoboken, New Jersey

Published simultaneously in Canada

For general information on our other products and services, please contact our Customer Care Department within the U.S. at 877-762-2974, outside the U.S. at 317-572-3993, or fax 317-572-4002. For technical support, please visit www.wiley.com/techsupport.

Wiley publishes in a variety of print and electronic formats and by print-on-demand. Some material included with standard print versions of this book may not be included in e-books or in print-on-demand. If this book refers to media such as a CD or DVD that is not included in the version you purchased, you may download this material at http://booksupport.wiley.com. For more information about Wiley products, visit www.wiley.com.

Library of Congress Control Number: 2013954209

ISBN: 978-1-118-60755-8 (pbk); ISBN 978-1-118-65220-6 (ebk); ISBN 978-1-118-70503-2 (ebk)

Manufactured in the United States of America

10 9 8 7 6 5 4 3 2 1

Contents at a Glance

Table of Contents

Introduction

Welcome to *Hadoop for Dummies*! Hadoop is an exciting technology, and this book will help you cut through the hype and wrap your head around what it's good for and how it works. We've included examples and plenty of practical advice so you can get started with your own Hadoop cluster.

About this Book

In our own Hadoop learning activities, we're constantly struck by how little beginner-level content is available. For almost any topic, we see two things: high-level marketing blurbs with pretty pictures; and dense, low-level, narrowly focused descriptions. What are missing are solid entry-level explanations that add substance to the marketing fluff and help someone with little or no background knowledge bridge the gap to the more advanced material. Every chapter in this book was written with this goal in mind: to clearly explain the chapter's concept, explain why it's significant in the Hadoop universe, and show how you can get started with it.

No matter how much (or how little) you know about Hadoop, getting started with the technology is not exactly easy for a number of reasons. In addition to the lack of entry-level content, the rapid pace of change in the Hadoop eco-system makes it difficult to keep on top of standards. We find that most discussions on Hadoop either cover the older interfaces, and are never updated; or they cover the newer interfaces with little insight into how to bridge the gap from the old technology. In this book, we've taken care to describe the current interfaces, but we also discuss previous standards, which are still commonly used in environments where some of the older interfaces are entrenched.

Here are a few things to keep in mind as you read this book:

- Bold text means that you're meant to type the text just as it appears in the book. The exception is when you're working through a steps list: Because each step is bold, the text to type is not bold.

- Web addresses and programming code appear in monofont. If you're reading a digital version of this book on a device connected to the Internet, note that you can click the web address to visit that website, like this: www.dummies.com

Foolish Assumptions

We've written this book so that anyone with a basic understanding of computers and IT can learn about Hadoop. But that said, some experience with databases, programming, and working with Linux would be helpful.

There are some parts of this book that require deeper skills, like the Java coverage in Chapter 6 on MapReduce; but if you haven't programmed in Java before, don't worry. The explanations of how MapReduce works don't require you to be a Java programmer. The Java code is there for people who'll want to try writing their own MapReduce applications. In Part 3, a database background would certainly help you understand the significance of the various Hadoop components you can use to integrate with existing databases and work with relational data. But again, we've written in a lot of background to help provide context for the Hadoop concepts we're describing.

How This Book Is Organized

This book is composed of five parts, with each part telling a major chunk of the Hadoop story. Every part and every chapter was written to be a self-contained unit, so you can pick and choose whatever you want to concentrate on. Because many Hadoop concepts are intertwined, we've taken care to refer to whatever background concepts you might need so you can catch up from other chapters, if needed. To give you an idea of the book's layout, here are the parts of the book and what they're about:

Part I: Getting Started With Hadoop

As the beginning of the book, this part gives a rundown of Hadoop and its ecosystem and the most common ways Hadoop's being used. We also show you how you can set up your own Hadoop environment and run the example code we've included in this book.

Part II: How Hadoop Works

This is the meat of the book, with lots of coverage designed to help you understand the nuts and bolts of Hadoop. We explain the storage and processing architecture, and also how you can write your own applications.

Part III: Hadoop and Structured Data

How Hadoop deals with structured data is arguably the most important debate happening in the Hadoop community today. There are many competing SQL-on-Hadoop technologies, which we survey, but we also take a deep look at the more established Hadoop community projects dedicated to structured data: HBase, Hive, and Sqoop.

Part IV: Administering and Configuring Hadoop

When you're ready to get down to brass tacks and deploy a cluster, this part is a great starting point. Hadoop clusters sink or swim depending on how they're configured and deployed, and we've got loads of experience-based advice here.

Part V: The Part Of Tens: Getting More Out of Your Hadoop Cluster

To cap off the book, we've given you a list of additional places where you can bone up on your Hadoop skills. We've also provided you an additional set of reasons to adopt Hadoop, just in case you weren't convinced already.

Icons Used in This Book

The Tip icon marks tips (duh!) and shortcuts that you can use to make working with Hadoop easier.

Remember icons mark the information that's especially important to know. To siphon off the most important information in each chapter, just skim through these icons.

The Technical Stuff icon marks information of a highly technical nature that you can normally skip over.

The Warning icon tells you to watch out! It marks important information that may save you headaches.

Beyond the Book

We have written a lot of extra content that you won't find in this book. Go online to find the following:

✔ **The Cheat Sheet for this book is at**

www.dummies.com/cheatsheet/hadoop

Here you'll find quick references for useful Hadoop information we've brought together and keep up to date. For instance, a handy list of the most common Hadoop commands and their syntax, a map of the various Hadoop ecosystem components, and what they're good for, and listings of the various Hadoop distributions available in the market and their unique offerings. Since the Hadoop ecosystem is continually evolving, we've also got instructions on how to set up the *Hadoop for Dummies* environment with the newest production-ready versions of the Hadoop and its components.

✔ **Updates to this book, if we have any, are at**

www.dummies.com/extras/hadoop

✔ **Code samples used in this book are also at**

www.dummies.com/extras/hadoop

All the code samples in this book are posted to the website in Zip format; just download and unzip them and they're ready to use with the *Hadoop for Dummies* environment described in Chapter 3. The Zip files, which are named according to chapter, contain one or more files. Some files have application code (Java, Pig, and Hive) and others have series of commands or scripts. (Refer to the downloadable Read Me file for a detailed description of the files.) Note that not all chapters have associated code sample files.

Where to Go from Here

If you're starting from scratch with Hadoop, we recommend you start at the beginning and truck your way on through the whole book. But Hadoop does a lot of different things, so if you come to a chapter or section that covers an area you won't be using, feel free to skip it. Or if you're not a total newbie, you can bypass the parts you're familiar with. We wrote this book so that you can dive in anywhere.

If you're a selective reader and you just want to try out the examples in the book, we strongly recommend looking at Chapter 3. It's here that we describe how to set up your own Hadoop environment in a Virtual Machine (VM) that you can run on your own computer. All the examples and code samples were tested using this environment, and we've laid out all the steps you need to download, install, and configure Hadoop.

Part I

Getting Started
with Hadoop

In this part . . .

- ✔ See what makes Hadoop-sense — and what doesn't.
- ✔ Look at what Hadoop is doing to raise productivity in the real world.
- ✔ See what's involved in setting up a Hadoop environment
- ✔ Visit www.dummies.com for great Dummies content online.

Chapter 1

Introducing Hadoop and Seeing What It's Good For

- -

In This Chapter

▶ Seeing how Hadoop fills a need

▶ Digging (a bit) into Hadoop's history

▶ Getting Hadoop for yourself

▶ Looking at Hadoop application offerings

- -

*O*rganizations are flooded with data. Not only that, but in an era of incredibly cheap storage where everyone and everything are interconnected, the nature of the data we're collecting is also changing. For many businesses, their critical data used to be limited to their transactional databases and data warehouses. In these kinds of systems, data was organized into orderly rows and columns, where every byte of information was well understood in terms of its nature and its business value. These databases and warehouses are still extremely important, but businesses are now differentiating themselves by how they're finding value in the large volumes of data that are *not* stored in a tidy database.

The variety of data that's available now to organizations is incredible: Internally, you have website clickstream data, typed notes from call center operators, e-mail and instant messaging repositories; externally, open data initiatives from public and private entities have made massive troves of raw data available for analysis. The challenge here is that traditional tools are poorly equipped to deal with the scale and complexity of much of this data. That's where Hadoop comes in. It's tailor-made to deal with all sorts of messiness. CIOs everywhere have taken notice, and Hadoop is rapidly becoming an established platform in any serious IT department.

This chapter is a newcomer's welcome to the wonderful world of Hadoop — its design, capabilities, and uses. If you're new to big data, you'll also find important background information that applies to Hadoop and other solutions.

Big Data and the Need for Hadoop

Like many buzzwords, what people mean when they say "big data" is not always clear. This lack of clarity is made worse by IT people trying to attract attention to their own projects by labeling them as "big data," even though there's nothing big about them.

At its core, big data is simply a way of describing data problems that are unsolvable using traditional tools. To help understand the nature of big data problems, we like the "the three Vs of big data," which are a widely accepted characterization for the factors behind what makes a data challenge "big":

- **Volume:** High volumes of data ranging from dozens of terabytes, and even petabytes.

- **Variety:** Data that's organized in multiple structures, ranging from raw text (which, from a computer's perspective, has little or no discernible structure — many people call this *unstructured data*) to log files (commonly referred to as being *semistructured*) to data ordered in strongly typed rows and columns (*structured* data). To make things even more confusing, some data sets even include portions of all three kinds of data. (This is known as *multistructured* data.)

- **Velocity:** Data that enters your organization and has some kind of value for a limited window of time — a window that usually shuts well before the data has been transformed and loaded into a data warehouse for deeper analysis (for example, financial securities ticker data, which may reveal a buying opportunity, but only for a short while). The higher the volumes of data entering your organization per second, the bigger your velocity challenge.

Each of these criteria clearly poses its own, distinct challenge to someone wanting to analyze the information. As such, these three criteria are an easy way to assess big data problems and provide clarity to what has become a vague buzzword. The commonly held rule of thumb is that if your data storage and analysis work exhibits any of these three characteristics, chances are that you've got yourself a big data challenge.

Failed attempts at coolness: Naming technologies

The co-opting of the big data label reminds us when Java was first becoming popular in the early 1990s and every IT project had to have Java support or something to do with Java. At the same time, web site application development was becoming popular and Netscape named their scripting language "JavaScript," even though it had nothing to do with Java. To this day, people are confused by this shallow naming choice.

Origin of the "3 Vs"

In 2001, years before marketing people got ahold of the term "big data," the analyst firm META Group published a report titled *3-D Data Management: Controlling Data Volume, Velocity and Variety*. This paper was all about data warehousing challenges, and ways to use relational technologies to overcome them. So while the definitions of the 3Vs in this paper are quite different from the big data 3Vs, this paper does deserve a footnote in the history of big data, since it originated a catchy way to describe a problem.

As you'll see in this book, Hadoop is anything but a traditional information technology tool, and it is well suited to meet many big data challenges, especially (as you'll soon see) with high volumes of data and data with a variety of structures. But there are also big data challenges where Hadoop isn't well suited — in particular, analyzing high-velocity data the instant it enters an organization. Data velocity challenges involve the analysis of data while it's in motion, whereas Hadoop is tailored to analyze data when it's at rest. The lesson to draw from this is that although Hadoop is an important tool for big data analysis, it will by no means solve all your big data problems. Unlike some of the buzz and hype, the entire big data domain isn't synonymous with Hadoop.

Exploding data volumes

It is by now obvious that we live in an advanced state of the information age. Data is being generated and captured electronically by networked sensors at tremendous volumes, in ever-increasing velocities and in mind-boggling varieties. Devices such as mobile telephones, cameras, automobiles, televisions, and machines in industry and health care all contribute to the exploding data volumes that we see today. This data can be browsed, stored, and shared, but its greatest value remains largely untapped. That value lies in its potential to provide insight that can solve vexing business problems, open new markets, reduce costs, and improve the overall health of our societies.

In the early 2000s (we like to say "the oughties"), companies such as Yahoo! and Google were looking for a new approach to analyzing the huge amounts of data that their search engines were collecting. Hadoop is the result of that effort, representing an efficient and cost-effective way of reducing huge analytical challenges to small, manageable tasks.

Varying data structures

Structured data is characterized by a high degree of organization and is typically the kind of data you see in relational databases or spreadsheets. Because of its defined structure, it maps easily to one of the standard data types (or user-defined types that are based on those standard types). It can be searched using standard search algorithms and manipulated in well-defined ways.

Semistructured data (such as what you might see in log files) is a bit more difficult to understand than structured data. Normally, this kind of data is stored in the form of text files, where there is some degree of order — for example, tab-delimited files, where columns are separated by a tab character. So instead of being able to issue a database query for a certain column and knowing exactly what you're getting back, users typically need to explicitly assign data types to any data elements extracted from semistructured data sets.

Unstructured data has none of the advantages of having structure coded into a data set. (To be fair, the unstructured label is a bit strong — all data stored in a computer has some degree of structure. When it comes to so-called unstructured data, there's simply too little structure in order to make much sense of it.) Its analysis by way of more traditional approaches is difficult and costly at best, and logistically impossible at worst. Just imagine having many years' worth of notes typed by call center operators that describe customer observations. Without a robust set of text analytics tools, it would be extremely tedious to determine any interesting behavior patterns. Moreover, the sheer volume of data in many cases poses virtually insurmountable challenges to traditional data mining techniques, which, even when conditions are good, can handle only a fraction of the valuable data that's available.

A playground for data scientists

A *data scientist* is a computer scientist who loves data (lots of data) and the sublime challenge of figuring out ways to squeeze every drop of value out of that abundant data. A *data playground* is an enterprise store of many terabytes (or even petabytes) of data that data scientists can use to develop, test, and enhance their analytical "toys."

Now that you know what big data is all about, what it is, and why it's important, it's time to introduce Hadoop, the granddaddy of these nontraditional analytical toys. Understanding how this amazing platform for the analysis of big data came to be, and acquiring some basic principles about how it works, will help you to master the details we provide in the remainder of this book.

The Origin and Design of Hadoop

So what exactly is this thing with the funny name — Hadoop? At its core, Hadoop is a framework for storing data on large clusters of *commodity* hardware — everyday computer hardware that is affordable and easily available — and running applications against that data. A *cluster* is a group of interconnected computers (known as *nodes*) that can work together on the same problem. Using networks of affordable compute resources to acquire business insight is the key value proposition of Hadoop.

As for that name, Hadoop, don't look for any major significance there; it's simply the name that Doug Cutting's son gave to his stuffed elephant. (Doug Cutting is, of course, the co-creator of Hadoop.) The name is unique and easy to remember — characteristics that made it a great choice.

Hadoop consists of two main components: a distributed processing framework named MapReduce (which is now supported by a component called YARN, which we describe a little later) and a distributed file system known as the Hadoop distributed file system, or HDFS.

An application that is running on Hadoop gets its work divided among the nodes (machines) in the cluster, and HDFS stores the data that will be processed. A Hadoop cluster can span thousands of machines, where HDFS stores data, and MapReduce jobs do their processing near the data, which keeps I/O costs low. MapReduce is extremely flexible, and enables the development of a wide variety of applications.

As you might have surmised, a Hadoop cluster is a form of *compute cluster,* a type of cluster that's used mainly for computational purposes. In a compute cluster, many computers (*compute nodes*) can share computational workloads and take advantage of a very large aggregate bandwidth across the cluster. Hadoop clusters typically consist of a few *master nodes,* which control the storage and processing systems in Hadoop, and many *slave nodes,* which store all the cluster's data and is also where the data gets processed.

Distributed processing with MapReduce

MapReduce involves the processing of a sequence of operations on distributed data sets. The data consists of key-value pairs, and the computations have only two phases: a map phase and a reduce phase. User-defined MapReduce jobs run on the compute nodes in the cluster.

A look at the history books

Hadoop was originally intended to serve as the infrastructure for the Apache Nutch project, which started in 2002. Nutch, an open source web search engine, is a part of the Lucene project. What are these projects? Apache projects are created to develop open source software and are supported by the Apache Software Foundation (ASF), a nonprofit corporation made up of a decentralized community of developers. *Open source software,* which is usually developed in a public and collaborative way, is software whose source code is freely available to anyone for study, modification, and distribution.

Nutch needed an architecture that could scale to billions of web pages, and the needed architecture was inspired by the Google file system

(GFS), and would ultimately become HDFS. In 2004, Google published a paper that introduced MapReduce, and by the middle of 2005 Nutch was using both MapReduce and HDFS.

In early 2006, MapReduce and HDFS became part of the Lucene subproject named Hadoop, and by February 2008, the Yahoo! search index was being generated by a Hadoop cluster. By the beginning of 2008, Hadoop was a top-level project at Apache and was being used by many companies. In April 2008, Hadoop broke a world record by sorting a terabyte of data in 209 seconds, running on a 910-node cluster. By May 2009, Yahoo! was able to use Hadoop to sort 1 terabyte in 62 seconds!

Generally speaking, a MapReduce job runs as follows:

1. During the Map phase, input data is split into a large number of fragments, each of which is assigned to a map task.

2. These map tasks are distributed across the cluster.

3. Each map task processes the key-value pairs from its assigned fragment and produces a set of intermediate key-value pairs.

4. The intermediate data set is sorted by key, and the sorted data is partitioned into a number of fragments that matches the number of reduce tasks.

5. During the Reduce phase, each reduce task processes the data fragment that was assigned to it and produces an output key-value pair.

6. These reduce tasks are also distributed across the cluster and write their output to HDFS when finished.

The Hadoop MapReduce framework in earlier (pre-version 2) Hadoop releases has a single master service called a JobTracker and several slave services called TaskTrackers, one per node in the cluster. When you submit a MapReduce job to the JobTracker, the job is placed into a queue and then runs according to the scheduling rules defined by an administrator. As you might expect, the JobTracker manages the assignment of map-and-reduce tasks to the TaskTrackers.

With Hadoop 2, a new resource management system is in place called YARN (short for *Yet Another Resource Manager*). YARN provides generic scheduling and resource management services so that you can run more than just Map Reduce applications on your Hadoop cluster. The JobTracker/TaskTracker architecture could only run MapReduce.

We describe YARN and the JobTracker/TaskTracker architectures in Chapter 7.

HDFS also has a master/slave architecture:

- ✔ **Master service:** Called a *NameNode,* it controls access to data files.

- ✔ **Slave services:** Called *DataNodes,* they're distributed one per node in the cluster. DataNodes manage the storage that's associated with the nodes on which they run, serving client read and write requests, among other tasks.

For more information on HDFS, see Chapter 4.

Apache Hadoop ecosystem

This section introduces other open source components that are typically seen in a Hadoop deployment. Hadoop is more than MapReduce and HDFS: It's also a family of related projects (an ecosystem, really) for distributed computing and large-scale data processing. Most (but not all) of these projects are hosted by the Apache Software Foundation. Table 1-1 lists some of these projects.

Table 1-1	Related Hadoop Projects
Project Name	*Description*
Ambari	An integrated set of Hadoop administration tools for installing, monitoring, and maintaining a Hadoop cluster. Also included are tools to add or remove slave nodes.
Avro	A framework for the efficient *serialization* (a kind of transformation) of data into a compact binary format
Flume	A data flow service for the movement of large volumes of log data into Hadoop
HBase	A distributed columnar database that uses HDFS for its underlying storage. With HBase, you can store data in extremely large tables with variable column structures
HCatalog	A service for providing a relational view of data stored in Hadoop, including a standard approach for tabular data

(continued)

Table 1-1 *(continued)*

Project Name	Description
Hive	A distributed data warehouse for data that is stored in HDFS; also provides a query language that's based on SQL (HiveQL)
Hue	A Hadoop administration interface with handy GUI tools for browsing files, issuing Hive and Pig queries, and developing Oozie workflows
Mahout	A library of machine learning statistical algorithms that were implemented in MapReduce and can run natively on Hadoop
Oozie	A workflow management tool that can handle the scheduling and chaining together of Hadoop applications
Pig	A platform for the analysis of very large data sets that runs on HDFS and with an infrastructure layer consisting of a compiler that produces sequences of MapReduce programs and a language layer consisting of the query language named Pig Latin
Sqoop	A tool for efficiently moving large amounts of data between relational databases and HDFS
ZooKeeper	A simple interface to the centralized coordination of services (such as naming, configuration, and synchronization) used by distributed applications

The Hadoop ecosystem and its commercial distributions (see the "Comparing distributions" section, later in this chapter) continue to evolve, with new or improved technologies and tools emerging all the time.

Figure 1-1 shows the various Hadoop ecosystem projects and how they relate to one-another:

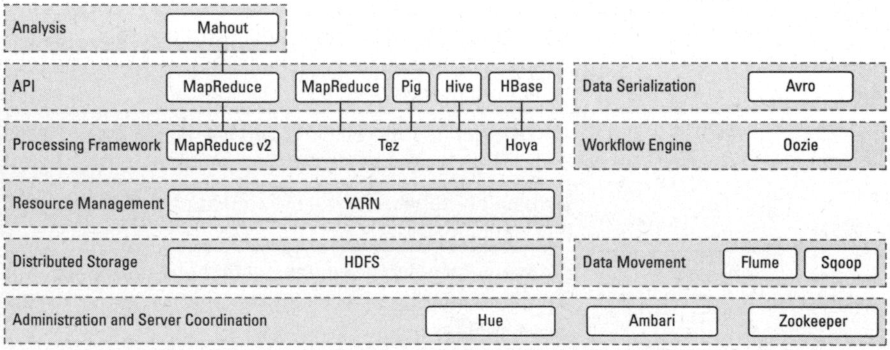

Figure 1-1: Hadoop ecosystem components.

Examining the Various Hadoop Offerings

Hadoop is available from either the Apache Software Foundation or from companies that offer their own Hadoop distributions.

Only products that are available directly from the Apache Software Foundation can be called Hadoop releases. Products from other companies can include the official Apache Hadoop release files, but products that are "forked" from (and represent modified or extended versions of) the Apache Hadoop source tree are not supported by the Apache Software Foundation.

Apache Hadoop has two important release series:

✔ **1.x:** At the time of writing, this release is the most stable version of Hadoop available (1.2.1).

Even after the 2.x release branch became available, this is still commonly found in production systems. All major Hadoop distributions include solutions for providing high availability for the NameNode service, which first appears in the 2.x release branch of Hadoop.

✔ **2.x:** At the time of writing, this is the current version of Apache Hadoop (2.2.0), including these features:

- *A MapReduce architecture, named MapReduce 2 or YARN (Yet Another Resource Negotiator):* It divides the two major functions of the JobTracker (resource management and job life-cycle management) into separate components.

- *HDFS availability and scalability:* The major limitation in Hadoop 1 was that the NameNode was a single point of failure. Hadoop 2 provides the ability for the NameNode service to fail over to an active standby NameNode. The NameNode is also enhanced to scale out to support clusters with very large numbers of files. In Hadoop 1, clusters could typically not expand beyond roughly 5000 nodes. By adding multiple active NameNode services, with each one responsible for managing specific partitions of data, you can scale out to a much greater degree.

Some descriptions around the versioning of Hadoop are confusing because both Hadoop 1.x and 2.x are at times referenced using different version numbers: Hadoop 1.0 is occasionally known as Hadoop 0.20.205, while Hadoop 2.x is sometimes referred to as Hadoop 0.23. As of December 2011, the Apache Hadoop project was deemed to be production-ready by the open source community, and the Hadoop 0.20.205 version number was officially changed to 1.0.0. Since then, legacy version numbering (below version 1.0) has persisted, partially because work on Hadoop 2.x was started well before the version numbering jump to 1.0 was made, and the Hadoop 0.23 branch was already created. Now that Hadoop 2.2.0 is production-ready, we're seeing the old numbering less and less, but it still surfaces every now and then.

Comparing distributions

You'll find that the Hadoop ecosystem has many component parts, all of which exist as their own Apache projects. (See the previous section for more about them.) Because Hadoop has grown considerably, and faces some significant further changes, different versions of these open source community components might not be fully compatible with other components. This poses considerable difficulties for people looking to get an independent start with Hadoop by downloading and compiling projects directly from Apache.

Red Hat is, for many people, the model of how to successfully make money in the open source software market. What Red Hat has done is to take Linux (an open source operating system), bundle all its required components, build a simple installer, and provide paid support to any customers. In the same way that Red Hat has provided a handy packaging for Linux, a number of companies have bundled Hadoop and some related technologies into their own Hadoop distributions. This list describes the more prominent ones:

early adopters of beta & alpha code

- **Cloudera (www.cloudera.com/):** Perhaps the best-known player in the field, Cloudera is able to claim Doug Cutting, Hadoop's co-founder, as its chief architect. Cloudera is seen by many people as the market leader in the Hadoop space because it released the first commercial Hadoop distribution and it is a highly active contributor of code to the Hadoop ecosystem.

  Cloudera Enterprise, a product positioned by Cloudera at the center of what it calls the "Enterprise Data Hub," includes the Cloudera Distribution for Hadoop (CDH), an open-source-based distribution of Hadoop and its related projects as well as its proprietary Cloudera Manager. Also included is a technical support subscription for the core components of CDH.

  Cloudera's primary business model has long been based on its ability to leverage its popular CDH distribution and provide paid services and support. In the fall of 2013, Cloudera formally announced that it is focusing on adding proprietary value-added components on top of open source Hadoop to act as a differentiator. Also, Cloudera has made it a common practice to accelerate the adoption of alpha- and beta-level open source code for the newer Hadoop releases. Its approach is to take components it deems to be mature and retrofit them into the existing production-ready open source libraries that are included in its distribution.

- **EMC (www.gopivotal.com):** Pivotal HD, the Apache Hadoop distribution from EMC, natively integrates EMC's massively parallel processing (MPP) database technology (formerly known as Greenplum, and now known as HAWQ) with Apache Hadoop. The result is a high-performance Hadoop distribution with true SQL processing for Hadoop. SQL-based queries and other business intelligence tools can be used to analyze data that is stored in HDFS.

✔ **Hortonworks (www.hortonworks.com):** Another major player in the Hadoop market, Hortonworks has the largest number of committers and code contributors for the Hadoop ecosystem components. (Committers are the gatekeepers of Apache projects and have the power to approve code changes.) Hortonworks is a spin-off from Yahoo!, which was the original corporate driver of the Hadoop project because it needed a large-scale platform to support its search engine business. Of all the Hadoop distribution vendors, Hortonworks is the most committed to the open source movement, based on the sheer volume of the development work it contributes to the community, and because all its development efforts are (eventually) folded into the open source codebase.

The Hortonworks business model is based on its ability to leverage its popular HDP distribution and provide paid services and support. However, it does not sell proprietary software. Rather, the company enthusiastically supports the idea of working within the open source community to develop solutions that address enterprise feature requirements (for example, faster query processing with Hive).

Hortonworks has forged a number of relationships with established companies in the data management industry: Teradata, Microsoft, Informatica, and SAS, for example. Though these companies don't have their own, in-house Hadoop offerings, they collaborate with Hortonworks to provide integrated Hadoop solutions with their own product sets.

The Hortonworks Hadoop offering is the Hortonworks Data Platform (HDP), which includes Hadoop as well as related tooling and projects. Also unlike Cloudera, Hortonworks releases only HDP versions with production-level code from the open source community.

✔ **IBM (www.ibm.com/software/data/infosphere/biginsights):** Big Blue offers a range of Hadoop offerings, with the focus around value added on top of the open source Hadoop stack:

InfoSphere BigInsights: This software-based offering includes a number of Apache Hadoop ecosystem projects, along with additional software to provide additional capability. The focus of InfoSphere BigInsights is on making Hadoop more readily consumable for businesses. As such, the proprietary enhancements are focused on standards-based SQL support, data security and governance, spreadsheet-style analysis for business users, text analytics, workload management, and the application development life cycle.

PureData System for Hadoop: This hardware- and software-based appliance is designed to reduce complexity, the time it takes to start analyzing data, as well as IT costs. It integrates InfoSphere BigInsights (Hadoop-based software), hardware, and storage into a single, easy-to-manage system.

✔ **Intel (`hadoop.intel.com`):** The Intel Distribution for Apache Hadoop (Intel Distribution) provides distributed processing and data management for enterprise applications that analyze big data. Key features include excellent performance with optimizations for Intel Xeon processors, Intel SSD storage, and Intel 10GbE networking; data security via encryption and decryption in HDFS, and role-based access control with cell-level granularity in HBase (you can control who's allowed to see what data down to the cell level, in other words); improved Hive query performance; support for statistical analysis with a connector for R, the popular open source statistical package; and analytical graphics through Intel Graph Builder.

It may come as a surprise to see Intel here among a list of software companies that have Hadoop distributions. The motivations for Intel are simple, though: Hadoop is a strategic platform, and it will require significant hardware investment, especially for larger deployments. Though much of the initial discussion around hardware reference architectures for Hadoop — the recommended patterns for deploying hardware for Hadoop clusters — have focused on commodity hardware, increasingly we are seeing use cases where more expensive hardware can provide significantly better value. It's with this situation in mind that Intel is keenly interested in Hadoop. It's in Intel's best interest to ensure that Hadoop is optimized for Intel hardware, on both the higher end and commodity lines.

The Intel Distribution comes with a management console designed to simplify the configuration, monitoring, tuning, and security of Hadoop deployments. This console includes automated configuration with Intel Active Tuner; simplified cluster management; comprehensive system monitoring and logging; and systematic health checking across clusters.

✔ **MapR (`www.mapr.com`):** For a complete distribution for Apache Hadoop and related projects that's independent of the Apache Software Foundation, look no further than MapR. Boasting no Java dependencies or reliance on the Linux file system, MapR is being promoted as the only Hadoop distribution that provides full data protection, no single points of failure, and significant ease-of-use advantages. Three MapR editions are available: M3, M5, and M7. The M3 Edition is free and available for unlimited production use; MapR M5 is an intermediate-level subscription software offering; and MapR M7 is a complete distribution for Apache Hadoop and HBase that includes Pig, Hive, Sqoop, and much more.

The MapR distribution for Hadoop is most well-known for its file system, which has a number of enhancements not included in HDFS, such as NFS access and POSIX compliance (long story short, this means you can mount the MapR file system like it's any other storage device in your Linux instance and interact with data stored in it with any standard file applications or commands), storage volumes for specialized management of data policies, and advanced data replication tools. MapR also ships a specialized version of HBase, which claims higher reliability, security, and performance than Apache HBase.

Working with in-database MapReduce

When MapReduce processing occurs on structured data in a relational database, the process is referred to as *in-database* MapReduce. One implementation of a hybrid technology that combines MapReduce and relational databases for the analysis of analytical workloads is HadoopDB, a research project that originated a few years ago at Yale University. HadoopDB was designed to be a free, highly scalable, open source, parallel database management system. Tests at Yale showed that HadoopDB could achieve the performance of parallel databases, but with the scalability, fault tolerance, and flexibility of Hadoop-based systems.

[handwritten: Hadoop DB. = Hadoop + Relational DB]

More recently, Oracle has developed an in-database Hadoop prototype that makes it possible to run Hadoop programs written in Java naturally from SQL. Users with an existing database infrastructure can avoid setting up a Hadoop cluster and can execute Hadoop jobs within their relational databases.

Looking at the Hadoop toolbox

A number of companies offer tools designed to help you get the most out of your Hadoop implementation. Here's a sampling:

- **Amazon (aws.amazon.com/ec2):** The Amazon Elastic MapReduce (Amazon EMR) web service enables you to easily process vast amounts of data by provisioning as much capacity as you need. Amazon EMR uses a hosted Hadoop framework running on the web-scale infrastructure of Amazon Elastic Compute Cloud (Amazon EC2) and Amazon Simple Storage Service (Amazon S3). Amazon EMR lets you analyze data without having to worry about setting up, managing, or tuning Hadoop clusters.

REMEMBER

Cloud-based deployments of Hadoop applications like those offered by Amazon EMR are somewhat different from on-premise deployments. You would follow these steps to deploy an application on Amazon EMR:

1. Script a job flow in your language of choice, including a SQL-like language such as Hive or Pig. *[handwritten: flow makes no sense]*

2. Upload your data and application to Amazon S3, which provides reliable storage for your data.

3. Log in to the AWS Management Console to start an Amazon EMR job flow by specifying the number and type of Amazon EC2 instances that you want, as well as the location of the data on Amazon S3.

4. Monitor the progress of your job flow, and then retrieve the output from Amazon S3 using the AWS management console, paying only for the resources that you consume.

Stop reading

Though Hadoop is an attractive platform for many kinds of workloads, it needs a significant hardware footprint, especially when your data approaches scales of hundreds of terabytes and beyond. This is where Amazon EMR is most practical: as a platform for short term, Hadoop-based analysis or for testing the viability of a Hadoop-based solution before committing to an investment in on-premise hardware.

✔ **Hadapt (www.hadapt.com):** Look for the product Adaptive Analytical Platform, which delivers an ANSI SQL compliant query engine to Hadoop. Hadapt enables interactive query processing on huge data sets (Hadapt Interactive Query), and the Hadapt Development Kit (HDK) lets you create advanced SQL analytic functions for marketing campaign analysis, full text search, customer sentiment analysis (seeing whether comments are happy or sad, for example), pattern matching, and predictive modeling. Hadapt uses Hadoop as the parallelization layer for query processing. Structured data is stored in relational databases, and unstructured data is stored in HDFS. Consolidating multistructured data into a single platform facilitates more efficient, richer analytics.

✔ **Karmasphere (www.karmasphere.com):** Karmasphere provides a collaborative work environment for the analysis of big data that includes an easy-to-use interface with self-service access. The environment enables you to create projects that other authorized users can access. You can use a personalized home page to manage projects, monitor activities, schedule queries, view results, and create visualizations. Karmasphere has self-service wizards that help you to quickly transform and analyze data. You can take advantage of SQL syntax highlighting and code completion features to ensure that only valid queries are submitted to the Hadoop cluster. And you can write SQL scripts that call ready-to-use analytic models, algorithms, and functions developed in MapReduce, SPSS, SAS, and other analytic languages. Karmasphere also provides an administrative console for system-wide management and configuration, user management, Hadoop connection management, database connection management, and analytics asset management.

✔ **WANdisco (www.wandisco.com):** The WANdisco Non-Stop NameNode solution enables multiple active NameNode servers to act as synchronized peers that simultaneously support client access for batch applications (using MapReduce) and real-time applications (using HBase). If one NameNode server fails, another server takes over automatically with no downtime. Also, WANdisco Hadoop Console is a comprehensive, easy-to-use management dashboard that lets you deploy, monitor, manage, and scale a Hadoop implementation

✔ **Zettaset (www.zettaset.com):** Its Orchestrator platform automates, accelerates, and simplifies Hadoop installation and cluster management. It is an independent management layer that sits on top of an Apache Hadoop distribution. As well as simplifying Hadoop deployment and cluster management, Orchestrator is designed to meet enterprise security, high availability, and performance requirements.

Chapter 2

Common Use Cases for Big Data in Hadoop

*B*y writing this book, we want to help our readers answer the questions "What is Hadoop?" and "How do I use Hadoop?" Before we delve too deeply into the answers to these questions, though, we want to get you excited about some of the tasks that Hadoop excels at. In other words, we want to provide answers to the eternal question "What should I use Hadoop for?" In this chapter, we cover some of the most popular use cases we've seen in the Hadoop space, but first we have a couple thoughts on how you can make your Hadoop project successful.

The Keys to Successfully Adopting Hadoop (Or, "Please, Can We Keep Him?")

We strongly encourage you *not* to go looking for a "science project" when you're getting started with Hadoop. By that, we mean that you shouldn't try to find an open-ended problem that, despite being interesting, has neither clearly defined milestones nor measurable business value. We've seen some shops set up nifty, 100-node Hadoop clusters, but all that effort did little or nothing to add value to their businesses (though its implementers still seemed proud of themselves). Businesses want to see value from their IT investments, and with Hadoop it may come in a variety of ways. For example, you may pursue a project whose goal is to create lower licensing and storage costs for warehouse data or to find insight from large-scale data analysis. The best way to request resources to fund interesting Hadoop projects is by working with your business's leaders. In any serious Hadoop project, you should start by teaming IT with business leaders from VPs on down to help solve your business's *pain points* — those problems (real or perceived) that loom large in everyone's mind.

Also examine the perspectives of people and processes that are adopting Hadoop in your organization. Hadoop deployments tend to be most successful when adopters make the effort to create a culture that's supportive of data science by fostering experimentation and data exploration. Quite simply, after you've created a Hadoop cluster, you still have work to do — you still need to enable people to experiment in a hands-on manner. Practically speaking, you should keep an eye on these three important goals:

- ✔ **Ensure that your business users and analysts have access to as much data as possible.** Of course, you still have to respect regulatory requirements for criteria such as data privacy.

- ✔ **Mandate that your Hadoop developers expose their logic so that results are accessible through standard tools in your organization.** The logic and any results must remain easily consumed and reusable.

- ✔ **Recognize the governance requirements for the data you plan to store in Hadoop.** Any data under governance control in a relational database management system (RDBMS) also needs to be under the same controls in Hadoop. After all, personally identifiable information has the same privacy requirements no matter where it's stored. Quite simply, you should ensure that you can pass a data audit for both RDBMS and Hadoop!

All the uses cases we cover in this chapter have Hadoop at their core, but it's when you combine it with the broader business and its repositories like databases and document stores that you can build a more complete picture of what's happening in your business. For example, social sentiment analysis performed in Hadoop might alert you to *what* people are saying, but do you know *why* they're saying it? This concept requires thinking beyond Hadoop and linking your company's systems of record (sales, for example) with its systems of engagement (like call center records — the data where you may draw the sentiment from).

Log Data Analysis

Log analysis is a common use case for an inaugural Hadoop project. Indeed, the earliest uses of Hadoop were for the large-scale analysis of *clickstream* logs — logs that record data about the web pages that people visit and in which order they visit them. We often refer to all the logs of data generated by your IT infrastructure as *data exhaust.* A log is a by-product of a functioning server, much like smoke coming from a working engine's exhaust pipe. Data exhaust has the connotation of pollution or waste, and many enterprises undoubtedly approach this kind of data with that thought in mind. Log data often grows quickly, and because of the high volumes produced, it can be tedious to analyze. And, the potential value of this data is often unclear. So the temptation in IT departments is to store this log data for as little time as reasonably possible. (After all, it costs money to retain data, and if there's no perceived business value, why store it?) But Hadoop changes the math: The cost of storing data is comparatively inexpensive, and Hadoop was originally developed especially for the large-scale batch processing of log data.

TIP

The log data analysis use case is a useful place to start your Hadoop journey because the chances are good that the data you work with is being deleted, or "dropped to the floor." We've worked with companies that consistently record a terabyte (TB) or more of customer web activity per week, only to discard the data with no analysis (which makes you wonder why they bothered to collect it). For getting started quickly, the data in this use case is likely easy to get and generally doesn't encompass the same issues you'll encounter if you start your Hadoop journey with other (governed) data.

When industry analysts discuss the rapidly increasing volumes of data that exist (4.1 exabytes as of 2014 — more than 4 million 1TB hard drives), log data accounts for much of this growth. And no wonder: Almost every aspect of life now results in the generation of data. A smartphone can generate hundreds of log entries per day for an active user, tracking not only voice, text, and data transfer but also geolocation data. Most households now have smart meters that log their electricity use. Newer cars have thousands of sensors that record aspects of their condition and use. Every click and mouse movement we make while browsing the Internet causes a cascade of log entries to be generated. Every time we buy something — even without using a credit card or debit card — systems record the activity in databases — and in logs. You can see some of the more common sources of log data: IT servers, web clickstreams, sensors, and transaction systems.

Every industry (as well as all the log types just described) have the huge potential for valuable analysis — especially when you can zero in on a specific kind of activity and then correlate your findings with another data set to provide context.

As an example, consider this typical web-based browsing and buying experience:

1. You surf the site, looking for items to buy.

2. You click to read descriptions of a product that catches your eye.

3. Eventually, you add an item to your shopping cart and proceed to the checkout (the buying action).

After seeing the cost of shipping, however, you decide that the item isn't worth the price and you close the browser window. Every click you've made — and then stopped making — has the potential to offer valuable insight to the company behind this e-commerce site.

In this example, assume that this business collects clickstream data (data about every mouse click and page view that a visitor "touches") with the aim of understanding how to better serve its customers. One common challenge among e-commerce businesses is to recognize the key factors behind abandoned shopping carts. When you perform deeper analysis on the clickstream data and examine user behavior on the site, patterns are bound to emerge.

Does your company know the answer to the seemingly simple question, "Are certain products abandoned more than others?" Or the answer to the question, "How much revenue can be recaptured if you decrease cart abandonment by 10 percent?" Figure 2-1 gives an example of the kind of reports you can show to your business leaders to seek their investment in your Hadoop cause.

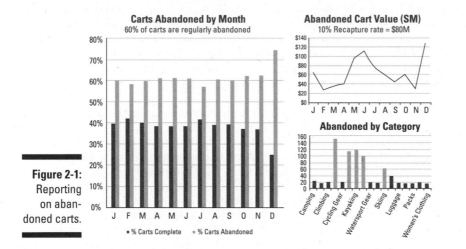

Figure 2-1: Reporting on abandoned carts.

To get to the point where you can generate the data to build the graphs shown in Figure 2-1, you isolate the web browsing sessions of individual users (a process known as *sessionization*), identify the contents of their shopping carts, and then establish the state of the transaction at the end of the session — all by examining the clickstream data.

In Figure 2-2, we give you an example of how to assemble users' web browsing sessions by grouping all clicks and URL addresses by IP address. (The example is a simple one in order to illustrate the point.) Remember: In a Hadoop context, you're always working with keys and values — each phase of MapReduce inputs and outputs data in sets of keys and values. (We discuss this in greater detail in Chapter 6.) In Figure 2-2, the key is the IP address, and the value consists of the timestamp and the URL. During the map phase, user sessions are assembled in parallel for all file blocks of the clickstream data set that's stored in your Hadoop cluster.

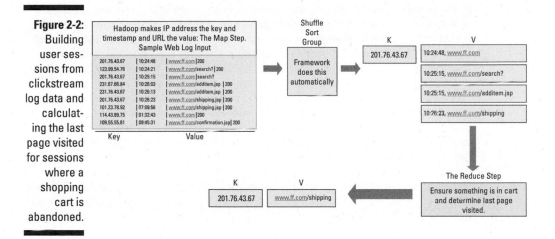

Figure 2-2: Building user sessions from clickstream log data and calculating the last page visited for sessions where a shopping cart is abandoned.

The map phase returns these elements:

- ✔ The final page that's visited
- ✔ A list of items in the shopping cart
- ✔ The state of the transaction for each user session (indexed by the IP address key)

The reducer picks up these records and performs aggregations to total the number and value of carts abandoned per month and to provide totals of the most common final pages that someone viewed before ending the user session.

This single example illustrates why Hadoop is a great fit for analyzing log data. The range of possibilities is limitless, and by leveraging some of the simpler interfaces such as Pig and Hive, basic log analysis makes for a simple initial Hadoop project.

Data Warehouse Modernization

Data warehouses are now under stress, trying to cope with increased demands on their finite resources. The rapid rise in the amount of data generated in the world has also affected data warehouses because the volumes of data they manage are increasing — partly because more *structured* data — the kind of data that is strongly typed and slotted into rows and columns — is generated but also because you often have to deal with regulatory requirements designed to maintain queryable access to historical data. In addition, the processing power in data warehouses is often used to perform transformations of the relational data as it either enters the warehouse itself or is loaded into a *child data mart* (a separate subset of the data warehouse) for a specific analytics application. In addition, the need is increasing for analysts to issue new queries against the structured data stored in warehouses, and these ad hoc queries can often use significant data processing resources. Sometimes a one-time report may suffice, and sometimes an exploratory analysis is necessary to find questions that haven't been asked yet that may yield significant business value. The bottom line is that data warehouses are often being used for purposes beyond their original design.

Hadoop can provide significant relief in this situation. Figure 2-3 shows, using high-level architecture, how Hadoop can live alongside data warehouses and fulfill some of the purposes that they aren't designed for.

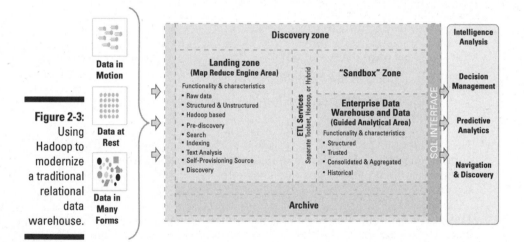

Figure 2-3:
Using Hadoop to modernize a traditional relational data warehouse.

Our view is that Hadoop is a warehouse *helper,* not a warehouse replacement. Later, in Chapter 11, we describe four ways that Hadoop can modernize a data warehousing ecosystem, here they are in summary:

✔ Provide a landing zone for all data.

✔ Persist the data to provide a queryable archive of cold data.

✔ Leverage Hadoop's large-scale batch processing efficiencies to preprocess and transform data for the warehouse.

✔ Enable an environment for ad hoc data discovery.

Fraud Detection

Fraud is a major concern across all industries. You name the industry
ing, insurance, government, health care, or retail, for example) and you'll find
fraud. At the same time, you'll find folks who are willing to invest an incredible
amount of time and money to try to prevent fraud. After all, if fraud were easy
to detect, there wouldn't be so much investment around it. In today's interconnected world, the sheer volume and complexity of transactions makes it
harder than ever to find fraud. What used to be called "finding a needle in a
haystack" has become the task of "finding a specific needle in stacks of nee-
dles." Though the sheer volume of transactions makes it harder to spot fraud
because of the volume of data, ironically, this same challenge can help create
better fraud predictive models — an area where Hadoop shines. (We tell you
more about statistical analysis in Chapter 9.)

Traditional approaches to fraud prevention aren't particularly efficient. For
example, the management of improper payments is often managed by analysts auditing what amounts to a very small sample of claims paired with
requesting medical documentation from targeted submitters. The industry
term for this model is pay and chase: Claims are accepted and paid out and
processes look for intentional or unintentional overpayments by way of post-
payment review of those claims. (The U.S. Internal Revenue Service (IRS)
operation uses the pay-and-chase approach on tax returns.)

Of course, you may wonder why businesses don't simply apply extra due dili-
gence to every transaction proactively. They don't do so because it's a balancing
act. Fraud detection can't focus only on stopping fraud when it happens, or
on detecting it quickly, because of the customer satisfaction component. For
example, traveling outside your home country and finding that your credit
card has been invalidated because the transactions originated from a geographical location that doesn't match your purchase patterns can place you in
a bad position, so vendors try to avoid false-positive results. They don't want
to anger clients by stopping transactions that seem suspicious but turn out to
be legitimate.

So how is fraud detection done now? Because of the limitations of traditional
technologies, fraud models are built by sampling data and using the sample
to build a set of fraud-prediction and -detection models. When you contrast
this model with a Hadoop-anchored fraud department that uses the full data
set — no sampling — to build out the models, you can see the difference.

The most common recurring theme you see across most Hadoop use cases is
that it assists business in breaking through the glass ceiling on the volume and
variety of data that can be incorporated into decision analytics. The more data
you have (and the more history you store), the better your models can be.

Mixing nontraditional forms of data with your set of historical transactions can make your fraud models even more robust. For example, if a worker makes a worker's compensation claim for a bad back from a slip-and-fall incident, having a pool of millions of patient outcome cases that detail treatment and length of recovery helps create a detection pattern for fraud.

As an example of how this model can work, imagine trying to find out whether patients in rural areas recover more slowly than those in urban areas. You can start by examining the proximity to physiotherapy services. Is there a pattern correlation between recovery times and geographical location? If your fraud department determines that a certain injury takes three weeks of recovery but that a farmer with the same diagnosis lives one hour from a physiotherapist and the office worker has a practitioner in her office, that's another variable to add to the fraud-detection pattern. When you harvest social network data for claimants and find a patient who claims to be suffering from whiplash is boasting about completing the rugged series of endurance events known as Tough Mudder, it's an example of mixing new kinds of data with traditional data forms to spot fraud.

If you want to kick your fraud-detection efforts into a higher gear, your organization can work to move away from market segment modeling and move toward at-transaction or at-person level modeling. Quite simply, making a forecast based on a segment is helpful, but making a decision based on particular information about an individual transaction is (obviously) better. To do this, you work up a larger set of data than is conventionally possible in the traditional approach. In our experiences with customers, we estimate that only (a maximum of) 30 percent of the available information that may be useful for fraud modeling is being used.

For creating fraud-detection models, Hadoop is well suited to

- **Handle volume:** That means processing the full data set — no data sampling.

- **Manage new varieties of data:** Examples are the inclusion of proximity-to-care-services and social circles to decorate the fraud model.

- **Maintain an agile environment:** Enable different kinds of analysis and changes to existing models.

Fraud modelers can add and test new variables to the model without having to make a proposal to your database administrator team and then wait a couple of weeks to approve a schema change and place it into their environment. This process is critical to fraud detection because dynamic environments commonly have cyclical fraud patterns that come and go in hours, days, or weeks. If the data used to identify or bolster new fraud-detection models isn't available at a moment's notice, by the time you discover these new patterns, it could be too late to prevent damage. Evaluate the benefit to your business of not only building out more comprehensive models with more types of data but also being able to refresh and enhance those models faster than ever. We'd bet that the company that can refresh and enhance models daily will fare better than those that do it quarterly.

You may believe that this problem has a simple answer — just ask your CIO for operational expenditure (OPEX) and capital expenditure (CAPEX) approvals to accommodate more data to make better models and load the other 70 percent of the data into your decision models. You may even believe that this investment will pay for itself with better fraud detection; however, the problem with this approach is the high up-front costs that need to be sunk into *unknown* data, where you don't know whether it contains any truly valuable insight. Sure, tripling the size of your data warehouse, for example, will give you more access to structured historical data to fine-tune your models, but they can't accommodate social media bursts. As we mention earlier in this chapter, traditional technologies aren't as agile, either. Hadoop makes it easy to introduce new variables into the model, and if they turn out not to yield improvements to the model, you can simply discard the data and move on.

Risk Modeling

Risk modeling is another major use case that's energized by Hadoop. We think you'll find that it closely matches the use case of fraud detection in that it's a model-based discipline. The more data you have and the more you can "connect the dots," the more often your results will yield better risk-prediction models.

The all-encompassing word *risk* can take on a lot of meanings. For example, customer churn prediction is the risk of a client moving to a competitor; the risk of a loan book relates to the risk of default; risk in health care spans the gamut from outbreak containment to food safety to the probability of reinfection and more.

The financial services sector (FSS) is now investing heavily in Hadoop-based risk modeling. This sector seeks to increase the automation and accuracy of its risk assessment and exposure modeling. Hadoop offers participants the opportunity to extend the data sets that are used in their risk models to include underutilized sources (or sources that are never utilized), such as e-mail, instant messaging, social media, and interactions with customer service representatives, among other data sources. Risk models in FSS pop up everywhere. They're used for customer churn prevention, trade manipulation modeling, corporate risk and exposure analytics, and more.

When a company issues an insurance policy against natural disasters at home, one challenge is clearly seeing how much money is potentially at risk. If the insurer fails to reserve money for possible payouts, regulators will intervene (the insurer doesn't want that); if the insurer puts too much money into its reserves to pay out future policy claims, they can't then invest your premium money and make a profit (the insurer doesn't want that, either). We know of companies that are "blind" to the risk they face because they have been unable to run an adequate amount of catastrophic simulations pertaining to variance in wind speed or precipitation rates (among other variables) as they relate to their exposure. Quite simply, these companies have difficulty stress-testing their risk models. The ability to fold in more data — for example, weather patterns or the ever-changing socioeconomic distribution of their client base — gives them a lot more insight and capability when it comes to building better risk models.

Building and stress-testing risk models like the one just described is an ideal task for Hadoop. These operations are often computationally expensive and, when you're building a risk model, likely impractical to run against a data warehouse, for these reasons:

✔ The warehouse probably isn't optimized for the kinds of queries issued by the risk model. (Hadoop isn't bound by the data models used in data warehouses.)

✔ A large, ad hoc batch job such as an evolving risk model would add load to the warehouse, influencing existing analytic applications. (Hadoop can assume this workload, freeing up the warehouse for regular business reporting.)

✔ More advanced risk models may need to factor in unstructured data, such as raw text. (Hadoop can handle that task efficiently.)

Social Sentiment Analysis

Social sentiment analysis is easily the most overhyped of the Hadoop use cases we present, which should be no surprise, given that we live in a world with a constantly connected and expressive population. This use case leverages content from forums, blogs, and other social media resources to develop a sense of what people are doing (for example, life events) and how they're reacting to the world around them (sentiment). Because text-based data doesn't naturally fit into a relational database, Hadoop is a practical place to explore and run analytics on this data.

Language is difficult to interpret, even for human beings at times — especially if you're reading text written by people in a social group that's different from your own. This group of people may be speaking your language, but their expressions and style are completely foreign, so you have no idea whether they're talking about a good experience or a bad one. For example, if you hear the word *bomb* in reference to a movie, it might mean that the movie was bad (or good, if you're part of the youth movement that interprets "It's da bomb" as a compliment); of course, if you're in the airline security business, the word *bomb* has quite a different meaning. The point is that language is used in many variable ways and is constantly evolving.

Social sentiment analysis is, in reality, text analysis

Though this section focuses on the "fun" aspects of using social media, the ability to extract understanding and meaning from unstructured text is an important use case. For example, corporate earnings are published to the web, and the same techniques that you use to build social sentiment extractors may be used to try to extract meaning from financial disclosures or to auto-assemble intrasegment earnings reports that compare the services revenue in a specific sector. In fact, some hedge fund management teams are now doing this to try to get a leg up on their competition.

Perhaps your entertainment company wants to crack down on violations of intellectual property on your event's video footage. You can use the same techniques outlined in this use case to extract textual clues from various web postings and teasers such as *Watch for free* or *Free on your PC*. You can use a library of custom-built text extractors (built and refined on data stored in Hadoop) to crawl the web to generate a list of links to pirated video feeds of your company's content.

These two examples don't demonstrate sentiment analysis; however, they do a good job of illustrating how social text analytics doesn't focus only on sentiment, despite the fun in illustrating the text analytics domain using sentiment analysis.

When you analyze sentiment on social media, you can choose from multiple approaches. The basic method programmatically parses the text, extracts strings, and applies rules. In simple situations, this approach is reasonable. But as requirements evolve and rules become more complex, manually coding text-extractions quickly becomes no longer feasible from the perspective of code maintenance, especially for performance optimization. Grammar- and rules-based approaches to text processing are computationally expensive, which is an important consideration in large-scale extraction in Hadoop. The more involved the rules (which is inevitable for complex purposes such as sentiment extraction), the more processing that's needed.

Alternatively, a statistics-based approach is becoming increasingly common for sentiment analysis. Rather than manually write complex rules, you can use the classification-oriented machine-learning models in Apache Mahout. (See Chapter 9 for more on these models.) The catch here is that you'll need to train your models with examples of positive and negative sentiment. The more training data you provide (for example, text from tweets and your classification), the more accurate your results.

Like the other use cases in this chapter, the one for social sentiment analysis can be applied across a wide range of industries. For example, consider food safety: Trying to predict or identify the outbreak of foodborne illnesses as quickly as possible is extremely important to health officials. Figure 2-4 shows a Hadoop-anchored application that ingests tweets using extractors based on the potential illness: FLU or FOOD POISONING. (We've anonymized the tweets so that you don't send a message asking how they're doing; we didn't clean up the grammar, either.)

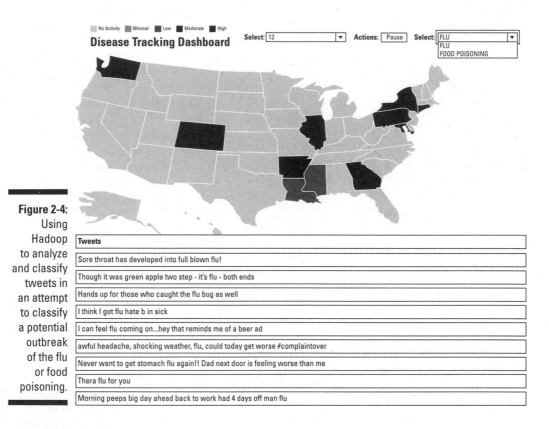

Figure 2-4: Using Hadoop to analyze and classify tweets in an attempt to classify a potential outbreak of the flu or food poisoning.

Do you see the generated heat map that shows the geographical location of the tweets? One characteristic of data in a world of big data is that most of it is *spatially enriched:* It has locality information (and temporal attributes, too). In this case, we reverse-engineered the Twitter profile by looking up the published location. As it turns out, lots of Twitter accounts have geographic locations as part of their public profiles (as well as disclaimers clearly stating that their thoughts are their own as opposed to speaking for their employers).

How good of a prediction engine can social media be for the outbreak of the flu or a food poisoning incident? Consider the anonymized sample data shown in Figure 2-5.

You can see that social media signals trumped all other indicators for predicting a flu outbreak in a specific U.S. county during the late summer and into early fall.

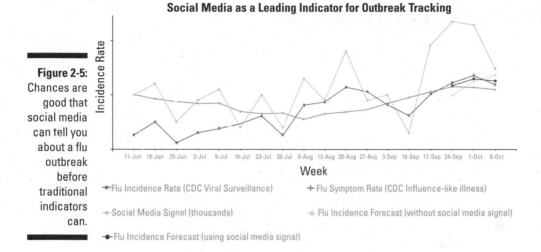

Figure 2-5:
Chances are
good that
social media
can tell you
about a flu
outbreak
before
traditional
indicators
can.

This example shows another benefit that accrues from analyzing social media: It gives you an unprecedented opportunity to look at attribute information in posters' profiles. Granted, what people say about themselves in their Twitter profiles is often incomplete (for example, the location code isn't filled in) or not meaningful (the location code might say *cloud nine*). But you can learn a lot about people over time, based on what they say. For example, a client may have *tweeted* (posted on Twitter) the announcement of the birth of her baby, an Instagram picture of her latest painting, or a Facebook posting stating that she can't believe Walter White's behavior in last night's *Breaking Bad* finale. (Now that many people watch TV series in their entirety, even long after they've ended, we wouldn't want to spoil the ending for you.) In this ubiquitous example, your company can extract a life event that populates a family-graph (a new child is a valuable update for a person-based Master Data Management profile), a hobby (painting), and an interest attribute (you love the show *Breaking Bad*). By analyzing social data in this way, you have the opportunity to flesh out personal attributes with information such as hobbies, birthdays, life events, geographical locations (country, state, and city, for example), employer, gender, marital status, and more.

Assume for a minute that you're the CIO of an airline. You can use the postings of happy or angry frequent travelers to not only ascertain sentiment but also round out customer profiles for your loyalty program using social media information. Imagine how much better you could target potential customers with the information that was just shared — for example, an e-mail telling the client that Season 5 of *Breaking Bad* is now available on the plane's media system or announcing that children under the age of two fly for free. It's also a good example of how systems of record (say, sales or subscription databases) can meet systems of engagement (say, support channels). Though the loyalty members' redemption and travel history is in a relational database, the system of engagement can update records (for example, a HAS_KIDS column).

Image Classification

Image classification starts with the notion that you build a training set and that computers learn to identify and classify what they're looking at. In the same way that having more data helps build better fraud detection and risk models, it also helps systems to better classify images. This requires a significant amount of data processing resources, however, which has limited the scale of deployments. Image classification is a hot topic in the Hadoop world because no mainstream technology was capable — until Hadoop came along — of opening doors for this kind of expensive processing on such a massive and efficient scale.

In this use case, the data is referred to as the training set as well as the models are classifiers. *Classifiers* recognize features or patterns within sound, image, or video and classify them appropriately. Classifiers are built and iteratively refined from training sets so that their precision scores (a measure of exactness) and recall scores (a measure of coverage) are high. Hadoop is well suited for image classification because it provides a massively parallel processing environment to not only create classifier models (iterating over training sets) but also provide nearly limitless scalability to process and run those classifiers across massive sets of unstructured data volumes. Consider multimedia sources such as YouTube, Facebook, Instagram, and Flickr — all are sources of unstructured binary data. Figure 2-6 shows one way you can use Hadoop to scale the processing of large volumes of stored images and video for multimedia semantic classification.

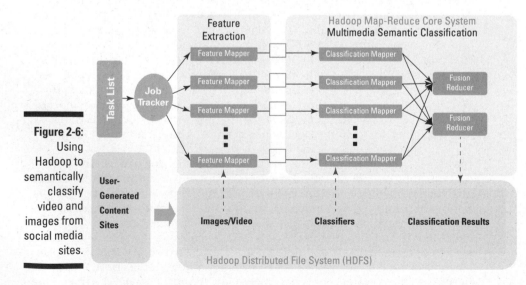

Figure 2-6: Using Hadoop to semantically classify video and images from social media sites.

In Figure 2-6, you can see how all the concepts relating to the Hadoop processing framework that are outlined in this book are applied to this data. Notice how images are loaded into HDFS. The classifier models, built over time, are now applied to the extra image-feature components in the Map phase of this solution. As you can see in the lower-right corner of Figure 2-6, the output of this processing consists of image classifications that range from cartoons to sports and locations, among others.

Though this section focuses on image analysis, Hadoop can be used for audio or voice analytics, too. One security industry client we work with creates an audio classification system to classify sounds that are heard via acoustic-enriched fiber optic cables laid around the perimeter of nuclear reactors. For example, this system knows how to nearly instantaneously classify the whisper of the wind as compared to the whisper of a human voice or to distinguish the sound of human footsteps running in the perimeter parklands from that of wildlife.

We realize that this description may have sort of a *Star Trek* feel to it, but you can now see live examples. In fact, IBM makes public one of the largest image-classification systems in the world, via the IBM Multimedia Analysis and Retrieval System (IMARS). Try it for yourself at

```
http://researcher.watson.ibm.com/researcher/view_project.
        php?id=877
```

Figure 2-7 shows the result of an IMARS search for the term *alpine skiing*. At the top of the figure, you can see the results of the classifiers mapped to the image set that was processed by Hadoop, along with an associated tag cloud. Note the more coarsely defined parent classifier `Wintersports`, as opposed to the more granular `Sailing`. In fact, notice the multiple classification tiers: `Alpine_Skiing` rolls into `Snow_Sports`, which rolls into `Wintersports` — all generated automatically by the classifier model, built and scored using Hadoop.

Figure 2-7:
The result of an IMARS search.

None of these pictures has any added metadata. No one has opened iPhoto and tagged an image as a winter sport to make it show up in this classification. It's the winter sport classifier that was built to recognize image attributes and characteristics of sports that are played in a winter setting.

Image classification has many applications, and being able to perform this classification at a massive scale using Hadoop opens up more possibilities for analysis as other applications can use the classification information generated for the images. To see what we mean, look at this example from the health industry. We worked with a large health agency in Asia that was focused on delivering health care via mobile clinics to a rural population distributed across a large land mass. A significant problem that the agency faced was the logistical challenge of analyzing the medical imaging data that was generated in its mobile clinics. A radiologist is a scarce resource in this part of the world, so it made sense to electronically transmit the medical images to a central point and have an army of doctors examine them. The doctors examining the images were quickly overloaded, however. The agency is now working on a classification system to help identify possible conditions to effectively provide suggestions for the doctors to verify. Early testing has shown this strategy to help reduce the number of missed or inaccurate diagnoses, saving time, money, and — most of all — lives.

Graph Analysis

Elsewhere in this chapter, we talk about log data, relational data, text data, and binary data, but you'll soon hear about another form of information: graph data. In its simplest form, a graph is simply a collection of nodes (an entity, for example — a person, a department, or a company), and the lines connecting them are edges (this represents a relationship between two entities, for example two people who know each other). What makes graphs interesting is that they can be used to represent concepts such as relationships in a much more efficient way than, say, a relational database. Social media is an application that immediately comes to mind — indeed, today's leading social networks (Facebook, Twitter, LinkedIn, and Pinterest) are all making heavy use of graph stores and processing engines to map the connections and relationships between their subscribers.

In Chapter 11, we discuss the NoSQL movement, and the graph database is one major category of alternative data-storage technologies. Initially, the predominant graph store was Neo4j, an open source graph database. But now the use of Apache Giraph, a graph processing engine designed to work in Hadoop, is increasing rapidly. Using YARN, we expect Giraph adoption to increase even more because graph processing is no longer tied to the traditional MapReduce model, which was inefficient for this purpose. Facebook is reportedly the world's largest Giraph shop, with a massive *trillion-edge* graph. (It's the Six Degrees of Kevin Bacon game on steroids.)

Graphs can represent any kind of relationship — not just people. One of the most common applications for graph processing now is mapping the Internet. When you think about it, a graph is the perfect way to store this kind of data, because the web itself is essentially a graph, where its websites are nodes and the hyperlinks between them are edges. Most PageRank algorithms use a form of graph processing to calculate the weightings of each page, which is a function of how many other pages point to it.

To Infinity and Beyond

This chapter easily could have been expanded into an entire book — there are that many places where Hadoop is a game changer. Before you apply one of the use cases from this chapter to your own first project and start seeing how to use Hadoop in Chapter 3, we want to reiterate some repeating patterns that we've noticed when organizations start taking advantage of the potential value of Hadoop:

- ✔ When you use more data, you can make better decisions and predictions and guide better outcomes.

- ✔ In cases where you need to retain data for regulatory purposes and provide a level of query access, Hadoop is a cost-effective solution.

- ✔ The more a business depends on new and valuable analytics that are discovered in Hadoop, the more it wants. When you initiate successful Hadoop projects, your clusters will find new purposes and grow!

Chapter 3

Setting Up Your Hadoop Environment

In This Chapter

▶ Deciding on a Hadoop distribution

▶ Checking out the *Hadoop For Dummies* environment

▶ Creating your first Hadoop program: Hello Hadoop!

This chapter is an overview of the steps involved in actually getting started with Hadoop. We start with some of the things you need to consider when deciding which Hadoop distribution to use. It turns out that you have quite a few distributions to choose from, and any of them will make it easier for you to set up your Hadoop environment than if you were to go it alone, assembling the various components that make up the Hadoop ecosystem and then getting them to "play nice with one another." Nevertheless, the various distributions that are available *do* differ in the features that they offer, and the trick is to figure out which one is best for you.

This chapter also introduces you to the *Hadoop For Dummies* environment that we used to create and test all examples in this book. (If you're curious, we based our environment on Apache Bigtop.)

We round out this chapter with information you can use to create your first MapReduce program, after your Hadoop cluster is installed and running.

Choosing a Hadoop Distribution

Commercial Hadoop distributions offer various combinations of open source components from the Apache Software Foundation and elsewhere — the idea is that the various components have been integrated into a single product, saving you the effort of having to assemble your own set of integrated components. In addition to open source software, vendors typically offer proprietary software, support, consulting services, and training.

How do you go about choosing a Hadoop distribution from the numerous options that are available? We provide an overview in Chapter 1 of the more prominent distributions, but when it comes to setting up your own environment, you're the one who has to choose, and that choice should be based on a set of criteria designed to help you make the best decision possible.

Not all Hadoop distributions have the same components (although they all have Hadoop's core capabilities), and not all components in one particular distribution are compatible with other distributions.

The criteria for selecting the most appropriate distribution can be articulated as this set of important questions:

✔ What do you want to achieve with Hadoop?

✔ How can you use Hadoop to gain business insight?

✔ What business problems do you want to solve?

✔ What data will be analyzed?

✔ Are you willing to use proprietary components, or do you prefer open source offerings?

✔ Is the Hadoop infrastructure that you're considering flexible enough for all your use cases?

✔ What existing tools will you want to integrate with Hadoop?

✔ Do your administrators need management tools? (Hadoop's core distribution doesn't include administrative tools.)

✔ Will the offering you choose allow you to move to a different product without obstacles such as vendor lock-in? (Application code that's not transferrable to other distributions or data stored in proprietary formats represent good examples of lock-in.)

✔ Will the distribution you're considering meet your future needs, insofar as you're able to anticipate those needs?

One approach to comparing distributions is to create a *feature matrix* — a table that details the specifications and features of each distribution you're considering. Your choice can then depend on the set of features and specs that best addresses the requirements around your specific business problems.

On the other hand, if your requirements include prototyping and experimentation, choosing the latest official Apache Hadoop distribution might prove to be the best approach. The most recent releases certainly have the newest most exciting features, but if you want stability you don't want excitement. For stability, look for an older release branch that's been available long enough to have some incremental releases (these typically include bug fixes and minor features).

Whenever you think about open source Hadoop distributions, give a moment's thought (or perhaps many moments' thought) to the concept of *open source fidelity* — the degree to which a particular distribution is compatible with the open source components on which it depends. High fidelity facilitates integration with other products that are designed to be compatible with those open source components. Low fidelity? Not so much.

The open source approach to software development itself is an important part of your Hadoop plans because it promotes compatibility with a host of third-party tools that you can leverage in your own Hadoop deployment. The open source approach also enables engagement with the Apache Hadoop community, which gives you, in turn, the opportunity to tap into a deeper pool of skills and innovation to enrich your Hadoop experience.

Because Hadoop is a fast-growing ecosystem, some parts continue to mature as the community develops tooling to meet industry demands. One aspect of this evolution is known as *backporting*, where you apply a new software modification or patch to a version of the software that's older than the version to which the patch is applicable. An example is NameNode failover: This capability is a part of Hadoop 2 but was backported (in its beta form) by a number of distributions into their Hadoop-1-based offerings for as much as a year before Hadoop 2 became generally available.

Not every distribution engages actively in backporting new content to the same degree, although most do it for items such as bug fixes. If you want a production license for bleeding-edge technology, this is certainly an option; for stability, however, it's not a good idea.

The majority of Hadoop distributions include proprietary code of some kind, which frequently comes in the form of installers and a set of management tools. These distributions usually emerge from different business models. For example, one business model can be summarized this way: "Establish yourself as an open source leader and pioneer, market your company as having the best expertise, and sell that expertise as a service." Red Hat, Inc. is an example of a vendor that uses this model. In contrast to this approach, the embrace-and-extend business model has vendors building capabilities that extend the capabilities of open source software. MapR and IBM, which both offer alternative file systems to the Hadoop Distributed File System (HDFS), are good examples.

People sometimes mistakenly throw the "fork" label at these innovations, making use of jargon used by software programmers to describe situations where someone takes a copy of an open source program as the starting point for their own (independent) development. The alternative file systems offered by MapR and IBM are completely different file systems, not a fork of the open source HDFS. Both companies enable their customers to choose either their proprietary distributed file system or HDFS. Nevertheless, in this approach, compatibility is critical, and the vendor must stay up to date with evolving interfaces. Customers need to know that vendors can be relied on to support their extensions.

Choosing a Hadoop Cluster Architecture

Hadoop is designed to be deployed on a large cluster of networked computers, featuring master nodes (which host the services that control Hadoop's storage and processing) and slave nodes (where the data is stored and processed). You can, however, run Hadoop on a single computer, which is a great way to learn the basics of Hadoop by experimenting in a controlled space.

Hadoop has two deployment modes: pseudo-distributed mode and fully distributed mode, both of which are described below.

Pseudo-distributed mode (single node)

A single-node Hadoop deployment is referred to as running Hadoop in *pseudo-distributed* mode, where all the Hadoop services, including the master and slave services, all run on a single compute node. This kind of deployment is useful for quickly testing applications while you're developing them without having to worry about using Hadoop cluster resources someone else might need. It's also a convenient way to experiment with Hadoop, as most of us don't have clusters of computers at our disposal. With this in mind, the *Hadoop for Dummies* environment is designed to work in pseudo-distributed mode.

Fully distributed mode (a cluster of nodes)

A Hadoop deployment where the Hadoop master and slave services run on a cluster of computers is running in what's known as *fully distributed mode*. This is an appropriate mode for production clusters and development clusters. A further distinction can be made here: a *development cluster* usually has a small number of nodes and is used to prototype the workloads that will eventually run on a *production cluster*.

Chapter 16 provides extensive guidance on the hardware requirements for fully distributed Hadoop clusters with special considerations for both master and slave nodes as they have different requirements.

The Hadoop For Dummies Environment

To help you get started with Hadoop, we're providing instructions on how to quickly download and set up Hadoop on your own laptop computer. As we mention earlier in the chapter, your cluster will be running in pseudo-distributed mode on a virtual machine, so you won't need special hardware.

A *virtual machine* (VM) is a simulated computer that you can run on a real computer. For example, you can run a program on your laptop that "plays" a VM, which opens a window that looks like it's running another computer. In effect, a pretend computer is running inside your real computer.

We'll be downloading a VM, and while running it, we'll install Hadoop.

As you make your way through this book, enhance your learning by trying the examples and experimenting on your own!

The Hadoop For Dummies distribution: Apache Bigtop

We've done our best to provide a vendor-agnostic view of Hadoop with this book. It's with this in mind that we built the *Hadoop For Dummies* environment using Apache Bigtop, a great alternative if you want to assemble your own Hadoop components. Bigtop gathers the core Hadoop components for you and ensures that your configuration works. Apache Bigtop is a 100 percent open source distribution.

The primary goal of Bigtop — itself an Apache project, just like Hadoop — is to build a community around the packaging, deployment, and integration of projects in the Apache Hadoop ecosystem. The focus is on the system as a whole rather than on individual projects.

Using Bigtop, you can easily install and deploy Hadoop components without having to track them down in a specific distribution and match them with a specific Hadoop version. As new versions of Hadoop components are released, they sometimes do not work with the newest releases of other projects. If you're on your own, significant testing is required. With Bigtop (or a commercial Hadoop release) you can trust that Hadoop experts have done this testing for you. To give you an idea of how expansive Bigtop has gotten, see the following list of all the components included in Bigtop:

- ✔ Apache Crunch
- ✔ Apache Flume
- ✔ Apache Giraph
- ✔ Apache HBase
- ✔ Apache HCatalog
- ✔ Apache Hive
- ✔ Apache Mahout
- ✔ Apache Oozie

- Apache Pig
- Apache Solr
- Apache Sqoop
- Apache Whirr
- Apache Zookeeper
- Cloudera Hue
- LinkedIn DataFu

This collection of Hadoop ecosystem projects is about as expansive as it gets, as both major and minor projects are included. See Chapter 1 for summary descriptions of the more prominent projects.

Apache Bigtop is continuously evolving, so the list that's presented here was current at the time of writing. For the latest release information about Bigtop, visit `http://blogs.apache.org/bigtop`.

Setting up the Hadoop For Dummies environment

This section describes all the steps involved in creating your own *Hadoop For Dummies* working environment. If you're comfortable working with VMs and Linux, feel free to install Bigtop on a different VM than what we recommend. If you're really bold and have the hardware, go ahead and try installing Bigtop on a cluster of machines in fully distributed mode!

Step 1: Downloading a VM

Hadoop runs on all popular Linux distributions, so we need a Linux VM. There is a freely available (and legal!) CentOS 6 image available here:

`http://sourceforge.net/projects/centos-6-vmware`

You will need a 64-bit operating system on your laptop in order to run this VM. Hadoop needs a 64-bit environment.

After you've downloaded the VM, extract it from the downloaded Zip file into the destination directory. Do ensure you have around 50GB of space available as Hadoop and your sample data will need it.

If you don't already have a VM player, you can download one for free from here:

`https://www.vmware.com/go/downloadplayer`

After you have your VM player set up, open the player, go to File⇨Open, then go to the directory where you extracted your Linux VM. Look for a file called `centos-6.2-x64-virtual-machine-org.vmx` and select it. You'll see information on how many processors and how much memory it will use. Find out how much memory your computer has, and allocate half of it for the VM to use. Hadoop needs lots of memory.

Once you're ready, click the Play button, and your Linux instance will start up. You'll see lots of messages fly by as Linux is booting and you'll come to a login screen. The user name is already set to "Tom." Specify the password as "tomtom" and log in.

Step 2: Downloading Bigtop

From within your Linux VM, right-click on the screen and select Open in Terminal from the contextual menu that appears. This opens a Linux terminal, where you can run commands. Click inside the terminal so you can see the cursor blinking and enter the following command:

```
su -
```

You'll be asked for your password, so type "tomtom" like you did earlier. This command switches the user to root, which is the master account for a Linux computer — we'll need this in order to install Hadoop.

With your root access (don't let the power get to your head), run the following command:

```
wget -O /etc/yum.repos.d/bigtop.repo \
    http://www.apache.org/dist/bigtop/bigtop-0.7.0/repos/centos6/bigtop.repo
```

The `wget` command is essentially a web request, which requests a specific file in the URL we can see and writes it to a specific path — in our case, that's `/etc/yum.repos.d/bigtop.repo`.

Step 3: Installing Bigtop

The geniuses behind Linux have made life quite easy for people like us who need to install big software packages like Hadoop. What we downloaded in the last step wasn't the entire Bigtop package and all its dependencies. It was just a *repository file* (with the extension `.repo`), which tells an installer program which software packages are needed for the Bigtop installation.

Like any big software product, Hadoop has lots of prerequisites, but you don't need to worry. A well-designed `.repo` file will point to any dependencies, and the installer is smart enough to see if they're missing on your computer and then download and install them.

The installer we're using is called yum, which you get to see in action now:

```
yum install hadoop\* mahout\* oozie\* hbase\* hive\* hue\* pig\* zookeeper\*
```

Notice that we're picking and choosing the Hadoop components to install. There are a number of other components available in Bigtop, but these are the only ones we'll be using in this book. Since the VM we're using is a fresh Linux install, we'll need many dependencies, so you'll need to wait a bit. The yum installer is quite verbose, so you can watch exactly what's being downloaded and installed to pass the time. When the install process is done, you should see a message that says "Complete!"

Step 4: Starting Hadoop

Before we start running applications on Hadoop, there are a few basic configuration and setup things we need to do. Here they are in order:

1. Download and install Java:

   ```
   yum install java-1.7.0-openjdk-devel.x86_64
   ```

2. Format the NameNode:

   ```
   sudo /etc/init.d/hadoop-hdfs-namenode init
   ```

3. Start the Hadoop services for your pseudodistributed cluster:

   ```
   for i in hadoop-hdfs-namenode hadoop-hdfs-datanode ; \
       do sudo service $i start ; done
   ```

4. Create a sub-directory structure in HDFS:

   ```
   sudo /usr/lib/hadoop/libexec/init-hdfs.sh
   ```

5. Start the YARN daemons:

   ```
   sudo service hadoop-yarn-resourcemanager start
   sudo service hadoop-yarn-nodemanager start
   ```

And with that, you're done. Congratulations! You've installed a working Hadoop deployment!

The Hadoop For Dummies Sample Data Set: Airline on-time performance

Throughout this book, we'll be running examples based on the Airline On-time Performance data set — we call it the flight data set for short. This data set is a collection of all the logs of domestic flights from the period of October 1987 to April 2008. Each record represents an individual flight, where various details are captured, such as the time and date of arrival and departure, the originating and destination airports, and the amount of time taken to taxi from the runway to the gate. For more information about this data set see this page: http://stat-computing.org/dataexpo/2009/.

Many of us on the author team for this book spend a lot of time on planes, so this example data set is close to our hearts.

Step 5: Downloading the sample data set

To download the sample data set, open the Firefox browser from within the VM, and go to the following page: http://stat-computing.org/dataexpo/2009/the-data.html.

You won't need the entire data set, so we recommend you start with a single year, so select 1987. When you're about to download, select the Open with Archive Manager option.

After your file has downloaded, extract the 1987.csv file into your home directory where you'll easily be able to find it. Click on the Extract button, and then select the Desktop directory.

Step 6: Copying the sample data set into HDFS

Remember that your Hadoop programs can only work with data once it's stored in HDFS. So what we're going to do now is copy the flight data file for 1987 into HDFS. Enter the following command:

```
hdfs dfs -copyFromLocal 1987.csv /user/root
```

Your First Hadoop Program: Hello Hadoop!

After the Hadoop cluster is installed and running, you can run your first Hadoop program.

This application is very simple, and calculates the total miles flown for all flights flown in one year. The year is defined by the data file you read in your application. We will look at MapReduce programs in more detail in Chapter 6, but to keep things a bit simpler here, we'll run a Pig script to calculate the total miles flown. You will see the map and reduce phases fly by in the output.

Here is the code for this Pig script:

```
records = LOAD '2013_subset.csv' USING PigStorage(',') AS
          (Year,Month,DayofMonth,DayOfWeek,DepTime,CRSDepTime,ArrTime,\
          CRSArrTime,UniqueCarrier,FlightNum,TailNum,ActualElapsedTime,\
          CRSElapsedTime,AirTime,ArrDelay,DepDelay,Origin,Dest,\
          Distance:int,TaxiIn,TaxiOut,Cancelled,CancellationCode,\
          Diverted,CarrierDelay,WeatherDelay,NASDelay,SecurityDelay,\
          LateAircraftDelay);
milage_recs = GROUP records ALL;
tot_miles = FOREACH milage_recs GENERATE SUM(records.Distance);
STORE tot_miles INTO /user/root/totalmiles;
```

We want to put this code in a file on our VM, so let's first create a file. Right-click on the desktop of your VM and select Create Document from the contextual menu that appears and name the document totalmiles.pig. Then open the document in an editor, paste in the above code, and save the file.

From the command line, run the following command to run the Pig script:

```
pig totalmiles.pig
```

You will see many lines of output, and then finally a "Success!" message, followed by more statistics, and then finally the command prompt. After your Pig job has completed, you can see your output:

```
hdfs dfs -cat /user/root/totalmiles/part-r-00000
```

Drumroll, please. . . And the answer is:

```
775009272
```

And with that, you've run your first Hadoop application! The examples in this book use the flight data set, and will work in this environment, so do be sure to try them out yourself.

Part II
How Hadoop Works

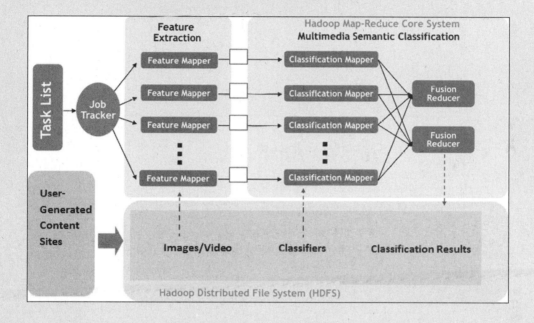

In this part . . .

- ✔ Find out why folks are excited about HDFS.

- ✔ See how file management works in HDFS.

- ✔ Explore the mysteries of MapReduce.

- ✔ Discover how funny names like YARN and Pig can make your Hadoop world a lot easier.

- ✔ Master statistical analysis in a Hadoop environment

- ✔ Work on workflows with Oozie

- ✔ Check out the article "Securing your data in Hadoop" (and more) online at www.dummies.com/extras/hadoop.

Chapter 4

Storing Data in Hadoop: The Hadoop Distributed File System

*W*hen it comes to the core Hadoop infrastructure, you have two components: storage and processing. The Hadoop Distributed File System (HDFS) is the storage component. In short, HDFS provides a distributed architecture for extremely large scale storage, which can easily be extended by scaling out.

Let us remind you why this is a big deal. In the late 1990s, after the Internet established itself as a fixture in society, Google was facing the major challenge of having to be able to store and process not only all the pages on the Internet but also Google users' web log data. Google's major claim to fame, then and now, was its expansive and current index of the Internet's many pages, and its ability to return highly relevant search results to its users. The key to its success was being able to process and analyze both the Internet data *and* its user data. At the time, Google was using a *scale-up* architecture model — a model where you increase system capacity by adding CPU cores, RAM, and disk to an existing server — and it had two major problems:

✔ **Expense:** Scaling up the hardware by using increasingly bigger servers with more storage was becoming incredibly expensive. As computer systems increased in their size, their cost increased at an even higher rate. In addition, Google needed a *highly available environment* — one that would ensure its mission critical workloads could continue running in the event of a failure — so a failover system was also needed, doubling the IT expense.

✔ **Structural limitations:** Google engineers were reaching the limits of what a scale-up architecture could sustain. For example, with the increasing data volumes Google was seeing, it was taking much longer for data sets to be transferred from SANs to the CPUs for processing. And all the while, the Internet's growth and usage showed no sign of slowing down.

Rather than scale *up,* Google engineers decided to scale *out* by using a cluster of smaller servers they could continually add to if they needed more power or capacity. To enable a scale-out model, they developed the Google File System (GFS), which was the inspiration for the engineers who first developed HDFS. The early use cases, for both the Google and HDFS engineers, were solely based on the batch processing of large data sets. This concept is reflected in the design of HDFS, which is optimized for large-scale batch processing workloads. Since Hadoop came on the scene in 2005, it has emerged as the premier platform for large-scale data storage and processing. There's a growing demand for the optimization of interactive workloads as well, which involve queries that involve small subsets of the data. Though today's HDFS still works best for batch workloads, features are being added to improve the performance of interactive workloads.

Data Storage in HDFS

Just to be clear, storing data in HDFS is not entirely the same as saving files on your personal computer. In fact, quite a number of differences exist — most having to do with optimizations that make HDFS able to scale out easily across thousands of slave nodes and perform well with batch workloads.

The most noticeable difference initially is the size of files. Hadoop is designed to work best with a modest number of extremely large files. Average file sizes that are larger than 500MB are the norm.

Here's an additional bit of background information on how data is stored: HDFS has a Write Once, Read Often model of data access. That means the contents of individual files cannot be modified, other than appending new data to the end of the file.

Don't worry, though: There's still lots you can do with HDFS files, including

✔ Create a new file

✔ Append content to the end of a file

✔ Delete a file

✔ Rename a file

✔ Modify file attributes like owner

Taking a closer look at data blocks

When you store a file in HDFS, the system breaks it down into a set of individual blocks and stores these blocks in various slave nodes in the Hadoop cluster, as shown in Figure 4-1. This is an entirely normal thing to do, as all file systems break files down into blocks before storing them to disk. HDFS has no idea (and doesn't care) what's stored inside the file, so raw files are not split in accordance with rules that we humans would understand. Humans, for example, would want *record boundaries* — the lines showing where a record begins and ends — to be respected. HDFS is often blissfully unaware that the final record in one block may be only a partial record, with the rest of its content shunted off to the following block. HDFS only wants to make sure that files are split into evenly sized blocks that match the predefined block size for the Hadoop instance (unless a custom value was entered for the file being stored). In Figure 4-1, that block size is 128MB.

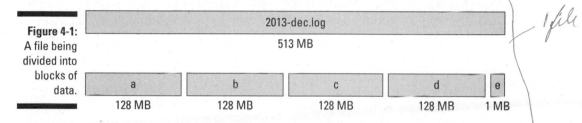

Figure 4-1: A file being divided into blocks of data.

Not every file you need to store is an exact multiple of your system's block size, so the final data block for a file uses only as much space as is needed. In the case of Figure 4-1, the final block of data is 1MB.

The concept of storing a file as a collection of blocks is entirely consistent with how file systems normally work. But what's different about HDFS is the scale. A typical block size that you'd see in a file system under Linux is 4KB, whereas a typical block size in Hadoop is 128MB. This value is configurable, and it can be customized, as both a new system default and a custom value for individual files.

Hadoop was designed to store data at the petabyte scale, where any potential limitations to scaling out are minimized. The high block size is a direct consequence of this need to store data on a massive scale. First of all, every data block stored in HDFS has its own metadata and needs to be tracked by a central server so that applications needing to access a specific file can be directed to wherever all the file's blocks are stored. If the block size were in the kilobyte range, even modest volumes of data in the terabyte scale would overwhelm the metadata server with too many blocks to track. Second, HDFS is designed to enable high throughput so that the parallel processing of these large data sets happens as quickly as possible. The key to Hadoop's scalability on the data processing side is, and always will be, *parallelism* — the ability to process the individual blocks of these large files in parallel. To enable efficient processing, a balance needs to be struck. On one hand, the block size needs to be large enough to warrant the resources dedicated to an individual unit of data processing (for instance, a map or reduce task, which we look at in Chapter 6). On the other hand, the block size can't be so large that the system is waiting a very long time for one last unit of data processing to finish its work. These two considerations obviously depend on the kinds of work being done on the data blocks.

Replicating data blocks

HDFS is designed to store data on inexpensive, and more unreliable, hardware. (We say more on that topic later in this chapter.) *Inexpensive* has an attractive ring to it, but it does raise concerns about the reliability of the system as a whole, especially for ensuring the high availability of the data. Planning ahead for disaster, the brains behind HDFS made the decision to set up the system so that it would store three (count 'em — three) copies of every data block.

HDFS assumes that every disk drive and every slave node is inherently unreliable, so, clearly, care must be taken in choosing where the three copies of the data blocks are stored. Figure 4-2 shows how data blocks from the earlier file are *striped* across the Hadoop cluster — meaning they are evenly distributed between the slave nodes so that a copy of the block will still be available regardless of disk, node, or rack failures.

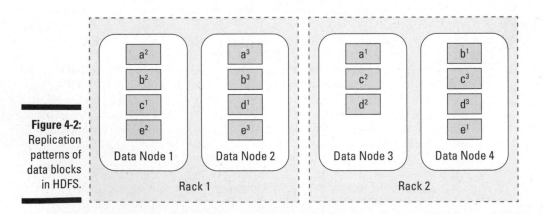

Figure 4-2: Replication patterns of data blocks in HDFS.

The file shown in Figure 4-2 has five data blocks, labeled a, b, c, d, and e. If you take a closer look, you can see this particular cluster is made up of two racks with two nodes apiece, and that the three copies of each data block have been spread out across the various slave nodes.

Every component in the Hadoop cluster is seen as a potential failure point, so when HDFS stores the replicas of the original blocks across the Hadoop cluster, it tries to ensure that the block replicas are stored in different failure points. For example, take a look at Block A. At the time it needed to be stored, Slave Node 3 was chosen, and the first copy of Block A was stored there. For multiple rack systems, HDFS then determines that the remaining two copies of block A need to be stored in a different rack. So the second copy of block A is stored on Slave Node 1. The final copy can be stored on the same rack as the second copy, but not on the same slave node, so it gets stored on Slave Node 2.

Slave node and disk failures

Like death and taxes, disk failures (and given enough time, even node or rack failures), are inevitable. Given the example in Figure 4-2, even if one rack were to fail, the cluster could continue functioning. Performance would suffer because you've lost half your processing resources, but the system is still online and all data is still available.

In a scenario where a disk drive or a slave node fails, the central metadata server for HDFS (called the NameNode) eventually finds out that the file blocks stored on the failed resource are no longer available. For example, if Slave Node 3 in Figure 4-2 fails, it would mean that Blocks A, C, and D are *underreplicated*. In other words, too few copies of these blocks are available in HDFS. When HDFS senses that a block is underreplicated, it orders a new copy.

To continue the example, let's say that Slave Node 3 comes back online after a few hours. Meanwhile, HDFS has ensured that there are three copies of all the file blocks. So now, Blocks A, C, and D have four copies apiece and are *overreplicated*. As with underreplicated blocks, the HDFS central metadata server will find out about this as well, and will order one copy of every file to be deleted.

One nice result of the availability of data is that when disk failures do occur, there's no need to immediately replace failed hard drives. This can more effectively be done at regularly scheduled intervals.

Sketching Out the HDFS Architecture

The core concept of HDFS is that it can be made up of dozens, hundreds, or even thousands of individual computers, where the system's files are stored in directly attached disk drives. Each of these individual computers is a self-contained server with its own memory, CPU, disk storage, and installed operating system (typically Linux, though Windows is also supported). Technically speaking, HDFS is a *user-space-level file system* because it lives on top of the file systems that are installed on all individual computers that make up the Hadoop cluster. Figure 4-3 illustrates this concept.

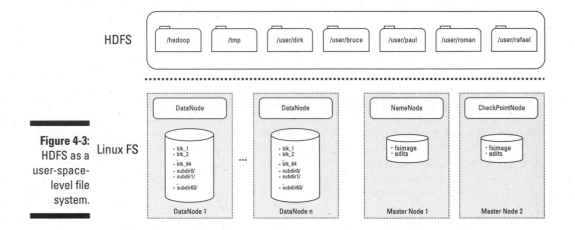

Figure 4-3:
HDFS as a user-space-level file system.

Figure 4-3 shows that a Hadoop cluster is made up of two classes of servers: *slave nodes*, where the data is stored and processed, and *master nodes*, which govern the management of the Hadoop cluster. On each of the master nodes and slave nodes, HDFS runs special services and stores raw data to capture the state of the file system. In the case of the slave nodes, the raw data consists of the blocks stored on the node, and with the master nodes, the raw data consists of metadata that maps data blocks to the files stored in HDFS.

Looking at slave nodes

In a Hadoop cluster, each data node (also known as a *slave node*) runs a background process named DataNode. This background process (also known as a *daemon*) keeps track of the slices of data that the system stores on its computer. It regularly talks to the master server for HDFS (known as the NameNode) to report on the health and status of the locally stored data.

Data blocks are stored as raw files in the local file system. From the perspective of a Hadoop user, you have no idea which of the slave nodes has the pieces of the file you need to process. From within Hadoop, you don't see data blocks or how they're distributed across the cluster — all you see is a listing of files in HDFS. The complexity of how the file blocks are distributed across the cluster is hidden from you — you don't know how complicated it all is, and you don't *need* to know. Actually, the slave nodes themselves don't even know what's inside the data blocks they're storing. It's the NameNode server that knows the mappings of which data blocks compose the files stored in HDFS.

Better living through redundancy

One core design principle of HDFS is the concept of minimizing the cost of the individual slave nodes by using commodity hardware components. For massively scalable systems, this idea is a sensible one because costs escalate quickly when you need hundreds or thousands of slave nodes. Using lower-cost hardware has a consequence, though, in that individual components aren't as reliable as more expensive hardware.

When you're choosing storage options, consider the impact of using commodity drives rather than more expensive enterprise-quality drives. Imagine that you have a 750-node cluster, where each node has 12 hard disk drives dedicated to HDFS storage. Based on an annual failure rate (AFR) of 4 percent for commodity disk drives (a given hard disk drive has a 4 percent likelihood of failing in a given year, in other words), your cluster will likely experience a hard disk failure every day of the year.

Because there can be so many slave nodes, their failure is also a common occurrence in larger clusters with hundreds or more nodes. With this information in mind, HDFS has been engineered on the assumption that *all* hardware components, even at the slave node level, are unreliable. HDFS overcomes the unreliability of individual hardware components by way of redundancy: That's the idea behind those three copies of every file stored in HDFS, distributed throughout the system. More specifically, each file block stored in HDFS has a total of three replicas. If one system breaks with a specific file block that you need, you can turn to the other two.

Sketching out slave node server design

To balance such important factors as total cost of ownership, storage capacity, and performance, you need to carefully plan the design of your slave nodes. Chapter 16 covers this topic in greater detail, but we want to take a quick look in this section at what a typical slave node looks like.

We commonly see slave nodes now where each node typically has between 12 and 16 locally attached 3TB hard disk drives. Slave nodes use moderately fast dual-socket CPUs with six to eight cores each — no speed demons, in other words. This is accompanied by 48GB of RAM. In short, this server is optimized for dense storage.

Because HDFS is a user-space-level file system, it's important to optimize the local file system on the slave nodes to work with HDFS. In this regard, one high-impact decision when setting up your servers is choosing a file system for the Linux installation on the slave nodes. Ext3 is the most commonly deployed file system because it has been the most stable option for a number of years. Take a look at Ext4, however. It's the next version of Ext3, and it has been available long enough to be widely considered stable and reliable. More importantly for our purposes, it has a number of optimizations for handling large files, which makes it an ideal choice for HDFS slave node servers.

 Don't use the Linux Logical Volume Manager (LVM) — it represents an additional layer between the Linux file system and HDFS, which prevents Hadoop from optimizing its performance. Specifically, LVM aggregates disks, which hampers the resource management that HDFS and YARN do, based on how files are distributed on the physical drives.

Keeping track of data blocks with NameNode

When a user stores a file in HDFS, the file is divided into data blocks, and three copies of these data blocks are stored in slave nodes throughout the Hadoop cluster. That's a lot of data blocks to keep track of. The NameNode acts as the address book for HDFS because it knows not only which blocks make up individual files but also where each of these blocks and their replicas are stored. As you might expect, knowing where the bodies are buried makes the NameNode a critically important component in a Hadoop cluster. If the NameNode is unavailable, applications cannot access any data stored in HDFS.

If you take another look at Figure 4-3, you can see the NameNode daemon running on a master node server. All mapping information dealing with the data blocks and their corresponding files is stored in a file named `fsimage`. HDFS is a journaling file system, which means that any data changes are logged in an edit journal that tracks events since the last *checkpoint* — the last time when the edit log was merged with `fsimage`. In HDFS, the edit journal is maintained in a file named `edits` that's stored on the NameNode.

NameNode startup and operation

To understand how the NameNode works, it's helpful to take a look at how it starts up. Because the purpose of the NameNode is to inform applications of how many data blocks they need to process and to keep track of the exact location where they're stored, it needs all the block locations and block-to-file mappings that are available in RAM. These are the steps the NameNode takes. To load all the information that the NameNode needs after it starts up, the following happens:

1. The NameNode loads the `fsimage` file into memory.

2. The NameNode loads the `edits` file and re-plays the journaled changes to update the block metadata that's already in memory.

3. The DataNode daemons send the NameNode block reports.

   For each slave node, there's a block report that lists all the data blocks stored there and describes the health of each one.

After the startup process is completed, the NameNode has a complete picture of all the data stored in HDFS, and it's ready to receive application requests from Hadoop clients. As data files are added and removed based on client requests, the changes are written to the slave node's disk volumes, journal updates are made to the `edits` file, and the changes are reflected in the block locations and metadata stored in the NameNode's memory (see Figure 4-4).

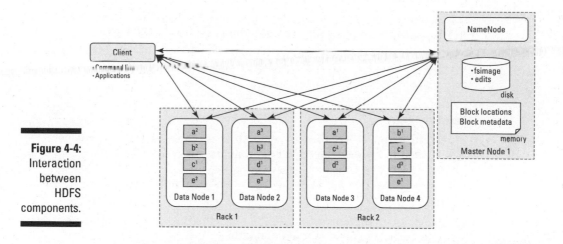

Figure 4-4:
Interaction
between
HDFS
components.

Throughout the life of the cluster, the DataNode daemons send the NameNode heartbeats (a quick signal) every three seconds, indicating they're active. (This default value is configurable.) Every six hours (again, a configurable default), the DataNodes send the NameNode a block report outlining which file blocks are on their nodes. This way, the NameNode always has a current view of the available resources in the cluster.

Writing data

To create new files in HDFS, the following process would have to take place (refer to Figure 4-4 to see the components involved):

1. The client sends a request to the NameNode to create a new file.

   The NameNode determines how many blocks are needed, and the client is granted a *lease* for creating these new file blocks in the cluster. As part of this lease, the client has a time limit to complete the creation task. (This time limit ensures that storage space isn't taken up by failed client applications.)

2. The client then writes the first copies of the file blocks to the slave nodes using the lease assigned by the NameNode.

   The NameNode handles write requests and determines where the file blocks and their replicas need to be written, balancing availability and performance. The first copy of a file block is written in one rack, and the second and third copies are written on a different rack than the first copy, but in different slave nodes in the same rack. This arrangement minimizes network traffic while ensuring that no data blocks are on the same failure point.

3. As each block is written to HDFS, a special process writes the remaining replicas to the other slave nodes identified by the NameNode.

4. After the DataNode daemons acknowledge the file block replicas have been created, the client application closes the file and notifies the NameNode, which then closes the open lease.

Reading Data

To read files from HDFS, the following process would have to take place (again, refer to Figure 4-4 for the components involved):

1. The client sends a request to the NameNode for a file.

   The NameNode determines which blocks are involved and chooses, based on overall proximity of the blocks to one another and to the client, the most efficient access path.

2. The client then accesses the blocks using the addresses given by the NameNode.

Balancing data in the Hadoop cluster

Over time, with combinations of uneven data-ingestion patterns (where some slave nodes might have more data written to them) or node failures, data is likely to become unevenly distributed across the racks and slave nodes in your Hadoop cluster. This uneven distribution can have a detrimental impact on performance because the demand on individual slave nodes will become unbalanced; nodes with little data won't be fully used; and nodes with many blocks will be overused. (*Note:* The overuse and underuse are based on disk activity, not on CPU or RAM.) HDFS includes a balancer utility to redistribute blocks from overused slave nodes to underused ones while maintaining the policy of putting blocks on different slave nodes and racks. Hadoop administrators should regularly check HDFS health, and if data becomes unevenly distributed, they should invoke the balancer utility.

NameNode master server design

Because of its mission-critical nature, the master server running the NameNode daemon needs markedly different hardware requirements than the ones for a slave node. Most significantly, enterprise-level components need to be used to minimize the probability of an outage. Also, you'll need enough RAM to load into memory all the metadata and location data about all the data blocks stored in HDFS. See Chapter 16 for a full discussion on this topic.

Checkpointing updates

Earlier in this chapter, we say that HDFS is a journaled file system, where new changes to files in HDFS are captured in an edit log that's stored on the NameNode in a file named edits. Periodically, when the edits file reaches a certain threshold or after a certain period has elapsed, the journaled entries need to be committed to the master fsimage file. The NameNode itself doesn't do this, because it's designed to answer application requests as quickly as possible. More importantly, considerable risk is involved in having this metadata update operation managed by a single master server.

If the metadata describing the mappings between the data blocks and their corresponding files becomes corrupted, the original data is as good as lost.

Checkpointing services for a Hadoop cluster are handled by one of four possible daemons, which need to run on their own dedicated master node alongside the NameNode daemon's master node:

- ✔ **Secondary NameNode:** Prior to Hadoop 2, this was the only checkpointing daemon, performing the checkpointing process described in this section. The Secondary NameNode has a notoriously inaccurate name because it is in no way "secondary" or a "standby" for the NameNode.

- ✔ **Checkpoint Node:** The Checkpoint Node is the replacement for the Secondary NameNode. It performs checkpointing and nothing more.

- ✔ **Backup Node:** Provides checkpointing service, but also maintains a backup of the fsimage and edits file.

- ✔ **Standby NameNode:** Performs checkpointing service and, unlike the old Secondary NameNode, the Standby NameNode is a true standby server, enabling a hot-swap of the NameNode process to avoid any downtime.

The checkpointing process

The following steps, depicted in Figure 4-5, describe the checkpointing process as it's carried out by the NameNode and the checkpointing service (note that four possible daemons can be used for checkpointing — see above):

1. When it's time to perform the checkpoint, the NameNode creates a new file to accept the journaled file system changes.

   It names the new file `edits.new`.

2. As a result, the `edits` file accepts no further changes and is copied to the checkpointing service, along with the `fsimage` file.

3. The checkpointing service merges these two files, creating a file named `fsimage.ckpt`.

4. The checkpointing service copies the `fsimage.ckpt` file to the NameNode.

5. The NameNode overwrites the file `fsimage` with `fsimage.ckpt`.

6. The NameNode renames the `edits.new` file to `edits`.

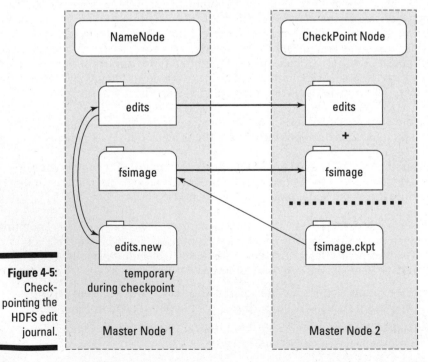

Figure 4-5: Checkpointing the HDFS edit journal.

Backup Node considerations

In addition to providing checkpointing functionality, the Backup Node maintains the current state of all the HDFS block metadata in memory, just like the NameNode. In this sense, it maintains a real-time backup of the NameNode's state. As a result of keeping the block metadata in memory, the Backup Node is far more efficient than the Checkpoint Node at performing the checkpointing task, because the `fsimage` and `edits` files don't need to be transferred and then merged. These changes are already merged in memory.

Another benefit of using the Backup Node is that the NameNode can be configured to delegate the Backup Node so that it persists journal data to disk.

If you're using the Backup Node, you can't run the Checkpoint Node. There's no need to do so, because the checkpointing process is already being taken care of.

Standby NameNode considerations

The Standby NameNode is the designated hot standby master server for the NameNode. While serving as standby, it also performs the checkpointing process. As such, you can't run the Backup Node or Standby Node.

Secondary NameNode, Checkpoint Node, Backup Node, and Standby NameNode Master server design

The master server running the Secondary NameNode, Checkpoint Node, Backup Node, or Standby NameNode daemons have the same hardware requirements as the ones deployed for the NameNode master server. The reason is that these servers also load into memory all the metadata and location data about all the data blocks stored in HDFS. See Chapter 16 for a full discussion on this topic.

HDFS Federation

Before Hadoop 2 entered the scene, Hadoop clusters had to live with the fact that NameNode placed limits on the degree to which they could scale. Few clusters were able to scale beyond 3,000 or 4,000 nodes. NameNode's need to maintain records for every block of data stored in the cluster turned out to be the most significant factor restricting greater cluster growth. When you have too many blocks, it becomes increasingly difficult for the NameNode to scale up as the Hadoop cluster scales out.

The solution to expanding Hadoop clusters indefinitely is to *federate* the NameNode. Specifically, you must set it up so that you have multiple NameNode instances running on their own, dedicated master nodes and then making each NameNode responsible only for the file blocks in its own name space. In Figure 4-6, you can see a Hadoop cluster with two NameNodes serving a single cluster. The slave nodes all contain blocks from both name spaces.

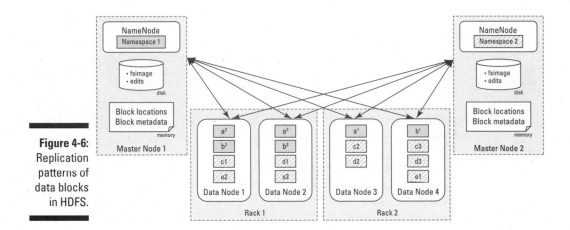

Figure 4-6: Replication patterns of data blocks in HDFS.

HDFS High Availability

Often in Hadoop's infancy, a great amount of discussion was centered on the NameNode's representation of a single point of failure. Hadoop, overall, has always had a robust and failure-tolerant architecture, with the exception of this key area. As we mention earlier in this chapter, without the NameNode, there's no Hadoop cluster.

Using Hadoop 2, you can configure HDFS so that there's an Active NameNode and a Standby NameNode (see Figure 4-7). The Standby NameNode needs to be on a dedicated master node that's configured identically to the master node used by the Active NameNode (refer to Figure 4-7).

The Standby NameNode isn't sitting idly by while the NameNode handles all the block address requests. The Standby NameNode, charged with the task of keeping the state of the block locations and block metadata in memory, handles the HDFS checkpointing responsibilities. The Active NameNode writes journal entries on file changes to the majority of the JournalNode services, which run on the master nodes. (*Note:* The HDFS high availability solution requires at least three master nodes, and if there are more, there can be only an odd number.) If a failure occurs, the Standby Node first reads all completed journal entries (where a majority of Journal Nodes have an entry, in other words), to ensure that the new Active NameNode is fully consistent with the state of the cluster.

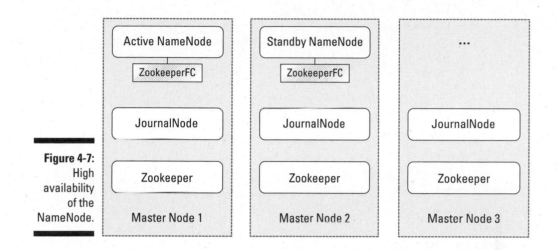

Figure 4-7:
High
availability
of the
NameNode.

Zookeeper is used to monitor the Active NameNode and to handle the failover logistics if the Active NameNode becomes unavailable. Both the Active and Standby NameNodes have dedicated Zookeeper Failover Controllers (ZFC) that perform the monitoring and failover tasks. In the event of a failure, the ZFC informs the Zookeeper instances on the cluster, which then elect a new Active NameNode.

Apache Zookeeper provides coordination and configuration services for distributed systems, so it's no wonder we see it used all over the place in Hadoop. See Chapter 12 for more information about Zookeeper.

Chapter 5

Reading and Writing Data

*T*his chapter tells you all about getting data in and out of Hadoop, which are basic operations along the path of big data discovery.

We begin by describing the importance of data compression for optimizing the performance of your Hadoop installation, and we briefly outline some of the available compression utilities that are supported by Hadoop. We also give you an overview of the Hadoop file system (FS) shell (a command-line interface), which includes a number of shell-like commands that you can use to directly interact with the Hadoop Distributed File System (HDFS) and other file systems that Hadoop supports. Finally, we describe how you can use Apache Flume — the Hadoop community technology for collecting large volumes of log files and storing them in Hadoop — to efficiently ingest huge volumes of log data.

We use the word "ingest" all over this chapter and this book. In short, ingesting data simply means to accept data from an outside source and store it in Hadoop. With Hadoop's scalable, reliable, and inexpensive storage, we think you'll understand why people are so keen on this.

Compressing Data

The huge data volumes that are realities in a typical Hadoop deployment make compression a necessity. Data compression definitely saves you a great deal of storage space and is sure to speed up the movement of that data throughout your cluster. Not surprisingly, a number of available compression schemes, called codecs, are out there for you to consider.

In a Hadoop deployment, you're dealing (potentially) with quite a large number of individual slave nodes, each of which has a number of large disk drives. It's not uncommon for an individual slave node to have upwards of 45TB of raw storage space available for HDFS. Even though Hadoop slave nodes are designed to be inexpensive, they're not free, and with large volumes of data that have a tendency to grow at increasing rates, compression is an obvious tool to control extreme data volumes.

First, some basic terms: A *codec,* which is a shortened form of *co*mpressor/ *de*compressor, is technology (software or hardware, or both) for compressing and decompressing data; it's the implementation of a compression/decompression algorithm. You need to know that some codecs support something called splittable compression and that codecs differ in both the speed with which they can compress and decompress data and the degree to which they can compress it.

Splittable compression is an important concept in a Hadoop context. The way Hadoop works is that files are split if they're larger than the file's block size setting, and individual file splits can be processed in parallel by different mappers. With most codecs, text file splits cannot be decompressed independently of other splits from the same file, so those codecs are said to be non-splittable, so MapReduce processing is limited to a single mapper. Because the file can be decompressed only as a whole, and not as individual parts based on splits, there can be no parallel processing of such a file, and performance might take a huge hit as a job waits for a single mapper to process multiple data blocks that can't be decompressed independently. (For more on how MapReduce processing works, see Chapter 6.)

Splittable compression is only a factor for text files. For binary files, Hadoop compression codecs compress data within a binary-encoded container, depending on the file type (for example, a SequenceFile, Avro, or ProtocolBuffer).

Speaking of performance, there's a cost (in terms of processing resources and time) associated with compressing the data that is being written to your Hadoop cluster. With computers, as with life, nothing is free. When compressing data, you're exchanging processing cycles for disk space. And when that data is being read, there's a cost associated with decompressing the data as well. Be sure to weigh the advantages of storage savings against the additional performance overhead.

If the input file to a MapReduce job contains compressed data, the time that is needed to read that data from HDFS is reduced and job performance is enhanced. The input data is decompressed automatically when it is being read by MapReduce. The input filename extension determines which supported codec is used to automatically decompress the data. For example, a `.gz` extension identifies the file as a gzip-compressed file.

It can also be useful to compress the intermediate output of the map phase in the MapReduce processing flow. Because map function output is written to disk and shipped across the network to the reduce tasks, compressing the output can result in significant performance improvements. And if you want to store the MapReduce output as history files for future use, compressing this data can significantly reduce the amount of needed space in HDFS.

There are many different compression algorithms and tools, and their characteristics and strengths vary. The most common trade-off is between compression ratios (the degree to which a file is compressed) and compress/decompress speeds. The Hadoop framework supports several codecs. The framework transparently compresses and decompresses most input and output file formats.

The following list identifies some common codecs that are supported by the Hadoop framework. Be sure to choose the codec that most closely matches the demands of your particular use case (for example, with workloads where the speed of processing is important, choose a codec with high decompression speeds):

- **Gzip:** A compression utility that was adopted by the GNU project, Gzip (short for GNU zip) generates compressed files that have a `.gz` extension. You can use the `gunzip` command to decompress files that were created by a number of compression utilities, including Gzip.

- **Bzip2:** From a usability standpoint, Bzip2 and Gzip are similar. Bzip2 generates a better compression ratio than does Gzip, but it's much slower. In fact, of all the available compression codecs in Hadoop, Bzip2 is by far the slowest. If you're setting up an archive that you'll rarely need to query and space is at a high premium, then maybe would Bzip2 be worth considering. (The *B* in Bzip comes from its use of the Burrows-Wheeler algorithm, in case you're curious.)

- **Snappy:** The Snappy codec from Google provides modest compression ratios, but fast compression and decompression speeds. (In fact, it has the fastest decompression speeds, which makes it highly desirable for data sets that are likely to be queried often.) The Snappy codec is integrated into Hadoop Common, a set of common utilities that supports other Hadoop subprojects. You can use Snappy as an add-on for more recent versions of Hadoop that do not yet provide Snappy codec support.

- **LZO:** Similar to Snappy, LZO (short for Lempel-Ziv-Oberhumer, the trio of computer scientists who came up with the algorithm) provides modest compression ratios, but fast compression and decompression speeds. LZO is licensed under the GNU Public License (GPL). This license is incompatible with the Apache license, and as a result, LZO has been removed from some distributions. (Some distributions, such as IBM's BigInsights, have made an end run around this restriction by releasing GPL-free versions of LZO.)

LZO supports splittable compression, which, as we mention earlier in this chapter, enables the parallel processing of compressed text file splits by your MapReduce jobs. LZO needs to create an index when it compresses a file, because with variable-length compression blocks, an index is required to tell the mapper where it can safely split the compressed file. LZO is only really desirable if you need to compress text files. For binary files, which are not impacted by non-splittable codecs, Snappy is your best option.

Table 5-1 summarizes the common characteristics of some of the codecs that are supported by the Hadoop framework.

Table 5-1		Hadoop Codecs		
Codec	*File Extension*	*Splittable?*	*Degree of Compression*	*Compression Speed*
Gzip	.gz	No	Medium	Medium
Bzip2	.bz2	Yes	High	Slow
Snappy	.snappy	No	Medium	Fast
LZO	.lzo	No, unless indexed	Medium	Fast

All compression algorithms must make trade-offs between the degree of compression and the speed of compression that they can achieve. The codecs that are listed in Table 5-1 provide you with some control over what the balance between the compression ratio and speed should be at compression time. For example, Gzip lets you regulate the speed of compression by specifying a negative integer (or keyword), where –1 (or --fast) indicates the fastest compression level, and –9 (or --best) indicates the slowest compression level. The default compression level is –6.

Managing Files with the Hadoop File System Commands

HDFS is one of the two main components of the Hadoop framework; the other is the computational paradigm known as MapReduce. A *distributed file system* is a file system that manages storage across a networked cluster of machines.

HDFS stores data in *blocks*, units whose default size is 64MB. Files that you want stored in HDFS need to be broken into block-size chunks that are then stored independently throughout the cluster. You can use the `fsck` line command to list the blocks that make up each file in HDFS, as follows:

```
% hadoop fsck / -files -blocks
```

Because Hadoop is written in Java, all interactions with HDFS are managed via the Java API. Keep in mind, though, that you don't need to be a Java guru to work with files in HDFS. Several Hadoop interfaces built on top of the Java API are now in common use (and hide Java), but the simplest one is the command-line interface; we use the command line to interact with HDFS in the examples we provide in this chapter.

You access the Hadoop file system shell by running one form of the `hadoop` command. (We tell you more about that topic later.) All `hadoop` commands are invoked by the `bin/hadoop` script. (To retrieve a description of all `hadoop` commands, run the hadoop script without specifying any arguments.) The `hadoop` command has the syntax

```
hadoop [--config confdir] [COMMAND] [GENERIC_OPTIONS]
          [COMMAND_OPTIONS]
```

The `--config confdir` option overwrites the default configuration directory (`$HADOOP_HOME/conf`), so you can easily customize your Hadoop environment configuration. The generic options and command options are a common set of options that are supported by several commands.

Hadoop file system shell commands (for command line interfaces) take uniform resource identifiers (URIs) as arguments. A *URI* is a string of characters that's used to identify a name or a web resource. The string can include a *scheme name* — a qualifier for the nature of the data source. For HDFS, the scheme name is `hdfs`, and for the local file system, the scheme name is `file`. If you don't specify a scheme name, the default is the scheme name that's specified in the configuration file. A file or directory in HDFS can be specified in a fully qualified way, such as in this example:

```
hdfs://namenodehost/parent/child
```

Or it can simply be /parent/child if the configuration file points to hdfs://namenodehost.

The Hadoop file system shell commands, which are similar to Linux file commands, have the following general syntax:

```
hadoop hdfs -file_cmd
```

Readers with some prior Hadoop experience might ask, "But what about the hadoop fs command?" The fs command is deprecated in the Hadoop 0.2 release series, but it does still work in Hadoop 2. We recommend that you use hdfs dfs instead.

As you might expect, you use the mkdir command to create a directory in HDFS, just as you would do on Linux or on Unix-based operating systems. Though HDFS has a default working directory, /user/$USER, where $USER is your login username, you need to create it yourself by using the syntax

```
$ hadoop hdfs dfs -mkdir /user/login_user_name
```

For example, to create a directory named "joanna", run this mkdir command:

```
$ hadoop hdfs dfs -mkdir /user/joanna
```

Use the Hadoop put command to copy a file from your local file system to HDFS:

```
$ hadoop hdfs dfs -put file_name /user/login_user_name
```

For example, to copy a file named data.txt to this new directory, run the following put command:

```
$ hadoop hdfs dfs -put data.txt /user/joanna
```

Run the ls command to get an HDFS file listing:

```
$ hadoop hdfs dfs -ls .
Found 2 items
drwxr-xr-x - joanna supergroup 0 2013-06-30 12:25 /user/joanna
-rw-r--r-- 1 joanna supergroup 118 2013-06-30 12:15 /user/joanna/data.txt
```

The file listing itself breaks down as described in this list:

- ✔ **Column 1 shows the *file mode* ("d" for directory and "–" for normal file, followed by the permissions).** The three permission types — read (r), write (w), and execute (x) — are the same as you find on Linux- and Unix-based systems. The execute permission for a file is ignored because you cannot execute a file on HDFS. The permissions are grouped by owner, group, and public (everyone else).

- ✔ **Column 2 shows the replication factor for files. (The concept of replication doesn't apply to directories.)** The blocks that make up a file in HDFS are replicated to ensure fault tolerance. The *replication factor,* or the number of replicas that are kept for a specific file, is configurable. You can specify the replication factor when the file is created or later, via your application.

- ✔ **Columns 3 and 4 show the file *owner* and *group*.** *Supergroup* is the name of the group of superusers, and a *superuser* is the user with the same identity as the NameNode process. If you start the NameNode, you're the superuser for now. This is a special group – regular users will have their userids belong to a group without special characteristics — a group that's simply defined by a Hadoop administrator.

- ✔ **Column 5 shows the size of the file, in bytes, or 0 if it's a directory.**

- ✔ **Columns 6 and 7 show the date and time of the last modification, respectively.**

- ✔ **Column 8 shows the unqualified name (meaning that the scheme name isn't specified) of the file or directory.**

Use the Hadoop `get` command to copy a file from HDFS to your local file system:

```
$ hadoop hdfs dfs -get file_name /user/login_user_name
```

Use the Hadoop `rm` command to delete a file or an empty directory:

```
$ hadoop hdfs dfs -rm file_name /user/login_user_name
```

Use the `hadoop hdfs dfs -help` command to get detailed help for every option.

Table 5-2 summarizes the Hadoop file system shell commands.

Table 5-2		File System Shell Commands	
Command	*What It Does*	*Usage*	*Examples*
dcat	Copies source paths to stdout.	hdfs dfs -cat URI [URI ...]	hdfs dfs -cat hdfs://<path>/ file1; hdfs dfs -cat file:/// file2 /user/ hadoop/file3
chgrp	Changes the group association of files. With -R, makes the change recursively by way of the directory structure. The user must be the file owner or the superuser.	hdfs dfs -chgrp [-R] GROUP URI [URI ...]	hdfs dfs -chgrp analysts test/ data1.txt
chmod	Changes the permissions of files. With -R, makes the change recursively by way of the directory structure. The user must be the file owner or the superuser.	hdfs dfs -chmod [-R] <MODE[,MODE]... | OCTALMODE> URI [URI ...]	hdfs dfs -chmod 777 test/data1.txt
chown	Changes the owner of files. With -R, makes the change recursively by way of the directory structure. The user must be the superuser.	hdfs dfs -chown [-R] [OWNER] [:[GROUP]] URI [URI]	hdfs dfs -chown -R hduser2 /opt/hadoop/ logs
copyFrom Local	Works similarly to the put command, except that the source is restricted to a local file reference.	hdfs dfs -copyFromLocal <localsrc> URI	hdfs dfs -copyFromLocal input/docs/ data2.txt hdfs:// localhost/ user/rosemary/ data2.txt
copyTo Local	Works similarly to the get command, except that the destination is restricted to a local file reference.	hdfs dfs -copyToLocal [-ignorecrc] [-crc] URI <localdst>	hdfs dfs -copyToLocal data2.txt data2.copy.txt
count	Counts the number of directories, files, and bytes under the paths that match the specified file pattern.	hdfs dfs -count [-q] <paths>	hdfs dfs -count hdfs://nn1. example.com/ file1 hdfs:// nn2.example .com/file2

cp	Copies one or more files from a specified source to a specified destination. If you specify multiple sources, the specified destination must be a directory.	`hdfs dfs -cp`
		`URI [URI ...]`
		`<dest>`
			`hdfs dfs -cp`
			`/user/hadoop/`
			`file1 /user/`
			`hadoop/file2`
			`/user/hadoop/`
			`dir`

du	Displays the size of the specified file, or the sizes of files and directories that are contained in the specified directory. If you specify the `-s` option, displays an aggregate summary of file sizes rather than individual file sizes. If you specify the `-h` option, formats the file sizes in a "human-readable" way.	`hdfs dfs -du`
		`[-s] [-h] URI`
		`[URI ...]`
			`hdfs dfs -du`
			`/user/hadoop/`
			`dir1 /user/`
			`hadoop/file1`

expunge	Empties the trash. When you delete a file, it isn't removed immediately from HDFS, but is renamed to a file in the `/trash` directory. As long as the file remains there, you can undelete it if you change your mind, though only the latest copy of the deleted file can be restored.	`hdfs dfs` `-expunge`	`hdfs dfs` `-expunge`

get	Copies files to the local file system. Files that fail a cyclic redundancy check (CRC) can still be copied if you specify the `-ignorecrc` option. The CRC is a common technique for detecting data transmission errors. CRC checksum files have the `.crc` extension and are used to verify the data integrity of another file. These files are copied if you specify the `-crc` option.	`hdfs dfs -get`
		`[-ignorecrc]`
		`[-crc] <src>`
		`<localdst>`
			`hdfs dfs -get`
			`/user/hadoop/`
			`file3 localfile`

(continued)

Table 5-2 *(continued)*

Command	What It Does	Usage	Examples
`getmerge`	Concatenates the files in `src` and writes the result to the specified local destination file. To add a newline character at the end of each file, specify the `addnl` option.	`hdfs dfs -getmerge <src> <localdst> [addnl]`	`hdfs dfs -getmerge/ user/hadoop/ mydir/ ~/result_file addnl`
`ls`	Returns statistics for the specified files or directories.	`hdfs dfs -ls <args>`	`hdfs dfs -ls /user/hadoop/ file1`
`lsr`	Serves as the recursive version of `ls`; similar to the Unix command `ls -R`.	`hdfs dfs -lsr <args>`	`hdfs dfs -lsr /user/hadoop`
`mkdir`	Creates directories on one or more specified paths. Its behavior is similar to the Unix `mkdir -p` command, which creates all directories that lead up to the specified directory if they don't exist already.	`hdfs dfs -mkdir <paths>`	`hdfs dfs -mkdir /user/hadoop/ dir5/temp`
`moveFrom Local`	Works similarly to the `put` command, except that the source is deleted after it is copied.	`hdfs dfs -moveFromLocal <localsrc> <dest>`	`hdfs dfs -moveFromLocal localfile1 localfile2 /user/hadoop/ hadoopdir`
`mv`	Moves one or more files from a specified source to a specified destination. If you specify multiple sources, the specified destination must be a directory. Moving files across file systems isn't permitted.	`hdfs dfs -mv URI [URI ...] <dest>`	`hdfs dfs -mv /user/hadoop/ file1 /user/ hadoop/file2`
`put`	Copies files from the local file system to the destination file system. This command can also read input from `stdin` and write to the destination file system.	`hdfs dfs -put <localsrc> ... <dest>`	`hdfs dfs -put localfile1 localfile2 /user/hadoop/ hadoopdir; hdfs dfs -put - /user/hadoop/ hadoopdir (reads input from stdin)`

rm	Deletes one or more speci-fied files. This command doesn't delete empty direc-tories or files. To bypass the trash (if it's enabled) and delete the specified files immediately, specify the -skipTrash option.	`hdfs dfs -rm [-skipTrash] URI [URI ...]`	`hdfs dfs -rm hdfs://nn. example.com/ file9`
rmr	Serves as the recursive version of −rm.	`hdfs dfs -rmr [-skipTrash] URI [URI ...]`	`hdfs dfs -rmr /user/hadoop/ dir`
setrep	Changes the replication factor for a specified file or directory. With -R, makes the change recursively by way of the directory structure.	`hdfs dfs -setrep <rep> [-R] <path>`	`hdfs dfs -setrep 3 -R /user/hadoop/ dir1`
stat	Displays information about the specified path.	`hdfs dfs -stat URI [URI ...]`	`hdfs dfs -stat /user/hadoop/ dir1`
tail	Displays the last kilobyte of a specified file to stdout. The syntax supports the Unix -f option, which enables the specified file to be monitored. As new lines are added to the file by another process, tail updates the display.	`hdfs dfs -tail [-f] URI`	`hdfs dfs -tail /user/hadoop/ dir1`
test	Returns attributes of the specified file or directory. Specifies -e to determine whether the file or direc-tory exists; -z to deter-mine whether the file or directory is empty; and -d to determine whether the URI is a directory.	`hdfs dfs -test -[ezd] URI`	`hdfs dfs -test /user/hadoop/ dir1`
text	Outputs a specified source file in text format. Valid input file formats are zip and TextRecord InputStream.	`hdfs dfs -text <src>`	`hdfs dfs -text /user/hadoop/ file8.zip`
touchz	Creates a new, empty file of size 0 in the specified path.	`hdfs dfs -touchz <path>`	`hdfs dfs -touchz /user/ hadoop/file12`

Ingesting Log Data with Flume

Some of the data that ends up in HDFS might land there via database load operations or other types of batch processes, but what if you want to capture the data that's flowing in high-throughput data streams, such as application log data? Apache Flume is the current standard way to do that easily, efficiently, and safely.

Apache Flume, another top-level project from the Apache Software Foundation, is a distributed system for aggregating and moving large amounts of streaming data from different sources to a centralized data store. Put another way, Flume is designed for the continuous ingestion of data into HDFS. The data can be any kind of data, but Flume is particularly well-suited to handling log data, such as the log data from web servers. Units of the data that Flume processes are called *events*; an example of an event is a log record.

To understand how Flume works within a Hadoop cluster, you need to know that Flume runs as one or more agents, and that each agent has three pluggable components: sources, channels, and sinks, as shown in Figure 5-1 and described in this list:

- *Sources* retrieve data and send it to channels.

- *Channels* hold data queues and serve as conduits between sources and sinks, which is useful when the incoming flow rate exceeds the outgoing flow rate.

- *Sinks* process data that was taken from channels and deliver it to a destination, such as HDFS.

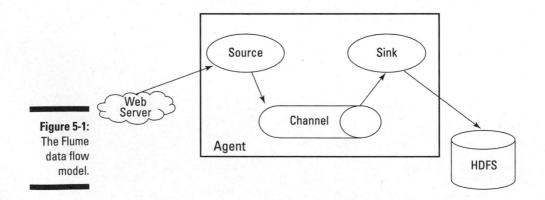

Figure 5-1:
The Flume
data flow
model.

An agent must have at least one of each component to run, and each agent is contained within its own instance of the Java Virtual Machine (JVM).

An event that is written to a channel by a source isn't removed from that channel until a sink removes it by way of a transaction. If a network failure occurs, channels keep their events queued until the sinks can write them to the cluster. An in-memory channel can process events quickly, but it is volatile and cannot be recovered, whereas a file-based channel offers persistence and can be recovered in the event of failure.

Each agent can have several sources, channels, and sinks, and although a source can write to many channels, a sink can take data from only one channel.

An agent is just a JVM that's running Flume, and the sinks for each *agent node* in the Hadoop cluster send data to *collector nodes*, which aggregate the data from many agents before writing it to HDFS, where it can be analyzed by other Hadoop tools.

Agents can be chained together so that the sink from one agent sends data to the source from another agent. Avro, Apache's remote call-and-serialization framework, is the usual way of sending data across a network with Flume, because it serves as a useful tool for the efficient serialization or transformation of data into a compact binary format. In the context of Flume, compatibility is important: An Avro event requires an Avro source, for example, and a sink must deliver events that are appropriate to the destination.

What makes this great chain of sources, channels, and sinks work is the Flume agent configuration, which is stored in a local text file that's structured like a Java properties file. You can configure multiple agents in the same file. Let's look at an sample file, which we name `flume-agent.conf` — it's set to configure an agent we named `shaman`:

```
# Identify the components on agent shaman:
shaman.sources = netcat_s1
shaman.sinks = hdfs_w1
shaman.channels = in-mem_c1

# Configure the source:
shaman.sources.netcat_s1.type = netcat
shaman.sources.netcat_s1.bind = localhost
shaman.sources.netcat_s1.port = 44444

# Describe the sink:
shaman.sinks.hdfs_w1.type = hdfs
shaman.sinks.hdfs_w1.hdfs.path = hdfs://<path>
shaman.sinks.hdfs_w1.hdfs.writeFormat = Text
shaman.sinks.hdfs_w1.hdfs.fileType = DataStream
```

```
# Configure a channel that buffers events in memory:
shaman.channels.in-mem_c1.type = memory
shaman.channels.in-mem_c1.capacity = 20000
shaman.channels.in-mem_c1.transactionCapacity = 100

# Bind the source and sink to the channel:
shaman.sources.netcat_s1.channels = in-mem_c1
shaman.sinks.hdfs_w1.channels = in-mem_c1
```

The configuration file includes properties for each source, channel, and sink in the agent and specifies how they're connected. In this example, agent shaman has a source that listens for data (messages to netcat) on port 44444, a channel that buffers event data in memory, and a sink that logs event data to the console. This configuration file could have been used to define several agents; we're configuring only one to keep things simple.

To start the agent, use a shell script called flume-ng, which is located in the bin directory of the Flume distribution. From the command line, issue the agent command, specifying the path to the configuration file and the agent name.

The following sample command starts the Flume agent that we showed you how to configure:

```
flume-ng agent -f /<path to flume-agent.conf> -n shaman
```

The Flume agent's log should have entries verifying that the source, channel, and sink started successfully.

To further test the configuration, you can telnet to port 44444 from another terminal and send Flume an event by entering an arbitrary text string. If all goes well, the original Flume terminal will output the event in a log message that you should be able to see in the agent's log.

Chapter 6

MapReduce Programming

After you've stored reams and reams of data in HDFS (a distributed storage system spread over an expandable cluster of individual slave nodes), the first question that comes to mind is "How can I analyze or query my data?" Transferring all this data to a central node for processing isn't the answer, since you'll be waiting forever for the data to transfer over the network (not to mention waiting for everything to be processed serially). So what's the solution? MapReduce!

As we describe in Chapter 1, Google faced this exact problem with their distributed Google File System (GFS), and came up with their MapReduce data processing model as the best possible solution. Google needed to be able to grow their data storage and processing capacity, and the only feasible model was a distributed system. In Chapter 4, we look at a number of the benefits of storing data in the Hadoop Distributed File System (HDFS): low cost, fault-tolerant, and easily scalable, to name just a few. In Hadoop, MapReduce integrates with HDFS to provide the exact same benefits for data processing.

At first glance, the strengths of Hadoop sound too good to be true — and overall the strengths truly are good! But there is a cost here: writing applications for distributed systems is completely different from writing the same code for centralized systems. For applications to take advantage of the distributed slave nodes in the Hadoop cluster, the application logic will need to run in parallel.

Thinking in Parallel

Let's say you want to do something simple, like count the number of flights for each carrier in our flight data set — this will be our example scenario for this chapter. For a normal program that runs serially, this is a simple operation. Listing 6-1 shows the pseudocode, which is fairly straightforward: set up the array to store the number of times you run across each carrier, and then, as you read each record in sequence, increment the applicable airline's counter.

Listing 6-1:   Pseudocode for Calculating The Number of Flights By Carrier Serially

```
create a two-dimensional array
  create a row for every airline carrier
    populate the first column with the carrier code
    populate the second column with the integer zero

for each line of flight data
  read the airline carrier code
  find the row in the array that matches the carrier code
    increment the counter in the second column by one

print the totals for each row in the two-dimensional array
```

The thing is, you would not be able to take this (elegantly simple) code and run it successfully on flight data stored in a distributed system. Even though this is a simple example, you need to think in parallel as you code your application. Listing 6-2 shows the pseudocode for calculating the number of flights by carrier in parallel.

Listing 6-2:   Pesudocode for Calculating The Number of Flights By Carrier in Parallel

```
Map Phase:
  for each line of flight data
    read the current record and extract the airline carrier code
    output the airline carrier code and the number one as a key/value pair

Shuffle and Sort Phase:
  read the list of key/value pairs from the map phase
  group all the values for each key together
    each key has a corresponding array of values
  sort the data by key
  output each key and its array of values

Reduce Phase:
  read the list of carriers and arrays of values from the shuffle and sort phase
  for each carrier code
    add the total number of ones in the carrier code's array of values together

print the totals for each row in the two-dimensional array
```

The code in Listing 6-2 shows a completely different way of thinking about how to process data. Since we need totals, we had to break this application up into phases. The first phase is the *map phase*, which is where every record in the data set is processed individually. Here, we extract the carrier code from the flight data record it's assigned, and then export a key/value pair, with the carrier code as the key and the value being an integer one. The map operation is run against every record in the data set. After every record is processed, you need to ensure that all the values (the integer ones) are grouped together for each key, which is the airline carrier code, and then sorted by key. This is known as the *shuffle and sort phase*. Finally, there is the reduce phase, where you add the total number of ones together for each airline carrier, which gives you the total flights for each airline carrier.

As you can see, there is little in common between the serial version of the code and the parallel version. Also, even though this is a simple example, developing the parallel version requires an altogether different approach. What's more, as the computation problems get even a little more difficult, they become even harder when they need to be parallelized.

Seeing the Importance of MapReduce

For most of Hadoop's history, MapReduce has been the only game in town when it comes to data processing. The availability of MapReduce has been the reason for Hadoop's success and at the same time a major factor in limiting further adoption.

As we'll see later in this chapter, MapReduce enables skilled programmers to write distributed applications without having to worry about the underlying distributed computing infrastructure. This is a very big deal: Hadoop and the MapReduce framework handle all sorts of complexity that application developers don't need to handle. For example, the ability to transparently scale out the cluster by adding nodes and the automatic failover of both data storage and data processing subsystems happen with zero impact on applications.

The other side of the coin here is that although MapReduce hides a tremendous amount of complexity, you can't afford to forget what it is: an interface for parallel programming. This is an advanced skill — and a barrier to wider adoption. There simply aren't yet many MapReduce programmers, and not everyone has the skill to master it.

The goal of this chapter is to help you understand how MapReduce applications work, how to think in parallel, and to provide a basic entry point into the world of MapReduce programming.

In Hadoop's early days (Hadoop 1 and before), you could only run MapReduce applications on your clusters. In Hadoop 2, the YARN component changed all that by taking over resource management and scheduling from the MapReduce framework, and providing a generic interface to facilitate applications to run on a Hadoop cluster. (See Chapter 7 for our discussion of YARN's framework-agnostic resource management.) In short, this means MapReduce is now just one of many application frameworks you can use to develop and run applications on Hadoop. Though it's certainly possible to run applications using other frameworks on Hadoop, it doesn't mean that we can start forgetting about MapReduce. At the time we wrote this book, MapReduce was still the only production-ready data processing framework available for Hadoop. Though other frameworks will eventually become available, MapReduce has almost a decade of maturity under its belt (with almost 4,000 JIRA issues completed, involving hundreds of developers, if you're keeping track). There's no dispute: MapReduce is Hadoop's most mature framework for data processing. In addition, a significant amount of MapReduce code is now in use that's unlikely to go anywhere soon. Long story short: MapReduce is an important part of the Hadoop story.

Later in this book, we cover certain programming abstractions to MapReduce, such as Pig (see Chapter 8) and Hive (see Chapter 13), which hide the complexity of parallel programming. The Apache Hive and Apache Pig projects are highly popular because they're easier entry points for data processing on Hadoop. For many problems, especially the kinds that you can solve with SQL, Hive and Pig are excellent tools. But for a wider-ranging task such as statistical processing or text extraction, and especially for processing unstructured data, you need to use MapReduce.

Doing Things in Parallel: Breaking Big Problems into Many Bite-Size Pieces

If you're a programmer, chances are good that you're at least aware of reddit, a popular discussion site — perhaps you're even a full-blown redditor. Its Ask Me Anything subreddit features a notable person logging in to reddit to answer redditor's questions. In a running gag, someone inevitably asks the question, "Would you rather fight 1 horse-sized duck or 100 duck-sized horses?" The answers and the rationale behind them are sources of great amusement, but they create a mental picture of what Hadoop and MapReduce are all about: scaling out as opposed to scaling up. Of course you'd rather defend yourself against 1 horse-sized duck — a herd of duck-sized horses would overwhelm you in seconds!

Looking at MapReduce application flow

At its core, MapReduce is a programming model for processing data sets that are stored in a distributed manner across a Hadoop cluster's slave nodes. The key concept here is *divide and conquer*. Specifically, you want to break a large data set into many smaller pieces and process them in parallel with the same algorithm. With the Hadoop Distributed File System (HDFS), the files are already divided into bite-sized pieces. MapReduce is what you use to process all the pieces.

MapReduce applications have multiple phases, as spelled out in this list:

1. Determine the exact data sets to process from the data blocks. This involves calculating where the records to be processed are located within the data blocks.

2. Run the specified algorithm against each record in the data set until all the records are processed. The individual instance of the application running against a block of data in a data set is known as a *mapper task*. (This is the mapping part of MapReduce.)

3. Locally perform an interim reduction of the output of each mapper. (The outputs are provisionally combined, in other words.) This phase is optional because, in some common cases, it isn't desirable.

4. Based on partitioning requirements, group the applicable partitions of data from each mapper's result sets.

5. Boil down the result sets from the mappers into a single result set — the Reduce part of MapReduce. An individual instance of the application running against mapper output data is known as a *reducer task*. (As strange as it may seem, since "Reduce" is part of the MapReduce name, this phase can be optional; applications without a reducer are known as *map-only jobs*, which can be useful when there's no need to combine the result sets from the map tasks.)

Understanding input splits

The way HDFS has been set up, it breaks down very large files into large blocks (for example, measuring 128MB), and stores three copies of these blocks on different nodes in the cluster. HDFS has no awareness of the content of these files. (If this business about HDFS doesn't ring a bell, check out Chapter 4.)

In YARN, when a MapReduce job is started, the Resource Manager (the cluster resource management and job scheduling facility) creates an Application Master daemon to look after the lifecycle of the job. (In Hadoop 1, the JobTracker monitored individual jobs as well as handling job scheduling and cluster resource management. For more on this, see Chapter 7.) One of the first things the Application Master does is determine which file blocks are needed for processing. The Application Master requests details from the NameNode on where the replicas of the needed data blocks are stored. Using the location data for the file blocks, the Application Master makes requests to the Resource Manager to have map tasks process specific blocks on the slave nodes where they're stored.

The key to efficient MapReduce processing is that, wherever possible, data is processed *locally* — on the slave node where it's stored.

Before looking at how the data blocks are processed, you need to look more closely at how Hadoop stores data. In Hadoop, files are composed of individual records, which are ultimately processed one-by-one by mapper tasks. For example, the sample data set we use in this book contains information about completed flights within the United States between 1987 and 2008. We have one large file for each year, and within every file, each individual line represents a single flight. In other words, one line represents one record. Now, remember that the block size for the Hadoop cluster is 64MB, which means that the light data files are broken into chunks of exactly 64MB.

Do you see the problem? If each map task processes all records in a specific data block, what happens to those records that span block boundaries? File blocks are exactly 64MB (or whatever you set the block size to be), and because HDFS has no conception of what's inside the file blocks, it can't gauge when a record might spill over into another block. To solve this problem, Hadoop uses a logical representation of the data stored in file blocks, known as *input splits*. When a MapReduce job client calculates the input splits, it figures out where the first whole record in a block begins and where the last record in the block ends. In cases where the last record in a block is incomplete, the input split includes location information for the next block and the byte offset of the data needed to complete the record. Figure 6-1 shows this relationship between data blocks and input splits.

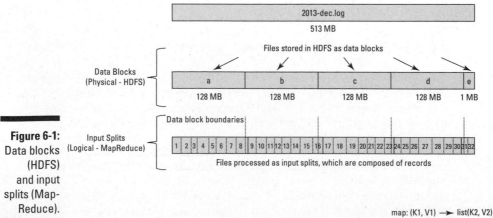

Figure 6-1: Data blocks (HDFS) and input splits (Map-Reduce).

You can configure the Application Master daemon (or JobTracker, if you're in Hadoop 1) to calculate the input splits instead of the job client, which would be faster for jobs processing a large number of data blocks.

MapReduce data processing is driven by this concept of input splits. The number of input splits that are calculated for a specific application determines the number of mapper tasks. Each of these mapper tasks is assigned, where possible, to a slave node where the input split is stored. The Resource Manager (or JobTracker, if you're in Hadoop 1) does its best to ensure that input splits are processed locally.

Seeing how key/value pairs fit into the MapReduce application flow

You may be wondering what happens in the processing of all these input splits. To answer this question, you need to understand that a MapReduce application processes the data in input splits on a *record-by-record* basis and that each record is understood by MapReduce to be a *key/value* pair. (In more technical descriptions of Hadoop, you see key/value pairs referred to as *tuples*.)

Obviously, when you're processing data, not everything needs to be represented as a key/value pair, so in cases where it isn't needed, you can provide a dummy key or value.

We describe the phases of a MapReduce application in the "Looking at MapReduce application flow" section, earlier in this chapter. Figure 6-2 fills out that description by showing how our sample MapReduce application (complete with sample flight data) makes its way through these phases. The next few sections of this chapter walk you through the process shown in Figure 6-2.

Map phase

After the input splits have been calculated, the mapper tasks can start processing them — that is, right after the Resource Manager's scheduling facility assigns them their processing resources. (In Hadoop 1, the JobTracker assigns mapper tasks to specific processing slots.) The mapper task itself processes its input split one record at a time — in Figure 6-2, this lone record is represented by the key/value pair (K1,V1). In the case of our flight data, when the input splits are calculated (using the default file processing method for text files), the assumption is that each row in the text file is a single record. For each record, the text of the row itself represents the value, and the byte offset of each row from the beginning of the split is considered to be the key.

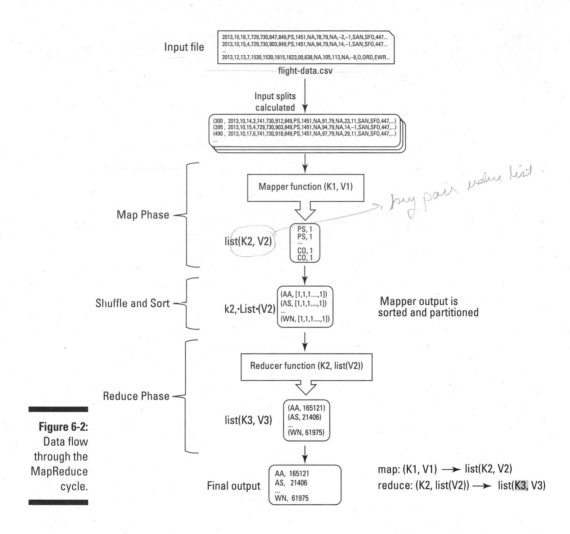

Input file

2013,10,18,7,729,730,847,849,PS,1451,NA,78,79,NA,−2,−1,SAN,SFO,447...
2013,10,15,4,729,730,903,849,PS,1451,NA,94,79,NA,14,−1,SAN,SFO,447...
...
2013,12,13,7,1530,1530,1815,1823,00,638,NA,105,113,NA,−8,0,ORD,EWR...

flight-data.csv

Input splits
calculated

(300 , 2013,10,14,3,741,730,912,849,PS,1451,NA,91,79,NA,23,11,SAN,SFO,447...)
(395 , 2013,10,15,4,729,730,903,849,PS,1451,NA,94,79,NA,14,−1,SAN,SFO,447...)
(490 , 2013,10,17,6,741,730,918,849,PS,1451,NA,97,79,NA,29,11,SAN,SFO,447...)
...

Map Phase

Mapper function (K1, V1)

hay pair value list

list(K2, V2)

PS, 1
PS, 1
...
CO, 1
CO, 1

Shuffle and Sort

k2,·List·(V2)

(AA, [1,1,1....,1])
(AS, [1,1,1....,1])
...
(WN, [1,1,1....,1])

Mapper output is
sorted and partitioned

Reduce Phase

Reducer function (K2, list(V2))

list(K3, V3)

(AA, 165121)
(AS, 21406)
...
(WN, 61975)

Final output

AA, 165121
AS,   21406
...
WN,   61975

map: (K1, V1) ⟶ list(K2, V2)
reduce: (K2, list(V2)) ⟶ list(K3, V3)

Figure 6-2:
Data flow
through the
MapReduce
cycle.

You might be wondering why the row number isn't used instead of the byte offset. When you consider that a very large text file is broken down into many individual data blocks, and is processed as many splits, the row number is a risky concept. The number of lines in each split vary, so it would be impossible to compute the number of rows preceding the one being processed. However, with the byte offset, you can be precise, because every block has a fixed number of bytes.

As a mapper task processes each record, it generates a new key/value pair: (K2, V2). The key and the value here can be completely different from the input pair. The output of the mapper task is the full collection of all these key/value pairs. In Figure 6-2, the output is represented by list(K2,V2).

Before the final output file for each mapper task is written, the output is partitioned based on the key and sorted. This partitioning means that all of the values for each key are grouped together, resulting in the following output: `K2, list(V2)`.

In the case of our fairly basic sample application, there is only a single reducer, so all the output of the mapper task is written to a single file. But in cases with multiple reducers, every mapper task may generate multiple output files as well. The breakdown of these output files is based on the partitioning key. For example, if there are only three distinct partitioning keys output for the mapper tasks and you have configured three reducers for the job, there will be three mapper output files. In this example, if a particular mapper task processes an input split and it generates output with two of the three keys, there will be only two output files.

Always compress your mapper tasks' output files. The biggest benefit here is in performance gains, because writing smaller output files minimizes the inevitable cost of transferring the mapper output to the nodes where the reducers are running. Enable compression by setting the `mapreduce.map.output.compress` property to `true` and assigning a compression codec to the `mapred.map.output.compress.codec` property. (This property can be found in the `mapred-site.xml` file, which is stored in Hadoop's `conf` directory. For details on configuring Hadoop, see Chapter 3.)

The default partitioner is more than adequate in most situations, but sometimes you may want to customize how the data is partitioned before it's processed by the reducers. For example, you may want the data in your result sets to be sorted by the key and their values — known as a *secondary* sort. To do this, you can override the default partitioner and implement your own. This process requires some care, however, because you'll want to ensure that the number of records in each partition is uniform. (If one reducer has to process much more data than the other reducers, you'll wait for your MapReduce job to finish while the single overworked reducer is slogging through its disproportionally large data set.) Using uniformly sized intermediate files, you can better take advantage of the parallelism available in MapReduce processing.

Shuffle phase

After the Map phase and before the beginning of the Reduce phase is a hand-off process, known as *shuffle and sort*. Here, data from the mapper tasks is prepared and moved to the nodes where the reducer tasks will be run. When the mapper task is complete, the results are sorted by key, partitioned if there are multiple reducers, and then written to disk. You can see this concept in Figure 6-3, which shows the MapReduce data processing flow and its interaction with the physical components of the Hadoop cluster. (One quick note about Figure 6-3: Data in memory is represented by white squares, and data stored to disk is represented by gray squares.) To speed up the overall MapReduce process, data is immediately moved to the reducer tasks' nodes, to avoid a flood of network activity when the final mapper task finishes its work. This transfer happens while the mapper task is running, as the outputs for each record — remember (K2,V2) — are stored in the memory of a waiting reducer task. (You can configure whether this happens — or doesn't happen — and also the number of threads involved.) Keep in mind that even though a reducer task might have most of the mapper task's output, the reduce task's processing cannot begin until all mapper tasks have finished.

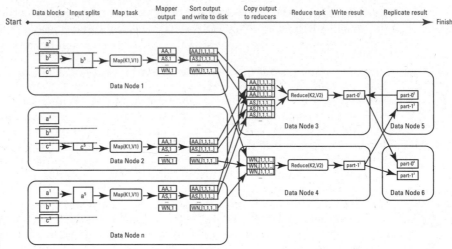

Figure 6-3:
MapReduce
processing
flow.

map: (K1, V1) ➤ list(K2, V2)
reduce: (K2, list(V2)) ➤ list(K3, V3)

To avoid scenarios where the performance of a MapReduce job is hampered by one straggling mapper task that's running on a poorly performing slave node, the MapReduce framework uses a concept called *speculative execution*. In case some mapper tasks are running slower than what's considered reasonable, the Application Master will spawn duplicate tasks (in Hadoop 1, the JobTracker does this). Whichever task finishes first — the duplicate or the original — its results are stored to disk, and the other task is killed. If you're monitoring your jobs closely and are wondering why there are more mapper tasks running than you expect, this is a likely reason.

The output from mapper tasks isn't written to HDFS, but rather to local disk on the slave node where the mapper task was run. As such, it's not replicated across the Hadoop cluster.

Aside from compressing the output, you can potentially boost performance by running a combiner task. This simple tactic, shown in Figure 6-4, involves performing a local reduce of the output for individual mapper tasks. In the majority of cases, no extra programming is needed, as you can tell the system to use the reducer function. If you're not using your reducer function, you need to ensure that the combiner function's output is identical to that of the reducer function. It's up to the MapReduce framework whether the combiner function needs to be run once, multiple times, or never, so it's critical that the combiner's code ensures that the final results are unaffected by multiple runs. Running the combiner can yield a performance benefit by lessening the amount of intermediate data that would otherwise need to be transferred over the network. This also lowers the amount of processing the reducer tasks would need to do. You are running an extra task here, so it is possible that any performance gain is negligible or may even result in worse overall performance. Your mileage may vary, so we recommend testing this carefully.

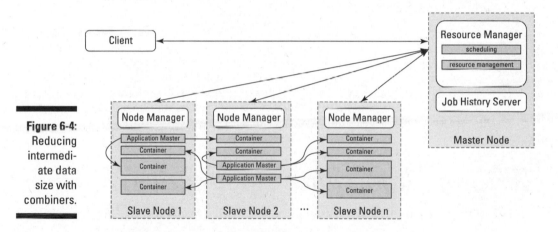

Figure 6-4: Reducing intermediate data size with combiners.

After all the results of the mapper tasks are copied to the reducer tasks' nodes, these files are merged and sorted.

Reduce phase

Here's the blow-by-blow so far: A large data set has been broken down into smaller pieces, called *input splits,* and individual instances of mapper tasks have processed each one of them. In some cases, this single phase of processing is all that's needed to generate the desired application output. For example, if you're running a basic transformation operation on the data — converting all text to uppercase, for example, or extracting key frames from video files — the lone phase is all you need. (This is known as a *map-only* job, by the way.) But in many other cases, the job is only half-done when the mapper tasks have written their output. The remaining task is boiling down all interim results to a single, unified answer.

The Reduce phase processes the keys and their individual lists of values so that what's normally returned to the client application is a set of key/value pairs. Similar to the mapper task, which processes each record one-by-one, the reducer processes each key individually. Back in Figure 6-2, you see this concept represented as K2, list(V2). The whole Reduce phase returns list(K3,V3). Normally, the reducer returns a single key/value pair for every key it processes. However, these key/value pairs can be as expansive or as small as you need them to be. In the code example later in this chapter, you see a minimalist case, with a simple key/value pair with one airline code and the corresponding total number of flights completed. But in practice, you could expand the sample to return a nested set of values where, for example, you return a breakdown of the number of flights per month for every airline code.

When the reducer tasks are finished, each of them returns a results file and stores it in HDFS. As shown in Figure 6-3, the HDFS system then automatically replicates these results.

Where the Resource Manager (or JobTracker if you're using Hadoop 1) tries its best to assign resources to mapper tasks to ensure that input splits are processed locally, there is no such strategy for reducer tasks. It is assumed that mapper task result sets need to be transferred over the network to be processed by the reducer tasks. This is a reasonable implementation because, with hundreds or even thousands of mapper tasks, there would be no practical way for reducer tasks to have the same locality prioritization.

Writing MapReduce Applications

The MapReduce API is written in Java, so MapReduce applications are primarily Java-based. The following list specifies the components of a MapReduce application that you can develop:

- **Driver (mandatory):** This is the application shell that's invoked from the client. It configures the MapReduce Job class (which you do not customize) and submits it to the Resource Manager (or JobTracker if you're using Hadoop 1).

- Mapper **class (mandatory):** The Mapper class you implement needs to define the formats of the key/value pairs you input and output as you process each record. This class has only a single method, named map, which is where you code how each record will be processed and what key/value to output. To output key/value pairs from the mapper task, write them to an instance of the Context class.

✔ Reducer **class (optional):** The reducer is optional for map-only applications where the Reduce phase isn't needed.

✔ Combiner **class (optional):** A combiner can often be defined as a reducer, but in some cases it needs to be different. (Remember, for example, that a reducer may not be able to run multiple times on a data set without mutating the results.)

✔ Partitioner **class (optional):** Customize the default partitioner to perform special tasks, such as a secondary sort on the values for each key or for rare cases involving sparse data and imbalanced output files from the mapper tasks.

✔ RecordReader **and** RecordWriter **classes (optional):** Hadoop has some standard data formats (for example, text files, sequence files, and databases), which are useful for many cases. For specifically formatted data, implementing your own classes for reading and writing data can greatly simplify your mapper and reducer code.

From within the driver, you can use the MapReduce API, which includes factory methods to create instances of all components in the preceding list. (In case you're not a Java person, a factory method is a tool for creating objects.)

A generic API named Hadoop Streaming lets you use other programming languages (most commonly, C, Python, and Perl). Though this API enables organizations with non-Java skills to write MapReduce code, using it has some disadvantages. Because of the additional abstraction layers that this streaming code needs to go through in order to function, there's a performance penalty and increased memory usage. Also, you can code mapper and reducer functions only with Hadoop Streaming. Record readers and writers, as well as all your partitioners, need to be written in Java. A direct consequence — and additional disadvantage — of being unable to customize record readers and writers is that Hadoop Streaming applications are well suited to handle only text-based data.

In this book, we've made two critical decisions around the libraries we're using and how the applications are processed on the Hadoop cluster. We're using the MapReduce framework in the YARN processing environment (often referred to as MRv2), as opposed to the old JobTracker / TaskTracker environment from before Hadoop 2 (referred to as MRv1). Also, for the code libraries, we're using what's generally known as the new MapReduce API, which belongs to the org.apache.hadoop.mapreduce package. The old MapReduce API uses the org.apache.hadoop.mapred package. We still see code in the wild using the old API, but it's deprecated, and we don't recommend writing new applications with it.

Getting Your Feet Wet: Writing a Simple MapReduce Application

It's time to take a look at a simple application. As we do throughout this book, we'll analyze data for commercial flights in the United States. In this MapReduce application, the goal is to simply calculate the total number of flights flown for every carrier.

The FlightsByCarrier driver application

As a starting point for the FlightsByCarrier application, you need a client application driver, which is what we use to launch the MapReduce code on the Hadoop cluster. We came up with the driver application shown in Listing 6-3, which is stored in the file named `FlightsByCarrier.java`.

Listing 6-3:   The FlightsByCarrier Driver Application

```
@@1
import org.apache.hadoop.fs.Path;
import org.apache.hadoop.io.*;
import org.apache.hadoop.mapreduce.Job;
import org.apache.hadoop.mapreduce.lib.input.TextInputFormat;
import org.apache.hadoop.mapreduce.lib.output.TextOutputFormat;

public class FlightsByCarrier {
        public static void main(String[] args) throws Exception {
                @@2
                Job job = new Job();
                job.setJarByClass(FlightsByCarrier.class);
                job.setJobName("FlightsByCarrier");

                @@3
                TextInputFormat.addInputPath(job, new Path(args[0]));
                job.setInputFormatClass(TextInputFormat.class);

                @@4
                job.setMapperClass(FlightsByCarrierMapper.class);
                job.setReducerClass(FlightsByCarrierReducer.class);

                @@5
                TextOutputFormat.setOutputPath(job, new Path(args[1]));
                job.setOutputFormatClass(TextOutputFormat.class);
                job.setOutputKeyClass(Text.class);
                job.setOutputValueClass(IntWritable.class);
```

```
           @@6
           job.waitForCompletion(true);
     }
}
```

The code in most MapReduce applications is more or less similar. The driver's job is essentially to define the structure of the MapReduce application and invoke it on the cluster — none of the application logic is defined here.

As you walk through the code, take note of these principles:

- ✔ **The import statements that follow the bold @@1 in the code pull in all required Hadoop classes.** Note that we used the new MapReduce API, as indicated by the use of the `org.apache.hadoop.mapreduce` package.

- ✔ **The first instance of the `Job` class (see the code that follows the bolded @@2) represents the entire MapReduce application.** Here, we've set the class name that will run the job and an identifier for it. By default, job properties are read from the configuration files stored in `/etc/hadoop/conf`, but you can override them by setting your `Job` class properties.

- ✔ **Using the input path we catch from the `main` method, (see the code that follows the bolded @@3), we identify the HDFS path for the data to be processed.** We also identify the expected format of the data. The default input format is `TextInputFormat` (which we've included for clarity).

- ✔ **After identifying the HDFS path, we want to define the overall structure of the MapReduce application.** We do that by specifying both the `Mapper` and `Reducer` classes. (See the code that follows the bolded @@4.) If we wanted a map-only job, we would simply omit the definition of the `Reducer` class and set the number of reduce tasks to zero with the following line of code:

```
job.setNumReduceTasks(0)
```

- ✔ **After specifying the app's overall structure, we need to indicate the HDFS path for the application's output as well as the format of the data.** (See the code following the bolded @@5.) The data format is quite specific here because both the key and value formats need to be identified.

- ✔ **Finally, we run the job and wait.** (See the code following the bolded @@6.) The driver waits at this point until the `waitForCompletion` function returns. As an alternative, if you want your driver application to run the lines of code following the submission of the job, you can use the `submit` method instead.

The FlightsByCarrier mapper

Listing 6-4 shows the mapper code, which is stored in the file named
`FlightsByCarrierMapper.java`.

Listing 6-4: The FlightsByCarrier Mapper Code

```
@@1
import java.io.IOException;
import au.com.bytecode.opencsv.CSVParser;
import org.apache.hadoop.io.*;
import org.apache.hadoop.mapreduce.Mapper;

@@2
public class FlightsByCarrierMapper extends
                              Mapper<LongWritable, Text, Text, IntWritable> {
    @Override
    @@3
    protected void map(LongWritable key, Text value, Context context)
             throws IOException, InterruptedException {
        @@4
        if (key.get() > 0) {
              String[] lines = new
        CSVParser().parseLine(value.toString());
              @@5
              context.write(new Text(lines[8]), new IntWritable(1));
        }
    }
}
```

The code for mappers is where you see the most variation, though it has
standard boilerplate. Here are the high points:

- **The import statements that follow the bold @@1 in the code pull in
  all the required Hadoop classes.** The `CSVParser` class isn't a standard
  Hadoop class, but we use it to simply the parsing of CSV files.

- The specification of the `Mapper` class (see the code after the bolded
  @@2) explicitly identifies the formats of the key/value pairs that the
  mapper will input and output.

- The `Mapper` class has a single method, named `map`. (See the code after
  the bolded @@3.) The `map` method names the input key/value pair variables and the `Context` object, which is where output key/value pairs
  are written.

✔ The block of code in the if statement is where all data processing happens. (See the code after the bolded @@4.) We use the if statement to indicate that we don't want to parse the first line in the file, because it's the header information describing each column. It's also where we parse the records using the CSVParser class's parseLine method.

✔ With the array of strings that represent the values of the flight record being processed, the ninth value is returned to the Context object as the key. (See the code after the bolded @@5.) This value represents the carrier that completed the flight. For the value, we return a value of one because this represents one flight.

The FlightsByCarrier reducer

Listing 6-5 shows the reducer code, which is stored in the file named FlightsByCarrierReducer.java.

Listing 6-5: The FlightsByCarrier Reducer Code

```
@@1
import java.io.IOException;
import org.apache.hadoop.io.*;
import org.apache.hadoop.mapreduce.Reducer;

@@2
public class FlightsByCarrierReducer extends
          Reducer<Text, IntWritable, Text, IntWritable> {
     @Override
     @@3
     protected void reduce(Text token, Iterable<IntWritable> counts,
               Context context) throws IOException, InterruptedException {
          int sum = 0;

          @@4
          for (IntWritable count : counts) {
               sum+= count.get();
          }
          @@5
          context.write(token, new IntWritable(sum));
     }
}
```

The code for reducers also has a fair amount of variation, but it also has common patterns. For example, the counting exercise is quite common. Again, here are the high points:

- ✔ The import statements that follow the bold @@1 in the code pull in all required Hadoop classes.

- ✔ The specification of the Reducer class (see the code after the bolded @@2) explicitly identifies the formats of the key/value pairs that the reducer will input and output.

- ✔ The Reducer class has a single method, named reduce. The reduce method names the input key/value pair variables and the Context object, which is where output key/value pairs are written. (See the code after the bolded @@3.)

- ✔ The block of code in the for loop is where all data processing happens. (See the code after the bolded @@4.) Remember that the reduce function runs on individual keys and their lists of values. So for the particular key, (in this case, the carrier), the for loop sums the numbers in the list, which are all ones. This provides the total number of flights for the particular carrier.

- ✔ This total is written to the context object as the value, and the input key, named token, is reused as the output key. (See the code after the bolded @@5.)

Running the FlightsByCarrier application

To run the FlightsByCarrier application, follow these steps:

1. **Go to the directory with your Java code and compile it using the following command:**

```
javac -classpath $CLASSPATH MapRed/FlightsByCarrier/*.java
```

2. **Build a JAR file for the application by using this command:**

```
jar cvf FlightsByCarrier.jar *.class
```

3. **Run the driver application by using this command:**

```
hadoop jar FlightsByCarrier.jar FlightsByCarrier /user/root/airline-
        data/2008.csv /user/root/output/flightsCount
```

Note that we're running the application against data from the year 2008. For this application to work, we clearly need the flight data to be stored in HDFS in the path identified in the command

```
/user/root/airline-data
```

The application runs for a few minutes. (Running it on a virtual machine on a laptop computer may take a little longer, especially if the machine has less than 8GB of RAM and only a single processor.) Listing 6-6 shows the status messages you can expect in your terminal window. You can usually safely ignore the many warnings and informational messages strewn throughout this output.

4. Show the job's output file from HDFS by running the command

```
hadoop fs -cat /user/root/output/flightsCount/part-r-00000
```

You see the total counts of all flights completed for each of the carriers in 2008:

```
AA        165121
AS        21406
CO        123002
DL        185813
EA        108776
HP        45399
NW        108273
PA (1)    16785
PI        116482
PS        41706
TW        69650
UA        152624
US        94814
WN        61975
```

Listing 6-6:   The FlightsByCarrier Application Output

```
...
14/01/30 19:58:39 INFO mapreduce.Job: The url to track the job:
  http://localhost.localdomain:8088/proxy/application_1386752664246_0017/
14/01/30 19:58:39 INFO mapreduce.Job: Running job: job_1386752664246_0017
14/01/30 19:58:47 INFO mapreduce.Job: Job job_1386752664246_0017 running in uber
  mode : false
14/01/30 19:58:47 INFO mapreduce.Job:  map 0% reduce 0%
14/01/30 19:59:03 INFO mapreduce.Job:  map 83% reduce 0%
14/01/30 19:59:04 INFO mapreduce.Job:  map 100% reduce 0%
14/01/30 19:59:11 INFO mapreduce.Job:  map 100% reduce 100%
14/01/30 19:59:11 INFO mapreduce.Job: Job job_1386752664246_0017 completed
  successfully
14/01/30 19:59:11 INFO mapreduce.Job: Counters: 43
    File System Counters
        FILE: Number of bytes read=11873580
        FILE: Number of bytes written=23968326
        FILE: Number of read operations=0
```

(continued)

Listing 6-6 *(continued)*

```
        FILE: Number of large read operations=0
        FILE: Number of write operations=0
        HDFS: Number of bytes read=127167274
        HDFS: Number of bytes written=137
        HDFS: Number of read operations=9
        HDFS: Number of large read operations=0
        HDFS: Number of write operations=2
    Job Counters
        Launched map tasks=2
        Launched reduce tasks=1
        Data-local map tasks=2
        Total time spent by all maps in occupied slots (ms)=29786
        Total time spent by all reduces in occupied slots (ms)=6024
    Map-Reduce Framework
        Map input records=1311827
        Map output records=1311826
        Map output bytes=9249922
        Map output materialized bytes=11873586
        Input split bytes=236
        Combine input records=0
        Combine output records=0
        Reduce input groups=14
        Reduce shuffle bytes=11873586
        Reduce input records=1311826
        Reduce output records=14
        Spilled Records=2623652
        Shuffled Maps =2
        Failed Shuffles=0
        Merged Map outputs=2
        GC time elapsed (ms)=222
        CPU time spent (ms)=8700
        Physical memory (bytes) snapshot=641634304
        Virtual memory (bytes) snapshot=2531708928
        Total committed heap usage (bytes)=496631808
    Shuffle Errors
        BAD_ID=0
        CONNECTION=0
        IO_ERROR=0
        WRONG_LENGTH=0
        WRONG_MAP=0
        WRONG_REDUCE=0
    File Input Format Counters
        Bytes Read=127167038
    File Output Format Counters
 Bytes Written=137
```

There you have it. You've just seen how to program and run a basic MapReduce application. What we've done is read the flight data set and calculated the total number of flights flown for every carrier. To make this work in MapReduce, we had to think about how to program this calculation so that the individual pieces of the larger data set could be processed in parallel. And, not to put too fine a point on it, the thoughts we came up with turned out to be pretty darn good!

Chapter 7

Frameworks for Processing Data in Hadoop: YARN and MapReduce

• •

In This Chapter

▶ Examining distributed data processing in Hadoop

▶ Looking at MapReduce execution

▶ Venturing into YARN architecture

▶ Anticipating future directions for data processing on Hadoop

• •

My, how time flies. If we had written this book a year (well, a few months) earlier, this chapter on data processing would have talked only about MapReduce, for the simple reason that MapReduce was then the only way to process data in Hadoop. With the release of Hadoop 2, however, YARN was introduced, ushering in a whole new world of data processing opportunities.

YARN stands for Yet Another Resource Negotiator — a rather modest label considering its key role in the Hadoop ecosystem. (The Yet Another label is a long-running gag in computer science that celebrates programmers' propensity to be lazy about feature names.) A (Hadoop-centric) thumbnail sketch would describe YARN as a tool that enables other data processing frameworks to run on Hadoop. A more substantive take on YARN would describe it as a general-purpose resource management facility that can schedule and assign CPU cycles and memory (and in the future, other resources, such as network bandwidth) from the Hadoop cluster to waiting applications.

At the time of this writing, only batch-mode MapReduce applications were supported in production. A number of additional application frameworks being ported to YARN are in various stages of development, however, and many of them will soon be production ready.

For us authors, as Hadoop enthusiasts, YARN raises exciting possibilities. Singlehandedly, YARN has converted Hadoop from simply a batch processing engine into a platform for many different modes of data processing, from traditional batch to interactive queries to streaming analysis.

Running Applications Before Hadoop 2

Because many existing Hadoop deployments still aren't yet using YARN, we take a quick look at how Hadoop managed its data processing before the days of Hadoop 2. We concentrate on the role that JobTracker master daemons and TaskTracker slave daemons played in handling MapReduce processing.

Before tackling the daemons, however, let us back up and remind you that the whole point of employing distributed systems is to be able to deploy computing resources in a network of self-contained computers in a manner that's fault-tolerant, easy, and inexpensive. In a distributed system such as Hadoop, where you have a cluster of self-contained compute nodes all working in parallel, a great deal of complexity goes into ensuring that all the pieces work together. As such, these systems typically have distinct layers to handle different tasks to support parallel data processing. This concept, known as the *separation of concerns,* ensures that if you are, for example, the application programmer, you don't need to worry about the specific details for, say, the failover of map tasks. In Hadoop, the system consists of these four distinct layers, as shown in Figure 7-1:

- **Distributed storage:** The Hadoop Distributed File System (HDFS) is the storage layer where the data, interim results, and final result sets are stored.

- **Resource management:** In addition to disk space, all slave nodes in the Hadoop cluster have CPU cycles, RAM, and network bandwidth. A system such as Hadoop needs to be able to parcel out these resources so that multiple applications and users can share the cluster in predictable and tunable ways. This job is done by the JobTracker daemon.

- **Processing framework:** The MapReduce process flow defines the execution of all applications in Hadoop 1. As we saw in Chapter 6, this begins with the map phase; continues with aggregation with shuffle, sort, or merge; and ends with the reduce phase. In Hadoop 1, this is also managed by the JobTracker daemon, with local execution being managed by TaskTracker daemons running on the slave nodes.

- **Application Programming Interface (API):** Applications developed for Hadoop 1 needed to be coded using the MapReduce API. In Hadoop 1, the Hive and Pig projects provide programmers with easier interfaces for writing Hadoop applications, and underneath the hood, their code compiles down to MapReduce.

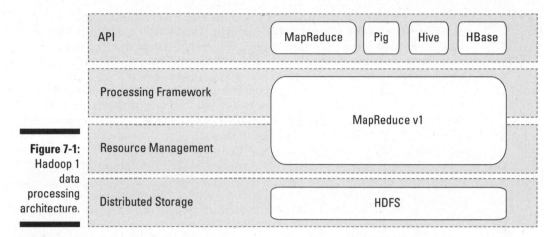

Figure 7-1:
Hadoop 1
data
processing
architecture.

In the world of Hadoop 1 (which was the only world we had until quite recently), all data processing revolved around MapReduce.

Tracking JobTracker

MapReduce processing in Hadoop 1 is handled by the JobTracker and TaskTracker daemons. The JobTracker maintains a view of all available processing resources in the Hadoop cluster and, as application requests come in, it schedules and deploys them to the TaskTracker nodes for execution. As applications are running, the JobTracker receives status updates from the TaskTracker nodes to track their progress and, if necessary, coordinate the handling of any failures. The JobTracker needs to run on a master node in the Hadoop cluster as it coordinates the execution of all MapReduce applications in the cluster, so it's a mission-critical service.

Tracking TaskTracker

An instance of the TaskTracker daemon runs on every slave node in the Hadoop cluster, which means that each slave node has a service that ties it to the processing (TaskTracker) and the storage (DataNode), which enables Hadoop to be a distributed system. As a slave process, the TaskTracker receives processing requests from the JobTracker. Its primary responsibility is to track the execution of MapReduce workloads happening locally on its slave node and to send status updates to the JobTracker.

TaskTrackers manage the processing resources on each slave node in the form of processing slots — the slots defined for map tasks and reduce tasks, to be exact. The total number of map and reduce slots indicates how many map and reduce tasks can be executed at one time on the slave node.

When it comes to tuning a Hadoop cluster, setting the optimal number of map and reduce slots is critical. The number of slots needs to be carefully configured based on available memory, disk, and CPU resources on each slave node. Memory is the most critical of these three resources from a performance perspective. As such, the total number of task slots needs to be balanced with the maximum amount of memory allocated to the Java heap size. Keep in mind that every map and reduce task spawns its own Java virtual machine (JVM) and that the heap represents the amount of memory that's allocated for each JVM. The ratio of map slots to reduce slots is also an important consideration. For example, if you have too many map slots and not enough reduce slots for your workloads, map slots will tend to sit idle, while your jobs are waiting for reduce slots to become available.

Distinct sets of slots are defined for map tasks and reduce tasks because they use computing resources quite differently. Map tasks are assigned based on data locality, and they depend heavily on disk I/O and CPU. Reduce tasks are assigned based on availability, not on locality, and they depend heavily on network bandwidth because they need to receive output from map tasks.

Launching a MapReduce application

To see how the JobTracker and TaskTracker work together to carry out a MapReduce action, take a look at the execution of a MapReduce application, as shown in Figure 7-2. The figure shows the interactions, and the following step list lays out the play-by-play:

1. The client application submits an application request to the JobTracker.

2. The JobTracker determines how many processing resources are needed to execute the entire application. This is done by requesting the locations and names of the files and data blocks that the application needs from the NameNode, and calculating how many map tasks and reduce tasks will be needed to process all this data.

3. The JobTracker looks at the state of the slave nodes and queues all the map tasks and reduce tasks for execution.

4. As processing slots become available on the slave nodes, map tasks are deployed to the slave nodes. Map tasks assigned to specific blocks of data are assigned to nodes where that same data is stored.

5. The JobTracker monitors task progress, and in the event of a task failure or a node failure, the task is restarted on the next available slot. If the same task fails after four attempts (which is a default value and can be customized), the whole job will fail.

6. After the map tasks are finished, reduce tasks process the interim result sets from the map tasks.

7. The result set is returned to the client application.

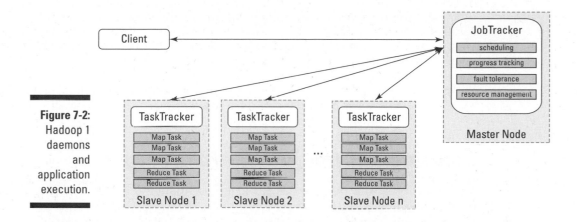

Figure 7-2:
Hadoop 1
daemons
and
application
execution.

More complicated applications can have multiple rounds of map/reduce phases, where the result of one round is used as input for the second round. This is quite common with SQL-style workloads, where there are, for example, join and group-by operations.

Seeing a World beyond MapReduce

MapReduce has been (and continues to be) a successful batch-oriented programming model. You need look no further than the wide adoption of Hadoop to recognize the truth of this statement. But Hadoop itself has been hitting a glass ceiling in terms of wider use. The most significant factor in this regard has been Hadoop's exclusive tie to MapReduce, which means that it could be used only for batch-style workloads and for general-purpose analysis. Hadoop's success has created demand for additional data processing modes: graph analysis, for example, or streaming data processing or message passing. To top it all off, demand is growing for real-time and ad-hoc analysis, where analysts ask many smaller questions against subsets of the data and need a near-instant response. This approach, which is what analysts are accustomed to using with relational databases, is a significant departure from the kind of batch processing Hadoop can currently support.

When you start noticing a technology's limitations, you're reminded of all its other little quirks that bother you, such as Hadoop 1's restrictions around scalability — the limitation of the number of data blocks that the NameNode could track, for example. (See Chapter 4 for more on these — and other — restrictions.) The JobTracker also has a practical limit to the amount of processing resources and running tasks it can track – this (like the NameNode's limitations) is between 4,000 and 5,000 nodes.

And finally, to the extent that Hadoop could support different kinds of workloads other than MapReduce — largely with HBase and other third-party services running on slave nodes — there was no easy way to handle competing requests for limited resources.

Where there's a will, there's often a way, and the will to move beyond the limitations of a Hadoop 1/MapReduce world led to a way out — the YARN way.

Scouting out the YARN architecture

YARN, for those just arriving at this particular party, stands for Yet Another Resource Negotiator, a tool that enables other data processing frameworks to run on Hadoop. The glory of YARN is that it presents Hadoop with an elegant solution to a number of longstanding challenges, many of which are outlined in some detail in the previous section. If you can't be bothered to reread that section, just know that YARN is meant to provide a more efficient and flexible workload scheduling as well as a resource management facility, both of which will ultimately enable Hadoop to run more than just MapReduce jobs.

Figure 7-3 shows in general terms how YARN fits into Hadoop and also makes clear how it has enabled Hadoop to become a truly general-purpose platform for data processing. The following list gives the lyrics to the melody — and it wouldn't hurt to compare Figure 7-3 with Figure 7-1:

- **Distributed storage:** Nothing has changed here with the shift from MapReduce to YARN — HDFS is still the storage layer for Hadoop.

- **Resource management:** The key underlying concept in the shift to YARN from Hadoop 1 is decoupling resource management from data processing. This enables YARN to provide resources to any processing framework written for Hadoop, including MapReduce.

- **Processing framework:** Because YARN is a general-purpose resource management facility, it can allocate cluster resources to any data processing framework written for Hadoop. The processing framework then handles application runtime issues. To maintain compatibility for all the code that was developed for Hadoop 1, MapReduce serves as the first framework available for use on YARN. At the time of this writing, the Apache Tez project was an incubator project in development as an alternative framework for the execution of Pig and Hive applications. Tez will likely emerge as a standard Hadoop configuration.

- **Application Programming Interface (API):** With the support for additional processing frameworks, support for additional APIs will come. At the time of this writing, Hoya (for running HBase on YARN), Apache Giraph (for graph processing), Open MPI (for message passing in parallel systems), Apache Storm (for data stream processing) are in active development.

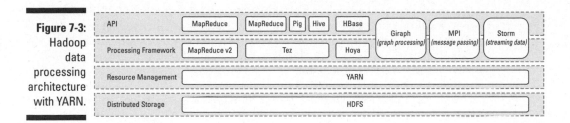

Figure 7-3:
Hadoop
data
processing
architecture
with YARN.

YARN's Resource Manager

The core component of YARN is the Resource Manager, which governs all the
data processing resources in the Hadoop cluster. Simply put, the Resource
Manager is a dedicated scheduler that assigns resources to requesting
applications. Its only tasks are to maintain a global view of all resources in
the cluster, handling resource requests, scheduling the request, and then
assigning resources to the requesting application.

The Resource Manager, a critical component in a Hadoop cluster, should run
on a dedicated master node.

Even though the Resource Manager is basically a pure scheduler, it relies
on scheduler modules for the actual scheduling logic. You can choose from
the same schedulers that were available in Hadoop 1, which have all been
updated to work with YARN: FIFO (first in, first out), Capacity, or Fair Share.
We'll discuss these schedulers in greater detail in Chapter 17.

The Resource Manager is completely agnostic with regard to both applications and frameworks — it doesn't have any dogs in those particular hunts,
in other words. It has no concept of map or reduce tasks, it doesn't track the
progress of jobs or their individual tasks, and it doesn't handle failovers. In
short, the Resource Manager is a complete departure from the JobTracker
daemon we looked at for Hadoop 1 environments. What the Resource
Manager does do is schedule workloads, and it does that job well. This high
degree of separating duties — concentrating on one aspect while ignoring
everything else — is exactly what makes YARN much more scalable, able to
provide a generic platform for applications, and able to support a *multi-tenant*
Hadoop cluster — multi-tenant because different business units can share the
same Hadoop cluster.

YARN's Node Manager

Each slave node has a Node Manager daemon, which acts as a slave for the
Resource Manager. As with the TaskTracker, each slave node has a service
that ties it to the processing service (Node Manager) and the storage service
(DataNode) that enable Hadoop to be a distributed system. Each Node Manager
tracks the available data processing resources on its slave node and sends
regular reports to the Resource Manager.

The processing resources in a Hadoop cluster are consumed in bite-size pieces called containers. A *container* is a collection of all the resources necessary to run an application: CPU cores, memory, network bandwidth, and disk space. A deployed container runs as an individual process on a slave node in a Hadoop cluster.

The concept of a container may remind you of a *slot,* the unit of processing used by the JobTracker and TaskTracker, but they have some notable differences. Most significantly, containers are generic and can run whatever application logic they're given, unlike slots, which are specifically defined to run either map or reduce tasks. Also, containers can be requested with custom amounts of resources, while slots are all uniform. As long as the requested amount is within the minimum and maximum bounds of what's acceptable for a container (and as long as the requested amount of memory is a multiple of the minimum amount), the Resource Manager will grant and schedule that container.

All container processes running on a slave node are initially provisioned, monitored, and tracked by that slave node's Node Manager daemon.

YARN's Application Master

Unlike the YARN components we've described already, no component in Hadoop 1 maps directly to the Application Master. In essence, this is work that the JobTracker did for every application, but the implementation is radically different. Each application running on the Hadoop cluster has its own, dedicated Application Master instance, which actually runs in a container process on a slave node (as compared to the JobTracker, which was a single daemon that ran on a master node and tracked the progress of all applications).

Throughout its life (for example, while the application is running), the Application Master sends heartbeat messages to the Resource Manager with its status and the state of the application's resource needs. Based on the results of the Resource Manager's scheduling, it assigns *container resource leases* — basically reservations for the resources containers need — to the Application Master on specific slave nodes.

The Application Master oversees the full lifecycle of an application, all the way from requesting the needed containers from the Resource Manager to submitting container lease requests to the NodeManager.

Each application framework that's written for Hadoop must have its own Application Master implementation. MapReduce, for example, has a specific Application Master that's designed to execute map tasks and reduce tasks in sequence.

Job History Server

The Job History Server is another example of a function that the JobTracker used to handle, and it has been siphoned off as a self-contained daemon. Any client requests for a job history or the status of current jobs are served by the Job History Server.

Launching a YARN-based application

To show how the various YARN components work together, we walk you through the execution of an application. For the sake of argument, it can be a MapReduce application, such as the one we describe earlier in this chapter, with the JobTracker and TaskTracker architecture. Just remember that, with YARN, it can be any kind of application for which there's an application framework. Figure 7-4 shows the interactions, and the prose account is set down in the following step list:

1. The client application submits an application request to the Resource Manager.

2. The Resource Manager asks a Node Manager to create an Application Master instance for this application. The Node Manager gets a container for it and starts it up.

3. This new Application Master initializes itself by registering itself with the Resource Manager.

4. The Application Master figures out how many processing resources are needed to execute the entire application. This is done by requesting from the NameNode the names and locations of the files and data blocks the application needs and calculating how many map tasks and reduce tasks are needed to process all this data.

5. The Application Master then requests the necessary resources from the Resource Manager. The Application Master sends heartbeat messages to the Resource Manager throughout its lifetime, with a standing list of requested resources and any changes (for example, a kill request).

6. The Resource Manager accepts the resource request and queues up the specific resource requests alongside all the other resource requests that are already scheduled.

7. As the requested resources become available on the slave nodes, the Resource Manager grants the Application Master leases for containers on specific slave nodes.

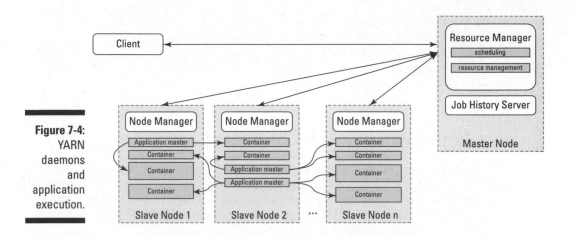

Figure 7-4:
YARN
daemons
and
application
execution.

8. The Application Master requests the assigned container from the Node Manager and sends it a Container Launch Context (CLC). The CLC includes everything the application task needs in order to run: environment variables, authentication tokens, local resources needed at runtime (for example, additional data files, or application logic in JARs), and the command string necessary to start the actual process. The Node Manager then creates the requested container process and starts it.

9. The application executes while the container processes are running. The Application Master monitors their progress, and in the event of a container failure or a node failure, the task is restarted on the next available slot. If the same task fails after four attempts (a default value which can be customized), the whole job will fail. During this phase, the Application Master also communicates directly with the client to respond to status requests.

10. Also, while containers are running, the Resource Manager can send a kill order to the Node Manager to terminate a specific container. This can be as a result of a scheduling priority change or a normal operation, such as the application itself already being completed.

11. In the case of MapReduce applications, after the map tasks are finished, the Application Master requests resources for a round of reduce tasks to process the interim result sets from the map tasks.

12. When all tasks are complete, the Application Master sends the result set to the client application, informs the Resource Manager that the application has successfully completed, deregisters itself from the Resource Manager, and shuts itself down.

Like the JobTracker and TaskTracker daemons and processing slots in Hadoop 1, all of the YARN daemons and containers are Java processes, running in JVMs. With YARN, you're no longer required to define how many map and reduce slots you need — you simply decide how much memory map and reduce tasks can have. The Resource Manager will allocate containers for map or reduce tasks on the cluster based on how much memory is available.

In this section, we have described what happens underneath the hood when applications run on YARN. When you're writing Hadoop applications, you don't need to worry about requesting resources and monitoring containers. Whatever application framework you're using does all that for you. It's always a good idea, however, to understand what goes on when your applications are running on the cluster. This knowledge can help you immensely when you're monitoring application progress or debugging a failed task.

Real-Time and Streaming Applications

The process flow we describe in our coverage of YARN looks an awful lot like a framework for batch execution. You might wonder, "What happened to this idea of flexibility for different modes of applications?" Well, the only application framework that was ready for production use at the time of this writing was MapReduce. Soon, the Apache Tez and Apache Storm will be ready for production use, and you can use Hadoop for more than just batch processing.

Tez, for example, will support *real-time* applications — an interactive kind of application where the user expects an immediate response. One design goal of Tez is to provide an interactive facility for users to issue Hive queries and receive a result set in just a few seconds or less.

Another example of a non-batch type of application is Storm, which can analyze streaming data. This concept is completely different from either MapReduce or Tez, both of which operate against data that is already persisted to disk — in other words, data at rest. Storm processes data that hasn't yet been stored to disk — more specifically, data that's streaming into an organization's network. It's data in motion, in other words.

In both cases, the interactive and streaming-data processing goals wouldn't work if Application Masters need to be instantiated, along with all the required containers, like we described in the steps involved in running a YARN application. What YARN allows here is the concept of an ongoing service (a session), where there's a dedicated Application Master that stays alive, waiting to coordinate requests. The Application Master also has open leases on reusable containers to execute any requests as they arrive.

Chapter 8

Pig: Hadoop Programming Made Easier

· ·

In This Chapter

▶ Looking at the Pig architecture

▶ Seeing the flow in the Pig Latin application flow

▶ Reciting the ABCs of Pig Latin

▶ Distinguishing between local and distributed modes of running Pig scripts

▶ Scripting with Pig Latin

· ·

*J*ava MapReduce programs (see Chapter 6) and the Hadoop Distributed File System (HDFS; see Chapter 4) provide you with a powerful distributed computing framework, but they come with one major drawback — relying on them limits the use of Hadoop to Java programmers who can think in Map and Reduce terms when writing programs. More developers, data analysts, data scientists, and all-around good folks could leverage Hadoop if they had a way to harness the power of Map and Reduce while hiding some of the Map and Reduce complexities.

As with most things in life, where there's a need, somebody is bound to come up with an idea meant to fill that need. A growing list of MapReduce *abstractions* is now on the market — programming languages and/or tools such as Hive and Pig, which hide the messy details of MapReduce so that a programmer can concentrate on the important work.

Hive, for example, provides a limited SQL-like capability that runs over MapReduce, thus making said MapReduce more approachable for SQL developers. Hive also provides a *declarative* query language (the SQL-like HiveQL), which allows you to focus on *which* operation you need to carry out versus *how* it is carried out.

Though SQL is the common accepted language for querying structured data, some developers still prefer writing *imperative* scripts — scripts that define a set of operations that change the state of the data — and also want to have more data processing flexibility than what SQL or HiveQL provides. Again, this need led the engineers at Yahoo! Research to come up with a product meant to fulfill that need — and so Pig was born. Pig's claim to fame was its status as a programming tool attempting to have the best of both worlds: a declarative query language inspired by SQL and a low-level procedural programming language that can generate MapReduce code. This lowers the bar when it comes to the level of technical knowledge needed to exploit the power of Hadoop.

By taking a look at some murky computer programming language history, we can say that Pig was initially developed at Yahoo! in 2006 as part of a research project tasked with coming up with ways for people using Hadoop to focus more on analyzing large data sets rather than spending lots of time writing Java MapReduce programs. The goal here was a familiar one: Allow users to focus more on what they want to do and less on how it's done. Not long after, in 2007, Pig officially became an Apache project. As such, it is included in most Hadoop distributions.

And its name? That one's easy to figure out. The Pig programming language is designed to handle any kind of data tossed its way — structured, semi-structured, unstructured data, you name it. Pigs, of course, have a reputation for eating anything they come across. (We suppose they could have called it Goat — or maybe that name was already taken.) According to the Apache Pig philosophy, pigs eat anything, live anywhere, are domesticated and can fly to boot. (Flying Apache Pigs? Now we've seen everything.) Pigs "living anywhere" refers to the fact that Pig is a parallel data processing programming language and is not committed to any particular parallel framework — including Hadoop. What makes it a domesticated animal? Well, if "domesticated" means "plays well with humans," then it's definitely the case that Pig prides itself on being easy for humans to code and maintain. (Hey, it's easily integrated with other programming languages and it's extensible. What more could you ask?) Lastly, Pig is smart and in data processing lingo this means there is an optimizer that figures out how to do the hard work of figuring out how to get the data quickly. Pig is not just going to be quick — it's going to fly. (To see more about the Apache Pig philosophy, check out `http://pig.apache.org/philosophy`.)

Admiring the Pig Architecture

"Simple" often means "elegant" when it comes to those architectural drawings for that new Silicon Valley mansion you have planned for when the money starts rolling in after you implement Hadoop. The same principle applies to software architecture. Pig is made up of two (count 'em, two) components:

- **The language itself:** As proof that programmers have a sense of humor, the programming language for Pig is known as Pig Latin, a high-level language that allows you to write data processing and analysis programs.

✔ **The Pig Latin compiler:** The Pig Latin compiler converts the Pig Latin code into executable code. The executable code is either in the form of MapReduce jobs or it can spawn a process where a virtual Hadoop instance is created to run the Pig code on a single node.

The sequence of MapReduce programs enables Pig programs to do data processing and analysis in parallel, leveraging Hadoop MapReduce and HDFS. Running the Pig job in the virtual Hadoop instance is a useful strategy for testing your Pig scripts.

Figure 8-1 shows how Pig relates to the Hadoop ecosystem.

Pig	Pig Latin Compiler		
Processing Framework	MapReduce v2	Tez	MapReduce v1
Resource Management	YARN		
Distributed Storage	HDFS		

Figure 8-1: Pig architecture.

Pig programs can run on MapReduce v1 or MapReduce v2 without any code changes, regardless of what mode your cluster is running. However, Pig scripts can also run using the Tez API instead. Apache Tez provides a more efficient execution framework than MapReduce. YARN enables application frameworks other than MapReduce (like Tez) to run on Hadoop. Hive can also run against the Tez framework. See Chapter 7 for more information on YARN and Tez.

Going with the Pig Latin Application Flow

At its core, Pig Latin is a *dataflow* language, where you define a data stream and a series of transformations that are applied to the data as it flows through your application. This is in contrast to a *control flow* language (like C or Java), where you write a series of instructions. In control flow languages, we use constructs like loops and conditional logic (like an `if` statement). You won't find loops and `if` statements in Pig Latin.

If you need some convincing that working with Pig is a significantly easier row to hoe than having to write Map and Reduce programs, start by taking a look at some real Pig syntax:

Listing 8-1: Sample Pig Code to illustrate the data processing dataflow

```
A = LOAD 'data_file.txt';
...
B = GROUP ... ;
...
C= FILTER ...;
...
DUMP B;
..
STORE C INTO 'Results';
```

Some of the text in this example actually looks like English, right? Not too scary, at least at this point. Looking at each line in turn, you can see the basic flow of a Pig program. (Note that this code can either be part of a script or issued on the interactive shell called Grunt — we learn more about Grunt in a few pages.)

1. **Load:** You first load (LOAD) the data you want to manipulate. As in a typical MapReduce job, that data is stored in HDFS. For a Pig program to access the data, you first tell Pig what file or files to use. For that task, you use the LOAD 'data_file' command.

   Here, 'data_file' can specify either an HDFS file or a directory. If a directory is specified, all files in that directory are loaded into the program.

   If the data is stored in a file format that isn't natively accessible to Pig, you can optionally add the USING function to the LOAD statement to specify a user-defined function that can read in (and interpret) the data.

2. **Transform:** You run the data through a set of transformations that, way under the hood and far removed from anything you have to concern yourself with, are translated into a set of Map and Reduce tasks.

   The transformation logic is where all the data manipulation happens. Here, you can FILTER out rows that aren't of interest, JOIN two sets of data files, GROUP data to build aggregations, ORDER results, and do much, much more.

3. **Dump:** Finally, you dump (DUMP) the results to the screen

   or

   Store (STORE) the results in a file somewhere.

You would typically use the DUMP command to send the output to the screen when you debug your programs. When your program goes into production, you simply change the DUMP call to a STORE call so that any results from running your programs are stored in a file for further processing or analysis.

Working through the ABCs of Pig Latin

Pig Latin is the language for Pig programs. Pig translates the Pig Latin script into MapReduce jobs that can be executed within Hadoop cluster. When coming up with Pig Latin, the development team followed three key design principles:

✔ **Keep it simple.** Pig Latin provides a streamlined method for interacting with Java MapReduce. It's an abstraction, in other words, that simplifies the creation of parallel programs on the Hadoop cluster for data flows and analysis. Complex tasks may require a series of interrelated data transformations — such series are encoded as *data flow sequences*.

Writing data transformation and flows as Pig Latin scripts instead of Java MapReduce programs makes these programs easier to write, understand, and maintain because a) you don't have to write the job in Java, b) you don't have to think in terms of MapReduce, and c) you don't need to come up with custom code to support rich data types. Pig Latin provides a simpler language to exploit your Hadoop cluster, thus making it easier for more people to leverage the power of Hadoop and become productive sooner.

✔ **Make it smart.** You may recall that the Pig Latin Compiler does the work of transforming a Pig Latin program into a series of Java MapReduce jobs. The trick is to make sure that the compiler can optimize the execution of these Java MapReduce jobs automatically, allowing the user to focus on semantics rather than on how to optimize and access the data.

For you SQL types out there, this discussion will sound familiar. SQL is set up as a declarative query that you use to access structured data stored in an RDBMS. The RDBMS engine first translates the query to a data access method and then looks at the statistics and generates a series of data access approaches. The cost-based optimizer chooses the most efficient approach for execution.

✔ **Don't limit development.** Make Pig extensible so that developers can add functions to address their particular business problems.

Traditional RDBMS data warehouses make use of the ETL data processing pattern, where you *e*xtract data from outside sources, *t*ransform it to fit your operational needs, and then *l*oad it into the end target, whether it's an operational data store, a data warehouse, or another variant of database. However, with big data, you typically want to reduce the amount of data you have moving about, so you end up bringing the processing to the data itself. The language for Pig data flows, therefore, takes a pass on the old ETL approach, and goes with ELT instead: *E*xtract the data from your various sources, *l*oad it into HDFS, and then *t*ransform it as necessary to prepare the data for further analysis.

Uncovering Pig Latin structures

To see how Pig Latin is put together, check out the following (bare-bones, training wheel) program for playing around in Hadoop. (To save time and money — hey, coming up with great examples can cost a pretty penny! — we'll reuse the Flight Data scenario from Chapter 6.) Compare and Contrast is often a good way to learn something new, so go ahead and review the problem we're solving in Chapter 6, and take a look at the code in Listings 6-3, 6-4, and 6-5.

The problem we're trying to solve involves calculating the total number of flights flown by every carrier. Following is the Pig Latin script we'll use to answer this question.

Listing 8-2:   Pig script calculating the total miles flown

```
records = LOAD '2013_subset.csv' USING PigStorage(',') AS
          (Year,Month,DayofMonth,DayOfWeek,DepTime,CRSDep
          Time,ArrTime,CRSArrTime,UniqueCarrier,FlightNum
          ,TailNum,ActualElapsedTime,CRSElapsedTime,AirTi
          me,ArrDelay,DepDelay,Origin,Dest,Distance:int,T
          axiIn,TaxiOut,Cancelled,CancellationCode,Divert
          ed,CarrierDelay,WeatherDelay,NASDelay,SecurityD
          elay,LateAircraftDelay);

milage_recs = GROUP records ALL;
tot_miles = FOREACH milage_recs GENERATE
          SUM(records.Distance);

DUMP tot_miles;
```

Before we walk through the code, here are a few high-level observations: The Pig script is a lot smaller than the MapReduce application you'd need to accomplish the same task — the Pig script only has 4 lines of code! Yes, that first line is rather long, but it's pretty simple, since we're just listing the names of the columns in the data set. And not only is the code shorter, but it's even semi-human readable. Just look at the key words in the script: LOADs the data, does a GROUP, calculates a SUM and finally DUMPs out an answer. You'll remember that one reason why SQL is so awesome is because it's a declarative query language, meaning you express queries on what you want the result to be, not how it is executed. Pig can be equally cool because it also gives you that declarative aspect and you don't have to tell it how to actually do it and in particular how to do the MapReduce stuff.

Ready for your walkthrough? As you make your way through the code, take note of these principles:

- ✔ **Most Pig scripts start with the LOAD statement to read data from HDFS.** In this case, we're loading data from a .csv file. Pig has a data model it uses, so next we need to map the file's data model to the Pig data mode. This is accomplished with the help of the USING statement. (More on the Pig data model in the next section.) We then specify that it is a comma-delimited file with the PigStorage(',') statement followed by the AS statement defining the name of each of the columns.

- ✔ **Aggregations are commonly used in Pig to summarize data sets.** The GROUP statement is used to aggregate the records into a single record mileage_recs. The ALL statement is used to aggregate all tuples into a single group. Note that some statements — including the following SUM statement — requires a preceding GROUP ALL statement for global sums.

- ✔ **FOREACH . . . GENERATE statements are used here to transform columns data.** In this case, we want to count the miles traveled in the records_Distance column. The SUM statement computes the sum of the record_Distance column into a single-column collection total_miles.

- ✔ **The DUMP operator is used to execute the Pig Latin statement and display the results on the screen.** DUMP is used in interactive mode, which means that the statements are executable immediately and the results are not saved. Typically, you will either use the DUMP or STORE operators at the end of your Pig script.

Looking at Pig data types and syntax

Pig's data types make up the data model for how Pig thinks of the structure of the data it is processing. With Pig, the data model gets defined when the data is loaded. Any data you load into Pig from disk is going to have a particular schema and structure. Pig needs to understand that structure, so when you do the loading, the data automatically goes through a mapping.

Luckily for you, the Pig data model is rich enough to handle most anything thrown its way, including table-like structures and nested hierarchical data structures. In general terms, though, Pig data types can be broken into two categories: scalar types and complex types. *Scalar* types contain a single value, whereas *complex* types contain other types, such as the Tuple, Bag, and Map types listed below.

Pig Latin has these four types in its data model:

- **Atom:** An *atom* is any single value, such as a string or a number — 'Diego', for example. Pig's atomic values are scalar types that appear in most programming languages — `int`, `long`, `float`, `double`, `chararray`, and `bytearray`, for example. See Figure 8-2 to see sample atom types.

- **Tuple:** A *tuple* is a record that consists of a sequence of fields. Each field can be of any type — 'Diego', 'Gomez', or 6, for example. Think of a tuple as a row in a table.

- **Bag:** A *bag* is a collection of non-unique tuples. The schema of the bag is flexible — each tuple in the collection can contain an arbitrary number of fields, and each field can be of any type.

- **Map:** A map is a collection of key value pairs. Any type can be stored in the value, and the key needs to be unique. The key of a map must be a `chararray` and the value can be of any type.

Figure 8-2 offers some fine examples of Tuple, Bag, and Map data types, as well.

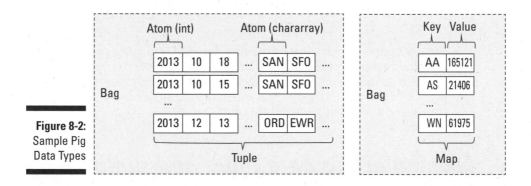

Figure 8-2:
Sample Pig
Data Types

The value of all these types can also be `null`. The semantics for `null` are similar to those used in SQL. The concept of `null` in Pig means that the value is unknown. Nulls can show up in the data in cases where values are unreadable or unrecognizable — for example, if you were to use a wrong data type in the LOAD statement. `Null` could be used as a placeholder until data is added or as a value for a field that is optional.

... simple syntax with powerful semantics you'll use to carry out ... cess and transform data. If you compare the Pig ... ing miles traveled by airline (Listing 8-1) with the ... tations (Listings 6-1, 6-2, and 6-3), they both come ... the Pig implementation has a lot less code and is

... *sing* data means allowing developers to load, store, ... *transforming* data means taking advantage of Pig's ... bine, split, filter, and sort data. Table 8-1 gives an ... associated with each operation.

Pig Latin Operators

	erator	*Explanation*
	AD/STORE	Read and Write data to file system
	UMP	Write output to standard output (stdout)
	REAM	Send all records through external binary
	FOREACH	Apply expression to each record and output one or more records
	FILTER	Apply predicate and remove records that don't meet condition
	GROUP/ COGROUP	Aggregate records with the same key from one or more inputs
	JOIN	Join two or more records based on a condition
Transformations	CROSS	Cartesian product of two or more inputs
	ORDER	Sort records based on key
	DISTINCT	Remove duplicate records
	UNION	Merge two data sets
	SPLIT	Divide data into two or more bags based on predicate
	LIMIT	subset the number of records

Pig also provides a few operators that are helpful for debugging and trouble-shooting, as shown in Table 8-2:

Table 8-2	Operators for Debugging and Troubleshooting	
Operation	*Operator*	*Description*
Debug	DESCRIBE	Return the schema of a relation.
	DUMP	Dump the contents of a relation to the screen.
	EXPLAIN	Display the MapReduce execution plans.

Part of the paradigm shift of Hadoop is that you apply your schema at Read instead of Load. According to the old way of doing things — the RDBMS way — when you load data into your database system, you must load it into a well-defined set of tables. Hadoop allows you to store all that raw data upfront and apply the schema at Read. With Pig, you do this during the load-ing of the data, with the help of the LOAD operator. Back in Listing 8-2, we used the LOAD operator to read the flight data from a file.

The optional USING statement defines how to map the data structure within the file to the Pig data model — in this case, the PigStorage () data struc-ture, which parses delimited text files. (This part of the USING statement is often referred to as a LOAD Func and works in a fashion similar to a custom deserializer.) The optional AS clause defines a schema for the data that is being mapped. If you don't use an AS clause, you're basically telling the default LOAD Func to expect a plain text file that is tab delimited. With no schema provided, the fields must be referenced by position because no name is defined.

Using AS clauses means that you have a schema in place at read-time for your text files, which allows users to get started quickly and provides agile schema modeling and flexibility so that you can add more data to your analytics.

The LOAD operator operates on the principle of *lazy evaluation,* also referred to as *call-by-need.* Now lazy doesn't sound particularly praiseworthy, but all it means is that you delay the evaluation of an expression until you really need it. In the context of our Pig example, that means that after the LOAD statement is executed, no data is moved — nothing gets shunted around — until a statement to write data is encountered. You can have a Pig script that is a page long filled with complex transformations, but nothing gets executed until the DUMP or STORE statement is encountered.

Evaluating Local and Distributed Modes of Running Pig scripts

Before you can run your first Pig script, you need to have a handle on how Pig programs can be packaged with the Pig server.

Pig has two modes for running scripts, as shown in Figure 8-3:

✔ **Local mode:** All scripts are run on a single machine without requiring Hadoop MapReduce and HDFS. This can be useful for developing and testing Pig logic. If you're using a small set of data to develope or test your code, then local mode could be faster than going through the MapReduce infrastructure.

Local mode doesn't require Hadoop. When you run in Local mode, the Pig program runs in the context of a local Java Virtual Machine, and data access is via the local file system of a single machine. Local mode is actually a local simulation of MapReduce in Hadoop's LocalJobRunner class.

✔ **MapReduce mode (also known as Hadoop mode):** Pig is executed on the Hadoop cluster. In this case, the Pig script gets converted into a series of MapReduce jobs that are then run on the Hadoop cluster.

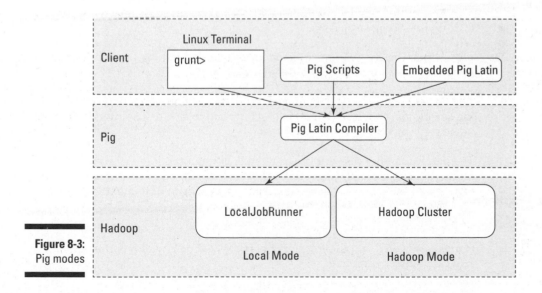

Figure 8-3:
Pig modes

If you have a terabyte of data that you want to perform operations on and you want to interactively develop a program, you may soon find things slowing down considerably, and you may start growing your storage. Local mode allows you to work with a subset of your data in a more interactive manner so that you can figure out the logic (and work out the bugs) of your Pig program. After you have things set up as you want them and your operations are running smoothly, you can then run the script against the full data set using MapReduce mode.

Checking Out the Pig Script Interfaces

Pig programs can be packaged in three different ways:

- ✔ **Script:** This method is nothing more than a file containing Pig Latin commands, identified by the `.pig` suffix (`FlightData.pig`, for example). Ending your Pig program with the `.pig` extension is a convention but not required. The commands are interpreted by the Pig Latin compiler and executed in the order determined by the Pig optimizer.

- ✔ **Grunt:** Grunt acts as a command interpreter where you can interactively enter Pig Latin at the Grunt command line and immediately see the response. This method is helpful for prototyping during initial development and with what-if scenarios.

- ✔ **Embedded:** Pig Latin statements can be executed within Java, Python, or JavaScript programs.

Pig scripts, Grunt shell Pig commands, and embedded Pig programs can run in either Local mode or MapReduce mode.

The Grunt shell provides an interactive shell to submit Pig commands or run Pig scripts. To start the Grunt shell in Interactive mode, just submit the command `pig` at your shell.

To specify whether a script or Grunt shell is executed locally or in Hadoop mode just specify it in the `-x` flag to the `pig` command. The following is an example of how you'd specify running your Pig script in local mode:

```
pig -x local milesPerCarrier.pig
```

Here's how you'd run the Pig script in Hadoop mode, which is the default if you don't specify the flag:

```
pig -x mapreduce milesPerCarrier.pig
```

By default, when you specify the `pig` command without any parameters, it starts the Grunt shell in Hadoop mode. If you want to start the Grunt shell in local mode just add the `-x local` flag to the command. Here is an example:

```
pig -x local
```

Scripting with Pig Latin

Hadoop is a rich and quickly evolving ecosystem with a growing set of new applications. Rather than try to keep up with all the requirements for new capabilities, Pig is designed to be extensible via *user-defined functions,* also known as UDFs. UDFs can be written in a number of programming languages, including Java, Python, and JavaScript. Developers are also posting and sharing a growing collection of UDFs online. (Look for Piggy Bank and DataFu, to name just two examples of such online collections.) Some of the Pig UDFs that are part of these repositories are LOAD/STORE functions (XML, for example), date time functions, text, math, and stats functions.

Pig can also be embedded in host languages such as Java, Python, and JavaScript, which allows you to integrate Pig with your existing applications. It also helps overcome limitations in the Pig language. One of the most commonly referenced limitations is that Pig doesn't support control flow statements: if/else, while loop, for loop, and condition statements. Pig natively supports data flow, but needs to be embedded within another language to provide control flow. There are tradeoffs, however of embedding Pig in a control-flow language. For example if a Pig statement is embedded in a loop, every time the loop iterates and runs the Pig statement, this causes a separate MapReduce job to run.

Chapter 9
Statistical Analysis in Hadoop

● ●

In This Chapter
▶ Scaling out statistical analysis with Hadoop
▶ Gaining an understanding of Mahout
▶ Working with R on Hadoop

● ●

*B*ig data is all about applying analytics to more data, for more people. To carry out this task, big data practitioners use new tools — such as Hadoop — to explore and understand data in ways that previously might not have been possible (problems that were "too difficult," "too expensive," or "too slow"). Some of the "bigger analytics" that you often hear mentioned when Hadoop comes up in a conversation revolve around concepts such as machine learning, data mining, and predictive analytics. Now, what's the common thread that runs through all these methods? That's right: they all use good old-fashioned statistical analysis.

In this chapter, we explore some of the challenges that arise when you try to use traditional statistical tools on a Hadoop-level scale — a *massive* scale, in other words. We also introduce you to some common, Hadoop-specific statistical tools and show you when it makes sense to use them.

Pumping Up Your Statistical Analysis

Statistical analytics is far from being a new kid on the block, and it is certainly old news that it depends on processing large amounts of data to gain new insight. However, the amount of data that's traditionally processed by these systems was in the range between 10 and 100 (or hundreds of) gigabytes — not the terabyte or petabyte ranges seen today, in other words. And it often required an expensive *symmetric multi-processing* (SMP) machine with as much memory as possible to hold the data being analyzed. That's because many of the algorithms used by the analytic approaches were quite "compute intensive" and were designed to run in memory — as they require multiple, and often frequent, passes through the data.

The limitations of sampling

Faced with expensive hardware and a pretty high commitment in terms of time and RAM, folks tried to make the analytics workload a bit more reasonable by analyzing only a sampling of the data. The idea was to keep the mountains upon mountains of data safely stashed in data warehouses, only moving a statistically significant sampling of the data from their repositories to a statistical engine.

While sampling is a good idea in theory, in practice this is often an unreliable tactic. Finding a statistically significant sampling can be challenging for sparse and/or skewed data sets, which are quite common. This leads to poorly judged samplings, which can introduce outliers and anomalous data points, and can, in turn, bias the results of your analysis.

Factors that increase the scale of statistical analysis

As we can see above, the reason people sample their data before running statistical analysis is that this kind of analysis often requires significant computing resources. This isn't just about data volumes: there are five main factors that influence the scale of statistical analysis:

- ✔ This one's easy, but we have to mention it: the volume of data on which you'll perform the analysis definitely determines the scale of the analysis.

- ✔ The number of transformations needed on the data set before applying statistical models is definitely a factor.

- ✔ The number of pairwise correlations you'll need to calculate plays a role.

- ✔ The degree of complexity of the statistical computations to be applied is a factor.

- ✔ The number of statistical models to be applied to your data set plays a significant role.

Hadoop offers a way out of this dilemma by providing a platform to perform massively parallel processing computations on data in Hadoop. In doing so, it's able to flip the analytic data flow; rather than move the data from its repository to the analytics server, Hadoop delivers analytics directly to the data. More specifically, HDFS allows you to store your mountains of data and then bring the computation (in the form of MapReduce tasks) to the slave nodes.

The common challenge posed by moving from traditional symmetric multi-processing statistical systems (SMP) to Hadoop architecture is the locality of the data. On traditional SMP platforms, multiple processors share access to a single main memory resource. In Hadoop, HDFS replicates partitions of data across multiple nodes and machines. Also, statistical algorithms that were designed for processing data in-memory must now adapt to datasets that span multiple nodes/racks and could not hope to fit in a single block of memory.

Running statistical models in MapReduce

Converting statistical models to run in parallel is a challenging task. In the traditional paradigm for parallel programming, memory access is regulated through the use of *threads* — sub-processes created by the operating system to distribute a single shared memory across multiple processors. Factors such as race conditions between competing threads — when two or more threads try to change shared data at the same time — can influence the performance of your algorithm, as well as affect the precision of the statistical results your program outputs — particularly for long-running analyses of large sample sets.

A pragmatic approach to this problem is to assume that not many statisticians will know the ins and outs of MapReduce (and vice-versa), nor can we expect they'll be aware of all the pitfalls that parallel programming entails. Contributors to the Hadoop project have (and continue to develop) statistical tools with these realities in mind. The upshot: Hadoop offers many solutions for implementing the algorithms required to perform statistical modeling and analysis, without overburdening the statistician with nuanced parallel programming considerations. We'll be looking at the following tools in greater detail:

✔ Mahout — and its wealth of statistical models and library functions

✔ The R language — and how to run it over Hadoop (including Big R)

Machine Learning with Mahout

Machine learning refers to a branch of artificial intelligence techniques that provides tools enabling computers to improve their analysis based on previous events. These computer systems leverage historical data from previous attempts at solving a task in order to improve the performance of future attempts at similar tasks. In terms of expected outcomes, machine learning may sound a lot like that other buzzword "data mining"; however, the former focuses on prediction through analysis of *prepared* training data, the latter is concerned with knowledge discovery from *unprocessed* raw data. For this reason, machine learning depends heavily upon statistical modelling techniques and draws from areas of probability theory and pattern recognition.

Mahout is an open source project from Apache, offering Java libraries for distributed or otherwise scalable machine-learning algorithms. (See Figure 9-1 for the Big Picture.) These algorithms cover classic machine learning tasks such as classification, clustering, association rule analysis, and recommendations. Although Mahout libraries are designed to work within an Apache Hadoop context, they are also compatible with any system supporting the MapReduce framework. For example, Mahout provides Java libraries for Java collections and common math operations (linear algebra and statistics) that can be used without Hadoop.

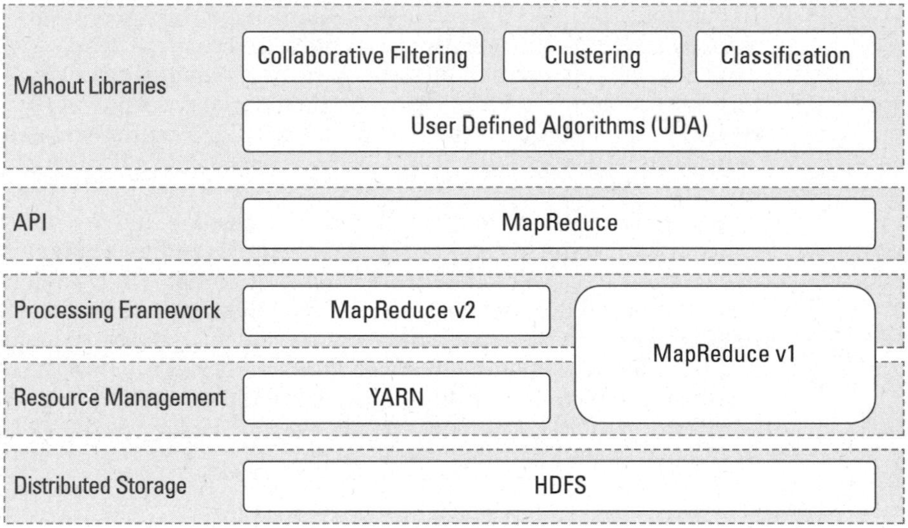

Mahout Libraries	Collaborative Filtering	Clustering	Classification
	User Defined Algorithms (UDA)		
API	MapReduce		
Processing Framework	MapReduce v2	MapReduce v1	
Resource Management	YARN		
Distributed Storage	HDFS		

Figure 9-1: High-level view of a Mahout deployment over the Hadoop framework.

As you can see in Figure 9-1, the Mahout libraries are implemented in Java MapReduce and run on your cluster as collections of MapReduce jobs on either YARN (with MapReduce v2), or MapReduce v1.

Mahout is an evolving project with multiple contributors. By the time of this writing, the collection of algorithms available in the Mahout libraries is by no means complete; however, the collection of algorithms implemented for use continues to expand with time.

There are three main categories of Mahout algorithms for supporting statistical analysis: collaborative filtering, clustering, and classification. The next few sections tackle each of these categories in turn.

Collaborative filtering

Mahout was specifically designed for serving as a recommendation engine, employing what is known as a *collaborative filtering* algorithm. Mahout combines the wealth of clustering and classification algorithms at its disposal to produce more precise recommendations based on input data. These recommendations are often applied against user preferences, taking into consideration the behavior of the user. By comparing a user's previous selections, it is possible to identify the nearest neighbors (persons with a similar decision history) to that user and predict future selections based on the behavior of the neighbors.

Consider a "taste profile" engine such as Netflix — an engine which recommends ratings based on that user's previous scoring and viewing habits. In this example, the behavioral patterns for a user are compared against the user's history — and the trends of users with similar tastes belonging to the same Netflix community — to generate a recommendation for content not yet viewed by the user in question.

Clustering

Unlike the supervised learning method described earlier for Mahout's recommendation engine feature, clustering is a form of *unsupervised* learning — where the labels for data points are unknown ahead of time and must be inferred from the data without human input (the *supervised* part). Generally, objects within a cluster should be similar; objects from different clusters should be dissimilar. Decisions made ahead of time about the number of clusters to generate, the criteria for measuring "similarity," and the representation of objects will impact the labelling produced by clustering algorithms.

For example, a clustering engine that is provided a list of news articles should be able to define clusters of articles within that collection which discuss similar topics. Suppose a set of articles about Canada, France, China, forestry, oil, and wine were to be clustered. If the maximum number of clusters were set to 2, our algorithm might produce categories such as "regions" and "industries." Adjustments to the number of clusters will produce different categorizations; for example, selecting for 3 clusters may result in pairwise groupings of nation-industry categories.

Classifications

Classification algorithms make use of human-labelled training data sets, where the categorization and classification of all future input is governed by these known labels. These classifiers implement what is known as *supervised learning* in the machine learning world. Classification rules — set by the training data, which has been labelled ahead of time by domain experts — are then applied against raw, unprocessed data to best determine their appropriate labelling.

These techniques are often used by e-mail services which attempt to classify spam e-mail before they ever cross your inbox. Specifically, given an e-mail containing a set of phrases known to commonly occur together in a certain class of spam mail — delivered from an address belonging to a known botnet — our classification algorithm is able to reliably identify the e-mail as malicious.

In addition to the wealth of statistical algorithms that Mahout provides natively, a supporting *User Defined Algorithms* (UDA) module is also available. Users can override existing algorithms or implement their own through the UDA module. This robust customization allows for performance tuning of native Mahout algorithms and flexibility in tackling unique statistical analysis challenges. If Mahout can be viewed as a statistical analytics extension to Hadoop, UDA should be seen as an extension to Mahout's statistical capabilities.

Traditional statistical analysis applications (such as SAS, SPSS, and R) come with powerful tools for generating workflows. These applications utilize intuitive graphical user interfaces that allow for better data visualization. Mahout scripts follow a similar pattern as these other tools for generating statistical analysis workflows. (See Figure 9-2.) During the final data exploration and visualization step, users can export to human-readable formats (JSON, CSV) or take advantage of visualization tools such as Tableau Desktop.

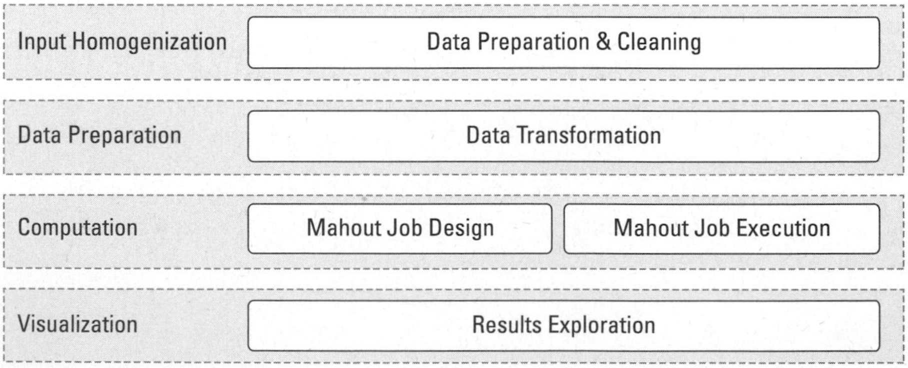

Figure 9-2: Generalized statistical analysis workflow for Mahout.

Input Homogenization	Data Preparation & Cleaning	
Data Preparation	Data Transformation	
Computation	Mahout Job Design	Mahout Job Execution
Visualization	Results Exploration	

Recall from Figure 9-1 that Mahout's architecture sits atop the Hadoop platform. Hadoop unburdens the programmer by separating the task of programming MapReduce jobs from the complex bookkeeping needed to manage parallelism across distributed file systems. In the same spirit, Mahout provides programmer-friendly abstractions of complex statistical algorithms, ready for implementation with the Hadoop framework.

R on Hadoop

The machine learning discipline has a rich and extensive catalogue of techniques. Mahout brings a range of statistical tools and algorithms to the table, but it only captures a fraction of those techniques and algorithms, as the task of converting these models to a MapReduce framework is a challenging one. Over time, Mahout is sure to continue expanding its statistical toolbox, but until then we advise all data scientists and statisticians out there to be aware of alternative statistical modelling software — which is where R comes in.

The R language

The R language is a powerful and popular open-source statistical language and development environment. It offers a rich analytics ecosystem that can assist data scientists with data exploration, visualization, statistical analysis and computing, modelling, machine learning, and simulation. The R language is commonly used by statisticians, data miners, data analysts, and (nowadays) data scientists.

R language programmers have access to the *Comprehensive R Archive Network* (CRAN) libraries which, as of the time of this writing, contains over 3000 statistical analysis packages. These add-ons can be pulled into any R project, providing rich analytical tools for running classification, regression, clustering, linear modelling, and more specialized machine learning algorithms. The language is accessible to those familiar with simple data structure types — vectors, scalars, data frames (matrices), and the like — commonly used by statisticians as well as programmers.

Out of the box, one of the major pitfalls with using the R language is the lack of support it offers for running concurrent tasks. Statistical language tools like R excel at rigorous analysis, but lack scalability and native support for parallel computations. These systems are non-distributable and were not developed to be scalable for the modern petabyte-world of big data. Proposals for overcoming these limitations need to extend R's scope beyond in-memory loading and single computer execution environments, while maintaining R's flair for easily-deployable statistical algorithms.

Hadoop Integration with R

In the beginning, big data and R were not natural friends. R programming requires that all objects be loaded into the main memory of a single machine. The limitations of this architecture are quickly realized when big data becomes a part of the equation. In contrast, distributed file systems such as Hadoop are missing strong statistical techniques but are ideal for scaling complex operations and tasks. Vertical scaling solutions — requiring investment in costly supercomputing hardware — often cannot compete with the cost-value return offered by distributed, commodity hardware clusters.

To conform to the in-memory, single-machine limitations of the R language, data scientists often had to restrict analysis to only a subset of the available sample data. Prior to deeper integration with Hadoop, R language programmers offered a scale-out strategy for overcoming the in-memory challenges posed by large data sets on single machines. This was achieved using message-passing systems and paging. This technique is able to facilitate work over data sets too large to store in main memory simultaneously; however, its low-level programming approach presents a steep learning curve for those unfamiliar with parallel programming paradigms.

Alternative approaches seek to integrate R's statistical capabilities with Hadoop's distributed clusters in two ways: interfacing with SQL query languages, and integration with Hadoop Streaming. With the former, the goal is to leverage existing SQL data warehousing platforms such as Hive (see Chapter 13) and Pig (see Chapter 8). These schemas simplify Hadoop job programming using SQL-style statements in order to provide high-level programming for conducting statistical jobs over Hadoop data. For programmers wishing to program MapReduce jobs in languages (including R) other than Java, a second option is to make use of Hadoop's Streaming API. User-submitted MapReduce jobs undergo data transformations with the assistance of UNIX standard streams and serialization, guaranteeing Java-compliant input to Hadoop — regardless of the language originally inputted by the programmer.

Developers continue to explore various strategies to leverage the distributed computation capability of MapReduce and the almost limitless storage capacity of HDFS in ways that can be exploited by R. Integration of Hadoop with R is ongoing, with offerings available from IBM (Big R as part of BigInsights) and Revolution Analytics (Revolution R Enterprise). Bridging solutions that integrate high-level programming and querying languages with Hadoop, such as RHive and RHadoop, are also available. Fundamentally, each system aims to deliver the deep analytical capabilities of the R language to much larger sets of data. In closing this chapter, we briefly examine some of these efforts to marry Hadoop's scalability with R's statistical capabilities.

RHive

The RHive framework serves as a bridge between the R language and Hive. RHive delivers the rich statistical libraries and algorithms of R to data stored in Hadoop by extending Hive's SQL-like query language (HiveQL) with R-specific functions. Through the RHive functions, you can use HiveQL to apply R statistical models to data in your Hadoop cluster that you have cataloged using Hive.

RHadoop

Another open source framework available to R programmers is RHadoop, a collection of packages intended to help manage the distribution and analysis of data with Hadoop. Three packages of note — rmr2, rhdfs, and rhbase — provide most of RHadoop's functionality:

- **rmr2:** The rmr2 package supports translation of the R language into Hadoop-compliant MapReduce jobs (producing efficient, low-level MapReduce code from higher-level R code).

- **rhdfs:** The rhdfs package provides an R language API for file management over HDFS stores. Using rhdfs, users can read from HDFS stores to an R data frame (matrix), and similarly write data from these R matrices back into HDFS storage.

- **rhbase:** rhbase packages provide an R language API as well, but their goal in life is to deal with database management for HBase stores, rather than HDFS files.

Revolution R

Revolution R (by Revolution Analytics) is a commercial R offering with support for R integration on Hadoop distributed systems. Revolution R promises to deliver improved performance, functionality, and usability for R on Hadoop. To provide deep analytics akin to R, Revolution R makes use of the company's ScaleR library — a collection of statistical analysis algorithms developed specifically for enterprise-scale big data collections.

ScaleR aims to deliver fast execution of R program code on Hadoop clusters, allowing the R developer to focus exclusively on their statistical algorithms and not on MapReduce. Furthermore, it handles numerous analytics tasks, such as data preparation, visualization, and statistical tests.

IBM BigInsights Big R

Big R offers end-to-end integration between R and IBM's Hadoop offering, BigInsights, enabling R developers to analyze Hadoop data. The aim is to exploit R's programming syntax and coding paradigms, while ensuring that the data operated upon stays in HDFS. R datatypes serve as proxies to these data stores, which means R developers don't need to think about low-level MapReduce constructs or any Hadoop-specific scripting languages (like Pig).

BigInsights Big R technology supports multiple data sources — including flat files, HBase, and Hive storage formats — while providing parallel and partitioned execution of R code across the Hadoop cluster. It hides many of the complexities in the underlying HDFS and MapReduce frameworks, allowing Big R functions to perform comprehensive data analytics — on both structured and unstructured data. Finally, the scalability of Big R's statistical engine allows R developers to make use of both pre-defined statistical techniques, as well as author new algorithms themselves.

Chapter 10

Developing and Scheduling Application Workflows with Oozie

• •

• •

*M*oving data and running different kinds of applications in Hadoop is great stuff, but it's only half the battle. For Hadoop's efficiencies to truly start paying off for you, start thinking about how you can tie together a number of these actions to form a cohesive workflow. This idea is appealing, especially after you and your colleagues have built a number of Hadoop applications and you need to mix and match them for different purposes. At the same time, you inevitably need to prepare or move data as you progress through your workflows and make decisions based on the output of your jobs or other factors. Of course, you can always write your own logic or hack an existing workflow tool to do this in a Hadoop setting — but that's a lot of work. Your best bet is to use Apache *Oozie,* a workflow engine and scheduling facility designed specifically for Hadoop.

As a workflow engine, Oozie enables you to run a set of Hadoop applications in a specified sequence known as a *workflow*. You define this sequence in the form of a directed acyclic graph (DAG) of actions. In this workflow, the nodes are actions and decision points (where the control flow will go in one direction, or another), while the connecting lines show the sequence of these actions and the directions of the control flow. Oozie graphs are acyclic (no cycles, in other words), which means you can't use loops in your workflows. In terms of the actions you can schedule, Oozie supports a wide range of job types, including Pig, Hive, and MapReduce, as well as jobs coming from Java programs and Shell scripts.

Oozie also provides a handy scheduling facility. An Oozie *coordinator job*, for example, enables you to schedule any workflows you've already created. You can schedule them to run based on specific time intervals, or even based on data availability. At an even higher level, you can create an Oozie *bundle job* to manage your coordinator jobs. Using a bundle job, you can easily apply policies against a set of coordinator jobs by using a *bundle* job.

For all three kinds of Oozie jobs (workflow, coordinator, and bundle), you start out by defining them using individual .xml files, and then you configure them using a combination of properties files and command-line options.

Figure 10-1 gives an overview of all the components you'd usually find in an Oozie server. Don't expect to understand all the elements in one fell swoop. We help you work through the various parts shown here throughout this chapter as we explain how all the components work together.

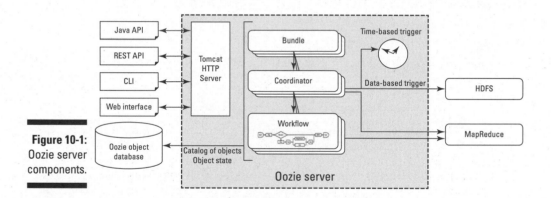

Figure 10-1: Oozie server components.

Getting Oozie in Place

Apache Oozie is included in every major Hadoop distribution, including Apache Bigtop, which is the basis of the distribution used by this book. In your Hadoop cluster, install the Oozie server on an edge node, where you would also run other client applications against the cluster's data, as shown in Figure 10-2.

Edge nodes are designed to be a gateway for the outside network to the Hadoop cluster. This makes them ideal for data transfer technologies (Flume, for example), but also client applications and other application infrastructure like Oozie. Oozie does not need a dedicated server, and can easily coexist with other services that are ideally suited for edge nodes, like Pig and Hive. For more information on Hadoop deployments, see Chapter 16.

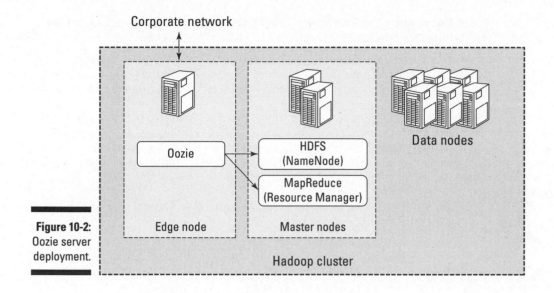

Figure 10-2: Oozie server deployment.

After Oozie is deployed, you're ready to start the Oozie server. Oozie's infrastructure is installed in the $OOZIE_HOME directory. From there, run the oozie-start.sh command to start the server. (As you might expect, stopping the server involves typing oozie-stop.sh.) You can test the status of your Oozie instance by running the command

```
oozie admin -status
```

After you have the Oozie server deployed and started, you can catalog and run your various workflow, coordinator, or bundle jobs. When working with your jobs, Oozie stores the catalog definitions — the data describing all the Oozie objects (workflow, coordinator, and bundle jobs) — as well as their states in a dedicated database.

By default, Oozie is configured to use the embedded Derby database, but you can use MySQL, Oracle, or PostgreSQL, if you need to.

A quick look at Figure 10-1 tells you that you have four options for interacting with the Oozie server:

✔ **The Java API:** This option is useful in situations where you have your own scheduling code in Java applications, and you need to control the execution of your Oozie workflows, coordinators, or bundles from within your application.

✔ **The REST API:** Again, this option works well in those cases where you want to use your own scheduling code as the basis of your Oozie workflows, coordinators, or bundles, or if you want to build your own interface or extend an existing one for administering the Oozie server.

✔ **Command Line Interface (CLI):** It's the traditional Linux command line interface for Oozie.

✔ **The Oozie Web Console:** Okay, maybe you can't do much interacting here, but the Oozie Web Console gives you a (read-only) view of the state of the Oozie server, which is useful for monitoring your Oozie jobs.

Hue, a Hadoop administration interface, provides another tool for working with Oozie. Oozie workflows, coordinators, and bundles are all defined using XML, which can be tedious to edit, especially for complex situations. Hue provides a GUI designer tool to graphically build workflows and other Oozie objects.

Underneath the covers, Oozie includes an embedded Tomcat web server, which handles its input and output.

Developing and Running an Oozie Workflow

Oozie workflows are, at their core, directed graphs, where you can define actions (Hadoop applications) and data flow, but with no looping — meaning you can't define a structure where you'd run a specific operation over and over until some condition is met (a `for` loop, for example). Oozie workflows are quite flexible in that you can define condition-based decisions and forked paths for parallel execution. You can also execute a wide range of actions.

Figure 10-3 shows a sample Oozie workflow.

Figure 10-3:
A sample
Oozie
workflow.

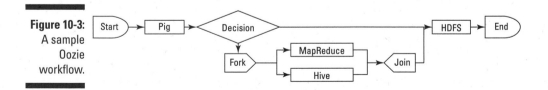

In this figure, we see a workflow showing the basic capabilities of Oozie workflows. First, a Pig script is run, and is immediately followed by a decision tree. Depending on the state of the output, the control flow can either go directly to an HDFS file operation (for example, a copyToLocal operation) or to a fork action. If the control flow passes to the fork action, two jobs are run concurrently: a MapReduce job, and a Hive query. The control flow then goes to the HDFS operation once both the MapReduce job and Hive query are finished running. After the HDFS operation, the workflow is complete.

Writing Oozie workflow definitions

Oozie workflow definitions are written in XML, based on the Hadoop Process Definition Language (hPDL) schema. This particular schema is, in turn, based on the XML Process Definition Language (XPDL) schema, which is a product-independent standard for modeling business process definitions.

An Oozie workflow is composed of a series of actions, which are encoded by XML nodes. There are different kinds of nodes, representing different kinds of actions or control flow directives. Each Oozie workflow has its own XML file, where every node and its interconnections are defined. Workflow nodes all require unique identifiers because they're used to identify the next node to be processed in the workflow. This means that the order in which the actions are executed depends on where an action's node appears in the workflow XML. To see how this concept would look, check out Listing 10-1, which shows an example of the basic structure of an Oozie workflow's XML file.

Listing 10-1:   A Sample Oozie XML File

```
<workflow-app name="SampleWorkflow" xmlns="uri:oozie:workflow:0.1">
  <start to="firstJob"/>
  <action name="firstJob">
    <pig>...</pig>
    <ok to="secondJob"/>
    <error to="kill"/>
  </action>
  <action name="secondJob">
    <map-reduce>...</map-reduce>
    <ok to="end" />
    <error to="kill" />
  </action>
  <end name="end"/>
  <kill name="kill">
    <message>"Killed job."</message>
  </kill>
</workflow-app>
```

In this example, aside from the start, end, and kill nodes, you have two action nodes. Each action node represents an application or a command being executed. The next few sections look a bit closer at each node type.

Start and end nodes

Each workflow XML file must have one matched pair of start and end nodes. The sole purpose of the start node is to direct the workflow to the first node, which is done using the to attribute. Because it's the automatic starting point for the workflow, no name identifier is required.

Action nodes need `name` identifiers, as the Oozie server uses them to track the current position of the control flow as well as to specify which action to execute next.

The sole purpose of the end node is to provide a termination point for the workflow. A `name` identifier is required, but there's no need for a `to` attribute.

Kill nodes

Oozie workflows can include *kill* nodes, which are a special kind of node dedicated to handling error conditions. Kill nodes are optional, and you can define multiple instances of them for cases where you need specialized handling for different kinds of errors. Action nodes can include error transition tags, which direct the control flow to the named kill node in case of an error. You can also direct decision nodes to point to a kill node based on the results of decision predicates, if needed. Like an end node, a kill node results in the workflow ending, and it does not need a `to` attribute.

Decision nodes

Decision nodes enable you to define conditional logic to determine the next step to be taken in the workflow — Listing 10-2 gives some examples:

Listing 10-2: A Sample Oozie XML File

```
<workflow-app name="SampleWorkflow" xmlns="uri:oozie:workflow:0.1">
  <start to="firstDecision"/>
  @@1
  <decision name="firstDecision">
  <switch>
    @@2
    <case to="firstJob">
    ${fs:fileSize('usr/dirk/ny-flights') gt 10 * GB}
    </case>
    @@3
    <case to="secondJob">
    ${fs:filSize('usr/dirk/ny-flights') lt 100 * MB}
    </case>
    @@4
    <default to="thirdJob"/>
  </switch>
  </decision>
  <action name="firstJob">...</action>
  <action name="secondJob">...</action>
  <action name="thirdJob">...</action>
  <end name="end"/>
</workflow-app>
```

In this workflow, we begin with a decision node (see the code following the bold @@1), which includes a case statement (called `switch`), where, depending on the size of the files in the `'usr/dirk/ny-flights'` directory, a different action is taken. Here, if the size of the files in the `'usr/dirk/ny-flights'` directory is greater than 10GB (see the code following the bold @@2), the control flow runs the action named `firstJob` next. If the size of the files in the `'usr/dirk/ny-flights'` directory is less than 100MB (see the code following the bold @@3), the control flow runs the action named `secondJob` next. And if neither case we've seen so far is true (in this case, if the size of the files in the `'usr/dirk/ny-flights'` directory is greater than 100MB and less than 10GB), we want the action named `thirdJob` to run.

Case statements (seen here as `switch`) are quite common in control flow programming languages. (We talk about the difference between *control flow* and *data flow* languages in Chapter 8.) They enable you to define the flow of a program based on a series of decisions. They're called case statements, because they're really a set of cases: for example, *in case* the first comparison is true, we'll run one function, or *in case* the second comparison is true, we'll run a different function.

As we just saw, a decision node consists of a `switch` operation, where you can define one or more cases and a single default case, which is mandatory. This is to ensure the workflow always has a next action. *Predicates* for the case statements — the logic inside the `<case>` tags — are written as JSP Expression Language (EL) expressions, which resolve to either a `true` or `false` value.

For the full range of EL expressions that are bundled in the Oozie, check out the related Oozie workflows specifications at this site:

```
http://oozie.apache.org/docs/4.0.0/WorkflowFunctionalSpec.
          html - a4.2_Expression_Language_Functions
```

Action nodes

Action nodes are where the actual work performed by the workflow is completed. You have a wide variety of actions to choose from — Hadoop applications (like Pig, Hive, and MapReduce), Java applications, HDFS operations, and even sending e-mail, to name just a few examples. You can also configure custom action types for operations that have no existing action.

Depending on the kind of action being used, a number of different tags need to be used. All actions, however, require transition tags: one for defining the next node after then successful completion of the action, and one for defining the next node if the action fails. In the following list, we describe the more commonly used action node types:

✔ **MapReduce:** MapReduce, as we discuss in Chapter 6, is a framework for distributed applications to run on Hadoop. For a MapReduce workflow to be successful, a couple things need to happen. MapReduce actions, for example, require that you specify the addresses of the processing and storage servers for your Hadoop cluster. We also need to specify the master services for both the processing and storage systems in Hadoop so that Oozie can properly submit this job for execution on the Hadoop cluster, and so that the input files can be found. Listing 10-3 shows the tagging for a MapReduce action:

Listing 10-3:   A Sample Oozie XML File to Run a MapReduce Job

```
<workflow-app name=" SampleWorkflow " xmlns="uri:oozie:workflow:0.1">
   ...
   <action name="firstJob">
      <map-reduce>
@@1      <job-tracker>serverName:8021</job-tracker>
         <name-node>serverName:8020</name-node>
@@2      <prepare>
            <delete path="hdfs://clientName:8020/usr/sample/output-data"/>
         </prepare>
@@3      <job-xml>jobConfig.xml</job-xml>
         <configuration>
            ...
            <property>
               <name>mapreduce.map.class</name>
               <value>dummies.oozie.FlightMilesMapper</value>
            </property>
            <property>
               <name>mapreduce.reduce.class</name>
               <value>dummies.oozie.FlightMilesReducer </value>
            </property>
            <property>
               <name>mapred.mapoutput.key.class</name>
               <value>org.apache.hadoop.io.Text</value>
            </property>
            <property>
               <name>mapred.mapoutput.value.class</name>
               <value>org.apache.hadoop.io.IntWritable</value>
            </property>
            <property>
               <name>mapred.output.key.class</name>
               <value>org.apache.hadoop.io.Text</value>
            </property>
            <property>
```

```
                <name>mapred.output.value.class</name>
                <value>org.apache.hadoop.io.IntWritable</value>
            </property>
            <property>
                <name>mapred.input.dir</name>
                <value>'/usr/dirk/flightdata'</value>
            </property>
            <property>
                <name>mapred.output.dir</name>
                <value>'/usr/dirk/flightmiles'</value>
            </property>
            ...
            </configuration>
        </map-reduce>
        <ok to="end"/>
        <error to="end"/>
    </action>
    ...
</workflow-app>
```

In this code, we just have a single action to illustrate how to invoke a
MapReduce job from an Oozie workflow. In the code following the bold
@@1, we need to define the master servers for the storage and processing systems in Hadoop. For the processing side, the old JobTracker term
is used, but you can enter the name for the Region Server if you're using
YARN to manage the processing in your cluster. (See Chapter 7 for more
information on the JobTracker and the Region Server and how they
manage the processing for Hadoop, both in Hadoop 1 and in Hadoop 2.)
Note that we also specify the server and port number for the NameNode
(again, so the MapReduce job can find its files).

In the code following the bold @@2, the <prepare> tag is used to delete
any residual information from previous runs of the same application.
You can also do other file movement operations here if needed.

All the definitions for the MapReduce applications are specified in configuration details. In the code following the bold @@3, we can see the first of
two options: the <job-xml> tag, which is optional, can point to a Hadoop
JobConf file, where you can define all your configuration details outside
the Oozie workflow XML document. This can be useful if you need to run
the same MapReduce application in many of your workflows, so if configurations need to change you only need to adjust the settings in one place.
You can also enter configuration details in the <configuration> tag,
as we've done in the example above. In the example, you can see that we
define all the key touch points for the MapReduce application: the data
types of the key/value pairs as they input and output the map and reduce
phases, the class names for the map and reduce code you have written,
and the paths for the input and output files. It's important to note that
configuration settings specified here would override any settings defined
in the file identified in the <job-xml> tag.

✔ **Hive:** Similar to MapReduce actions, as just described, Hive actions require that you specify the addresses of the processing and storage servers for your Hadoop cluster. Hive enables you to submit SQL-like queries against data in HDFS that you've cataloged as a Hive table. (For more information on Hive, see Chapter 13.) As Hive does its work, Hive queries get turned into MapReduce jobs, so we will need to specify the names of the processing and storage systems used in your Hadoop cluster. The following example shows the tagging for a Hive action:

Listing 10-4:   A Sample Oozie XML File to Run a Hive Query

```
<workflow-app name="SampleWorkflow" xmlns="uri:oozie:workflow:0.2">
    ...
    <action name="firstJob">
        <hive>
            <job-tracker>serverName:8021</job-tracker>
            <name-node>serverName:8020</name-node>
            <prepare>
                <delete path="hdfs://clientName:8020/usr/sample/output-
            data"/>
            </prepare>
            <job-xml>jobConfig.xml</job-xml>
            <configuration>...</configuration>
        @@1 <script>firstJob.hql</script>
        </hive>
        <ok to="end"/>
        <error to="end"/>
    </action>
    ...
</workflow-app>
```

In the code in Listing 10-4, we have defined similar definitions as we've done with the MapReduce action. The key difference here is that we can avoid the extensive configuration tags defining the MapReduce details and simply specify the location and name of the file containing the Hive query. (See the code following the bold @@1.)

To specify the Hive script being used, enter the filename and path in the `<script>` tag. Aside from this tag, the remaining tags shown are the same as for MapReduce.

✔ **Pig:** Pig scripts enable you to define a data flow (a series of actions you can apply to data) and the Pig compiler turns that code into MapReduce. (See Chapter 8 for more on Pig in general.) Pig actions require that you specify the addresses of the processing and storage servers for your

Hadoop cluster. Since the Hadoop processing and storage systems are used here, as they are in the Hive action, we need to specify their names here as well. Listing 10-5 shows the tagging for a Pig action:

Listing 10-5:   A Sample Oozie XML File to Run a Pig Script

```
<workflow-apfp name="SampleWorkflow" xmlns="uri:oozie:workflow:0.2">
    ...
    <action name="firstJob">
        <pig>
            <job-tracker>serverName:8021</job-tracker>
            <name-node>serverName:8020</name-node>
            <prepare>
                <delete path="hdfs://clientName:8020/usr/sample/output-
            data"/>
            </prepare>
            <job-xml>jobConfig.xml</job-xml>
            <configuration>...</configuration>
        @@1 <script>firstJob.pig</script>
        </pig>
        <ok to="end"/>
        <error to="end"/>
    </action>
    ...
</workflow-app>
```

Listing 10-5 looks a lot like Listing 10-4. Once again, we have defined similar definitions as we've done with the MapReduce action and once again the key difference here is that we can avoid the extensive configuration tags defining the MapReduce details. All we have to do is specify the location and name of the file containing the Pig script query. (See the code following the bold @@1.) To specify the `.pig` script being used, enter the filename and path in the `<script>` tag.

✔ **File System (FS):** The File System action enables you to run HDFS commands as part of your workflow, which is tremendously useful as you post-process and pre-preprocess data. *Note:* The HDFS commands enable you to perform the typical file movement operations people need to do when manipulating data inputs and outputs, like deleting, copying, renaming, and moving files. Listing 10-6 shows the tagging for a file system action where a file is deleted, a directory is created, a file is moved, and permissions are changed:

Listing 10-6: A Sample Oozie XML File to Run File System Commands

```
<workflow-app name="SampleWorkflow" xmlns="uri:oozie:workflow:0.1">
    ...
    <action name="firstJob">
        <fs>
            <delete path="hdfs://servername:8020/usr/sample/temp-data"/>
            <mkdir path="archives/${wf:id()}"/>
            <move source="${jobInput}"
          target="archives/${wf:id()}/processed-input"/>
            <chmod path="${jobOutput}" permissions="-rwxrw-rw-" dir-
          files="true"><recursive/></chmod>
        </fs>
        <ok to="end"/>
        <error to="end"/>
    </action>
    ...
</workflow-app>
```

Fork and join nodes

You can define parallel execution tracks for your workflows by using fork and join nodes together. This structure, which begins with a fork, can spawn two or more workflow paths, which would then be executed in parallel. Use the join node to merge the control flow back to a single path. See the code in Listing 10-7:

Listing 10-7: A Sample Oozie XML File to Fork a Control Flow

```
<workflow-app name="SampleWorkflow" xmlns="uri:oozie:workflow:0.1">
  <start to="fork"/>
  <fork name="fork">
    <path start="firstJob" />
    <path start="secondJob" />
  </fork>
  <action name="firstJob">
    ...
    <ok to="join" />
    <error to="end" />
  </action>
  <action name="secondJob">
    ...
    <ok to="join" />
    <error to="end" />
  </action>
  <join name="join" to="end" />
  <end name="end"/>
</workflow-app>
```

The actions and other control flow nodes must point to the join node to terminate the individual workflow paths that were spawned with the fork operation. Before the next node pointed to by the join node can be executed, all the actions and control flows in each of the paths must be finished.

Configuring Oozie workflows

You can configure Oozie workflows in one of three ways, depending on your particular circumstances. You can use

- ✔ **The** `config-default.xml` **file:** Defines parameters that don't change for the workflow.

- ✔ **The** `job.properties` **file:** Defines parameters that are common for a particular deployment of the workflow. Definitions here override those made in the `config-default.xml` file.

- ✔ **The command-line parameters:** Defines parameters that are specific for the workflow invocation. Definitions here override those made in the `job.properties` file and the `config-default.xml` file.

The configuration details will differ, depending on the action they're associated with. For example, as we saw in the MapReduce action (map-action) in Listing 10-3, you have many more things to configure there, as opposed to a file system (`fs`) action like the one shown in Listing 10-6.

Running Oozie workflows

Before running your Oozie workflows, all its components need to exist within a specified directory structure. Specifically, the workflow itself should have its own, dedicated directory, where `workflow.xml` is in the root directory, and any code libraries exist in the subdirectory named `lib`. The workflow directory and all its files must exist in HDFS for it to be executed.

If you'll be using the Oozie command-line interface to work with various jobs, be sure to set the `OOZIE_URL` environment variable. (This is easily done from a command line in a Linux terminal.) You can save yourself a lot of typing because the Oozie server's URL will now automatically be included with your requests. Here's a sample command one could use to set the `OOZIE_URL` environment variable from the command line:

```
export OOZIE_URL="http://localhost:8080/oozie"
```

To run an Oozie workload from the Oozie command-line interface, issue a command like the following, while ensuring that the `job.properties` file is *locally accessible* — meaning the account you're using can see it, meaning it has to be on the same system where you're running Oozie commands:

```
$ oozie job -config sampleWorkload/job.properties -run
```

After you submit a job, the workload is stored in the Oozie object database. (Refer to Figure 10-1.) On submission, Oozie returns an identifier to enable you to monitor and administer your workflow — `job:0000001-00000001234567-oozie-W`, for example:

To check the status of this job, you'd run the command

```
oozie job -info 0000001-00000001234567-oozie-W
```

Scheduling and Coordinating Oozie Workflows

After you've created a set of workflows, you can use a series of Oozie coordinator jobs to schedule when they're executed. You have two scheduling options for execution: a specific time and the availability of data in conjunction with a certain time. The following three sections take a look at each option.

Time-based scheduling for Oozie coordinator jobs

Oozie coordinator jobs can be scheduled to execute at a certain time, but after they're started, they can then be configured to run at specified intervals. The following example shows a coordinator job that starts running at a specified start time and date:

Listing 10-8:   A Sample Oozie XML File to Schedule a Workflow by Time

```
<coordinator-app name="sampleCoordinator"
            frequency="${coord:days(1)}"
            start="2014-06-01T00:01Z "
            end="2014-06-01T01:00Z "
            timezone="UTC"
            xmlns="uri:oozie:coordinator:0.1">
    <controls>...</controls>
```

```
    <action>
       <workflow>
          <app-path>${workflowAppPath}</app-path>
       </workflow>
    </action>
</coordinator-app>
```

Time and data availability-based scheduling for Oozie coordinator jobs

Oozie coordinator jobs can also be scheduled to execute at a certain time if specified data files or directories are available. Listing 10-9 shows an example of a coordinator that starts running at a specified start time and date, is executed once a day if the data set identified by triggerDatasetDir exists, and runs until the specified end time:

Listing 10-9:   A Sample Oozie XML File to Schedule a Workflow by Time and Data Availability

```
<coordinator-app name="sampleCoordinator"
                 frequency="${coord:days(1)}"
                 start="${startTime}"
                 end="${endTime}"
                 timezone="${timeZoneDef}"
                 xmlns="uri:oozie:coordinator:0.1">
   <controls>...</controls>
   <datasets>
      <dataset name="input" frequency="${coord:days(1)}" initial-
               instance="${startTime}" timezone="${timeZoneDef}">
         <uri-template>${triggerDatasetDir}</uri-template>
      </dataset>
   </datasets>
   <input-events>
         <data-in name="sampleInput" dataset="input">
         <instance>${startTime}</instance>
      </data-in>
   </input-events>
   <action>
      <workflow>
         <app-path>${workflowAppPath}</app-path>
      </workflow>
   </action>
</coordinator-app>
```

Running Oozie coordinator jobs

Similar to Oozie workflow jobs, coordinator jobs require a `job.properties` file, and the coordinator.xml file needs to be loaded in the HDFS. To run an Oozie coordinator job from the Oozie command-line interface, issue a command like the following while ensuring that the `job.properties` file is locally accessible:

```
$ oozie job -config sampleCoordinator/job.properties -run
```

After you submit the job, the coordinator is stored in the Oozie object database. (Refer to Figure 10-1.) On submission, Oozie returns an identifier to enable you to monitor and administer your coordinator — `job: 0000001-00000001234567-oozie-C`, for example:

To check the status of this job, run the command

```
oozie job -info 0000001-00000001234567-oozie-C
```

Part III
Hadoop and Structured Data

Check out the article "Roadmap of Hadoop Family Projects" (and more) online at www.dummies.com/extras/hadoop.

In this part . . .

- ✔ Examine how Hadoop can play nice with different kinds of data warehouses.
- ✔ See what HBase brings to the Hadoop table.
- ✔ Be busy as a bee with Hive.
- ✔ Get the scoop on Sqoop.
- ✔ Look into the (SQL) future of Hadoop
- ✔ Check out the article "Roadmap of Hadoop Family Projects" (and more) online at `www.dummies.com/extras/hadoop`.

Chapter 11

Hadoop and the Data Warehouse: Friends or Foes?

---

*I*T types like us tend to love the latest and greatest new technologies, and when compelling platforms like Hadoop emerge, they're often accompanied by a significant amount of hype. You might even say that this *For Dummies* book is part of that hype! When it comes to Hadoop, though, there's real substance behind the hype. Not convinced? Just look at the increasing numbers of code contributions in the Apache Hadoop projects as well as the adoption rates of Hadoop in medium-to large-size businesses. The consensus is overwhelming: Hadoop is here to stay.

It's important to understand how any new technology relates to existing technologies and business practices. In the case of Hadoop, you should know how it will impact the field of enterprise data management. In our experience, the IT market reacts in two distinct ways.

On one hand, the Hadoop hype machine is in full gear and bent on world domination. This camp sees Hadoop replacing the relational database products that now power the world's data warehouses. The argument here is compelling: Hadoop is cheap and scalable, and it has queryable interfaces that are becoming increasingly faster and more closely compliant with ANSI SQL — *the* standard for programming applications used with database systems.

On the other hand, many relational warehouse vendors have gone out of their way to resist the appeal of all the Hadoop hype. Understandably, they won't roll over and make way for Hadoop to replace their relational database offerings. They've adopted what we consider to be a protectionist stance, drawing a line between structured data, which they consider to be the exclusive domain of relational databases, and unstructured data, which is where they feel Hadoop can operate. In this model, they're positioning Hadoop as solely a tool to transform unstructured data into a structured form for relational databases to store.

We feel that the truth lies in the middle of these opposing views: there are many workloads and business applications where data warehouses powered by relational databases are still the most practical choice. At the same time, there are classes of data (both structured and unstructured) and workloads where Hadoop is the most practical option. The key consideration here is using tools that are best suited for the task at hand.

The focus of this chapter is on comparing and contrasting the relative strengths of Hadoop technologies and relational databases and then on exploring a family of use cases for how Hadoop's strengths can expand the capabilities of today's data warehouses.

Comparing and Contrasting Hadoop with Relational Databases

Database models and database systems have been around as long as computer systems have roamed the earth, and most of us IT people have at least been exposed to (or perhaps even used) some type of database technology for a very long time. The most prevalent database technology is the relational database management system (RDBMS), which can be traced back to Edgar F. Codd's groundbreaking work at IBM in the 1970s. Several well-known companies (IBM, Informix, Oracle, and Sybase, for example) capitalized on Codd's work and sold, or continue to sell, products based on his relational model. At roughly the same time, Donald D. Chamberlin and Raymond F. Boyce created the structured query language (SQL) as a way to provide a common programming language for managing data stored in an RDBMS.

The 1980s and 1990s saw the birth of the object database, which provided a better fit for a particular class of problems than the relational database, and now *another* new class of technologies, commonly referred to as NoSQL databases, is emerging. Because NoSQL databases play a significant role in the Hadoop story, they deserve a closer look, so be sure to read the next section.

NoSQL data stores

NoSQL data stores originally subscribed to the notion "Just Say No to SQL" (to paraphrase from an anti-drug advertising campaign in the 1980s), and they were a reaction to the perceived limitations of (SQL-based) relational databases. It's not that these folks hated SQL, but they were tired of forcing square pegs into round holes by solving problems that relational databases weren't designed for. A relational database is a powerful tool, but for some kinds of data (like key-value pairs, or graphs) and some usage patterns (like extremely large scale storage) a relational database just isn't practical. And when it comes to high-volume storage, relational database can be expensive, both in terms of database license costs and hardware costs. (Relational databases are designed to work with enterprise-grade hardware.) So, with the NoSQL movement, creative programmers developed dozens of solutions for different kinds of thorny data storage and processing problems. These NoSQL databases typically provide massive scalability by way of clustering, and are often designed to enable high throughput and low latency.

The name NoSQL is somewhat misleading because many databases that fit the category *do* have SQL support (rather than "NoSQL" support). Think of its name instead as "Not Only SQL."

The NoSQL offerings available today can be broken down into four distinct categories, based on their design and purpose:

- ✔ **Key-value stores:** This offering provides a way to store any kind of data without having to use a schema. This is in contrast to relational databases, where you need to define the schema (the table structure) before any data is inserted. Since key-value stores don't require a schema, you have great flexibility to store data in many formats. In a key-value store, a row simply consists of a key (an identifier) and a value, which can be anything from an integer value to a large binary data string. Many implementations of key-value stores are based on Amazon's Dynamo paper.

- ✔ **Column family stores:** Here you have databases in which columns are grouped into column families and stored together on disk.

Strictly speaking, many of these databases aren't column-oriented, because they're based on Google's BigTable paper, which stores data as a multidimensional sorted map. (For more on the role of Google's BigTable paper on database design, see Chapter 12.)

- ✔ **Document stores:** This offering relies on collections of similarly encoded and formatted documents to improve efficiencies. Document stores enable individual documents in a collection to include only a subset of fields, so only the data that's needed is stored. For sparse data sets, where many fields are often not populated, this can translate into significant space savings. By contrast, empty columns in relational database tables do take up space. Document stores also enables schema flexibility, because only the fields that are needed are stored, and new fields can be added. Again, in contrast to relational databases, table structures are defined up front before data is stored, and changing columns is a tedious task that impacts the entire data set.

✔ **Graph databases:** Here you have databases that store *graph structures* — representations that show collections of entities (vertices or nodes) and their relationships (edges) with each other. These structures enable graph databases to be extremely well suited for storing complex structures, like the linking relationships between all known web pages. (For example, individual web pages are nodes, and the edges connecting them are links from one page to another.) Google, of course, is all over graph technology, and invented a graph processing engine called Pregel to power its PageRank algorithm. (And yes, there's a white paper on Pregel.) In the Hadoop community, there's an Apache project called Giraph (based on the Pregel paper), which is a graph processing engine designed to process graphs stored in HDFS.

The data storage and processing options available in Hadoop are in many cases implementations of the NoSQL categories listed here. This will help you better evaluate solutions that are available to you and see how Hadoop can complement traditional data warehouses.

ACID versus BASE data stores

One hallmark of relational database systems is something known as *ACID compliance.* As you might have guessed, ACID is an acronym — the individual letters, meant to describe a characteristic of individual database transactions, can be expanded as described in this list:

✔ **Atomicity:** The database transaction must completely succeed or completely fail. Partial success is not allowed.

✔ **Consistency:** During the database transaction, the RDBMS progresses from one valid state to another. The state is never invalid.

✔ **Isolation:** The client's database transaction must occur in isolation from other clients attempting to transact with the RDBMS.

✔ **Durability:** The data operation that was part of the transaction must be reflected in *nonvolatile storage* (computer memory that can retrieve stored information even when not powered – like a hard disk) and persist after the transaction successfully completes. Transaction failures cannot leave the data in a partially committed state.

Certain use cases for RDBMSs, like online transaction processing, depend on ACID-compliant transactions between the client and the RDBMS for the system to function properly. A great example of an ACID-compliant transaction is a transfer of funds from one bank account to another. This breaks down into two database transactions, where the originating account shows a withdrawal, and the destination account shows a deposit. Obviously, these two transactions have to be tied together in order to be valid so that if either of them fail, the whole operation must fail to ensure both balances remain valid.

Hadoop itself has no concept of transactions (or even records, for that matter), so it clearly isn't an ACID-compliant system. Thinking more specifically about data storage and processing projects in the entire Hadoop ecosystem (we tell you more about these projects later in this chapter), none of them is fully ACID-compliant, either. However, they *do* reflect properties that you often see in NoSQL data stores, so there is some precedent to the Hadoop approach.

One key concept behind NoSQL data stores is that not every application truly needs ACID-compliant transactions. Relaxing on certain ACID properties (and moving away from the relational model) has opened up a wealth of possibilities, which have enabled some NoSQL data stores to achieve massive scalability and performance for their niche applications. Whereas ACID defines the key characteristics required for reliable transaction processing, the NoSQL world requires different characteristics to enable flexibility and scalability. These opposing characteristics are cleverly captured in the acronym BASE:

- ✔ **Basically Available:** The system is guaranteed to be available for querying by all users. (No isolation here.)

- ✔ **Soft State:** The values stored in the system may change because of the eventual consistency model, as described in the next bullet.

- ✔ **Eventually Consistent:** As data is added to the system, the system's state is gradually replicated across all nodes. For example, in Hadoop, when a file is written to the HDFS, the replicas of the data blocks are created in different data nodes after the original data blocks have been written. For the short period before the blocks are replicated, the state of the file system isn't consistent.

The acronym BASE is a bit contrived, as most NoSQL data stores don't completely abandon *all* the ACID characteristics — it's not really the polar opposite concept that the name implies, in other words. Also, the Soft State and Eventually Consistent characteristics amount to the same thing, but the point is that by relaxing consistency, the system can horizontally scale (many nodes) and ensure availability.

No discussion of NoSQL would be complete without mentioning the CAP theorem, which represents the three kinds of guarantees that architects aim to provide in their systems:

- ✔ **Consistency:** Similar to the C in ACID, all nodes in the system would have the same view of the data at any time.

- ✔ **Availability:** The system always responds to requests.

- ✔ **Partition tolerance:** The system remains online if network problems occur between system nodes.

The CAP theorem states that in distributed networked systems, architects have to choose two of these three guarantees — you can't promise your users all three. That leaves you with the three possibilities shown in Figure 11-1:

- ✔ **Systems using traditional relational technologies** normally aren't partition tolerant, so they can guarantee consistency and availability. In short, if one part of these traditional relational technologies systems is offline, the whole system is offline.

- ✔ **Systems where partition tolerance and availability are of primary importance** can't guarantee consistency, because updates (that destroyer of consistency) can be made on either side of the partition. The key-value stores Dynamo and CouchDB and the column-family store Cassandra are popular examples of partition tolerant/availability (PA) systems.

- ✔ **Systems where partition tolerance and consistency are of primary importance** can't guarantee availability because the systems return errors until the partitioned state is resolved.

Hadoop-based data stores are considered CP systems (consistent and partition tolerant). With data stored redundantly across many slave nodes, outages to large portions (partitions) of a Hadoop cluster can be tolerated. Hadoop is considered to be consistent because it has a central metadata store (the NameNode) which maintains a single, consistent view of data stored in the cluster. We can't say that Hadoop guarantees availability, because if the NameNode fails applications cannot access data in the cluster.

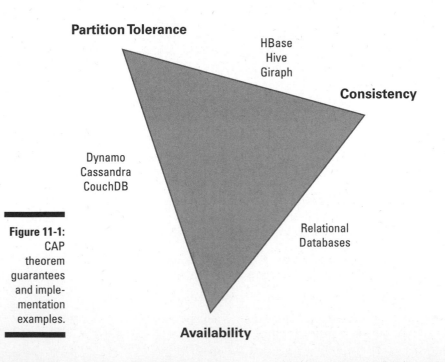

Figure 11-1:
CAP
theorem
guarantees
and imple-
mentation
examples.

Structured data storage and processing in Hadoop

When considering Hadoop's capabilities for working with structured data (or working with data of any type, for that matter), remember Hadoop's core characteristics: Hadoop is, first and foremost, a general-purpose data storage and processing platform designed to scale out to thousands of compute nodes and petabytes of data. There's no data model in Hadoop itself; data is simply stored on the Hadoop cluster as raw files. As such, the core components of Hadoop itself have no special capabilities for cataloging, indexing, or querying structured data.

The beauty of a general-purpose data storage system is that it can be extended for highly specific purposes. The Hadoop community has done just that with a number of Apache projects — projects that, in totality, make up the Hadoop *ecosystem*. When it comes to structured data storage and processing, the projects described in this list are the most commonly used:

- ✔ **Hive:** A data warehousing framework for Hadoop. Hive catalogs data in structured files and provides a query interface with the SQL-like language named HiveQL. (We tell you tons more about Hive in Chapter 13.)

- ✔ **HBase:** A *distributed* database — a NoSQL database that relies on multiple computers rather than on a single CPU, in other words — that's built on top of Hadoop. (For more on HBase, see Chapter 12.)

- ✔ **Giraph:** A graph processing engine for data stored in Hadoop. (See the earlier discussion in this chapter on NoSQL and graph databases.)

Many other Apache projects support different aspects of structured data analysis, and some projects focus on a number of frameworks and interfaces. Chapter 14 takes a look at another structured data analysis tool — the aptly named Sqoop — and Chapter 15 takes a look at SQL interfaces to Hadoop data.

When determining the optimal architecture for your analytics needs, be sure to evaluate the attributes and capabilities of the systems you're considering. Table 11-1 compares Hadoop-based data stores (Hive, Giraph, and HBase) with traditional RDBMS.

Table 11-1   A Comparison of Hadoop-Based Storage and RDBMS

Criteria	Hive	Giraph	HBase	RDBMS
Changeable data	No		Yes	Yes
Data layout	Raw files stored in HDFS; Hive supports proprietary row-oriented or column-oriented formats.		A sparse, distributed, persistent multidimensional sorted map	Row-oriented or column-oriented
Data types	Bytes; data types are interpreted on query.			Rich data type support
Hardware	Hadoop-clustered commodity x86 servers; five or more is typical because the underlying storage technology is HDFS, which by default requires three replicas.			Typically large, scalable multi-processor systems
High availability	Yes; built into the Hadoop architecture			Yes, if the hardware and RDBMS are configured correctly
Indexes	Yes	No	Row-key only or special table required	Yes
Query language	HiveQL	Giraph API	HBase API commands (get, put, scan, delete, increment, check), HiveQL	SQL

Criteria	Hive	Giraph	HBase	RDBMS
Schema	Schema defined as files are catalogued with the Hive Data Definition Language (DDL)	Schema on read	Variability in schema between rows	Schema on load
Throughput	Millions of reads and writes per second			Thousands of reads and writes per second
Transactions	None		Provides ACID support on only a single row	Provides multi-row and cross-table transactional support with full ACID property compliance
Transaction speed	Modest speed for interactive queries; fast for full table scans		Fast for interactive queries; fast for full table scans	Fast for interactive queries; slower for full table scans
Typical size	Ranges from terabytes to petabytes (from hundreds of millions to billions of rows)			From gigabytes to terabytes (from hundreds of thousands to millions of rows)

Modernizing the Warehouse with Hadoop

We want to stress the fact that Hadoop and traditional RDBMS technologies are more complementary than competitive. The sensationalist marketing and news media articles that pit these technologies against each other are missing the point: By using the strengths of these technologies together, you can build a highly flexible and scalable analytics environment.

Rather than have you simply trust us on that assertion, we use the rest of this chapter to lay out four (specific) ways that Hadoop can modernize the warehouse. Get ready to delve into the messy details of these use cases:

- ✔ Landing Zone for All Data
- ✔ Queryable Archive of Cold Data
- ✔ Preprocessing Engine
- ✔ Data Discovery Zone

The landing zone

When we try to puzzle out what an analytics environment might look like in the future, we stumble across the pattern of the Hadoop-based landing zone time and time again. In fact, it's no longer even a futures-oriented discussion because the landing zone has become *the* way that forward-looking companies now try to save IT costs, and provide a platform for innovative data analysis.

So what exactly is the landing zone? At the most basic level, the *landing zone* is merely the central place where data will land in your enterprise — weekly extractions of data from operational databases, for example, or from systems generating log files. Hadoop is a useful repository in which to land data, for these reasons:

- ✔ It can handle all kinds of data.
- ✔ It's easily scalable.
- ✔ It's inexpensive.
- ✔ Once you land data in Hadoop, you have the flexibility to query, analyze, or process the data in a variety of ways.

A Hadoop-based landing zone, seen in Figure 11-2, is the foundation of the other three use cases we describe later in this chapter.

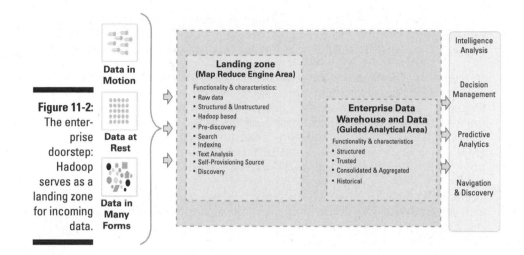

Figure 11-2:
The enter-
prise
doorstep:
Hadoop
serves as a
landing zone
for incoming
data.

This diagram only shows part of the story and is by no means complete. After all, you need to know how the data moves from the landing zone to the data warehouse, and so on. (We get around to answering such questions and filling in some of these blanks as we add more Hadoop use cases in this chapter.)

The starting point for the discussion on modernizing a data warehouse has to be how organizations use data warehouses and the challenges IT departments face with them. In the 1980s, once organizations became good at storing their operational information in relational databases (sales transactions, for example, or supply chain statuses), business leaders began to want reports generated from this relational data. The earliest relational stores were operational databases and were designed for Online Transaction Processing (OLTP), so that records could be inserted, updated, or deleted as quickly as possible. This is an impractical architecture for large scale reporting and analysis, so Relational Online Analytical Processing (ROLAP) databases were developed to meet this need. This led to the evolution of a whole new kind of RDBMS: a *data warehouse,* which is a separate entity and lives alongside an organization's operational data stores. This comes down to using purpose-built tools for greater efficiency: we have operational data stores, which are designed to efficiently process transactions, and data warehouses, which are designed to support repeated analysis and reporting.

Data warehouses are under increasing stress though, for the following reasons:

- ✔ Increased demand to keep longer periods of data online.

- ✔ Increased demand for processing resources to transform data for use in other warehouses and data marts.

- ✔ Increased demand for innovative analytics, which requires analysts to pose questions on the warehouse data, on top of the regular reporting that's already being done. This can incur significant additional processing.

The use cases we cover later in this chapter address these pain points, and actually frees data warehouses to do what they're designed to do, which is support the regular reporting activities that keep organizations running.

In Figure 11-2, we can see the data warehouse presented as the primary resource for the various kinds of analysis listed on the far right side of the figure. Here we also see the concept of a landing zone represented, where Hadoop will store data from a variety of incoming data sources. To enable a Hadoop landing zone, you'll need to ensure you can write data from the various data sources to HDFS. For relational databases, a good solution would be to use Sqoop, which we talk about in Chapter 14.

But landing the data is only the beginning. What you do with it is where the real value comes in, and that's what we'll get into with the remaining three use cases — all of which depend on a Hadoop-based landing zone populated with data from a variety of sources.

When you're moving data from many sources into your landing zone, one issue that you'll inevitably run into is data quality. It's common for companies to have many operational databases where key details are different, for example, that a customer might be known as "D. deRoos" in one database, and "Dirk deRoos" in another. Another quality problem lies in systems where there's a heavy reliance on manual data entry, either from customers or staff — here, it's not uncommon to find first names and last names switched around or other misinformation in the data fields. Data quality issues are a big deal for data warehouse environments, and that's why a lot of effort goes into cleansing and validation steps as data from other systems are processed as it's loaded into the warehouse. It all comes down to *trust*: if the data you're asking questions against is dirty, you can't trust the answers in your reports. So while there's huge potential in having access to many different data sets from different sources in your Hadoop landing zone, you have to factor in data quality and how much you can trust the data.

A queryable archive of cold warehouse data

A multitude of studies show that most data in an enterprise data warehouse is rarely queried. Database vendors have responded to such observations by implementing their own methods for sorting out what data gets placed where. One method orders the data universe into designations of hot, warm, or cold, where *hot* data (sometimes called *active* data) is used often, *warm* data is used from time to time; and *cold* data is rarely used. The proposed solution for many vendors is to store the cold data on slower disks within the data warehouse enclosures or to create clever caching strategies to keep the hot data in-memory, among others. The problem with this approach is that even though slower storage is used, it's still expensive to store cold, seldom used data in a warehouse. The costs here stems from both hardware and software licensing. At the same time, cold and dormant data is often archived to tape. This traditional model of archiving data breaks down when you want to query all cold data in a cost-effective and relatively efficient way — without having to request old tapes, in other words.

If you look at the cost and operational characteristics of Hadoop, indeed it seems that it's set to become the new backup tape. Hadoop is inexpensive largely because Hadoop systems are designed to use a lower grade of hardware than what's normally deployed in data warehouse systems. Another significant cost savings is software licensing. Commercial Hadoop distribution licenses require a fraction of the cost of relational data warehouse software licenses, which are notorious for being expensive. From an operational perspective, Hadoop is designed to easily scale just by adding additional slave nodes to an existing cluster. And as slave nodes are added and data sets grow in volume, Hadoop's data processing frameworks enable your applications to seamlessly handle the increased workload. Hadoop represents a simple, flexible, and inexpensive way to push processing across literally thousands of servers. To put this statement into perspective: In 1955, 1 megabyte of storage cost about US$6,235. By the middle of 1993, the price per megabyte dipped below US$1. The cost to purchase 1 megabyte of storage is now US$0.0000467 — in other words, at the time this book was published, US$1 could get you about 22 gigabytes of storage.

With its scalable and inexpensive architecture, Hadoop would seem to be a perfect choice for archiving warehouse data . . . except for one small matter: Most of the IT world runs on SQL, and SQL on its own doesn't play well with Hadoop. Sure, the more Hadoop-friendly NoSQL movement is alive and well, but most power users now use SQL by way of common, off-the-shelf toolsets that generate SQL queries under the hood — products such as Tableau, Microsoft Excel, and IBM Cognos BI. It's true that the Hadoop ecosystem includes Hive, but Hive supports only a subset of SQL, and although performance is improving (along with SQL support), it's not nearly as fast at answering smaller queries as relational systems are. Recently, there has been major progress around SQL access to Hadoop, which has paved the way for Hadoop to become the new destination for online data warehouse archives.

Depending on the Hadoop vendor, SQL (or SQL-like) APIs are becoming available so that the more common off-the-shelf reporting and analytics tools can seamlessly issue SQL that executes on data stored in Hadoop. For example, IBM has its Big SQL API, Cloudera has Impala, and Hive itself, via the Hortonworks Stinger initiative, is becoming increasingly SQL compliant. Though various points of view exist (some aim to enhance Hive; some, to extend Hive; and others, to provide an alternative), all these solutions attempt to tackle two issues: MapReduce is a poor solution for executing smaller queries, and SQL access is — for now — the key to enabling IT workers to use their existing SQL skills to get value out of data stored in Hadoop.

To add it all up — the inexpensive cost of storage for Hadoop plus the ability to query Hadoop data with SQL — we think that Hadoop is the prime destination for archival data. We consider this use case to have a low impact on your organization because you can start building your Hadoop skill set on data that's not stored on performance-mission-critical systems. What's more, you don't have to work hard to get at the data. (Since archived data is normally stored on systems that have low usage, it's easier to get at than data that's in "the limelight" on performance-mission-critical systems, like data warehouses.) If you're already using Hadoop as a landing zone, you have the foundation for your archive! You simply keep what you want to archive and delete what you don't.

If you think about the Landing Zone use case (refer to Figure 11-2), the queryable archive, shown in Figure 11-3, extends the value of Hadoop and starts to integrate pieces that likely already exist in your enterprise. It's a great example of finding economies of scale and cost take-out opportunities using Hadoop.

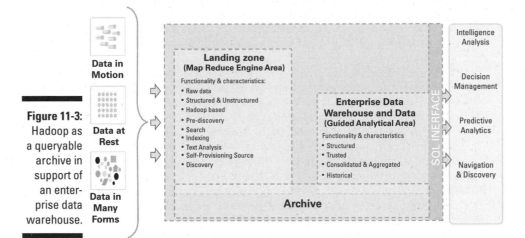

Figure 11-3: Hadoop as a queryable archive in support of an enterprise data warehouse.

In Figure 11-3, we show the archive component connecting the landing zone and the data warehouse. The data being archived originates in the warehouse and is then stored in the Hadoop cluster, which is also provisioning the landing zone. In short, you can use the same Hadoop cluster to archive data and act as your landing zone.

The key Hadoop technology you would use to perform the archiving is Sqoop, which can move the data to be archived from the data warehouse into Hadoop. You will need to consider what form you want the data to take in your Hadoop cluster. In general, compressed Hive files are a good choice. You can, of course, transform the data from the warehouse structures into some other form (for example, a normalized form to reduce redundancy), but this is generally not a good idea. Keeping the data in the same structure as what's in the warehouse will make it much easier to perform a full data set query across the archived data in Hadoop and the active data that's in the warehouse.

The concept of querying both the active and archived data sets brings up another consideration: how much data should you archive? There are really two common choices: archive everything as data is added and changed in the data warehouse, or only archive the data you deem to be cold. Archiving everything has the benefit of enabling you to easily issue queries from one single interface across the entire data set — without a full archive, you'll need to figure out a federated query solution where you would have to union the results from the archive and the active data warehouse. But the downside here is that regular updates of your data warehouse's hot data would cause headaches for the Hadoop-based archive. This is because any changes to data in individual rows and columns would require wholesale deletion and re-cataloging of existing data sets.

Now that archival data is stored in your Hadoop-based landing zone (assuming you're using an option like the compressed Hive files mentioned above), you can query it. This is where the SQL on Hadoop solutions we talk about in Chapter 15 can become interesting. An excellent example of what's possible is for the analysis tools we see on the right in Figure 11-3 to directly run reports or analysis on the archived data stored in Hadoop. This is not to replace the data warehouse — after all, Hadoop would not be able to match the warehouse's performance characteristics for supporting hundreds or more concurrent users asking complex questions. The point here is that you can use reporting tools against Hadoop to experiment and come up with new questions to answer in a dedicated warehouse or mart.

When you start your first Hadoop-based project for archiving warehouse data, don't break the current processes until you've fully tested them on your new Hadoop solution. In other words, if your current warehousing strategy is to archive to tape, keep that process in place, and dual-archive the data into Hadoop and tape until you've fully tested the scenario (which would typically include restoring the warehouse data in case of a warehouse failure). Though you're maintaining (in the short term) two archive repositories, you'll have a robust infrastructure in place and tested before you decommission a tried-and-true process. Personal observation makes us believe that this process can ensure that you remain employed — with your current employer.

This use case is simple because there's no change to the existing warehouse. The business goal is still the same: cheaper storage and licensing costs by migrating rarely-used data to an archive. The difference in this case is that the technology behind the archive is Hadoop rather than offline storage, like tape. In addition, we've seen various archive vendors start to incorporate Hadoop into their solutions (for example, allowing their proprietary archive files to reside on HDFS), so expect capabilities in this area to expand soon.

As you develop Hadoop skills (like exchanging data between Hadoop and relational databases and querying data in HDFS) you can use them to tackle bigger problems, such as analysis projects, which could provide additional value for your organization's Hadoop investment. This will be especially relevant in the data discovery sandbox use case we describe a bit later.

Hadoop as a data preprocessing engine

One of the earliest use cases for Hadoop in the enterprise was as a programmatic transformation engine used to preprocess data bound for a data warehouse. Essentially, this use case leverages the power of the Hadoop ecosystem to manipulate and apply transformations to data *before* it's loaded into a data warehouse. Though the actual transformation engine is new (it's Hadoop, so transformations and data flows are coded in Pig or MapReduce, among other languages), the approach itself has been in use awhile. What we're talking about here is Extract, Transform, Load (ETL) processes.

Think back for a minute to our description of the evolution of OLTP and ROLAP databases in the Landing Zone section earlier in the chapter. The outcome of this is that many organizations with operational databases also deployed data warehouses. So how do IT departments get data from their operational databases into their data warehouses? (Remember that the operational data is typically not in a form that lends itself to analysis.) The answer here is ETL, and as data warehouses increased in use and importance, the steps in the process became well understood and best practices were developed. Also, a number of software companies started offering interesting ETL solutions so that IT departments could minimize their own custom code development.

The basic ETL process is fairly straightforward: you *E*xtract data from an operational database, *T*ransform it into the form you need for your analysis and reporting tools, and then you *L*oad this data into your data warehouse.

One common variation to ETL is ELT — Extract, Load, and Transform. In the ELT process, you perform transformations (in contrast to ETL) *after* loading the data into the target repository. This approach is often used when the transformation stands to greatly benefit from a very fast SQL processing engine on structured data. (Relational databases may not excel at processing unstructured data, but they perform very fast processing of — guess what? — structured data.) If the data you're transforming is destined for a data warehouse, and many of those transformations can be done in SQL, you may choose to run the transformations in the data warehouse itself. ELT is especially appealing if the bulk of your skill set lies with SQL-based tooling. With Hadoop now able to process SQL queries, both ETL and ELT workloads can be hosted on Hadoop. In Figure 11-4 we show ETL services added to our reference architecture.

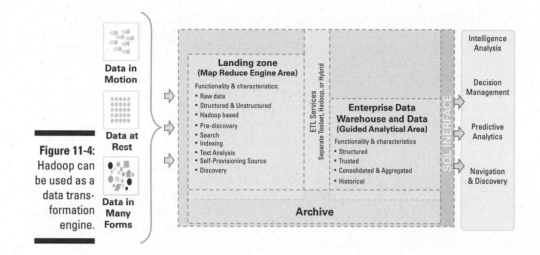

Figure 11-4: Hadoop can be used as a data transformation engine.

If you've deployed a Hadoop-based landing zone, which you can again see in Figure 11-4, you've got almost everything you need in place to use Hadoop as a transformation engine. You're already landing data from your operational systems into Hadoop using Sqoop, which covers the extraction step. At this point you'll need to implement your transformation logic into MapReduce or Pig applications. After the data is transformed, you can load the data into the data warehouse using Sqoop.

Thinking back to the archive use case we just discussed, using Hadoop as a data transformation engine raises possibilities there as well. What we described initially was a scenario where the archive consists of warehouse data that's dumped into the landing zone. But if your data warehouse doesn't modify its data (it's for reporting only), you can simply keep the data you generate with the transformation process. In this model, data only flows from left-to-right in Figure 11-4, where data is extracted from operational databases, transformed in the landing zone, and then loaded into the data warehouse. With all the transformed data already in the landing zone, there's no need to copy it back to Hadoop — unless, of course, the data gets modified in the warehouse.

The hybrid data preprocess option (Or, hybrids aren't just for cars)

In addition to having to store larger volumes of cold data, one pressure we see in traditional data warehouses is that increasing amounts of processing resources are being used for transformation (ELT) workloads. The idea behind using Hadoop as a preprocessing engine to handle data transformation means that precious processing cycles are freed up, allowing the data warehouse to adhere to its original purpose: Answer repeated business questions to support analytic applications. Again, we're seeing how Hadoop can complement traditional data warehouse deployments and enhance their productivity.

Perhaps a tiny, imaginary light bulb has lit up over your head and you're thinking, "Hey, maybe there *are* some transformation tasks perfectly suited for Hadoop's data processing ability, but I know there's also a lot of transformation work steeped in algebraic, step-by-step tasks where running SQL on a relational database engine would be the better choice. Wouldn't it be cool if I could run SQL on Hadoop?" As we've been hinting, SQL on Hadoop is already here, and you can see the various offerings in Chapter 15. With the ability to issue SQL queries against data in Hadoop, you're not stuck with only an ETL approach to your data flows — you can also deploy ELT-like applications.

Another hybrid approach to consider is where to run your transformation logic: in Hadoop or in the data warehouse? Although some organizations are concerned about running anything but analytics in their warehouses, the fact remains that relational databases are excellent at running SQL, and could be a more practical place to run a transformation than Hadoop.

Data transformation is more than just data transformation

The idea of Hadoop-inspired ETL engines has gained a lot of traction in recent years. After all, Hadoop is a flexible data storage and processing platform that can support huge amounts of data and operations on that data. At the same time, it's fault tolerant, and it offers the opportunity for capital and software cost reductions.

Despite Hadoop's popularity as an ETL engine, however, many folks (including a famous firm of analysts) don't recommend Hadoop as the sole piece of technology for your ETL strategy. This is largely because developing ETL flows requires a great deal of expertise about your organization's existing database systems, the nature of the data itself, and the reports and applications dependent on it. In other words, the DBAs, developers, and architects in your IT department would need to become familiar enough with Hadoop to implement the needed ETL flows. For example, a lot of intensive hand coding with Pig, Hive, or even MapReduce may be necessary to create even the simplest of data flows — which puts your company on

the hook for those skills if it follows this path. You have to code elements such as parallel debugging, application management services (such as check pointing and error and event handling). Also, consider enterprise requirements such as glossarization and being able to show your data's lineage. There are regulatory requirements for many industry standard reports, where data lineage is needed; the reporting organization must be able to show where the data points in the report come from, how the data got to you, and what has been done to the data.

Even for relational database systems, ETL is complex enough that there are popular specialized products that provide interfaces for managing and developing ETL flows. Some of these products now aid in Hadoop-based ETL and other Hadoop-based development. However, depending on your requirements, you may need to write some of your own code to support your transformation logic.

Data discovery and sandboxes

Data discovery is becoming an increasingly important activity for organizations that rely on their data to be a differentiator. Today, that describes most businesses, as the ability to see trends and extract meaning from available data sets applies to almost any industry. What this requires is two critical components: analysts with the creativity to think of novel ways of analyzing data sets to ask new questions (often these kinds of analysts are called *data scientists*); and to provide these analysts with access to as much data as possible.

Consider the traditional approach to analytics in today's IT landscape: The business user community now typically determines the business questions to ask — they submit a request, and the IT team builds a system that answers specific questions. From a technical perspective, because this work has traditionally been done in a relational database, it has been the IT team's responsibility to build schemas, remove data duplication, and so on. They're investing a lot of time into making this data queryable and to quickly answering preplanned questions that the business unit wants answered. This is why relational databases are typically considered schema-on-write because you have to do a lot of work in order to write to the database. (In many cases, the amount of work is worth the investment; however, in a world of big data, the value and quality of many newer types of data you work with is unknown.)

This relational database approach is well suited to many common business processes, such as monitoring sales by geography, product, or channel; extracting insight from customer surveys, cost and profitability analyses, and more — basically, the questions are asked time and time again. Data is typically highly structured and is most likely highly trusted in this environment (see the paragraph on trusted data in the earlier section describing the landing zone for more on the concept of *trust*) in this environment; we refer to this activity as *guided analytics* (as shown in Figure 11-5 and as you may have noticed in the use cases described earlier in this chapter).

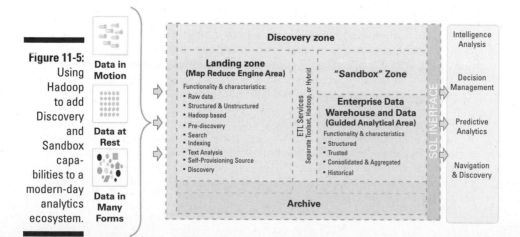

Figure 11-5: Using Hadoop to add Discovery and Sandbox capabilities to a modern-day analytics ecosystem.

As an analogy, it's as though your 8-year-old child is taking a break for recess at school. For the most part, she can do whatever she wants within the school's grounds — as long as she remains within the fenced perimeter; however, she can't jump the fence to discover what's on the outside. Specifically, your child can explore a known, safeguarded (within the schema) area and analyze whatever can be found within that area.

Now imagine that your analytics environment has a discovery zone, as shown in Figure 11-5. In this scenario, IT delivers data (it's likely not to be fully trusted, and it's likely "dirty") on a flexible discovery platform for business users to ask virtually any question they want. In our analogy, your child is allowed to climb the schoolyard fence (this area is schema-less), venture into the forest, and return with whatever items she discovers. (Of course, in the IT world, you don't have to worry about business users getting lost or getting poison ivy.)

If you think about it, data discovery mirrors in some respects the evolution of gold mining. During the gold rush years of old, gold strikes would spark resource investment because someone discovered gold — it was visible to the naked eye, it had clear value, and it therefore warranted the investment. Fifty years ago, no one could afford to mine low-grade ore for gold because cost-effective or capable technology didn't exist (equipment to move and handle vast amounts of ore wasn't available) and rich-grade ore was still available (compared to today, gold was relatively easier to find). Quite simply, it wasn't cost effective (or even possible) to work through the noise (low-grade ore) to find the signals (the gold). With Hadoop, IT shops now have the capital equipment to process millions of tons of ore (data with a low value per byte) to find gold that's nearly invisible to the naked eye (data with high value per byte). And that's exactly what discovery is all about. It's about having a low-cost, flexible repository where next-to-zero investment is made to enrich the data until a discovery is made. After a discovery is made, it might make sense to ask for more resources (to mine the gold discovery) and formalize it into an analytics process that can be deployed in a data warehouse or specialized data mart.

When insights are made in the discovery zone, that's likely a good time to engage the IT department and formalize a process, or have those folks lend assistance to more in-depth discovery. In fact, this new pattern could even move into the area of guided analytics. The point is that IT provisioned the discovery zone for business users to ask and invent questions they haven't thought about before. Because that zone resides in Hadoop, it's agile and allows for users to venture into the wild blue yonder.

Notice that Figure 11-5 has a sandbox zone. In some reference architectures, this zone is combined with the discovery zone. We like to keep these zones separate because we see this area being used by application developers and IT shops to do their own research, test applications, and, perhaps, formalize conclusions and findings in the Discovery Zone when IT assistance is required after a potential discovery is made.

Looking to the future

The relational database, as we know it, isn't going away any time soon. Pundits will always claim, "RDBMS will go the way of the dinosaur," but we think (at least for now) that IT needs both systems. More importantly, IT needs both systems to work together and complement each other. Suppose that you need to derive client attributes from social media feeds. Assume that your company underwrites a life insurance policy to an individual with a family. Your processes likely run the gamut of medical tests and smoker / nonsmoker classifications, but your actuaries might be better able to assess risk and costs if they know that this particular client participates in extreme sports such as hang gliding. If you could extract this information from social media data that you've stored in a Hadoop landing zone, you could analyze this information and create a risk multiplier based on social activities that your client openly shares with the world via Facebook and Twitter, for example. This information could be updated in your system of record, where the actual policy costs are itemized and maintained. This example explains systems of engagement meeting systems of record, which is a key tenet to a next-generation analytics ecosystem.

We'd be remiss not to note that our reference architecture is flexible, and can easily be tweaked. Nothing is cast in stone: you can take what you need, leave what you don't, and add your own nuances. For instance, some organizations may choose to co-locate all zones into a single Hadoop cluster, some may choose to leverage a single cluster designed for multiple purposes; and others may physically separate them. None of this affects the use cases that we've built into the final reference architecture shown in Figure 11-5.

Chapter 12

Extremely Big Tables: Storing Data in HBase

Do you remember your first surfing experience on the World Wide Web? You just knew that it was an incredible innovation for the IT industry. Having this vast ocean of knowledge at your fingertips was transformational. Times change, though, and now the Internet is truly just another part of everyday life that many people take for granted. You open your favorite browser and visit a search engine, and — in a matter of seconds — you're learning something new.

In this chapter, we ask you to take a step back and ponder the immensity of the web and, more specifically, how exactly an entity such as Google stores all those references and web pages for your use? If the picture in your mind includes the concept of a database, you're right, but what kind of database? Every database administrator has thought about limits at one time or another. Storing gigabytes (or even terabytes) of data using your database of choice is common, but you may be faced with petabytes of data as Google was when it sought to index the web. The company's strategy was to use BigTable — Google researchers even published an important paper outlining their vision of BigTable in 2006.

You may wonder what all this has to do with the history of HBase. Well, HBase is an implementation of Google's BigTable distributed data storage system (DDSS, for short). After Google's release of the BigTable paper, Powerset, a company focused on building a natural language processing

(NLP) search engine for the Internet, became interested in creating its own implementation of BigTable. So when the University of Michigan's Mike Cafarella made his first code drop of HBase to the Apache Open Source community in early 2007, Powerset engineers decided to carry the work forward. By 2008 HBase had become a sub-project of Hadoop and in 2010 HBase became an Apache top-level project. HBase, which has an affinity to Hadoop, is referred to as "the Hadoop database" on its Apache web page. (Don't believe us? Check out the Welcome Apache HBase page at `http://hbase.apache.org`.)

After you know a bit of the history of HBase, you're on better footing to start understanding what HBase actually does. In subsequent sections of this chapter, you can see how HBase works and why it's vital in the age of big data.

Say Hello to HBase

HBase is a Java implementation of Google's BigTable. Google defines BigTable as a "sparse, distributed, persistent multidimensional sorted map." We're sure that you'll agree that it's quite a concise definition, but that you'll also agree that it's a bit on the complex side. To break down BigTable's complexity a bit, we discuss each attribute in this section.

Sparse

As you might have guessed, the BigTable distributed data storage system was designed to meet the demands of big data. Now, big data applications store lots of data but big data content is also often variable. Imagine a traditional table in a company database storing customer contact information, as shown in Table 12-1.

Table 12-1 Traditional Customer Contact Information Table

Customer ID	Last Name	First Name	Middle Name	E-mail Address	Street Address
00001	Smith	John	Timothy	`John.Smith@xyz.com`	1 Hadoop Lane, NY 11111
00002	Doe	Jane	NULL	NULL	7 HBase Ave, CA 22222

A company or individual may require a complete data record for each of its customers or constituents. A good example is your doctor, who needs all your contact information in order to provide you with proper care. Other companies or individuals may require only partial contact information or may need to learn that information over time. For example, a customer service company may process phone calls or e-mail messages for service requests. Clients may or may not choose to give service companies all their contact information. However, with each interaction over time, companies may learn more about their clients that will enable them to provide better service — by issuing proactive service alerts, for example.

In this context, *sparse* means that fields in rows can be empty or NULL but that doesn't bring HBase to a screeching halt. HBase can handle the fact that we don't (yet) know Jane Doe's middle name and e-mail address, for example.

Here's another example: a database for storing satellite images. It turns out that Google uses BigTable technology to store satellite imagery of the earth. In almost every case, whenever imagery is stored, metadata is also stored with it. The metadata may include the street address of the image or only the latitude and longitude if the image is captured from the wilderness. The metadata is variable in content so some fields will be NULL — and that's OK.

In both examples, the data sets that are collected can be extremely large — especially in the second example. Imagery databases are almost always measured in terabytes or sometimes in petabytes. We've already mentioned that HBase is designed for storing big data, but it's also designed for storing sparse data records at no cost. This concern is crucial when you're using big data applications! Storing a few NULL records over a million rows is wasteful, but try to imagine the waste over a quadrillion rows! Thankfully, this was a key consideration for Google designers and the HBase community. Sparse data is supported with no waste of costly storage space.

And it doesn't stop there. Consider the power of a schema-less data store. Table 12-1 shows you a classic customer contact table. When companies design these tables, they know up front what they want to store. In other words the schema is *fixed*; it's defined even before the first byte of information is stored in the table. Now what if, over time, a new field is needed for a customer? How about a Twitter handle or a new mobile phone number? You're seemingly stuck with a schema that no longer works for you. Well, HBase solves this challenge as well — you can not only skip fields at no cost when you don't have the data, but also dynamically add fields (or *columns* in the HBase vernacular — more on this later) over time without having to redesign the schema or disrupt operations. So you can think of HBase as a schema-less data store; that is, it's fluid — you can add to, subtract from or modify the schema as you go along.

It's distributed and persistent

BigTable is a distributed and persistent data store. *Persistent* simply means that the data you store in BigTable (and HBase, for that matter) will persist or remain after your program or session ends. That's pretty straightforward — persistent means that it persists — but you should spend a little more time thinking about *how* the data is persisted. In its BigTable paper, Google described the distributed file system known as Google File System or GFS. It turns out that, just as HBase is an open source implementation of BigTable, HDFS is an open source implementation of GFS. By default, HBase leverages HDFS to persist its data to disk storage. (For more on the mechanics of HDFS, see Chapter 3.) Though other distributed data stores can be used with HBase, the vast majority of HBase installations leverage HDFS. This makes perfect sense given that HBase is the "Hadoop Database" — hey, it's built into the name, for goodness sake.

REMEMBER

HDFS is a key enabling technology not only for Hadoop but also for HBase. By storing data in HDFS, HBase offers reliability, availability, seamless scalability, high performance and much more — all on cost effective distributed servers!

It has a multidimensional sorted map

Starting from the basics, a *map* (also known as an *associative array*) is an abstract collection of key-value pairs, where the key is unique. This definition is crucial to your understanding of HBase because the HBase data model is often described in different ways — often incompletely as a column-oriented store. HBase is, at bottom, a key-value data store where each key is unique — meaning it appears at most once in the HBase data store. Additionally, the map is sorted and multidimensional. The keys are stored in HBase and sorted in byte-lexicographical order. Each value can have multiple versions, which makes the data model multidimensional. By default, data versions are implemented with a timestamp.

Understanding the HBase Data Model

HBase data stores consist of one or more tables, which are indexed by row keys. Data is stored in rows with columns, and rows can have multiple versions. By default, data versioning for rows is implemented with time stamps. Columns are grouped into *column families*, which must be defined up front during table creation. Column families are stored together on disk, which is why HBase is referred to as a column-oriented data store. To show you a practical example, we've altered Table 12-1 to make it conform to an HBase data model — behold the logical view of information in Table 12-2.

Because the data model is critical to understanding HBase, we discuss Table 12-2 in detail in the following five sections.

Table 12-2   Logical View of Customer Contact Information in HBase

Row Key	Column Family: {Column Qualifier:Version:Value}
00001	CustomerName: {'FN': 1383859182496:'John',
	'LN': 1383859182858:'Smith',
	'MN': 1383859183001:'Timothy',
	'MN': 1383859182915:'T'}
	ContactInfo: {'EA': 1383859183030:'John.Smith@xyz.com',
	'SA': 1383859183073:'1 Hadoop Lane, NY 11111'}
00002	CustomerName: {'FN': 1383859183103:'Jane',
	'LN': 1383859183163:'Doe',
	ContactInfo: {
	'SA': 1383859185577:'7 HBase Ave, CA 22222'}

(handwritten annotation: → 2 Time stamps / Version)

Row keys

For the sake of illustration, Table 12-2 has two simple row keys: 00001 and 00002. Row keys are implemented as byte arrays, and are sorted in byte-lexicographical order, which simply means that the row keys are sorted, byte by byte, from left to right. If you think in terms of numeric values when designing row keys, then sorting is simple. Given two keys, if the byte at Index 1 in Key 1 is less than the byte at Index 1 in Key 2, Row Key 1 will always be stored before Row Key 2, no matter what's next in the sequence of bytes. However, it's common to use printable (ASCII) characters rather than numeric values for row keys in HBase and if you do, you need to understand that the Java language represents characters using the Unicode Standard. The following example illustrates this design consideration for Basic Latin (ASCII).

```
"RowA" precedes "RowA"
"Row-1" precedes "Row11"
"Row1" precedes "RowA"
```

If you're not sure of the order for ASCII characters, you can view an ordered table at www.unicode.org/.

You may wonder why you would bother with this fine detail with respect to row keys. The reason for this special attention is that proper row key design is crucial to achieving good performance in HBase — not doing so means you won't realize the full value of your HBase cluster. Our detailed discussion of Row key design at the end of this chapter can help you grasp the importance of the sorting scheme. For now, keep in mind that sorted row keys can help you access your data faster.

Column Families

Table 12-2 shows two column families: CustomerName and ContactInfo. When creating a table in HBase, the developer or administrator is required to define one or more column families using printable characters. (See the earlier section "Row keys" for more on printable characters.) Generally, column families remain fixed throughout the lifetime of an HBase table but new column families can be added by using administrative commands. At the time this book was written, the official recommendation for the number of column families per table was three or less. (We have that number on good authority — see the Apache HBase online documentation at `http://hbase.apache.org/book/number.of.cfs.html`.) In addition, you should store data with similar access patterns in the same column family — you wouldn't want a customer's middle name stored in a separate column family from the first or last name because you generally access all name data at the same time.

Column families are grouped together on disk, so grouping data with similar access patterns reduces overall disk access and increases performance.

Column Qualifiers

Column qualifiers are specific names assigned to your data values in order to make sure you're able to accurately identify them. Unlike column families, column qualifiers can be virtually unlimited in content, length and number. If you omit the column qualifier, the HBase system will assign one for you. Printable characters are not required, so any type and number of bytes can be used to create a column qualifier. Because the number of column qualifiers is variable, new data can be added to column families on the fly, making HBase flexible and highly scalable. But there's a cost to consider: HBase stores the column qualifier with your value (it's actually part of the key), and since HBase doesn't limit the number of column qualifiers you can have, creating long column qualifiers can be quite costly in terms of storage. That's why we decided to abbreviate the column qualifiers in Table 12-2 (for example, "LN:" was used instead of "LastName"). Notice in our logical representation of the customer contact information in HBase that the system is taking advantage of sparse data support in the case of Jane Doe (again, see Table 12-2). Assuming this table represents customer contact information from a service company, the company isn't too worried about Jane's middle name (abbreviated 'MN') and e-mail addresses (abbreviated 'EA') now, but hopes to (progressively) gather that information over time.

Versions

Looking back at Table 12-2, you can see a number between the column qualifier and value ('FN': 1383859182496:'John,' for example). That number is the *version* number for each value in the table. Values stored in HBase are time stamped by default, which means you have a way to identify different versions of your data right out of the box. It's possible to create a custom versioning scheme, but users typically go with a time stamp created using the current Unix time. (The Unix time or Unix *epoch* represents the number of milliseconds since midnight January 1, 1970 UTC.) The versioned data is stored in decreasing order, so that the most recent value is returned by default unless a query specifies a particular timestamp. You can see in Table 12-2 that our fictional service company at first only had an initial for John Smith's middle name but then later on they learned that the "T" stood for "Timothy." The most recent value for the 'MN' column is stored first in the table.

You can set a limit on the amount of time that data can stay in HBase with a variable called time to live (TTL). You can also set a variable which controls the number of versions per value. This can be done per column family. (You'll be learning more about these variables and how to set them later in the chapter.)

Key Value Pairs

If you're reading this chapter from start to finish, you should be developing a feel for the logical HBase data model. It's simple yet elegant, and it provides a natural data storage mechanism for all kinds of data — especially unstructured big data sets. A little later in this chapter, we cap our discussion of the data model by walking you through a hands-on example to create your first HBase table. First, though, we spend a little time explaining how all these parts of the data model converge into a key-value pair.

First off, in a world where you can think of the row key as the primary key for data stored in HBase, how do you end up leveraging the rest of the data model components? Well, it all depends on how much data you want returned in queries and how long you're willing to wait. Specifying only the row key can potentially return a ton of data, because an individual row can have millions of columns. Also, with only the row key to work from, HBase can return every column qualifier, version, and value related to the row key. What if you want only a particular column or version of your data? From the example shown in Table 12-2, can you see what happens if you want only the last name of a particular customer? The solution is to build a more complex key to specify exactly what you need. A key-value pair can look like this:

```
RowKey:(Column Family:Column Qualifier:Version) => Value
```

After you specify the key, the rest is optional. The more specific you make the query, however (moving from left to right), the more granular the results. Your performance will worsen, because the system has to spend more time locating the exact value or values you need, but less data is returned when the query is finished. So keys are more complex than you might imagine from studying Table 12-2. For example, if you want the most recent middle name (or the only middle name so far) of the customer in row '00001', the resulting key-value pair would look like this:

```
'00001:CustomerName:MN' => 'Timothy'
```

Remember that versions are implemented using time stamps by default and are sorted in decreasing order so that you automatically get the most recent value if you don't specify a version. If you want a prior middle initial for your customer (refer to Table 12-2), your resulting key-value pair would look like this:

```
'00001:CustomerName:MN:1383859182915' => 'T'
```

We hope that our various descriptions of HBase are starting to take shape in your mind. Specifically HBase is both a column family oriented data store and a key-value-pair data store. Referring to HBase as simply a "column oriented" data store leaves a lot to the imagination.

In case you were curious, there are no data types in HBase — values in HBase are just one or more bytes. Again, simple but powerful because you can store anything!

Understanding the HBase Architecture

The reason that folks such as chief financial officers are excited by the thought of using Hadoop is that it lets you store massive amounts of data across a cluster of low cost commodity servers — that's music to the ears of financially minded people. Well, HBase offers the same economic bang for the buck — it's a distributed data store, which leverages a network attached cluster of low-cost commodity servers to store and persist data.

HBase persists data by storing it in HDFS, but alternate storage arrangements are possible. For example, HBase can be deployed in standalone mode in the cloud (typically for educational purposes) or on expensive servers if the use case warrants it.

In most cases, though, HBase implementations look pretty much like the one shown in Figure 12-1.

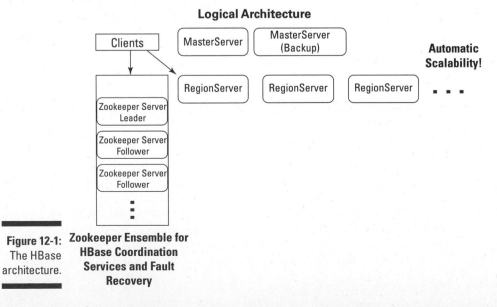

Figure 12-1: The HBase architecture.

As with the data model, understanding the components of the architecture is critical for successful HBase cluster deployment. In the next few sections we discuss the key components.

RegionServers

RegionServers are the software processes (often called daemons) you activate to store and retrieve data in HBase. In production environments, each RegionServer is deployed on its own dedicated compute node. When you start using HBase, you create a table and then begin storing and retrieving your data. However, at some point — and perhaps quite quickly in big data use cases — the table grows beyond a configurable limit. At this point, the HBase system automatically splits the table and distributes the load to another RegionServer.

In this process, often referred to as *auto-sharding*, HBase automatically scales as you add data to the system — a huge benefit compared to most database management systems, which require manual intervention to scale the overall system beyond a single server. With HBase, as long as you have in the rack another spare server that's configured, scaling is automatic!

Why set a limit on tables and then split them? After all, HDFS is the underlying storage mechanism, so all available disks in the HDFS cluster are available for storing your tables. (Not counting the replication factor, of course; see Chapter 3 for that wrinkle.) If you have an entire cluster at your disposal, why limit yourself to one RegionServer to manage your tables?

Simple. You may have any number of tables large or small and you'll want HBase to leverage all available RegionServers when managing your data. You want to take full advantage of the cluster's compute performance. Furthermore, with many clients accessing your HBase system, you'll want to use many RegionServers to meet the demand. HBase addresses all of these concerns for you and scales automatically in terms of storage capacity and compute power.

Regions

RegionServers are one thing, but you also have to take a look at how individual regions work. In HBase, a table is both spread across a number of RegionServers as well as being made up of individual regions. As tables are split, the splits become regions. Regions store a range of key-value pairs, and each RegionServer manages a configurable number of regions. But what do the individual regions look like? HBase is a column-family-oriented data store, so how do the individual regions store key-value pairs based on the column families they belong to? Figure 12-2 begins to answer these questions and helps you digest more vital information about the architecture of HBase.

HBase Regions in Detail

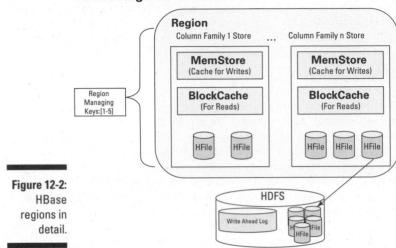

Figure 12-2:
HBase
regions in
detail.

HBase is written in Java — like the vast majority of Hadoop technologies. Java is an object oriented programming language and an elegant technology for distributed computing. So, as you continue to find out more about HBase, remember that all of the components in the architecture are ultimately Java objects.

First off, Figure 12-2 gives a pretty good idea of what region objects actually look like, generally speaking. Figure 12-2 also makes it clear that regions separate data into column families and store the data in the HDFS using HFile objects. When clients put key-value pairs into the system, the keys are processed so that data is stored based on the column family the pair belongs to. As shown in the figure, each column family store object has a read cache called the BlockCache and a write cache called the MemStore. The BlockCache helps with random read performance. Data is read in blocks from the HDFS and stored in the BlockCache. Subsequent reads for the data — or data stored in close proximity — will be read from RAM instead of disk, improving overall performance. The Write Ahead Log (WAL, for short) ensures that your HBase writes are reliable. There is one WAL per RegionServer.

Always heed the Iron Law of Distributed Computing: A failure isn't the exception — it's the norm, especially when clustering hundreds or even thousands of servers. Google followed the Iron Law in designing BigTable and HBase followed suit. If you're reading the entire chapter, you'll find out more about how node failures are handled in HBase and how the WAL is a key part of this overall strategy. When you write or modify data in HBase, the data is first persisted to the WAL, which is stored in the HDFS, and then the data is written to the MemStore cache. At configurable intervals, key-value pairs stored in the MemStore are written to HFiles in the HDFS and afterwards WAL entries are erased. If a failure occurs *after* the initial WAL write but *before* the final MemStore write to disk, the WAL can be replayed to avoid any data loss.

Figure 12-2 shows three HFile objects in one column family and two in the other. The design of HBase is to flush column family data stored in the MemStore to one HFile per flush. Then at configurable intervals HFiles are combined into larger HFiles. This strategy queues up the critical compaction operation in HBase, as described in the next section

Compactions major and minor

Compaction, the process by which HBase cleans up after itself, comes in two flavors: major and minor. Major compactions can be a big deal so we'll discuss managing them in detail in a bit, but first you need to understand minor compactions.

Minor compactions combine a configurable number of smaller HFiles into one larger HFile. You can tune the number of HFiles to compact and the frequency of a minor compaction. Minor compactions are important because without them, reading a particular row can require many disk reads and cause slow overall performance. Figure 12-3, which illustrates how this concept works, can help you visualize how Table 12-2 can be persisted on the HDFS.

HFiles and Minor Compaction

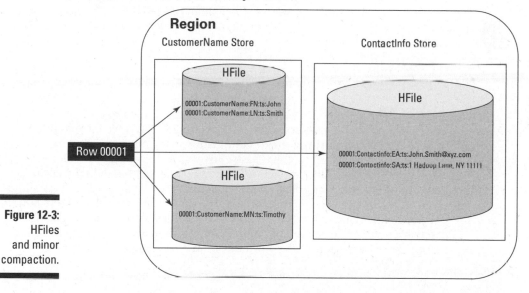

Figure 12-3:
HFiles
and minor
compaction.

Looking at Figure 12-3, notice how the CustomerName column family was written to the HDFS with two MemStore flushes and how the data in the ContactInfo column family was persisted to disk with only one MemStore flush. This example is hypothetical, but it's a likely scenario depending on the timing of the writes. Picture a service company that's gaining more and more customer contact information over time. The service company may know its client's first and last name but not learn about its middle name until hours or weeks later in subsequent service requests. This scenario would result in parts of Row 00001 being persisted to the HDFS in different HFiles. Until the HBase system performs a minor compaction, reading from Row 00001 would require three disk reads to retrieve the relevant HFile content! Minor compactions seek to minimize system overhead while keeping the number of HFiles under control. HBase designers took special care to give the HBase administrator as much tuning control as possible to make any system impact "minor."

As its name implies, a major compaction is different from the perspective of a system impact. However, the compaction is quite important to the overall functionality of the HBase system. A major compaction seeks to combine *all* HFiles into one large HFile. In addition, a major compaction does the cleanup work after a user deletes a record. When a user issues a Delete call, the HBase system places a marker in the key-value pair so that it can be permanently removed during the next major compaction. Additionally, because major compactions combine all HFiles into one large HFile, the time is right for the system to review the versions of the data and compare them against the time to live (TTL) property. Values older than the TTL are purged.

Time to live refers to the variable in HBase you can set in order to define how long data with multiple versions will remain in HBase. For more information on versions in HBase see the "Understanding the HBase Data Model" section, earlier in this chapter.

For a complete list of HBase tuning parameters see `http://hbase.apache.org/book/config.files.html`.

You may have guessed that a major compaction significantly affects the system response time. Users who are trying to add, retrieve or manipulate data in the system during a major compaction, they may see poor system response time. In addition, the HBase cluster may have to split regions at the same time that a major compaction is taking place *and* balance the regions across all RegionServers. This scenario would result in a significant amount of network traffic between RegionServers. For these reasons, your HBase administrator needs to have a major compaction strategy for your deployment. We discuss a solution to the major compaction challenge at the end of this chapter, but for now we continue your tour of the basic HBase architecture.

MasterServer

Starting our discussion of architecture by describing RegionServers instead of the MasterServer may surprise you. The term *RegionServer* would seem to imply that it depends on (and is secondary to) the MasterServer and that we should therefore describe the MasterServer first. As the old song goes, though, "it ain't necessarily so." The RegionServers do depend on the MasterServer for certain functions, but not in the sense of a master-slave relationship for data storage and retrieval. In the upper-left corner of Figure 12-1, notice that the clients do not point to the MasterServer, but point instead to the Zookeeper cluster and RegionServers.

The MasterServer isn't in the path for data storage and access — that's the job of the Zookeeper cluster and the RegionServers. We'll cover Zookeeper in the following section and describe client interaction later in this chapter; for now, take a look at the primary functions of the MasterServer, which is also a software process (or daemon) like the RegionServers. The MasterServer is there to

- ✔ **Monitor the RegionServers in the HBase cluster:** The MasterServer maintains a list of active RegionServers in the HBase cluster.

- ✔ **Handle metadata operations:** When a table is created or its attributes are altered (compression setting, cache settings, versioning, and more) the MasterServer handles the operation and stores the required metadata.

- ✔ **Assign regions:** The MasterServer assigns regions to RegionServers.

- ✔ **Manage RegionServer failover:** As with any distributed cluster, you hope that node failures don't occur and you plan for them anyway. When region servers fail, Zookeeper notifies the MasterServer so that failover and restore operations can be initiated. We discuss this topic in greater detail in the later section "Zookeeper and HBase reliability."

- ✔ **Oversee load balancing of regions across all available RegionServers:** You may recall that tables are comprised of regions which are evenly distributed across all available RegionServers. This is the work of the balancer thread (or *chore*, if you prefer) which the MasterServer periodically activates.

- ✔ **Manage (and clean) catalog tables:** Two key catalog tables — labeled ROOT- and .META — are used by the HBase system to help a client find a particular key value pair in the system.

  - The -ROOT- table keeps track of the .META table's location in the cluster.

  - The .META table keeps track of where each region is located in the cluster.

  The MasterServer provides management of these critical tables on behalf of the overall HBase system.

- ✔ **Clear the WAL:** The MasterServer interacts with the WAL during RegionServer failover and periodically cleans the logs.

- ✔ **Provide a coprocessor framework for observing master operations:** Here's another new term for your growing HBase glossary. *Coprocessors* run in the context of the MasterServer or RegionServers. For example, a MasterServer observer coprocessor allows you to change or extend the normal functionality of the server when operations such as table creation or table deletion take place. Often coprocessors are used to manage table indexes for advanced HBase applications.

A coprocessor, which runs in the context of the MasterServer and or RegionServer (or both) can be used to enhance security, create secondary indexes, and more. You can find more information about coprocessors at this HBase community blog: `https://blogs.apache.org/hbase/entry/coprocessor_introduction`.

As with all open source Hadoop technologies, MasterServer operations will likely change over time as the community of engineers work on innovations designed to enhance HBase. As of this writing, however, you now have a fairly thorough list that serves as a high-level reference for the MasterServer

Finally, we have one more important point to make about the HBase MasterServer. There can and should be a backup MasterServer in any HBase cluster. (Refer to Figure 12-1.) There needs to be only one active MasterServer at any given time, so the backup MasterServer is for failover purposes. You may recall that the MasterServer isn't in the data access path for HBase clients. However, you may also recall (from the list of functions in this section) that the MasterServer is responsible for actions such as RegionServer failover and load balancing. The good news is that clients can continue to query the HBase cluster if the master goes down but for normal cluster operations, the master should not remain down for any length of time.

Zookeeper and HBase reliability

Zookeeper is a distributed cluster of servers that collectively provides reliable coordination and synchronization services for clustered applications. Admittedly, the name "Zookeeper" may seem at first to be an odd choice, but when you understand what it does for an HBase cluster, you can see the logic behind it. When you're building and debugging distributed applications "it's a zoo out there," so you should put Zookeeper on your team. (If you're like us, you love it when a technology is appropriately named.)

HBase clusters can be huge and coordinating the operations of the MasterServers, RegionServers, and clients can be a daunting task, but that's where Zookeeper enters the picture. As in HBase, Zookeeper clusters typically run on low-cost commodity x86 servers. Each individual x86 server runs a single Zookeeper software process (hereafter referred to as a Zookeeper server), with one Zookeeper server elected by the ensemble as the leader and the rest of the servers are followers. Zookeeper ensembles are governed by the principle of a majority quorum. Configurations with one Zookeeper server are supported for test and development purposes, but if you want a reliable cluster that can tolerate server failure, you need to deploy at least three Zookeeper servers to achieve a majority quorum.

So, how many Zookeeper servers will you need? Five is the minimum recommended for production use, but you really don't want to go with the bare minimum. When you decide to plan your Zookeeper ensemble, follow this simple formula: 2F + 1 = N where F is the number of failures you can accept in your Zookeeper cluster and N is the total number of Zookeeper servers you must deploy. Five is recommended because one server can be shut down for maintenance but the Zookeeper cluster can still tolerate one server failure.

Zookeeper provides coordination and synchronization with what it calls *znodes*, which are presented as a directory tree and resemble the file path names you'd see in a Unix file system. Znodes *do* store data but not much to speak of — currently less than 1 MB by default. The idea here is that Zookeeper stores znodes in memory and that these memory-based znodes provide fast client access for coordination, status, and other vital functions required by distributed applications like HBase. Zookeeper replicates znodes across the ensemble so if servers fail, the znode data is still available as long as a majority quorum of servers is still up and running.

Another primary Zookeeper concept concerns how znode reads (versus writes) are handled. Any Zookeeper server can handle reads from a client, including the leader, but only the leader issues *atomic* znode writes — writes that either completely succeed or completely fail. When a znode write request arrives at the leader node, the leader broadcasts the write request to the follower nodes and then waits for a majority of followers to acknowledge znode write complete. After the acknowledgement, the leader issues the znode write itself and then reports the successful completion status to the client.

Znodes provide some very powerful guarantees. When a Zookeeper client (such as an HBase RegionServer) writes or reads a znode, the operation is *atomic*. It either completely succeeds or completely fails — there are no partial reads or writes. No other competing client can cause the read or write operation to fail. In addition, a znode has an access control lists (ACL) associated with it for security, and it supports versions, timestamps and notification to clients when it changes.

Zookeeper replicates znodes across the ensemble so if servers fail, the znode data is still available as long as a majority quorum of servers is still up and running. This means that writes to any znode from any Zookeeper server must be propagated across the ensemble. The Zookeeper leader manages this operation.

This znode write approach can cause followers to fall behind the leader for short periods. Zookeeper solves this potential problem by providing a synchronization command. Clients that cannot tolerate this temporary lack of synchronization within the Zookeeper cluster may decide to issue a sync command before reading znodes.

In a znode world, you're going to come across what looks like the Unix-style pathnames. (Typically they begin with /hbase.) These pathnames, which are a subset of the znodes in the Zookeeper system created by HBase, are described in this list:

- ✔ master: Holds the name of the primary MasterServer,

- ✔ hbaseid: Holds the cluster's ID,

- ✔ root-region-server: Points to the RegionServer holding the -ROOT- table),

- ✔ Something called /hbase/rs.

So now you may wonder what's up with this rather vaguely defined /hbase/rs. In the previous section, we describe the various operations of the MasterServer and mention that Zookeeper notifies the MasterServer whenever a RegionServer fails. Now we help you take a closer look at how the process actually works in HBase — and you'd be right to assume that it has something to do with /hbase/rs. Zookeeper uses its *watches* mechanism to notify clients whenever a znode is created, accessed, or changed in some way. The MasterServers are Zookeeper clients as well as the RegionServers and can leverage these znode watches. When a RegionServer comes online in the HBase system, it connects to the Zookeeper ensemble and creates its own unique ephemeral znode under the znode pathname /hbase/rs. At the same time, the Zookeeper system establishes a session with the RegionServer and monitors the session for events. If the RegionServer breaks the session for whatever reason (by failing to send a heartbeat ping, for example), the ephemeral znode that it created is deleted. The action of deleting the RegionServer's child node under /hbase/rs will cause the MasterServer to be notified so that it can initiate RegionServer failover. This notification is accomplished by way of a watch that the MasterServer sets up on the /hbase/rs znode.

HBase provides a high degree of reliability. When configured with the proper redundancy (a backup MasterServer, proper Zookeeper configuration, and sufficient RegionServers), HBase is sometimes considered *fault tolerant*, meaning that HBase can tolerate any failure and still function properly. This is not exactly true, of course, since (for example) a cascading failure could cause the cluster to fail if the Zookeeper ensemble and or the MasterServers all failed at once. When thinking about HBase and fault tolerance, remember that HBase is a distributed system and that failure modes are quite different in distributed systems versus the traditional high-end scalable database server in a high availability (HA) configuration. To understand HBase fault tolerance and availability in more detail you need to consider the CAP theorem which we introduce in Chapter 11. No discussion of HBase and fault tolerance would be complete without at least mentioning the CAP theorem. CAP stands for "Consistency" (in the data stored), "Availability"(ready for use) and "Partition Tolerance" (tolerant of network failures). Remember, HBase provides "Consistency" and "Partition Tolerance" but is not always "Available." For example, you may have a RegionServer failure and when you do, the availability of your data may be delayed if the failed RegionServer was managing the key (or keys) you were querying at the time of failure. The good news is that the system, if configured properly, will recover (thanks to Zookeeper and the MasterServer) and your data will become available again without manual intervention. So HBase is consistent and tolerant of network failures but not highly available like traditional HA database systems.

Taking HBase for a Test Run

In this section, you find out how to download and deploy HBase in standalone mode. We think you'll agree that it's amazingly simple to install HBase and start using the technology. Just keep in mind that HBase is typically deployed on a cluster of commodity servers, though you can also easily deploy HBase in a standalone configuration instead, for learning or demonstration purposes.

For more information on the hardware requirements for HBase, check out the section "Deploying and Tuning HBase," later in this chapter. For Apache's official Quick Start Guide to HBase, check out `http://hbase.apache.org/book/quickstart.html`.

Like Apache Hadoop, HBase supports Linux primarily but you *can* use Windows in non-production environments if you first download Cygwin. Cygwin gives Microsoft Windows users a Unix shell with all its commands and utilities. So if you follow the Quick Start Guide — which we recommend you do — you'll want to download the latest HBase release (HBase 0.94.7 at the time of this writing).

You get to choose where to install HBase. We decided to install it on a nice little laptop that's currently running a 64-bit Linux kernel. You get to choose where you want to install your HBase. It turns out, though, that if you want things to run in standalone mode, you'll need to edit a couple of files before you can actually start HBase. Look for these files in the `$INSTALL DIR/hbase-0.94.7/conf` directory in the HBase release. The first file is the `hbase-site.xml` file shown in Listing 12-1. The changes you'll want to make are bolded to make them stand out:

Listing 12-1: The *hbase-site.xml* File

```
<configuration>
  <property>
    <name>hbase.rootdir</name>
    <value>file:///home/biadmin/my-local-hbase/hbase-data</value>
  </property>
  <property>
    <name>hbase.cluster.distributed</name>
    <value>true</value>
```

(continued)

Listing 12-1 *(continued)*

```
    </property>
    <property>
      <name>hbase.zookeeper.property.clientPort</name>
      <value>2222</value>
      <description>Property from ZooKeeper's config zoo.cfg.
        The port at which the clients will connect.
      </description>
    </property>
    <property>
      <name>hbase.zookeeper.property.dataDir</name>
      <value>/home/biadmin/my-local-hbase/zookeeper</value>
    </property>
     <property>
        <name>hbase.zookeeper.quorum</name>
        <value>bivm</value>
     </property>
 </configuration>
```

Using the `hbase.rootdir` property, you specify a directory in the local file system to store the HBase data. In production environments, this property would point to the HDFS for the data store. You also set the `hbase.cluster.distributed` property to `true` which causes HBase to start up in a pseudo-distributed mode. If you would choose not to set this property to `true`, HBase would run all of the necessary processes in a single Java Virtual Machine (JVM). However, for the sake of illustration, pseudo-distributed mode will cause HBase to start a RegionServer instance, a MasterServer instance, and a Zookeeper process. Additionally, you need to specify the `hbase.zookeeper.property.clientPort`, the directory where Zookeeper will store its data (`hbase.zookeeper.property.dataDir`) and a list of servers on which Zookeeper will run to form a quorum (`hbase.zookeeper.quorum`). For standalone, you specify only the single Zookeeper server `bivm`.

Getting started with HBase in standalone mode is very straightforward in part because HBase manages Zookeeper for you. You can download a separate Zookeeper release and point HBase to it, but for standalone installs, you'll find it much easier to let HBase manage Zookeeper for you.

To crystallize the decision to let HBase manage Zookeeper for you, we show you how to set an environment variable in yet another HBase file: the `hbase-env.sh` file, to be precise. Listing 12-2 shows what needs to be added:

Listing 12-2:   The *hbase-env.sh* File

```
# Tell HBase whether it should manage its own instance of Zookeeper or not.
export HBASE_MANAGES_ZK=true

# The java implementation to use. Java 1.6 required.
export JAVA_HOME=/opt/ibm/biginsights/jdk
```

In the listing, we've also set the JAVA_HOME environment variable to point to the IBM JDK we have on our system. You'll have to make sure you set JAVA_HOME to point to your chosen JDK. Finally, you need to specify the name of your Linux system in yet another file — the regionservers file. (In a fully distributed production environment, the regionservers file would have a line by line list of all servers on which HBase can start the RegionServer process on.)

With the hbase-site.xml file and the hbase-env.sh file configured, you can now start up HBase and test your install. To start HBase, use the start-hbase.sh script as spelled out in Listing 12-3. (We show you how to test the install below.)

Listing 12-3:   Starting HBase

```
$ cd $INSTALL_DIR/hbase-0.94.7/bin
$ ./start-hbase.sh
bivm: starting zookeeper, logging to /home/biadmin/my-local-hbase/hbase-0.94.7/
               bin/../logs/hbase-biadmin-zookeeper-bivm.out
starting master, logging to /home/biadmin/my-local-hbase/hbase-0.94.7/bin/../
               logs/hbase-biadmin-master-bivm.out
localhost: starting regionserver, logging to /home/biadmin/my-local-hbase/hbase-
               0.94.7/bin/../logs/hbase-biadmin-regionserver-bivm.out
```

Note that the first line has a cd (change directory) command that moves you to an environment variable called $INSTALL_DIR. You have to set that variable to your actual install directory for HBase or type out the full path.

In Listing 12-1 we set the hbase.cluster.distributed property to true which causes HBase to start up in a pseudo-distributed mode. We explained that this would cause HBase to start three processes: a RegionServer instance, a MasterServer instance, and a Zookeeper process. This is exactly what we see in Listing 12-3.

Next we use the JConsole tool, which comes bundled with Java, to perform a quick check on what processes are running after the start-hbase.sh script finishes. You can start the JConsole tool by typing the following command:

```
$JAVA_HOME/bin/jconsole
```

In Figure 12-4, JConsole reveals that the three processes that the start-hbase.sh script claimed to start are indeed running — the zookeeper, the master and the RegionServer processes.

To put HBase through its paces, you interact with all three HBase processes, starting with the MasterServer. By default, the MasterServer reports on the system status by way of a browser user interface on port number 60010. In the example, our server name is bivm so you can confirm that the MasterServer is running correctly by entering the following URL in a web browser: http://bivm:60010/. Doing so brings up the information you see in Figure 12-5.

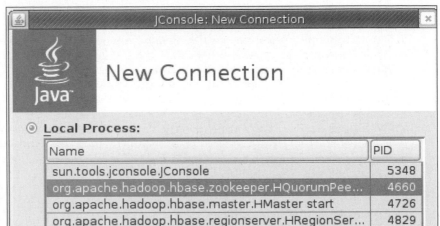

Figure 12-4: HBase Java processes running In pseudo-distributed mode.

Attribute Name	Value	Description
HBase Version	0.94.7, r1471806	HBase version and revision
HBase Compiled	Wed Apr 24 18:48:26 PDT 2013, lhofhans	When HBase version was compiled and by whom
Hadoop Version	1.0.4, r1393290	Hadoop version and revision
Hadoop Compiled	Thu Oct 4 20:40:32 UTC 2012, hortonfo	When Hadoop version was compiled and by whom
HBase Root Directory	file:/home/biadmin/my-local-hbase/hbase-data	Location of HBase home directory
HBase Cluster ID	9ed8fba6-d834-411c-9a91-f43d5749d5d7	Unique identifier generated for each HBase cluster
Load average	3	Average number of regions per regionserver. Naive computation.
Zookeeper Quorum	bivm:2222	Addresses of all registered ZK servers. For more, see zk dump.

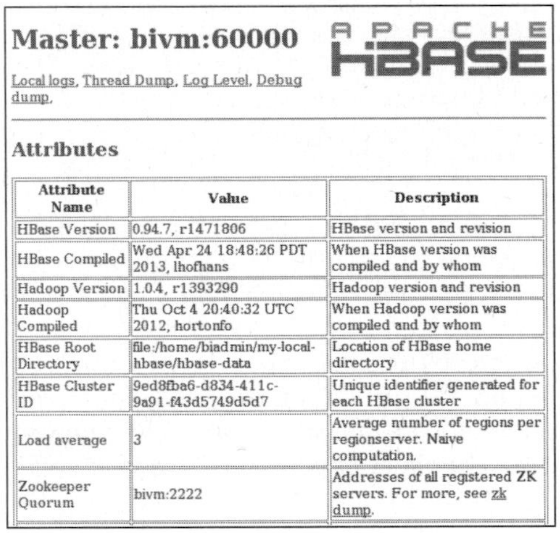

Figure 12-5: Master-Server user interface screenshot.

To keep the figure simple, we've captured only a portion of the MasterServer metrics, but you can see the HBase Root Directory we set in the `hbase-site.xml` file along with the Zookeeper Quorum port number. The RegionServers also report their status and provide critical metrics via a browser user interface on port 60030 by default. We tell you how to interact with the Zookeeper process shortly but first we want to show you how to leverage the RegionServer process and enter some data.

There are a growing number of approaches for clients to access HBase. In the next section entitled "Getting things done with HBase" you'll learn more about the various client options for interacting with HBase. In this section, we introduce you to the HBase shell. You can think of the HBase shell as a client program for interacting with HBase. To activate the HBase shell, first use the cd command to change to the $INSTALL-DIR/bin directory and then type this command:

```
./hbase shell
```

You should see output like the following example, depending on which version of HBase you've managed to download:

```
HBase Shell; enter 'help<RETURN>' for list of supported commands.
Type "exit<RETURN>" to leave the HBase Shell
Version 0.94.7, r1471806, Wed Apr 24 18:48:26 PDT 2013
```

Creating a table

And now the real work begins. The HBase shell provides you with a simple set of commands for creating, reading, writing or updating, and deleting tables. Commands to manage and configure tables are also provided. In this section you'll be learning about the create, put, get, scan and describe commands. (These HBase shell commands are implemented by a Java class called HTable that you'll get to try out in the section entitled "Working with an HBase Java API client example".) Start by building the Customer Contact Information table, using the information from Table 12-2.

```
hbase(main):002:0> create 'CustomerContactInfo', 'CustomerName', 'ContactInfo'
0 row(s) in 1.2080 seconds
```

This command creates two column families — 'CustomerName' and 'ContactInfo' — in a table called 'CustomerContactInfo'.

Now enter the records from Table 12-2 into the new table, using Listing 12-4 as a model:

Listing 12-4:   Entering Records

```
hbase(main):008:0> put 'CustomerContactInfo', '00001', 'CustomerName:FN', 'John'
0 row(s) in 0.2070 seconds

hbase(main):009:0> put 'CustomerContactInfo', '00001', 'CustomerName:LN', 'Smith'
0 row(s) in 0.0170 seconds

hbase(main):010:0> put 'CustomerContactInfo', '00001', 'CustomerName:MN', 'T'
0 row(s) in 0.0070 seconds

hbase(main):011:0> put 'CustomerContactInfo', '00001', 'CustomerName:MN', 'Timothy'
0 row(s) in 0.0050 seconds
```

(continued)

Listing 12-4 *(continued)*

```
hbase(main):012:0> put 'CustomerContactInfo', '00001', 'ContactInfo:EA', 'John.
          Smith@xyz.com'
0 row(s) in 0.0170 seconds

hbase(main):013:0> put 'CustomerContactInfo', '00001', 'ContactInfo:SA', '1
          Hadoop Lane, NY 11111'
0 row(s) in 0.0030 seconds

hbase(main):014:0> put 'CustomerContactInfo', '00002', 'CustomerName:FN', 'Jane'
0 row(s) in 0.0290 seconds

hbase(main):015:0> put 'CustomerContactInfo', '00002', 'CustomerName:LN', 'Doe'
0 row(s) in 0.0090 seconds

hbase(main):016:0> put 'CustomerContactInfo', '00002', 'ContactInfo:SA', '7
          HBase Ave, CA 22222'
0 row(s) in 0.0240 seconds
```

After you enter all the data from Table 12-2, you can retrieve the contents of the new table by using the HBase scan command. The result should look like Listing 12-5:

Listing 12-5: Scan Results

```
hbase(main):020:0> scan 'CustomerContactInfo', {VERSIONS => 2}
ROW                                 COLUMN+CELL
 00001                              column=ContactInfo:EA,
          timestamp=1383859183030, value=John.Smith@xyz.com
 00001                              column=ContactInfo:SA,
          timestamp=1383859183073, value=1 Hadoop Lane, NY 11111
 00001                              column=CustomerName:FN,
          timestamp=1383859182496, value=John
 00001                              column=CustomerName:LN,
          timestamp=1383859182858, value=Smith
 00001                              column=CustomerName:MN,
          timestamp=1383859183001, value=Timothy
 00001                              column=CustomerName:MN,
          timestamp=1383859182915, value=T
 00002                              column=ContactInfo:SA,
          timestamp=1383859185577, value=7 HBase Ave, CA 22222
 00002                              column=CustomerName:FN,
          timestamp=1383859183103, value=Jane
 00002                              column=CustomerName:LN,
          timestamp=1383859183163, value=Doe
2 row(s) in 0.0520 seconds
```

Notice that we specified that HBase should return *two* versions of our values if they exist in the table. This allows us to see the original middle initial of John Smith as well as the latest full middle name.

Now we want to show you how to retrieve individual key-value pairs from our Customer Contact Information table instead of retrieving the whole table with the scan command. This will also further illustrate the versioning in HBase. To retrieve data, you'll need to build a key using the shell's get command. As you saw earlier in the chapter, keys look like this:

```
RowKey:(Column Family:Column Qualifier:Version)
```

Now, if you just specify the row key (0001 or 0002, for example) then you get *all* the data associated with a row key — the row keys you're using are just not that granular. However, the more specific you get, the less data you get back. Listing 12-6 illustrates this principle in HBase.

Listing 12-6:   Using the *get* Command to Retrieve Entire Rows and Individual Values

```
(1) hbase(main):037:0> get 'CustomerContactInfo', '00001'
COLUMN                                 CELL
 ContactInfo:EA                        timestamp=1383859183030, value=John.
              Smith@xyz.com
 ContactInfo:SA                        timestamp=1383859183073, value=1 Hadoop
          Lane, NY 11111
 CustomerName:FN                       timestamp=1383859182496, value=John
 CustomerName:LN                       timestamp=1383859182858, value=Smith
 CustomerName:MN                       timestamp=1383859183001, value=Timothy
5 row(s) in 0.0150 seconds


(2) hbase(main):038:0> get 'CustomerContactInfo', '00001',
                        {COLUMN => 'CustomerName:MN'}
COLUMN                                 CELL
 CustomerName:MN                       timestamp=1383859183001, value=Timothy
1 row(s) in 0.0090 seconds


(3) hbase(main):039:0> get 'CustomerContactInfo', '00001',
                        {COLUMN => 'CustomerName:MN',
                        TIMESTAMP => 1383859182915}
COLUMN                                 CELL
 CustomerName:MN                       timestamp=1383859182915, value=T
1 row(s) in 0.0290 seconds
```

Note that, in Listing 12-6 above you can see how John Smith's full middle name (Timothy) is returned by default (lines 1 & 2) until we specify an exact timestamp to return the prior middle initial (T in line 3). Note as well that for the last get command (line 3), we constructed a full key to retrieve a specific value — in this case the prior middle initial for John Smith. We included the column family name (CustomerContactInfo), column qualifier (MN) and time stamp (1383859182915).

You may be wondering how many versions you can store in the Customer Contact Information table. To answer this question, you'd need to use the describe shell command to look at the table descriptors per column family. The first line of Listing 12-7 shows the syntax of the describe command and the bolded lines in the same listing give you the answer you're looking for.

Listing 12-7: Using the *describe* Command

```
hbase(main):018:0> describe 'CustomerContactInfo'
DESCRIPTION                                                         ENABLED
 'CustomerContactInfo', {NAME => 'ContactInfo', REPLICATION_SCOPE => '0', KE true
EP_DELETED_CELLS => 'false', COMPRESSION => 'NONE', ENCODE_ON_DISK => 'true
', BLOCKCACHE => 'true', MIN_VERSIONS => '0', DATA_BLOCK_ENCODING => 'NONE'
, IN_MEMORY => 'false', BLOOMFILTER => 'NONE', TTL => '2147483647', VERSION
S => '3', BLOCKSIZE => '65536'}, {NAME => 'CustomerName', REPLICATION_SCOPE
 => '0', KEEP_DELETED_CELLS => 'false', COMPRESSION => 'NONE', ENCODE_ON_DI
SK => 'true', BLOCKCACHE => 'true', MIN_VERSIONS => '0', DATA_BLOCK_ENCODIN
G => 'NONE', IN_MEMORY => 'false', BLOOMFILTER => 'NONE', TTL => '214748364
7', VERSIONS => '3', BLOCKSIZE => '65536'}
1 row(s) in 0.0350 seconds

hbase(main):022:0> quit
```

Notice that the default value for VERSIONS in both of our column families is 3. This descriptor and others can be modified with the alter command by disabling the table (via the disable command), altering it, and then enabling the table again with the help of the enable command.

Working with Zookeeper

After you've created the table, you should ensure that the Zookeeper process is working smoothly. The way the Zookeeper ensemble works is that it maintains critical data for HBase in data registers it calls *znodes*. If everything has been working correctly, you should now have some meaningful znodes to retrieve. It's time to see whether that assumption is correct.

You've set your Zookeeper port to 2222 in the hbase-site.xml file back in Listing 12-1, so using that port number you can bring up a Zookeeper command line interface as shown in Listing 12-8 using the command shown in line 1.

Listing 12-8: Testing Zookeeper

```
(1) ./hbase zkcli -server bivm:2222
Connecting to bivm:2222
13/06/30 12:54:44 INFO zookeeper.ZooKeeper: Client environment:zookeeper.
          version=3.4.5-1392090, built on 09/30/2012 17:52 GMT
13/06/30 12:54:44 INFO zookeeper.ZooKeeper: Client environment:host.name=bivm
. . .
(2) [zk: bivm:2222(CONNECTED) 0] ls /
[hbase, zookeeper]
```

```
(3) [zk: bivm:2222(CONNECTED) 1] ls /hbase
[root-region-server, rs, master, hbaseid, shutdown, backup-masters, unassigned,
            table92, draining, splitlog, online-snapshot, table]
(4) [zk: bivm:2222(CONNECTED) 2] ls /hbase/table
[CustomerContactInfo, .META., -ROOT-]
(5) [zk: bivm:2222(CONNECTED) 5] quit
Quitting...
```

Using the ls command (lines 2 & 3), you can browse through the znodes as set up by the MasterServer and RegionServer (line 3). Notice the results of line 4 ls /hbase/table. As expected, you can see the Customer Contact Information table that you created using the hbase shell. (We bolded it for you.)

Getting Things Done with HBase

HBase is written in Java, an elegant language for building distributed technologies like HBase, but let's face it — not everyone who wants to take advantage of HBase innovations is a Java developer. That's why there's a rich HBase client ecosystem out there whose sole purpose is to do the heavy Java lifting for you and let you concentrate on making HBase work for you.

Rich is usually a good characteristic, but when that adjective crosses the line into *overwhelming,* you start having a problem. In case the rich HBase client ecosystem strikes you as overwhelming, we thought we should do some pruning and highlight only the most popular clients available. To make things even easier, we start by giving you an overview of the client ecosystem in diagram form, as shown in Figure 12-6. Note that the diagram is similar to the HBase architecture diagram in Figure 12-1, with an exploded view of the client box.

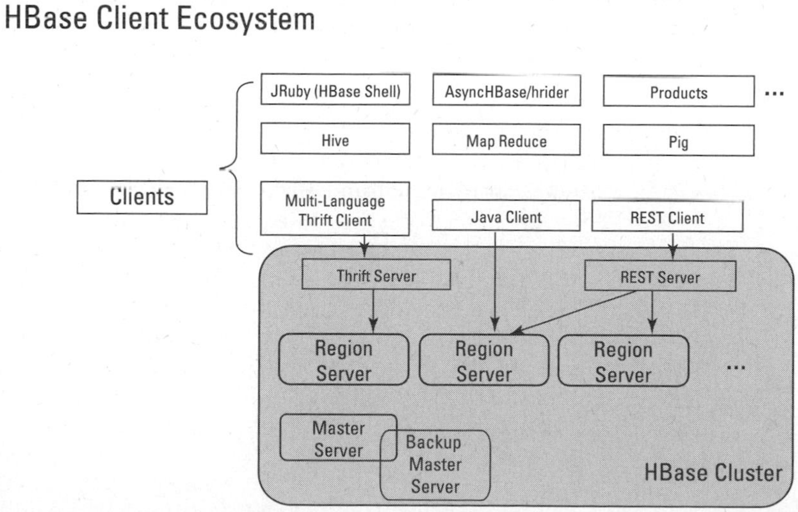

HBase Client Ecosystem

Figure 12-6: The HBase client ecosystem.

The following lists summarize your options, starting with the Apache Hadoop clients, more specifically those HBase clients which are part of the Apache Hadoop ecosystem along with those technologies bundled with HBase that are designed to help you build HBase clients:

- ✔ **Hive:** Hive is another top level Apache project and it happens to have an entire chapter in this book devoted to it. (Chapter 13, if you're curious.) Hive provides its own take on data warehousing capabilities on top of Apache Hadoop. It comes with a storage handler for HBase, and also provides the HiveQL query language, which is quite similar to SQL. With Hive, you can do all the querying of HBase that you want using HiveQL and — here's the kicker — no Java coding is required when you're using HBase with Hive.

- ✔ **MapReduce:** MapReduce is part of the Apache Hadoop framework (and gets some nice coverage in Chapter 6 of this book). MapReduce's claim to fame is that it's a programming model for processing data in parallel on a distributed cluster. In the Hadoop universe, HBase is (as the name implies) the "Hadoop Database." HBase leverages the Hadoop Distributed File System (HDFS) and can also be leveraged by MapReduce jobs. HBase tables can be a source or sink to parallel processing MapReduce jobs. This is an exciting feature included with HBase and has many applications.

- ✔ **Pig:** Pig is another technology included with Apache Hadoop and, as with Hive, Pig can leverage HBase. Pig takes you up a level by giving you a higher level programming language called Pig Latin, which can do the heavy MapReduce lifting for you. The details are a bit complicated, but you'll find out more in Chapter 8.

- ✔ **Multi-Language Thrift System:** Thrift provides a language-neutral approach to building HBase clients. Developed by Facebook, Thrift's Interface Definition Language (IDL) allows you to define data types and service interfaces so that two different systems written in different languages can communicate with one another. After the IDL is written, Thrift generates the code necessary for communication.

  Here's the really cool part — HBase comes with the Thrift IDL already written for you! As long as Thrift supports your language — and there are 14 supported languages as of this writing — you're well on your way to writing your own custom HBase client. HBase also includes the Thrift Server that's necessary to act as a gateway for your custom client. (That's why the Thrift Server is depicted inside the HBase cluster in Figure 12-6.) It doesn't have to run on a cluster node; it ships with HBase and only needs network access to the cluster. The Thrift server provides a gateway between your client and the HBase Java Client APIs. (More on those in a bit.) You start the Thrift gateway server pretty much like you'd start the HBase shell client — by using the `$INSTALL_DIR/ hbase-0.94.7/bin/hbase thrift start` command.

✔ **Java Client:** If you happen to be a Java developer — hey, we've got no problem with that! — and you understand the ins and outs of Java packages, then you'll want to check out the `org.apache.hadoop.hbase.client` package which comes bundled with the HBase distribution.

A little later in this chapter we show you a sample Java client that leverages this package, but if you just want to poke around a bit, a good place to start is with the package's `HTable` class. There you'll find the `get`, `put`, `checkAndPut`, `checkAndDelete`, and `delete` primitives, some of which you tried with the HBase shell in the hands-on example from the "Taking HBase for a test run" section, earlier in this chapter.

These primitives form the data manipulation language of HBase. (Okay, we need to add `scan` here as well; it's also part of the client package but in a separate class.) When you've mastered the package's `HTable` class, you'll want to check out its `HBaseAdmin` class so that you can manage your tables and, while you're at it, take a look at `HTablePool` as well, because it's an efficient way to leverage the Java client APIs.

✔ **REST System:** Probably the fastest approach for accessing a HBase table is to leverage the REST interface. REST, which stands for *R*epresentational *S*tate *T*ransfer, is the technology that makes your web browser work. Most folks just take web browsers for granted these days, so what could be more natural for anyone than just using your favorite browser as the gateway to an HBase cluster? As with the Thrift approach, the REST gateway server ships with HBase and you need to start at least one in order to enable browser interaction with your tables. To do that, just pick a port number for your gateway server (we'll use 7777) and type the following command:

```
$INSTALL_DIR/hbase-0.94.7/bin/hbase rest start _p 7777
```

If you continue leveraging the example of the Customer Contact Information table from earlier in this chapter, you can type `http://bivm:7777/CustomerContactInfo/schema/` in your browser to have the table schema returned to you — in effect mirroring what the `describe` command would do in the HBase shell (note that 'bivm' is the system name here so you'll need to enter the actual name of your system for this to work).

You can perform HBase client commands like `get`, `put`, `scan`, `delete`, and others using the Unix `curl` command. The `curl` command is often written as *cURL* because it lets you create web browser URLs using the command line. However, you'll need to do a little more work to get human readable results after you start retrieving your data. On its own, the browser returns base64 encoded data, since HBase is just storing bytes.

✔ **JRuby (HBase Shell):** The fastest way to roll up your sleeves and learn to use HBase is via the HBase shell. As you've probably already seen in the hands-on example of the HBase shell in the previous section, the shell is a powerful tool for interacting with HBase. The HBase shell is based on JRuby's Interactive Ruby Shell or IRB for short. (For more on

JRuby, check out `http://jruby.org`.) Keep in mind, however, that you can also write scripts and execute them in batch mode. (You see a use case for shell scripts in the "Deploying and Tuning HBase" section, later in this chapter, when we discuss major compactions.)

With the Apache Hadoop clients out of the way, it's time to turn to other HBase clients. The following list describes HBase clients which have been created by other open source communities and commercial companies.

- **AsyncHBase & hrider:** We're seeing lots of open source HBase clients springing up, so we want to introduce you to a pair that are really cool! The first is AsyncHBase which, as the name implies, is an asynchronous client. The standard bundled HBase client found in the `org.apache.hadoop.hbase.client` package is synchronous, which means that when you write a program using the standard package and it accesses an HBase table in some way, your program has to stop and wait for HBase to finish the operation. AsyncHBase provides an alternative to this Stop and Wait approach by letting your program do other things while HBase fulfills your request in the background. The second client is hrider which is a really cool little graphical user interface (GUI) on top of HBase. You know how we used the HBase shell earlier in our hands-on example? Well, hrider lets you interact with HBase through a GUI with a point and a click instead of typing out all of your HBase commands. You can find both of these projects and more on `http://github.com`.

- **Other Products:** As you would expect, plenty of commercial companies are creating innovative products for HBase — IBM, Cloudera, Hortonworks, and Amazon to name a few. To take just two examples, IBM created Big SQL which allows you to execute SQL against HBase tables, and Cloudera created Impala which improves HiveQL performance when querying data stored in HBase tables. You'll want to check out Chapter 14 for more on Big SQL and Impala.

Working with an HBase Java API client example

Here's a simple Java Client example to help you get started if you have your heart set on writing your own client. To run this code on the standalone pseudo-distributed install you've set up, set the Java CLASSPATH environment variable as follows:

```
CLASSPATH=$YOUR_HOME/HBaseClientApp:$INSTALL_DIR/hbase-0.94.7/hbase-
            0.94.7.jar:$INSTALL_DIR/hbase-0.94.7/conf:$INSTALL_DIR/
            hbase-0.94.7/lib/*
```

Your application needs to not only find the HBase `jar` files, but also know where your configuration files reside. Setting the Java `CLASSPATH` environment variable as shown takes care of that task for you. (Without the HBase configuration files, the Java Client APIs cannot find Zookeeper, which is Step # 1 for accessing the installation.)

Before you start working your way through the following sample code, you should know that one of the more powerful features in HBase for making data retrieval more efficient is filters. A *filter* lets you leverage the RegionServer's processing power to separate out the data you need — and the sample Java client example takes advantage of one of these built-in filters. This approach makes your queries faster and reduces the load on your network. Now clients don't have to sort through potentially huge chunks of data to find the record they need!

Listing 12-9 shows a simple Java client example in all its splendor. Note that the code below has been documented with comments — lines starting with `//`, that is — to help you understand how the HBaseClientApp class works. We labeled the comments with bold numbers so you can keep them straight:

Listing 12-9: A Simple Java Client Example

```java
import java.io.IOException;
import org.apache.hadoop.conf.Configuration;
import org.apache.hadoop.hbase.HBaseConfiguration;
import org.apache.hadoop.hbase.client.Get;
import org.apache.hadoop.hbase.client.HTable;
import org.apache.hadoop.hbase.client.Put;
import org.apache.hadoop.hbase.client.Result;
import org.apache.hadoop.hbase.client.ResultScanner;
import org.apache.hadoop.hbase.client.Scan;
import org.apache.hadoop.hbase.filter.*;
import org.apache.hadoop.hbase.util.Bytes;

public class HBaseClientApp {

    // Comment 1
    // HBase programming best practices call for declaring column
    // family names, column qualifiers and other frequently
    // used byte arrays once as constants instead of calling
    // Bytes.toBytes every time you need to create these byte
    // arrays.  Bytes.toBytes can be very costly in terms of
    // CPU cycles and can slow down your code especially if you
    // call the method inside a loop.

    private static final byte[] FIRSTROWKEY = Bytes.toBytes("00001");
    private static final byte[] ROWKEY = Bytes.toBytes("91000");
    private static final byte[] CF_CustomerName = Bytes.toBytes("CustomerName");
    private static final byte[] CF_ContactInfo = Bytes.toBytes("ContactInfo");
    private static final byte[] CQ_FirstName = Bytes.toBytes("FN");
    private static final byte[] CQ_LastName = Bytes.toBytes("LN");
```

(continued)

Listing 12-9 *(continued)*

```java
private static final byte[] CQ_EmailAddr = Bytes.toBytes("EA");
private static final byte[] CQ_StreetAddr = Bytes.toBytes("SA");

public static void main(String[] args) throws IOException {

    // Comment 2
    // Find the hbase-site.xml configuration
    // file from your CLASSPATH

    Configuration myConfig = HBaseConfiguration.create();

    // Comment 3
    // Create an HTable object and connect it
    // to your Customer Contact Information table

    HTable myTable = new HTable(myConfig, "CustomerContactInfo");

    // Comment 4
    // Create a Put object to enter some new
    // customer information into your Customer Contact Information table.
    // This code assumes that you_re keeping track
    // of your ROWKEY.
    Put myPutObject = new Put(ROWKEY);

    myPutObject.add(CF_CustomerName, CQ_FirstName,  Bytes.toBytes("Bruce"));
    myPutObject.add(CF_CustomerName, CQ_LastName,   Bytes.toBytes("Brown"));
    myPutObject.add(CF_ContactInfo,  CQ_EmailAddr,  Bytes.toBytes("brownb@
            client.com"));
    myPutObject.add(CF_ContactInfo,  CQ_StreetAddr, Bytes.toBytes("HBase
            Author Lane, CA 33333"));

    // Comment 5
    // Commit our new record to the 'CustomerContactInfo'
    // table.
    myTable.put(myPutObject);

    // Comment 6
    // In the example below you are leveraging one of the many
    // built-in filters to query the Customer Contact
    // Information table for customers that have a
    // particular email address. Only client records that have
    // a particular domain name in their email address
    // are returned to our Java Client.

    Filter companyFilter = new ValueFilter(CompareFilter.CompareOp.EQUAL,
            new SubstringComparator("@client.com"));
    Scan myScanner = new Scan(FIRSTROWKEY,companyFilter);
    ResultScanner myResults = myTable.getScanner(myScanner);
    for (Result res : myResults) {
        System.out.println(Bytes.toString(res.value()));
    }
}
}
```

Beginning with Comment 1, this block of Java code illustrates a best practice with HBase, namely that you want to define your byte arrays holding your HBase row keys, column family names, column qualifiers and data up front as constants. This saves valuable CPU cycles and makes your code run faster, especially if there are repeated loop constructs. If you were wondering how the main method that executes the HBase commands finds the Zookeeper ensemble and then RegionServers, Comment 2 explains this. However, the `HBaseConfiguration.create` method won't find your cluster if your `CLASSPATH` environment variable is not set correctly, so don't forget that task! Comment 3 explains how our `HBaseClientApp` class connects with the 'CustomerContactInfo' table and Comments 4 and 5 show you how you can place data in our 'CustomerContactInfo' table. Finally, Comment 6 explains how HBase filter technology can improve your table scans by allowing you to target specific data in the table. Without filters you would be pulling much more data out of the HBase cluster and across the network to your client where you would have to write code to sort through the results. Filters make HBase life a whole lot easier!

If you compile and run this example application, you'll have added a new customer name (Bruce Brown) and the customer's contact info (`brownb@ client.com`, residing at HBase Author Lane, CA 33333) to the Customer Contact Information table and you'll have used a filter to track down and print the e-mail address.

HBase and the RDBMS world

We think it's best to state right up front that HBase and relational database technology (like Oracle, DB2, and MySQL to name just a few) really don't compare all that well. Despite the cliché, it's truly a case of comparing apples to oranges. HBase is a *NoSQL* technology — we explain the meaning of this catchy nomenclature in detail in Chapter 11 and we discuss the major differences between relational database management systems (RDBMSs) and HBase in Chapter 11 as well. If your background is in relational database technology and you are wondering how you might convert some of your databases to HBase — or even if that makes sense — then this section is just for you! We'll start with a brief description (or refresher if you read Chapter 11) of the differences and then we'll discuss some considerations and guidelines for making the move.

BigTable, HBase's Google forebear, was born out of a need to manage massive amounts of data in a seamless, scalable fashion. HBase is a direct implementation of BigTable providing the same scalability properties, reliability, fault recovery, a rich client ecosystem, and a simple yet powerful programming model. The relational data model and the database systems that followed were built with different goals in mind. The relational model and accompanying structured query language (SQL) is a mathematical approach that enforces data integrity, defines how data is to be manipulated, provides a basis for efficient data storage and prevents update anomalies by way of the normalization process. Though HBase and the RDBMS have some commonalities, the design goals were different.

You may wonder why the examples earlier in this chapter center on mapping a relational table — our Customer Contact Information table — to an HBase table. The reason is two-fold:

- ✔ The relational model is the most prevalent, so using *that* model for the sake of comparisons often helps professionals coming from the world of RDBMSs better grasp the HBase data model.

- ✔ The innovations provided by BigTable and HBase are making this new NoSQL technology an attractive alternative for certain applications that don't necessarily fit the RDBMS model. (The ability of HBase to scale automatically is alone a huge innovation for the world of database technology!)

Knowing when HBase makes sense for you?

So, when should you consider using HBase? Though the answer to this question isn't necessarily straightforward for everyone, for starters you clearly must have

- ✔ **A big data requirement:** We're talking terabytes to petabytes here — otherwise you'll have a lot of idle servers in your racks.

- ✔ **Sufficient hardware resources:** Five servers is a good starting point, as described in the "Hardware Architecture" row in Table 12-4.

When considering which route to take — HBase versus RDBMS — consider other requirements such as transaction support, rich data types, indexes, and query language support — though these factors are not as black and white as the preceding two bullets. Rich data types, indexes and query language support can be added via other technologies, such as Hive or commercial products, as described in Chapter 13. "What about transactions?" you ask. The answer to that question is in the following section.

ACID Properties in HBase

Certain use cases for RDBMSs, like online transaction processing, depend on ACID-compliant transactions between the client and the RDBMS for the system to function properly. (We define the ACID acronym — **A**tomicity, **C**onsistency, **I**solation, and **D**urability — in Chapter 11.) When compared to an RDBMS, HBase isn't considered an ACID-compliant database as of this writing. HBase does not support ACID-compliant transactions over multiple rows or across tables. However, HBase does guarantee the following aspects:

- ✔ **Atomic:** All row level operations within a table are atomic. This guarantee is maintained even when there's more than one column family within a row. HBase provides, in addition to the `get`, `put`, `delete` and `scan` commands described earlier in this chapter, atomic `increment`, `checkAndPut` and `checkAndDelete` methods.

- ✔ **Consistency:** Scan operations return a consistent view of the data stored in HBase at some point in the past. Concurrent client interaction could update a row during a multi-row scan, but all rows returned by a scan operation will always contain valid data from some point in the past.

- ✔ **Durability:** Any data that can be retrieved from HBase has also been made *durable to disk* (persisted to HDFS, in other words).

One of the exciting aspects of HBase and other open source Apache projects is that someone in the community is always innovating and trying to improve the technology. HBase does support multi-row transactions if the rows are on the same RegionServer. This feature, which requires additional coding, was introduced in HBase version 0.94.0 documented at `https://issues.apache.org/jira/browse/HBASE-5229`. (If you're curious, the additional coding focused on HBase's split policy.)

When ACID properties are required by HBase clients, design the HBase schema such that cross row or cross table data operations are not required. Keeping data within a row provides atomicity.

Transitioning from an RDBMS model to HBase

If you're facing the design phase for your application and you believe that HBase would be a good fit, then designing your row keys and schema to fit the HBase data model and architecture is the right approach. However, sometimes it makes sense to move a database originally designed for an RDBMS to HBase. A common scenario where this approach makes sense is a MySQL database instance that has reached its limits of scalability. Techniques exist for horizontally scaling a MySQL instance (*sharding,* in other words) but this process is usually cumbersome and problematic because MySQL simply was not originally designed for sharding. If you're in this predicament yet you believe that the HBase differences are manageable, then read on. The tips in this section may save you some valuable time.

Transitioning from the relational model to the HBase model is a relatively new discipline. However, certain established patterns of thought are emerging and have coalesced into three key principles to follow when approaching a transition. These principles are *denormalization, duplication,* and *intelligent keys (DDI)*. The following list takes a closer look at each principle:

- ✔ **Denormalization:** The relational database model depends on a) a normalized database schema and b) joins between tables to respond to SQL operations. Database normalization is a technique which guards against data loss, redundancy, and other anomalies as data is updated and retrieved. There are a number of rules the experts follow to arrive at a normalized database schema (and database normalization is a whole study itself), but the process usually involves dividing larger tables into smaller tables and defining relationships between them. Database denormalization is the opposite of normalization, where smaller, more specific tables are joined into larger, more general tables. This is a common pattern when transitioning to HBase because joins are not provided across tables, and joins can be slow since they involve costly disk operations. Guarding against the update and retrieval anomalies is now the job of your HBase client application, since the protections afforded you by normalization are null and void.

- ✔ **Duplication:** As you denormalize your database schema, you will likely end up duplicating the data because it can help you avoid costly read operations across multiple tables. Don't be concerned about the extra storage (within reason of course); you can use the automatic scalability of HBase to your advantage. Be aware, though, that extra work will be required by your client application to duplicate the data and remember that natively HBase only provides row level atomic operations not cross row (with the exception described in the HBASE-5229 JIRA) or cross table.

- ✔ **Intelligent Keys:** Because the data stored in HBase is ordered by row key, and the row key is the only native index provided by the system, careful intelligent design of the row key can make a huge difference. For example, your row key could be a combination of a service order number and the customer's ID number that placed the service order. This row key design would allow you to look up data related to the service order or look up data related to the customer using the same row key in the same table. This technique will be faster for some queries and avoid costly table joins.

To clarify these particular patterns of thought, we expand on the example of the Customer Contact Information table by placing it within the context of a typical service order database. Figure 12-7 shows you what a normalized service order database schema might look like.

RDBMS Normalized Service Order Database

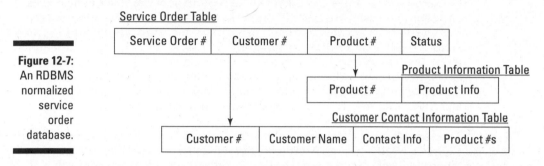

Figure 12-7:
An RDBMS
normalized
service
order
database.

Following the rules of RDBMS normalization, we set up the sample Customer Contact Information table so that it is separate from the service order table in order to avoid losing customer data when service orders are closed and possibly deleted. We took the same approach for the Products table, which means that new products can be added to the fictional company database independently of service orders. By relying on RDBMS join operations, this schema supports queries that reveal the number of service orders that are opened against a particular product along with the customer's location where the product is in use.

That's all fine and dandy, but it's a schema you'd use with RDBM. How do you transition this schema to an HBase schema? Figure 12-8 illustrates a possible HBase scheme — one that follows the DDI design pattern.

HBase Schema for the Service Order Database

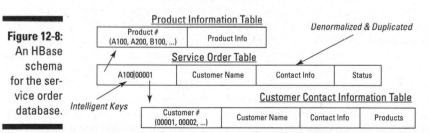

Figure 12-8:
An HBase
schema
for the ser-
vice order
database.

To avoid costly search operations and additional HBase `get` and/or `scan` operations (or both), the Customer Contact Information table has been denormalized by including the customer name and contact info in place of the foreign keys used previously. (See Figure 12-7.) Also, the data is duplicated by keeping the Customer Contact Information table as is. Now joins across the Service Order table and Customer Contact Information table are not necessary. Additionally, an intelligent row key design has been employed that combines the product number with the customer number to form the service order number (A100|00001, for example). Using this intelligent key, the service order table can provide vital reports about product deficiencies and customers who are currently experiencing product issues. All these queries can all be supported by HBase in a row level atomic fashion for the application. We don't have to worry about the lack of ACID compliant joins across the two tables. Additionally, because you know that HBase orders row keys and sorts them in a lexicographical fashion, your application can make certain educated guesses about data locality when issuing scans for reporting. (All A* series product numbers will be stored together, for example.)

The service order database represented by the HBase schema (refer to Figure 12-8) is a relatively simple example, but it illustrates how HBase can, in certain cases, intersect with the RDBMS world and provide significant value. If the fictional company has terabytes or even petabytes of service call data to store, HBase would make a huge difference in terms of cost, reliability, performance, and scale. You can, of course, design your service order HBase schema in several different ways. Admittedly, the design all depends on the queries that must be supported, but you have the ability to transition some relational databases to very powerful HBase applications for production use as long as you work from a solid understanding of HBase architecture and the DDI design pattern.

This example has assumed that queries were performed by a Java application leveraging the HBase client APIs, or perhaps via another language using Apache Thrift. This application model may fit the requirements just fine and provide useful performance and customization options for the fictional service company. However, the downside is that the service order database schema is tied pretty tightly to the application layer that issues the queries and manages the database integrity. (We say "tied pretty tightly" because changes to the HBase schema would require changes to the application code.) You might ask these two questions: "could either HiveQL or other commercial offerings providing SQL support for HBase be used to make this process easier for the engineers creating this HBase application?" (changing HiveQL or SQL is certainly easier and less costly than changing application code) and "could joins be performed when appropriate using Hadoop MapReduce?" (That might be easier than following the DDI pattern if the limited ACID properties provided by HBase fit your application.) The answer to these questions is "yes," so you'll want to check out Chapters 13 and 15 to see how HBase can be combined with other Hadoop and commercial products to create some very powerful big data applications.

Deploying and Tuning HBase

HBase is a powerful and flexible technology, but accompanying this flexibility is the requirement for proper configuration and tuning. Now, installing and running HBase in a standalone mode for learning purposes is seamless and very straightforward, but standalone mode for testing purposes in no way, shape, or form represents the real world. Admittedly, some applications of HBase simply involve ingesting large amounts of data and then querying that data occasionally over time at a leisurely pace — no strict deadlines, in other words, which means that you don't have to worry too much about efficiencies. Other possibilities might include running a Map Reduce job against the data for business analytics or machine learning applications. These use cases are batch oriented in nature and if your use case fits into this category, you probably don't need to configure and tune HBase all that much. Your main concerns are the proper hardware configuration and correct configuration files. Reviewing the Apache HBase online Quick Start guide (`http://hbase.apache.org/book/quickstart.html`) and following the guidance in the later section "Hardware requirements" is likely all you need to soon be on your way.

Most HBase deployments, however, are going to include performance expectations or performance requirements (or both) along with the expectation that you take advantage of freebies such as auto sharding and automatic recovery after node failures. Often new use cases arise after an organization becomes accustomed to the new and shiny database toy on the network and so the original expectations or requirements can change. So for all these reasons and more, deploying HBase at scale in production environments typically requires careful thought and an understanding of how to tune HBase. The good news is that, in our experience, a little tuning goes a long way, so don't feel overwhelmed. We've personally seen HBase performance improve by several orders of magnitude by simply following the suggestions in this section and in the online page "Apache HBase performance tuning" (`http://hbase.apache.org/book/performance.html`).

Hardware requirements

It's time for some general guidelines for configuring HBase clusters. Your "mileage" may vary, depending on specific compute requirements for your RegionServers (custom coprocessors, for example) and other applications you may choose to co-locate on your cluster.

RegionServers

The first temptation to resist when configuring your RegionServers is plunking down lots of cash for some high end enterprise systems. Don't do it! HBase is typically deployed on plain vanilla commodity x86 servers. Now, don't take that statement as license to deploy the cheapest, low quality servers. Yes, HBase is designed to recover from node failures but your availability suffers during recovery periods so hardware quality and redundancy *do* matter. Redundant power supplies as well as redundant network interface cards are a good idea for production deployments. Typically, organizations choose two socket machines with four to six cores each.

The second temptation to resist is configuring your server with the maximum storage and memory capacity. A common configuration would include from 6 to 12 terabytes (TB) of disk space and from 48 to 96 gigabytes (GB) of RAM. RAID controllers for the disks are unnecessary because HDFS provides data protection when disks fail.

HBase requires a read and write cache that's allocated from the Java heap. Keep this statement in mind as you read about the HBase configuration variables because you'll see that a direct relationship exists between a RegionServer's disk capacity and a RegionServer's Java heap. You can find an excellent discussion on HBase RegionServer memory sizing at

```
http://hadoop-hbase.blogspot.com/2013/01/hbase-region-
              server-memory-sizing.html
```

The article points out that you can estimate the ratio of raw disk space to Java heap by following this formula:

RegionSize *divided by* Memstoresize *multiplied by* HDFS Replication Factor *multiplied by* HeapFractionForMemstores

Using the default HBase configuration variables from `http://hbase.apache.org/book/config.files.html` provides this ratio:

10GB / 128MB * 3 * 0.4 = Ratio of 96MB disk space : 1 MB Java heap space.

The preceding line equates to 3TB of raw disk capacity per RegionServer with 32GB of RAM allocated to the Java heap.

What you end up with, then, is 1 terabyte of usable space per RegionServer since the default HDFS replication factor is 3. This number is still impressive in terms of database storage per node but not so impressive given that commodity servers can typically accommodate eight or more drives with a capacity of 2 to 4 terabyte a piece. The overarching problem as of this writing is the fact that current Java Virtual Machines (JVMs) struggle to provide efficient memory management (garbage collection, to be precise) with large heap spaces (spaces greater than 32GB, for example).

Yes, there are garbage collection tuning parameters you can use, and you should check with your JVM vendor to insure you have the latest options, but you won't be able to get very far using them at this time. The memory management issue will eventually be solved but for now be aware that you may encounter a problem if your HBase storage requirements are in the range of hundreds of terabytes to more than a petabyte. You can easily increase the `hbase.hregion.max.filesize` to 20GB to reach 6TB raw and 2TB usable. You can make other tweaks (reducing MemStore size for read heavy workloads, for example) but you won't make orders of magnitude leaps in the useable space until we have a JVM that efficiently handles garbage collection with massive heaps.

You can find ways around the JVM garbage collection issue for RegionServers but the solutions are new and are not yet part of the main HBase distribution as of this writing. If your HBase data store requirements are massive, check out the "bucket cache" article at `https://issues.apache.org/jira/browse/HBASE-7404` before you buy too many RegionServers.

Master servers

The MasterServer does not consume system resources like the RegionServers do. However, you should provide for hardware redundancy, including RAID to prevent system failure. For good measure, also configure a backup MasterServer into the cluster. A common configuration is 4 CPU cores, between 8GB and 16GB of RAM and 1 Gigabit Ethernet is a common configuration. If you co-locate MasterServers and Zookeeper nodes, 16GB of RAM is advisable.

Zookeeper

Like the MasterServer, Zookeeper doesn't require a large hardware configuration, but Zookeeper must not block (or be required to compete for) system resources. Zookeeper, which is the coordination service for an HBase cluster, sits in the data path for clients. If Zookeeper cannot do its job, time-outs will occur — and the results can be catastrophic. Zookeeper hardware requirements are the same as for the MasterServer except that a dedicated disk should be provided for the process. For small clusters you can co-locate Zookeeper with the master server but remember that Zookeeper needs sufficient system resources to run when ready.

Deployment Considerations

Now that you have a solid understanding of HBase hardware (HW) requirements, we have a couple of points for you regarding deployment:

- ✔ In this chapter, we're assuming that you're concerned primarily about setting up an HBase cluster. Though co-locating HBase with MapReduce is often done, it affects performance and sizing requirements. So if you're serious about maximum HBase performance, consider carefully the additional HW resources you may require or provision a separate cluster for MapReduce and other Hadoop jobs. Then you can keep your HBase cluster separate.

- ✔ Deploying Hadoop is the subject of Chapter 16 so we encourage you to check that chapter out. In Chapter 16, you'll find more detail on networking as well as physical HW deployment examples for HBase and Hadoop. We cover Hadoop 1 deployments as well as Hadoop 2 deployments.

Tuning prerequisites

Any serious HBase installation requires some standard setup on your cluster and on your individual nodes. We give you a few examples here and then point you to the sections in the Apache HBase online documentation you'll need to reference. First take a look at monitoring and management.

Tools to monitor your cluster

If you've had the privilege of engineering a system at some point in your career, you know you face the major challenge of coming up with a rigorous testing procedure to ensure that your system is ready for its production phase. If you don't plan for testing and debugging right up front, you'll likely miss your production deadlines or fail altogether. The HBase and Hadoop committers made sure that you would have a rich metrics subsystem to draw on during the debug and test phase. You can find all the messy details in the Apache HBase online documentation (`http://hbase.apache.org/book.html#ops_mgt`), especially the sections dealing with HBase Backup and Replication. In this section, we give you an overview of the available tools.

The Cluster Replication feature is a key tool when debugging, tuning or if you want to run Map Reduce against your tables without impacting performance. Obviously, you'll need it for disaster recover as well.

Getting started with the Hadoop management tools set is surprisingly easy. HBase leverages the Java Management Extensions (JMX) technology for exposing key metrics. And with the Java Virtual Machine, you also get the JConsole tool, a free JMX client that you can use to view HBase metrics. The HBase distribution we've been working with (0.94.7) enables access via JConsole by default, so in your standalone environment you simply select the HBase server that you want to monitor and JConsole then presents you with a graphical user interface for viewing key server metrics.

You can start the JConsole tool with the following command:

```
$JAVA_HOME/bin/jconsole
```

Additionally, you should familiarize yourself with these two other open source technologies for monitoring your HBase cluster:

- ✔ **Ganglia:** Often used to provide monitoring graphs over time, Ganglia can help you spot problems that occur occasionally or only after days of operation.
- ✔ **Nagios:** Nagios is useful if you're an HBase administrator and you want to receive a page on your pager or an e-mail if, say, a RegionServer goes down or you have a garbage collection issue in your cluster.

If you're leveraging HBase as part of a commercial product, be sure to check with your vendor for a tool to monitor and manage HBase.

Cluster setup

HBase typically deploys on a cluster, and you'll need to make some adjustments on each of your servers to accommodate HBase components. A good first step is insuring that the system clocks on each server in your cluster are in sync. Out of sync system clocks on your servers can really confuse HBase, so check out the Network Time Protocol or NTP for short. Running the NTP on your cluster will take care of any time synchronization issues. Furthermore, HBase is a unique application in certain respects because it stresses your system beyond the level that applications may do. The truth is that HBase is going to be opening a lot of files — that's just the nature of the beast. Given that fact, you need to ensure that your operating systems are configured to handle what is sure to be a far-from-typical file system load. Swapping in your Linux operating systems (moving between disk and memory, in other words) can have very adverse effects on Zookeeper. Finally there's the Java Virtual Machine (JVM) that ultimately runs on each of your nodes and executes the HBase processes. HBase also puts far-from-typical stress on the JVM. (For example, the MemStore cache, which heavily exercises the garbage collection system, is sure to be taxed to the max.)

When the MemStore is committed to HFiles on the HDFS, the Java heap is reclaimed. This can result in long garbage collection pauses if your JVM is not configured correctly.

So for all of these reasons and more you should review these two sections of the Apache HBase online documentation:

- ✔ **General Configuration Requirements:** Review Chapter 2 of the Apache HBase online documentation (`http://hbase.apache.org/book/configuration.html`) and especially section 2.5 entitled "The Important Configurations" - `http://hbase.apache.org/book/important_configurations.html`.

- ✔ **Java Virtual Machine:** Determine which JVM you're running and make sure that it has been tested for compatibility with HBase. As of this writing, the Apache HBase online documentation suggests Java 6 from Oracle because Java 7 hasn't been fully tested. Another JVM we've tested is IBM's J9. If you plan to use J9, review the IBM documentation for the latest command line options when starting your JVMs. If you plan to use Oracle's JVM, review the following sections of the HBase online documentation to familiarize yourself with the proper settings: `http://hbase.apache.org/book/jvm.html` and `http://hbase.apache.org/book/trouble.log.html#trouble.log.gc`

Enabling compression

Compression boosts HBase performance by reducing overall disk input/output. Consider enabling compression unless your data doesn't compress well (images, for example) or if your RegionServers cannot handle the additional CPU load that compression and decompression requires. Compression can be enabled via the HBase shell command, as we explain in the "Taking

HBase for a test run" section, earlier in this chapter, when we tell you how to leverage the `describe` shell command (see Listing 12-10) to view our Customer Contact Information table descriptors:

Listing 12-10: The *describe* Shell Command

```
hbase(main):018:0> describe 'CustomerContactInfo'
... {NAME => 'ContactInfo', REPLICATION_SCOPE => '0', KE true
 EP_DELETED_CELLS => 'false', COMPRESSION => 'NONE',...
```

By default, compression is disabled per column family. The supported compression types are Gzip, LZO and Snappy (with some other derivatives available and more on the way). GZIP is best overall for achieving a good compression ratio, but LZO and Snappy are faster. Keep in mind, though, that both LZO and Snappy compression codecs must be installed separately; only Gzip works without further configuration steps. Listing 12-11 shows the steps you'd need to enable Gzip compression on the Customer Contact Information table:

Listing 12-11: Enabling Gzip Compression

```
hbase(main):007:0> disable 'CustomerContactInfo'
hbase(main):010:0> alter 'CustomerContactInfo', { NAME => 'CustomerName',
                COMPRESSION => 'GZ' }
hbase(main):014:0> describe 'CustomerContactInfo'
... {NAME => 'CustomerName', REPLICATION_SC
 OPE => '0', KEEP_DELETED_CELLS => 'false', COMPRESSION => 'GZ',...
hbase(main):017:0> enable 'CustomerContactInfo'
```

Understanding your data access patterns

Achieving peak performance with HBase requires an understanding of your data access patterns. How will your application or clients query HBase? Is your data ingested in bulk or gradually over time? Are the patterns mostly reads or writes or a mix of both? Are the queries random or sequential? How much data is read or written per query? Often no clear answer to these questions emerges or the answer varies per table. However, the good news is that you can tune on a per table basis, so choosing a few key tables to tune can help a great deal.

It is beyond the scope of this section and somewhat unrealistic to cover all tuning scenarios, but we do want to provide some general guidance which will (hopefully) help you focus on the most important issues and tuning parameters:

✔ As mentioned earlier in this chapter, the Apache HBase online guide has a whole section on performance tuning that's worth your while to check out:

```
http://hbase.apache.org/book.html#performance
```

✔ While you're at it, review the online guide's Apache HBase configuration coverage, especially the section about HBase configuration variables:

```
http://hbase.apache.org/book/config.files.html
```

✔ Commonly used variables are in the section about performance tuning:

```
http://hbase.apache.org/book/perf.configurations.html
```

Here's what we recommend for some common situations:

✔ **Read Heavy Workloads:** If the read workload is random, consider increasing the `hfile.block.cache.size` setting and shrinking the `hbase.regionserver.global.memstore.upperLimit` and `hbase.regionserver.global.memstore.lowerLimit` settings.

You can also keep part or all of a column family in memory by setting the `in_memory` descriptor to `true` while disabling the block cache altogether for other tables' column families.

```
{ NAME => 'columnfamily', IN_MEMORY => 'true' }
{ NAME => 'columnfamily', BLOCKCACHE => 'false' }
```

If the read workload is sequential, caching will most likely not help your performance so look at increasing the HFile block size to achieve more data per read. The HBase API docs suggest numbers between 8KB and 1MB, with the default setting of 64KB. (We suggest going with 128KB in the example below.) Also review your `hbase.client.scanner.caching` setting to ensure that it fits your sequential read patterns.

```
{ NAME => 'columnfamily', BLOCKSIZE => 131072 }
```

✔ **Write Heavy Workloads:** With write heavy workloads, the MemStore configuration becomes quite important, so review all settings that affect the MemStore write cache — things like the `hbase.regionserver.global.memstore.lowerLimit` setting and the `hbase.regionserver.global.memstore.upperLimit` setting.

JVM garbage collection must also be configured correctly so that large garbage collection pauses don't occur — and slow your application. Worse yet, such large pauses can confuse Zookeeper into believing that your RegionServer has failed and then your HBase experience gets *ugly*. Finally you should have a strategy in place for handling region splits. HBase-generated region splits is a beautiful thing with respect to automatic scalability but if you're doing lots of writes, you'll want to control when your regions split. You can handle it in a couple of ways:

- *Increase the region size parameter,* `hbase.hregion.max.filesize`. The default size was increased to 10GB recently, though, so it depends on the amount of data you want to ingest.

- *Pre-split your regions to distribute them across the cluster.* You can do this if you have enough RegionServers. We discuss this technique in the next section.

✔ **Mixed workloads:** If your workload is mixed, you're in good company! Most clusters serve more than a single purpose. For mixed workloads, you need to follow best practices. First and foremost you'll need a good row key design to match your table access patterns. (We discuss row key design in the later section "The importance of row key design.") We've already discussed compression which improves performance.

Pre-Splitting your regions

HBase scales automatically by splitting regions when their size reaches the value configured in the `hbase.hregion.max.filesize` parameter. Regions are evenly distributed across the cluster by the load balancer process which runs on the MasterServer. This automation is very valuable for most HBase use cases, but you may (during bulk ingest operations or heavy writes, for example) want to manually control the whole process. In this case, you would set the `hbase.hregion.max.filesize` parameter to a very high value that you do not anticipate you will reach. After this is done, you can then manually split and compact your regions using the HBase shell commands. (See the "Tuning major compactions" section later in this chapter for more details.) You may also choose to pre-split your table(s) and distribute them across all available RegionServers right up front so that you can leverage the full power of the cluster immediately. If this tuning concept fits your application, then you can leverage one of the approaches in this list.

✔ **Use the HBase shell to create a table with pre-split regions, like this:**

```
hbase(main):021:0> create 'Pre-Splits-Table',
        'OneColumnFamily', { SPLITS => ['A999',
        'B999', 'C999', 'D999'] }
0 row(s) in 1.1720 seconds
```

✔ Note that you can also create a `splits` file where each line has a starting row key and then point to the file using the HBase shell `create table` command, as in this example.

```
hbase(main):021:0> create 'Pre-Splits-Table',
        'OneColumnFamily', { SPLITS_FILE =>
        'mySplitsFile' }
```

✔ **Leverage the** org.apache.hadoop.hbase.util.RegionSplitter **utility.**

For documentation on the utility go to: `http://hbase.apache.org/apidocs/org/apache/hadoop/hbase/util/RegionSplitter.html`.

✔ **Leverage a** createTable **method from the** org.apache.hadoop.hbase.client.HBaseAdmin **class**

If you decide that manual intervention into HBase region splitting is right for you, check out Hannibal, a very cool little tool for monitoring region splitting that helps you better manage the overall process. Hannibal is on GitHub at `https://github.com/sentric/hannibal`.

The importance of row key design

Proper row key design is central to creating any table in HBase. How you design the row key affects your performance, how you query your data, and the complexity of your application or client access approach. Also, if you find that you need to transition from a relational data model to an HBase model, you'll find that "intelligent" row keys are quite helpful. We stress this fact in the section "Transitioning from a RDBMS To HBase," earlier in this chapter. Given the importance of row key design, we could dedicate an entire section or even chapter to the subject but the point of this section is to highlight the key points around HBase deployment and performance tuning and then point you to further information where appropriate. So as you might expect by now, the Apache HBase online guide has an entire section dedicated to row key design case studies and you'll definitely want to review it for a thorough understanding of row key design. It's part of Apache's HBase and schema design overview; see `http://hbase.apache.org/book/schema.casestudies.html`.

What we want to do here is highlight the key points and considerations for proper row key design and introduce you to some tools at your disposal.

Making your row key fit your query patterns

The first thing you have to consider is how you intend to query data that's stored in the table. Will the row key enable targeted access to a particular row you're looking for or will you have to scan large numbers of rows and look for the key value pair you need? Remember that HBase is row level atomic (meaning operations like get, put, and scan are guaranteed to successfully complete or completely fail — no partial results allowed), so it may be critical to target individual rows rather than perform scans for certain queries. Can you combine two or more unique identifiers to create a composite row key? When we show you how to work with the service order database earlier in this chapter, we combined the service order number with the customer number to create an intelligent composite row key, like this

A100|00001 **Customer Name** **Contact Info** **Status**

This approach enables queries based only on product number or customer number. This can be accomplished by leveraging HBase row key filters. Listing 12-12 shows simple table that illustrates this row key design.

Listing 12-12: Illustrating Intelligent Row Key Design

```
hbase(main):124:0> scan 'RowKeyTest'
ROW                            COLUMN+CELL
 A100|00005                    column=cf:service-order, value=brokenc
 B100|00003                    column=cf:service-order,
             timestamp=1373463447048, value=brokeng
 B102|00004                    column=cf:service-order,
             timestamp=1373463409362, value=brokenb
 C201|00001                    column=cf:service-order,
             timestamp=1373463173365, value=brokena
4 row(s) in 0.0140 seconds
Now, use the <span cssStyle="text-decoration:line-through">scan</span> command
             to determine whether a service call has been placed for product
             number <span cssStyle="text-decoration:line-through">A100</span>.

hbase(main):127:0> scan 'RowKeyTest', { FILTER => PrefixFilter.new(Bytes.
             toBytes('A100')) }
ROW                            COLUMN+CELL
 A100|00005                    column=cf:service-order,
             timestamp=1373463418241, value=brokenc
1 row(s) in 0.0090 seconds
Use the same <span cssStyle="text-decoration:line-through">scan</span> command
             to determine whether customer number <span cssStyle="text-
             decoration:line-through">00001</span> has placed a service call.

hbase(main):128:0> scan 'RowKeyTest', { FILTER => RowFilter.
             new(CompareFilter::CompareOp.valueOf('EQUAL'),
             SubstringComparator.new('00001')) }
ROW                            COLUMN+CELL
 C201|00001                    column=cf:service-order,
             timestamp=1373463173365, value=brokena
1 row(s) in 0.0080 seconds
```

The two examples above illustrate how awesome composite row keys can be when combined with filters! Instead of having multiple tables or multiple rows to store customer and service order information, you can store it all in a single row and single table, thereby reducing overall disk and network traffic within your HBase cluster. Targeted or pointed HBase queries are the goal; you don't want to be doing extra IO operations while you search for your data.

Making your row key design leverage the performance potential of the cluster

A common challenge you face when designing your row keys is region *hotspotting,* where one or more RegionServers get overloaded with requests while the others sit idle. This is not what we want to see in HBase-land; we'd rather have every RegionServer pulling its own weight so users see the maximum performance! This performance issue will occur during large sequential writes or when you are reading continually from a small subsection of the table.

You learned about the MasterServer web interface at `http://bivm:60010/` in the "Taking HBase for a Test Run" section, and about the byte lexicographical sorting of row keys in the "Understanding the HBase Data Model" section. Now we're showing you some practical uses for this knowledge.

Now that the regions are pre-split (Step 1 we completed in the "Pre-Splitting your regions" section), Step 2 involves the row key. Keep in mind that, with byte lexicographical sorting, row keys are sorted from left to right. You can pre-split your tables, but if you don't ensure that your row keys are designed to distribute evenly across the splits, you'll still have a region hotspotting problem.

HBase is a highly configurable and therefore a flexible technology, and the Load Balancer is no exception. You can either let the MasterServer automatically balance your regions or manually control the balancer via the shell.

Tuning major compactions

We introduce you to minor and major *compactions* — the process by which HBase cleans up after itself — in the "Understanding the HBase Architecture" section, earlier in this chapter, but in this section we want to briefly explain how you can control major compactions, because the impact to cluster performance is "major" — pun intended!

The approach is very straightforward — simply turn off automatic major compactions and issue the command manually against your tables at an appropriate time. To turn off major compactions, set the `hbase.hregion.majorcompaction` parameter to 0 in your `hbase-site.xml` file and restart HBase. To manually run a major compaction, simply issue the `major_compact` command from the HBase shell.

```
hbase(main):018:0> major_compact 'CustomerContactInfo'
0 row(s) in 0.0480 seconds
```

An obvious solution would be to script the major compaction shell commands and run the script using a scheduling utility like cron at the appropriate time. Simply put the preceding command in a file, name it `major-compact.rb`, add an `exit` command and execute it with this command:

```
$INSTALL_DIR/bin/hbase shell major-compact.rb
```

You can also trigger a major compaction via one of several `major_compact` methods in the Java client `org.apache.hadoop.hbase.client.HBaseAdmin` class.

For a quick review of the HBaseAdmin class (it's well worth your time), see: `http://hbase.apache.org/apidocs/org/apache/hadoop/hbase/client/HBaseAdmin.html`.

How HBase is being used in the marketplace

The truly innovative technology HBase is a vital part of the Hadoop ecosystem. Here's a web page for you to check out: `http://wiki.apache.org/hadoop/Hbase/PoweredBy`. If you're wondering how HBase is now used in the marketplace, you'll be pleasantly surprised to know that you've probably already counted on HBase as part of your social media experience. Popular sites such as Facebook, Yahoo, Twitter, Meetup, StumbleUpon, Adobe, and many others now leverage HBase in production today. We trust that you'll be inspired to leverage HBase for your big data storage needs and start contributing to the ever growing and vibrant HBase community!

Chapter 13

Applying Structure to Hadoop Data with Hive

*I*f you were to look back at the history of the IT Industry, you'd soon see that every decade has had one or more watershed moments. Huge innovations have often dramatically impacted the industry as a whole, changing the course of certain companies and creating a "genesis moment" for others. Edgar F. Codd's groundbreaking work in the 1970s on the relational model that spawned the whole relational database management system (RDBMS) industry was definitely a significant innovation. Immediately following Codd's innovation was the introduction of structured query language (SQL), which was created by Donald D. Chamberlin and Raymond F. Boyce to provide a common programming language for managing data stored in a RDBMS. The RDBMS and SQL technologies became the de facto standards for data management and processing and have continued to hold sway over the industry.

Now, if you were to ask us to name the major innovation of the "noughties" (we're still getting used to this nickname for the aught years, from 2000 to 2009), we'd pick Apache Hadoop, of course — the amazing new technology for big data management, analysis, and processing. However, few if any new IT technologies, no matter how innovative and attractive, can uproot established standards and start over with a clean slate. For Hadoop to truly have a broad impact on the IT Industry and live up to its true potential, it needed to "play nice" with the older technologies: It had to support SQL; integrate with, and extend, the RDBMS; and enable IT professionals who lack skills in using Java MapReduce to take advantage of its features. For this reason (and others, which we discuss later in this chapter), Apache Hive was created at Facebook by a team of engineers who were led by Jeff Hammerbacher. Hive, a top-level Apache project and a vital component within the Apache Hadoop ecosystem, drives several leading big-data use cases and has brought Hadoop into data centers across the globe.

Saying Hello to Hive

To make a long story short, Hive provides Hadoop with a bridge to the RDBMS world and provides an SQL dialect known as Hive Query Language (HiveQL), which can be used to perform SQL-like tasks. That's the big news, but there's more to Hive than meets the eye, as they say, or more applications of this new technology than you can present in a standard elevator pitch. For example, Hive also makes possible the concept known as enterprise data warehouse (EDW) augmentation, a leading use case for Apache Hadoop, where data warehouses are set up as RDBMSs built specifically for data analysis and reporting. Now, some experts will argue that Hadoop (with Hive, HBase, Sqoop, and its assorted buddies) can replace the EDW, but we disagree. We believe that Apache Hadoop is a great *addition* to the enterprise and that it can *augment* (as mentioned earlier in this paragraph) and complement existing EDWs. This particular debate is also the subject of Chapter 10, so check out our discussion there. For now, we leave that debate alone and simply explain in this chapter how Hive, HBase, and Sqoop enable EDW augmentation.

Closely associated with RDBMS/EDW technology is extract, transform, and load (ETL) technology. To grasp what ETL does, it helps to know that, in many use cases, data cannot be immediately loaded into the relational database — it must first be extracted from its native source, transformed into an appropriate format, and then loaded into the RDBMS or EDW. For example, a company or an organization might extract unstructured text data from an Internet forum, transform the data into a structured format that's both valuable and useful, and then load the structured data into its EDW.

As you make your way through this chapter (if you choose to read it that way), you can see that Hive is a powerful ETL tool in its own right, along with the major player in this realm: Apache Pig. (See Chapter 8 for more on Apache's porcine offering.) Again, users may try to set up Hive and Pig as *the* new ETL tools for the data center. (Let them try.) As with the debate over

EDW versus Apache Hadoop, we see these Apache Hadoop technologies not as direct *replacements* for existing ETL tools but instead as powerful new ETL tools to be used when appropriate.

Last but not least, Apache Hive gives you powerful analytical tools, all within the framework of HiveQL. These tools should look and feel quite familiar to IT professionals who understand how to use SQL. We provide you with hands-on examples of Hive analytics later in this chapter, but first we discuss the architecture of Hive in the next section.

Seeing How the Hive is Put Together

In this section, we illustrate for you the architecture of Apache Hive and explain its various components, as shown in the illustration in Figure 13-1.

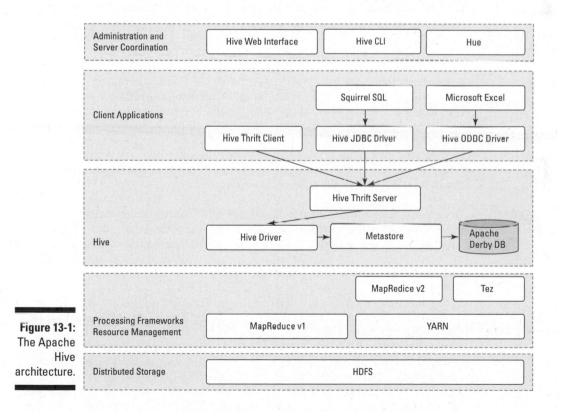

Figure 13-1:
The Apache
Hive
architecture.

As you examine the elements shown in Figure 13-1, you can see at the bottom that Hive sits on top of the Hadoop Distributed File System (HDFS) and MapReduce systems. In the case of MapReduce, Figure 13-1 shows both the Hadoop 1 and Hadoop 2 components. With Hadoop 1, Hive queries are converted to MapReduce code and executed using the MapReduce v1 (MRv1) infrastructure, like the JobTracker and TaskTracker. With Hadoop 2, YARN has decoupled resource management and scheduling from the MapReduce framework. (For more on MapReduce and YARN, check out Chapters 6 and 7.) Hive queries can still be converted to MapReduce code and executed, now with MapReduce v2 (MRv2) and the YARN infrastructure.

There is a new framework under development called Apache Tez, which is designed to improve Hive performance for batch-style queries and support smaller interactive (also known as *real-time*) queries. At the time of writing, the Apache Tez project is still in incubation, and doesn't yet have a production-ready release.

If it helps you visualize how all the pieces fit together, think of the HDFS (see Chapter 4) and MapReduce systems (see Chapter 6) as being parts of the Apache Hadoop operating system, with Hive — as well as other components, such as HBase, described in Chapter 12 — as higher-level functions or applications. (If you read the chapters in this part of the book, you can see a common theme emerge: HDFS provides the storage, and MapReduce provides the parallel processing capability for higher-level functions within the Hadoop ecosystem.) Moving up the diagram, you find the Hive Driver, which compiles, optimizes, and executes the HiveQL. The Hive Driver may choose to execute HiveQL statements and commands locally or spawn a MapReduce job, depending on the task at hand. (We discuss MapReduce within the context of Hive later in this chapter.) The Hive Driver stores table metadata in the metastore and its database.

We assume that you have some familiarity with SQL and the relational database model from the world of RDBMSs. A *table* or *relation* is composed of vertical columns and horizontal rows. *Cells* are stored where the rows and columns intersect. If you're not familiar with SQL and the relational database model, you can find helpful learning sources using your favorite search engine.

By default, Hive includes the Apache Derby RDBMS configured with the metastore in what's called embedded mode. *Embedded mode* means that the Hive Driver, the metastore, and Apache Derby are all running in one Java Virtual Machine (JVM). This configuration is fine for learning purposes, but embedded mode can support only a single Hive session, so it normally isn't used in multi-user production environments. Two other modes exist — *local* and *remote* — which can better support multiple Hive sessions in production environments. Also, you can configure any RDBMS that's compliant with the Java Database Connectivity (JDBC) Application Programming Interface (API) suite. (Examples here include MySQL and DB2.)

The key to application support is the Hive Thrift Server (see Figure 13-1), which enables a rich set of clients to access the Hive subsystem. We've included the open source SQuirreL SQL client, which can be found at `http://squirrel-sql.sourceforge.net`, as an example. The main point is that any JDBC-compliant application can access Hive via the bundled JDBC driver. The same statement applies to clients compliant with Open Database Connectivity (ODBC) — for example, unixODBC and the isql utility, which are typically bundled with Linux, enable access to Hive from remote Linux clients. Additionally, if you use Microsoft Excel, you'll be pleased to know that you can access Hive after you install the Microsoft ODBC driver on your client system. Finally, if you need to access Hive from programming languages other than Java (PHP or Python, for example), Apache Thrift is the answer. Apache Thrift clients connect to Hive via the Hive Thrift Server, just as the JDBC and ODBC clients do.

For more information on Apache Thrift see Chapter 12.

To continue with the Hive architecture drawing in Figure 13-1, note that Hive includes a Command Line Interface (CLI), where you can use a Linux terminal window to issue queries and administrative commands directly to the Hive Driver. (We use the Hive CLI several times in this chapter to demonstrate HiveQL.) If a graphical approach is more your speed, there's also a handy web interface so that you can access your Hive-managed tables and data via your favorite browser.

There is another web browser technology known as Hue that provides a graphical user interface (GUI) to Apache Hive. Some Hadoop users like to have a GUI at their disposal instead of just a command line interface (CLI). Along with Hive, Hue supports other key Hadoop technologies as well like HDFS, MapReduce/YARN, HBase, Zookeeper, Oozie, Pig, and Sqoop. We think you'll like the name for Hue's Apache Hive GUI – it's called Beeswax. Hue is also an open source project and you can find it at `http://gethue.com`.

Getting Started with Apache Hive

As with most technological matters, there's no better way to see what's what than to install the software and give it a test run — Hive is no exception. And, as with other technologies in the Hadoop ecosystem, it doesn't take long to get started.

If you have the time and the network bandwidth, it's always best to download an entire Apache Hadoop distribution with all the technologies integrated and ready to run. You can find a list of Apache Hadoop bundles at

```
http://wiki.apache.org/hadoop/Distributions%20and%20
          Commercial%20Support
```

If you take the full-distribution route, a popular approach for learning the ins and outs of Hive is to run your Hadoop distribution in a Linux virtual machine (VM) on a 64-bit-capable laptop with sufficient RAM. (Eight gigabytes or more of RAM tends to work well if Windows 7 is hosting your VM, although we've met engineers who live dangerously with less.) You also need Java 6 or later and — of course — a supported operating system: Linux, Mac OS X, or Cygwin, to provide a Linux shell for Windows users. (We use Red Hat Linux on Windows 7 in a VMware virtual machine for the sample environment.)

The setup steps run something like this:

1. **Download the latest Hive release from this site:**

   ```
   http://hive.apache.org/releases.html
   ```

   For this book, we downloaded Hive version 11.0. You also need the Hadoop and MapReduce subsystems, so be sure to complete Step 2.

2. **Download Hadoop version 1.2.1 from this site:**

   ```
   http://hadoop.apache.org/releases.html
   ```

3. **Using the commands in Listing 13-1 (the listing following this step list), place the releases in separate directories, and then uncompress and untar them. (*Untar* is one of those pesky Unix terms which simply means to expand an archived software package.)**

4. **Using the commands in Listing 13-2 (again, following this step list), set up your Apache Hive environment variables, including HADOOP_ HOME, JAVA_HOME, HIVE_HOME and PATH, in your shell profile script.**

5. **Create the Hive configuration file that you'll use to define specific Hive configuration settings.**

   The Apache Hive distribution includes a template configuration file that provides all default settings for Hive. To customize Hive for your environment, all you need to do is copy the template file to the file named `hive-site.xml` and edit it. Listing 13-3 shows the steps to accomplish this task.

   Because you're running Hive in stand-alone mode on a virtual machine rather than in a real-life Apache Hadoop cluster, configure the system to use local storage rather than the HDFS: Simply set the `hive. metastore.warehouse.dir` parameter. As we demonstrate in the next section, when you start a Hive client, the $HIVE_HOME environment variable tells the client that it should look for your configuration file (hive-site.xml) in the conf directory.

Listing 13-1:   Installing Apache Hadoop and Hive

```
$ mkdir hadoop; cp hadoop-1.2.1.tar.gz hadoop; cd hadoop
$ gunzip hadoop-1.2.1.tar.gz
$ tar xvf *.tar
$ mkdir hive; cp hive-0.11.0.tar.gz hive; cd hive
$ gunzip hive-0.11.0.tar.gz
$ tar xvf *.tar
```

Listing 13-2:   Setting Up Apache Hive Environment Variables in .bashrc

```
export HADOOP_HOME=/home/user/Hive/hadoop/hadoop-1.2.1
export JAVA_HOME=/opt/jdk
export HIVE_HOME=/home/user/Hive/hive-0.11.0
export PATH=$HADOOP_HOME/bin:$HIVE_HOME/bin:
          $JAVA_HOME/bin:$PATH
```

Listing 13-3:   Setting Up the hive-site.xml File

```
$ cd $HIVE_HOME/conf
$ cp hive-default.xml.template hive-site.xml

(Using your favorite editor, modify the hive-site.xml file
          so that it only includes the "hive.metastore.
          warehouse.dir" property for now. When finished
          it will look like the XML file below. Note
          that we removed the comments to shorten the
          listing):

<?xml version="1.0"?>
<?xml-stylesheet type="text/xsl"
          href="configuration.xsl"?>
<configuration>
<!-- Hive Execution Parameters -->
<property>
   <name>hive.metastore.warehouse.dir</name>
   <value>/home/biadmin/Hive/warehouse</value>
   <description>location of default database for the
          warehouse</description>
</property>
</configuration>
```

Both Hadoop and Hive support a local mode configuration, which is the approach we're leveraging in this chapter. If you already have a Hadoop cluster configured and running, you need to set the `hive.metastore.warehouse.dir` configuration variable to the HDFS directory where you intend to store your Hive warehouse, set the `mapred.job.tracker` configuration variable to point to your Hadoop JobTracker, and (most likely) set up a distributed metastore. For the latest up-to-date Hive installation instructions, see the page at

```
https://cwiki.apache.org/confluence/display/Hive/
        GettingStarted
```

That's all you need to do to get started with Apache Hive! In the next section, you meet several Hive clients and get to run your first Hive commands.

Examining the Hive Clients

Earlier in this chapter (refer to Figure 13-1), you can see that there are quite a number of client options for Hive. It's truly beyond the scope of this chapter to show you how to leverage all the client options, so we picked three that we believe should prove quite useful when the time comes to analyze data using HiveQL. The first client is the Hive command-line interface (CLI), followed by a web browser using the Hive Web Interface (HWI) Server, and, finally, the open source SQuirreL client using the JDBC driver. Each of these client options can play a particular role as you work with Hive to analyze data.

The Hive CLI client

To master the finer points of the Hive CLI client, it might help to revisit the (somewhat busy-looking) Hive architecture diagram shown in Figure 13-1. In Figure 13-2, we've streamlined the original figure to focus only on the components that are required when running the CLI.

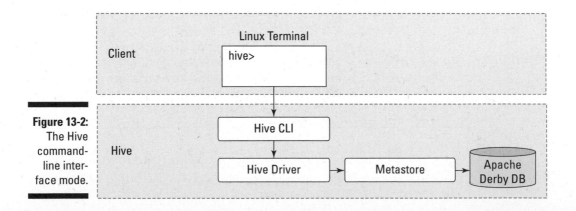

Figure 13-2:
The Hive command-line interface mode.

Figure 13-2 illustrates the components of Hive that are needed when running the CLI on a Hadoop cluster. In the examples in this chapter, you run Hive in local mode, which uses local storage, rather than the HDFS, for your data.

To run the Hive CLI, you execute the `hive` command and specify the CLI as the service you want to run. In Listing 13-4, you can see the command that's required as well as some of our first HiveQL statements. (We have included a steps annotation using the A-B-C model in the listing to direct your attention to the key commands.)

Listing 13-4: Using the Hive CLI to Create a Table

```
(A) $ $HIVE_HOME/bin hive --service cli
(B) hive> set hive.cli.print.current.db=true;
(C) hive (default)> CREATE DATABASE ourfirstdatabase;
OK
Time taken: 3.756 seconds
(D) hive (default)> USE ourfirstdatabase;
OK
Time taken: 0.039 seconds
(E) hive (ourfirstdatabase)> CREATE TABLE our_first_table
         (
                         > FirstName      STRING,
                         > LastName       STRING,
                         > EmployeeId     INT);
OK
Time taken: 0.043 seconds
hive (ourfirstdatabase)> quit;
(F) $ ls /home/biadmin/Hive/warehouse/ourfirstdatabase.db
our_first_table
```

The first command in Listing 13-4 (see Step A) starts the Hive CLI using the `$HIVE_HOME` environment variable (refer to Listing 13-2). The `-service cli` command-line option directs the Hive system to start the command-line interface, though you could have chosen other servers. (In fact, you can try a few later in this section.) Next, in Step B, you tell the Hive CLI to print your current working database so that you know where you are in the namespace. (This statement will make sense after we explain how to use the next command, so hold tight.) Continuing in Listing 13-4, in Step C you use HiveQL's data definition language (DDL) to create your first database. (Remember that databases in Hive are simply namespaces where particular tables reside; because a set of tables can be thought of as a database or schema, you could have used the term `SCHEMA` in place of `DATABASE` to accomplish the same result.) More specifically, you're using DDL to tell the system to create a database called `ourfirstdatabase` and then to make this database the default for subsequent HiveQL DDL commands using the `USE` command in Step D. In Step E, you create your first table and give it the (quite appropriate) name `our_first_table`. (Until now, you may have believed that it looks a lot like SQL, with perhaps a few minor differences in syntax depending on which RDBMS you're accustomed to — and you would have been right.)

The last command, in Step F, carries out a directory listing of your chosen Hive warehouse directory so that you can see that `our_first_table` has in fact been stored on disk.

You set the `hive.metastore.warehouse.dir` variable to point to the local directory `/home/biadmin/Hive/warehouse` in your Linux virtual machine rather than use the HDFS as you would on a proper Hadoop cluster.

After you've created a table, it's interesting to view the table's metadata. In production environments, you might have dozens of tables or more, so it's helpful to be able to review the table structure from time to time. You *can* use a HiveQL command to do this using the Hive CLI, but the Hive Web Interface (HWI) Server provides a helpful interface for this type of operation. (More on HWI in the next section.)

Using the HWI Server instead of the CLI can also be more secure. Careful consideration must be made when using the CLI in production environments because the machine running the CLI must have access to the entire Hadoop cluster. Therefore, system administrators typically put in place tools like the secure shell (`ssh`) in order to provide controlled and secure access to the machine running the CLI as well as to provide network encryption. However, when the HWI Server is employed, a user can only access Hive data allowed by the HWI Server via his or her web browser

The web browser as Hive client

Using the Hive CLI requires only one command to start the Hive shell, but when you want to access Hive using a web browser, you first need to start the HWI Server and then point your browser to the port on which the server is listening. Figure 13-3 illustrates how this type of Hive client configuration might work. (Note that even though you might not be using the Hive CLI, it's not an optional component and is still present.)

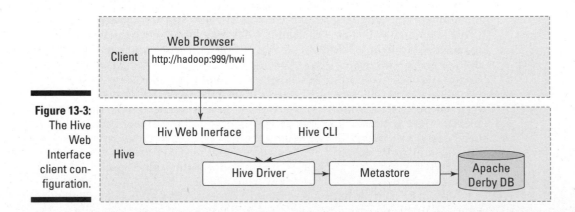

Figure 13-3:
The Hive Web Interface client configuration.

The following steps show you what you need to do before you can start the HWI Server:

1. **Using the commands in Listing 13-5 (following this list), configure the** `$HIVE_HOME/conf/hive-site.xml` **file to ensure that Hive can find and load the HWI's Java server pages.**

2. **The HWI Server requires Apache Ant libraries to run, so you need to download more files. Download Ant from the Apache site at** `http://ant.apache.org/bindownload.cgi`.

3. **Install Ant using the following commands:**

```
mkdir ant
cp apache-ant-1.9.2-bin.tar.gz ant; cd ant
gunzip apache-ant-1.9.2-bin.tar.gz
tar xvf apache-ant-1.9.2-bin.tar
```

4. **Set the** `$ANT_LIB` **environment variable and start the HWI Server by using the following commands:**

```
$ export ANT_LIB=/home/user/ant/apache-ant-1.9.2/lib
$ bin/hive --service hwi
13/09/24 16:54:37 INFO hwi.HWIServer: HWI is starting up
...
13/09/24 16:54:38 INFO mortbay.log: Started
        SocketConnector@0.0.0.0:9999
```

Listing 13-5:   Configuring the $HIVE_HOME/conf/hive-site.xml file

```
<property>
    <name>hive.hwi.war.file</name>
    <value>${HIVE_HOME}/lib/hive_hwi.war</value>
    <description>This is the WAR file with the
jsp
    content for Hive Web Interface</description>
</property>
```

In a production environment, you'd probably configure two other properties: `hive.hwi.listen.host` and `hive.hwi.listen.port`. You can use the first property to set the IP address of the system running your HWI Server, and use the second to set the port that the HWI Server listens on. In this exercise, you use the default settings: With the HWI Server now running, you simply enter the URL `http://localhost:9999/hwi/` into your web browser and view the metadata for `our_first_table` (refer to Listing 13-4). Figure 13-4 shows what the screen looks like after selecting the Browse Schema link followed by `ourfirstdatabase` and `our_first_table`.

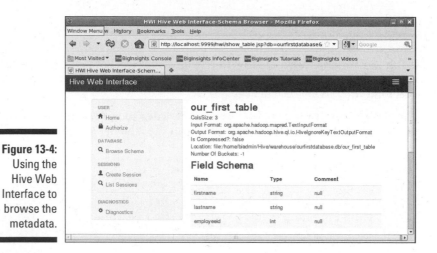

Figure 13-4:
Using the
Hive Web
Interface to
browse the
metadata.

In production environments, working with the HWI Server can save you the time of loading the Hive distribution on every client — instead, you just point your browser to the server running the HWI. Additionally, you can use the HWI Server to view Hive Thrift Server diagnostics and query tables. The HWI Server allows you to set up batch sessions for long-running queries. To set up a session, you simply click the Create Session link (refer to Figure 13-4).

SQuirreL as Hive client with the JDBC Driver

The last Hive client we discuss and demonstrate in this chapter is the open source tool SQuirreL SQL. You can download this universal SQL client from the SourceForge website: `http://sourceforge.net`. It provides a user interface to Hive and simplifies the tasks of querying large tables and analyzing data with Apache Hive.

Figure 13-5 illustrates how the Hive architecture would work when using tools such as SQuirreL.

In the figure, you can see that the SQuirreL client uses the JDBC APIs to pass commands to the Hive Driver by way of the Server.

For a helpful example of a Hive Java client connecting to the system via the JDBC interface, see

```
https://cwiki.apache.org/confluence/display/Hive/
        HiveClient#HiveClient-JDBC
```

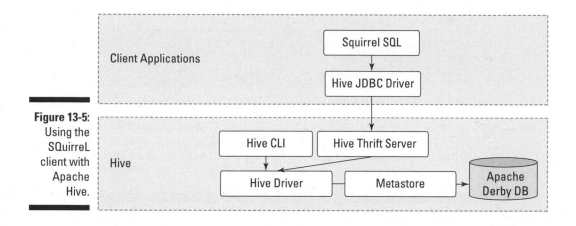

Figure 13-5:
Using the
SQuirreL
client with
Apache
Hive.

Follow these steps to get SQuirreL running:

1. **Start the Hive Thrift Server using the command in Listing 13-6 (follow-ing this list).**

2. **Download the latest SQuirreL distribution from the SourceForge site into a directory of your choice.**

   For this example, we downloaded `squirrel-sql-3.5.0-standard.tar.gz` from `http://sourceforge.net/projects/squirrel-sql/files/1-stable/3.5.0-plainzip`.

3. **Uncompress the SQuirreL package using the** gunzip **command and expand the archive using the** tar **command.**

   ```
   gunzip squirrel-sql-3.5.0-standard.tar.gz; tar
   xvf squirrel-sql-3.5.0-standard.tar.gz
   ```

4. **Change to the new SQuirreL release directory and start the tool using the following command.**

   ```
   $ cd squirrel-sql-3.5.0-standard;./squirrel-
   sql.sh
   ```

5. **Follow the directions for running SQuirreL with Apache Hive at**

   ```
   https://cwiki.apache.org/confluence/display/Hive/
       HiveJDBCInterface - HiveJDBCIntcrface-
       IntegrationwithSQuirrelSQLClient
   ```

   Note that the instructions for including the Hadoop core `.jar` file may differ depending on the Hadoop release. In this case, the Hadoop `.jar` file was named `hadoop-core-1.2.1.jar`, so including `$HADOOP_HOME/hadoop-*-core.jar` per the online instructions was incorrect. We had to use `$HADOOP_HOME/hadoop-core*.jar`.

Listing 13-6:   Starting the Hive Thrift Server

```
$ $HIVE_HOME/bin/hive --service hiveserver -p 10000 -v
Starting Hive Thrift Server
Starting Hive Thrift Server on port 10000 with 100 min
          worker threads and 2147483647 max worker
          threads
```

This is all that's required to begin using the SQuirreL graphical user interface. Figure 13-6 shows some HiveQL commands running against the Hive Driver — similar to the commands you ran earlier, with the CLI; refer to Listing 13-4.

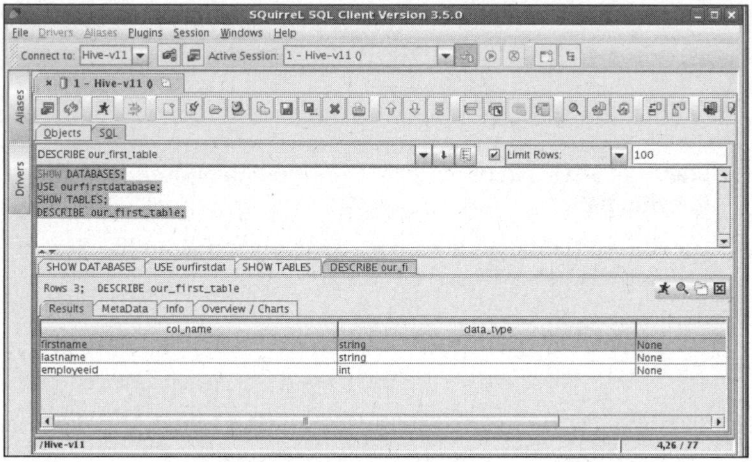

Figure 13-6:
Using the
SQuirreL
SQL client to
run HiveQL
commands.

The Apache Hive 0.11 release also includes a new Hive Thrift Server called HiveServer2. When configured correctly, HiveServer2 can support multiple clients (a CLI client and a SQuirreL client at the same time, for example) and it provides better security. For more information on HiveServer2 see: https://cwiki.apache.org/confluence/display/Hive/Setting+up+HiveServer2.

Now that you know how to leverage some indispensable Hive client technologies, we want to start you on your survey of the HiveQL. Your first stop: Hive data types.

Working with Hive Data Types

Listing 13-7 goes to the trouble of creating a table that leverages all (as of this writing) Hive-supported data types.

Listing 13-7: HiveQL-Supported Data Types

```
$ ./hive --service cli
hive> CREATE DATABASE data_types_db;
OK
Time taken: 0.119 seconds
hive> USE data_types_db;
OK
Time taken: 0.018 seconds
(1)Hive> CREATE TABLE data_types_table (
(2)  > our_tinyint    TINYINT     COMMENT '1 byte signed integer',
(3)  > our_smallint   SMALLINT    COMMENT '2 byte signed integer',
(4)  > our_int        INT         COMMENT '4 byte signed integer',
(5)  > our_bigint     BIGINT      COMMENT '8 byte signed integer',
(6)  > our_float      FLOAT       COMMENT 'Single precision floating point',
(7)  > our_double     DOUBLE      COMMENT 'Double precision floating point',
(8)  > our_decimal    DECIMAL     COMMENT 'Precise decimal type based
(9)  >                                    on Java BigDecimal Object',
(10) > our_timestamp  TIMESTAMP   COMMENT 'YYYY-MM-DD HH:MM:SS.fffffffff"
(11) >                                    (9 decimal place precision)',
(12) > our_boolean    BOOLEAN     COMMENT 'TRUE or FALSE boolean data type',
(13) > our_string     STRING      COMMENT 'Character String data type',
(14) > our_binary     BINARY      COMMENT 'Data Type for Storing arbitrary
(15) >                                    number of bytes',
(16) > our_array      ARRAY<TINYINT>  COMMENT 'A collection of fields all of
(17) >                                         the same data type indexed BY
(18) >                                         an integer',
(19) > our_map       MAP<STRING,INT> COMMENT 'A Collection of Key,Value Pairs
(20) >                                        where the Key is a Primitive
(21) >                                        Type and the Value can be
(22) >                                        anything.  The chosen data
(23) >                                        types for the keys and values
(24) >                                        must remain the same per map',
(25) > our_struct     STRUCT<first : SMALLINT, second : FLOAT, third : STRING>
(26) >                                COMMENT 'A nested complex data
(27) >                                        structure',
(28) > our_union      UNIONTYPE<INT,FLOAT,STRING>
(29) >                                COMMENT 'A Complex Data Type that can
(30) >                                        hold One of its Possible Data
(31) >                                        Types at Once')
(32) > COMMENT 'Table illustrating all Apache Hive data types'
(33) > ROW FORMAT DELIMITED
(34) > FIELDS TERMINATED BY ','
(35) > COLLECTION ITEMS TERMINATED BY '|'
(36) > MAP KEYS TERMINATED BY '^'
(37) > LINES TERMINATED BY '\n'
(38) > STORED AS TEXTFILE
(39) > TBLPROPERTIES ('creator'='Bruce Brown', 'created_at'='Sat Sep 21
             20:46:32 EDT 2013');
OK
Time taken: 0.886 seconds
```

We've included line numbers with the HiveQL to make it easier to study the table. You can see from the CREATE TABLE statement (refer to Line 1) all the various data types at your disposal (again, as of this writing) in Hive 0.11. One in particular, DECIMAL, is new as of Hive 0.11, so whenever Hive 0.12 is released, check to see whether it has more. (**Hint:** Watch for the type named DATE.)

Consult the Data Types page in the Apache Hive Language Manual (https://cwiki.apache.org/confluence/display/Hive/LanguageManual+Types) to watch for new data types as the Hive community continues to develop and create new, innovative features in Hive.

Notice in the table that after every column we created (see Lines 2–31), we wrote a comment (using the HiveQL reserved keyword - COMMENT) giving you information about the Hive data type of the column. Hive supports the Comment feature as a way to document the columns in your tables. Also, Line 32 allows you to add a comment for the entire table. Line 39 starts with the keyword TBLPROPERTIES, which provides a way for you to add metadata to the table. This information can be viewed later, after the table is created, with other HiveQL commands such as DESCRIBE EXTENDED table_name.

Keep in mind that Hive has primitive data types as well as complex data types. The last four columns (see Lines 16–31) in our_datatypes_table are complex data types: ARRAY, MAP, STRUCT, and UNIONTYPE. Their presence provides more proof (if proof is needed) that Hive supports a rich set of data types that enables you to manage diverse data, all under HiveQL.

Finally, Lines 33–38 in the CREATE TABLE statement show off a particularly powerful feature of Hive. Here, the lines let you define the file format when your table gets stored in HDFS and define how fields and rows are delimited. Actually Hive allows you to specify the file format and record format separately. We discuss this powerful feature of Hive in greater detail in the next section as we tell you more about creating Hive databases and tables.

Creating and Managing Databases and Tables

To fully grasp Hive database and table creation in all its splendor, you need a thorough grounding in what's referred to as Hive's data definition language (DDL). You get that grounding in this section, starting with database or schema creation.

Managing Hive databases

Earlier in this chapter, Listing 13-4 shows you the basics of creating data-bases or schemas with Hive, but they're just that — the basics. Quite a few more features are out there that you'll find useful; Listing 13-8 illustrates a few of them.

Listing 13-8:   Creating, Dropping, and Altering Databases in Apache Hive

```
(1) $ $HIVE_HOME/bin hive --service cli
(2) hive> set hive.cli.print.current.db=true;
(3) hive (default)> USE ourfirstdatabase;
(4) hive (ourfirstdatabase)> ALTER DATABASE
        ourfirstdatabase SET DBPROPERTIES
        ('creator'='Bruce Brown',
        'created_for'='Learning Hive DDL');
OK
Time taken: 0.138 seconds
(5) hive (ourfirstdatabase)> DESCRIBE DATABASE EXTENDED
        ourfirstdatabase;
OK
ourfirstdatabase
        file:/home/biadmin/Hive/warehouse/
        ourfirstdatabase.db   {created_for=Learning
        Hive DDL, creator=Bruce Brown}
Time taken: 0.084 seconds, Fetched: 1 row(s)CREATE
        (DATABASE|SCHEMA) [IF NOT EXISTS] database_name
(6) hive (ourfirstdatabase)> DROP DATABASE
        ourfirstdatabase CASCADE;
OK
Time taken: 0.132 seconds
```

Listing 13-8 picks up where Listing 13-4 left off, with you having already cre-ated a database aptly named ourfirstdatabase. In Line 4 of Listing 13-8, you're now altering the database to include two new metadata items: creator and created_for. As you can imagine, including custom metadata with your database (and tables, as we describe earlier) can be quite useful for docu-mentation purposes and coordination within your working group. On Line 5, you get the command to view the metadata, and on Line 6 you're dropping the entire database — removing it from the server, in other words — with the DROP command and CASCADE keyword. (Without the CASCADE keyword, you couldn't drop the database because the server has still stored our_first_ table — refer to Listing 13-4.) You can use the DROP TABLE command to delete individual tables or you can use the brute-force technique, as you do here, to forcefully remove everything from the namespace.

Creating and managing tables with Hive

After you have a good working knowledge of Hive database creation and management under your belt, it's time to turn your attention to table creation and management. Your first stop? Hive table file and record formats. Apache Hive lets you define the record format separately from the file format. This powerful feature — coupled with the complex data types you leveraged in Listing 13-7 — enables the Hive user to analyze and query unstructured and semistructured data that RDBMSs cannot handle!

Defining table file formats

In the "Working with Hive Data Types" section, earlier in this chapter, we describe how to create a table (`data_types_table`) that includes all Hive 0.11–supported data types. We point out there that Lines 33–38 illustrate a powerful feature in Hive, and we promise to discuss that feature in this chapter. Well, here we are, as promised. To refresh your memory, we've copied Lines 33–38 into Listing 13-9 so that you don't have to flip back and review the Hive Query Language (HiveQL) — refer to Listing 13-7.

Listing 13-9:   Defining the Hive Row Format for the `TEXTFILE` File Format

```
(1)Hive> CREATE TABLE data_types_table (
...
(33) > ROW FORMAT DELIMITED
(34) > FIELDS TERMINATED BY ','
(35) > COLLECTION ITEMS TERMINATED BY '|'
(36) > MAP KEYS TERMINATED BY '^'
(37) > LINES TERMINATED BY '\n'
(38) > STORED AS TEXTFILE
...
(39) > TBLPROPERTIES ('creator'='Bruce Brown',
            'created_at'='Sat Sep 21 20:46:32 EDT 2013');
```

Lines 33–37 define the Hive *row format* for your `data_types_table` and provide specifics on how fields will be separated or delimited whenever you insert or load data into the table. (You can find out more in the next section about the various techniques for loading data into tables.) Line 38 defines the Hive *file format* — a text file — when the data is stored in the HDFS (or local file system, in this case). You may be wondering why `our_first_table` (refer to Listing 13-4) lacks these extra keywords and delimiters. The reason is that Hive tables default to the configuration in Listing 13-10 unless you override the default settings, as we do above in Listing 13-9.

Listing 13-10:   Hive Table Default Row and File Format

```
CREATE TABLE ...
         ...
ROW FORMAT DELIMITED
FIELDS TERMINATED BY '\001'
COLLECTION ITEMS TERMINATED BY '\002'
MAP KEYS TERMINATED BY '\003'
LINES TERMINATED BY '\n'
STORED AS TEXTFILE
...
```

We chose to have you override the defaults in Listing 13-7 and 13-9 to make it easier to build a readable data file to load into the data_types_table, and to illustrate this powerful row formatting feature in Hive. We show you how to actually create a readable data file and load it into the data_types_ table later in this chapter, in the section entitled "Seeing How the Hive Data Manipulation Language Works" in Listing 13-13.

So far, we have been using the default TEXTFILE format for your Hive table records. However, as you know, text files are slower to process, and they consume a lot of disk space unless you compress them. For these reasons and more, the Apache Hive community came up with several choices for storing our tables on the HDFS. The following list describes the file formats you can choose from as of Hive version 0.11.

- ✔ **TEXTFILE:** The default file format for Hive records. Alphanumeric characters from the Unicode standard (see www.unicode.org) are used to store your data.

- ✔ **SEQUENCEFILE:** The format for binary files composed of key/value pairs. Sequence files, which are used heavily by Hadoop, are often good choices for Hive table storage, especially if you want to integrate Hive with other technologies in the Hadoop ecosystem.

- ✔ **RCFILE:** Stores records in a column-oriented fashion rather than a row-oriented fashion — like the TEXTFILE format approach. Using the RCFILE format makes sense when tables have a large number of columns, but only a few columns are typically accessed. (RCFILE stands for *record* columnar *file*.)

- ✔ **ORC:** A format (new as of Hive 0.11) that has significant optimizations to improve Hive reads and writes and the processing of tables. (ORC stands for *optimized* row columnar and has nothing to do goblins loyal to Lord Sauron.) For example, ORC files include optimizations for Hive complex types and new types such as DECIMAL. Also lightweight indexes are included with ORC files to improve performance. For a complete list of new ORC file format features, consult the Hive Language Manual at https://cwiki.apache.org/confluence/display/Hive/ LanguageManual+ORC

✔ **INPUTFORMAT, OUTPUTFORMAT:** Lets you specify the Java class that will read data from the Hive table. OUTPUTFORMAT does the same thing for writing data to the Hive table. The keywords in the earlier table entries (TEXTFILE, for example) provide shortened syntax so that you don't have to specify both INPUTFORMAT and OUTPUTFORMAT for every CREATE TABLE statement. Of course, it enables customization and can be quite powerful under the right circumstances. To see the default settings for the table, simply execute a DESCRIBE EXTENDED *tablename* HiveQL statement and you'll see the INPUTFORMAT and OUTPUTFORMAT classes for your table.

Defining table record formats

The Java technology that Hive uses to process records and map them to column data types in Hive tables (like you defined in Listing 13-7) is called *SerDe,* which is short for *SerializerDeserializer.* Figure 13-7 illustrates how SerDes are leveraged and it will help you understand how Hive keeps file formats separate from record formats.

How Hive Reads and Writes Records

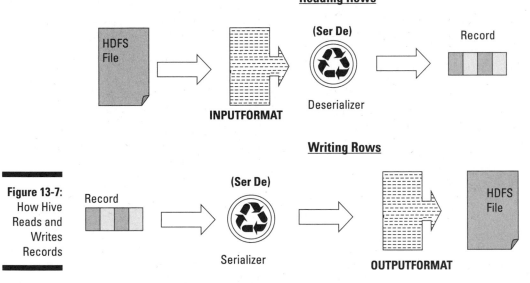

Figure 13-7: How Hive Reads and Writes Records

So the first thing to notice from Figure 13-7 is the INPUTFORMAT object. INPUTFORMAT allows you to specify your own Java class should you want Hive to read from a different file format. In the examples so far, you have been using STORED AS TEXTFILE, which is easier than writing INPUTFORMAT org.apache.hadoop.mapred.TextInputFormat — the whole Java package tree and class name for the default text file input format object, in other words. The same is true of the OUTPUTFORMAT object. Instead of writing out the whole Java package tree and class name, the STORED AS TEXTFILE statement takes care of all of that for you. Now, we've been saying that Hive allows you to separate your record format from your file format so how exactly do you accomplish this? Simple, you either replace STORED AS TEXTFILE with something like STORED AS RCFILE, or you can create your own Java class and specify the input and output classes using INPUTFORMAT packagepath.classname and OUTPUTFORMAT packagepath.classname.

Finally notice that when Hive is reading data from the HDFS (or local file system), a Java Deserializer formats the data into a record that maps to table column data types. This would characterize the data flow for a HiveQL SELECT statement which you'll be able to try out in "Querying and analyzing data" section below. When Hive is writing data, a Java Serializer accepts the record Hive uses and translates it such that the OUTPUTFORMAT class can write it to the HDFS (or local file system). This would characterize the data flow for a HiveQL CREATE-TABLE-AS-SELECT statement which you'll be able to try out in "Mastering the Hive data-manipulation language" section below. So the INPUTFORMAT, OUTPUTFORMAT and SerDe objects allow Hive to separate the table record format from the table file format. You'll be able to see this in action in two examples below but first we want to expose you to some SerDe options.

Hive bundles a number of SerDes for you to choose from, and you'll find a larger number available from third parties if you search online. You can also develop your own SerDes if you have a more unusual data type that you want to manage with a Hive table. (Possible examples here are video data and e-mail data.) In the list below, we describe some of the SerDes provided with Hive as well as one third-party option that you may find useful.

- ✔ **LazySimpleSerDe:** The default SerDe that's used with the TEXTFILE format; it would be used with our_first_table from Listing 13-4 and with data_types_table from Listing 13-7.

- ✔ **ColumnarSerDe:** Used with the RCFILE format.

- ✔ **RegexSerDe:** The regular expression SerDe, which ships with Hive to enable the parsing of text files, RegexSerDe can form a powerful approach for building structured data in Hive tables from unstructured blogs, semi-structured log files, e-mails, tweets, and other data from social media. Regular expressions allow you to extract meaningful information (an e-mail address, for example) with HiveQL from an unstructured or semi-structured text document incompatible with traditional SQL and RDBMSs.

- ✔ **HBaseSerDe:** Included with Hive to enables it to integrate with HBase. You can store Hive tables in HBase by leveraging this SerDe.

- ✔ **JSONSerDe:** A third-party SerDe for reading and writing JSON data records with Hive. We quickly found (via Google and GitHub) two JSON SerDes by searching online for the phrase *json serde for hive*.

- ✔ **AvroSerDe:** Included with Hive so that you can read and write Avro data in Hive tables.

Reviewing the Language Manual DDL (found at: `https://cwiki.apache.org/confluence/display/Hive/LanguageManual+DDL`) can be very helpful before you start creating your tables. We've included an excerpt from the manual below, which shows you (in bold print) all of the options we've been discussing in this section.

```
CREATE [EXTERNAL] TABLE [IF NOT EXISTS]
        [db_name.]table_name
  ...   (Skipping some lines for brevity)
  [ROW FORMAT row_format] [STORED AS file_format]
  | STORED BY 'storage.handler.class.name' [WITH
        SERDEPROPERTIES (...)] ]
  ...   (Skipping some lines for brevity)
row_format
  : DELIMITED [FIELDS TERMINATED BY char [ESCAPED BY
        char]] [COLLECTION ITEMS TERMINATED BY char]
      [MAP KEYS TERMINATED BY char] [LINES TERMINATED BY
        char] [NULL DEFINED AS char]
      | SERDE serde_name [WITH SERDEPROPERTIES
        (property_name=property_value, property_
        name=property_value, ...)]
file_format:
  : SEQUENCEFILE | TEXTFILE | RCFILE | ORC
  | INPUTFORMAT input_format_classname OUTPUTFORMAT
        output_format_classname
```

Tying it all together with an example

We want to tie things together in this section with two examples. In this first example, we revisit `data_types_table` from Listing 13-7. Here we leverage the `DESCRIBE EXTENDED data_types_table` HiveQL command to illustrate what Hive does with our `CREATE TABLE` statement under the hood.

```
hive> DESCRIBE EXTENDED data_types_table;
OK
our_tinyint            tinyint                1 byte
        signed integer
our_smallint           smallint               2 byte
        signed integer
...
(A)inputFormat:org.apache.hadoop.mapred.TextInputFormat,
outputFormat:
(B)org.apache.hadoop.hive.ql.io.
        HiveIgnoreKeyTextOutputFormat
, ...
serializationLib:
  org.apache.hadoop.hive.serde2.lazy.LazySimpleSerDe,
(C)parameters:{collection.delim=|, mapkey.delim=^, line.
        delim=
(D), serialization.format= ,, field.delim=,}),
...
```

Notice that Hive provides an INPUTFORMAT and OUTPUTFORMAT class for you when you specify STORED AS TEXTFILE, as we did in line 38 from Listing 13-7. Also note how Hive included the default LazySimpleSerDe. The row format delimiters that you specified in lines 33 through 37 from Listing 13-7 are inserted as parameters to the LazySimpleSerDe so the records in the text file can be parsed and translated into column types by the SerDe or written in proper format to the text file.

An example of how to use the HBase SerDe

In this last example of this section, we want to show you how to specify a SerDe instead of letting Hive pick a default SerDe for you. We want to show you an example that also dovetails with some of the concepts covered in Chapter 12 — the HBase Chapter. Hive includes an HBase SerDe, which is great news if you want to put a HiveQL front end on your HBase table. Without HiveQL, HBase users have to leverage the HBase shell or write Java code to query from and write to HBase tables. In the example in Listing 13-11, you create an EXTERNAL Hive table that connects with an HBase table. (The external table is another feature of Hive that lets you connect with data, then query and analyze the data with HiveQL, but when you delete the table, the data remains in its original location.) Listing 13-11 shows the schema and contents of the HBase table that you connect to with Hive using the HBase SerDe.

Listing 13-11:   Customer Information HBase Table

```
ROW      COLUMN+CELL
00001    column=ContactInfo:EA,   value=John.Smith@xyz.com
00001    column=ContactInfo:SA,   value=1 Hadoop Lane, NY
            11111
00001    column=CustomerName:FN,  value=John
00001    column=CustomerName:LN,  value=Smith
00001    column=CustomerName:MN,  value=Timothy
00002    column=ContactInfo:EA,   value=Jane.Doe@xyz.com
00002    column=ContactInfo:SA,   value=7 HBase Ave, CA 22222
00002    column=CustomerName:FN,  value=Jane
00002    column=CustomerName:LN,  value=Doe
00002    column=CustomerName:MN,  value=A
```

The Customer Information HBase table consists of two rows and two column families: ContactInfo and CustomerName. The ContactInfo column family has two columns storing the customer's e-mail address (EA) and street address (SA). The CustomerName column family has three rows storing the first name (FN), middle name (MN) and last name (LN) of the customer. You can find out much more about HBase in Chapter 12, but for now, what's important to understand is that HBase stores key value pairs just like the Hive map data type we demonstrate in Line 19 of Listing 13-7. In Listing 13-12, you see the HiveQL statements you need in order to create a table that connects to your HBase table (refer to Listing 13-11) using map data types.

Listing 13-12:   Creating an External Hive Table to Connect to the HBase Customer Information Table

```
(A) CREATE EXTERNAL TABLE hive_hbase_table (
key      INT,
name     map<STRING,STRING>,
info     map<STRING,STRING>)
STORED BY 'org.apache.hadoop.hive.hbase.
         HBaseStorageHandler'
WITH SERDEPROPERTIES ("hbase.columns.mapping" =
         ":key,CustomerName:,ContactInfo:")
TBLPROPERTIES ("hbase.table.name" = "customerinfo");

(B) hive> SELECT * FROM hive_hbase_table;
OK
1       {"FN":"John","LN":"Smith","MN":"Timothy"}
        {"EA":"John.Smith@xyz.com","SA":"1 Hadoop Lane, NY
           11111"}
2       {"FN":"Jane","LN":"Doe","MN":"A"}
        {"EA":"Jane.Doe@xyz.com","SA":"6 Novice HBase Ave,
           CA 22222"}
Time taken: 1.422 seconds
(C) hive> SELECT info["EA"] FROM hive_hbase_table WHERE
         name["FN"] = "Jane" AND name["LN"] = "Doe";
Total MapReduce jobs = 1
...
OK
Jane.Doe@xyz.com
```

In Step (A), you create an external table with a Key field to link up with the HBase row keys (00001 and 00002 from Listing 13-11), and two map data types (name and info) to link up with the two column families (ContactInfo and CustomerName). Note the syntax for providing this linkage via the WITH SERDEPROPERTIES keywords. This SerDe configuration technique is quite common in Hive DDL. Note as well that the TBLPROPERTIES keyword is crucial for connecting the new external hive_hbase_table with the actual customerinfo HBase table name.

Step (B) shows how the key value pairs in HBase ({"FN","John"}, for example) are now available for querying with the help of the HiveQL. Note the syntax for accessing the Hive map data type in Step (C). You can select the value of the info map type using the notation info ["EA"] where "EA" is the key.

If you're already familiar with SQL, you'll notice that the SELECT . . . FROM . . . WHERE statement shown in Step (C) is almost identical to the types of queries you can form using SQL and MySQL, or DB2 and others.

Seeing How the Hive Data Manipulation Language Works

In the first half of this chapter, we walk you through a couple of CREATE TABLE examples using the Hive CLI (refer to Listings 13-4 and 13-7), and you can see how Hive allows you to control your table's file and record storage formats. Now it's time to delve into Hive's data manipulation language (DML) — it lets you load and insert data into tables and create tables from other tables. We even go all out and provide examples that illustrate *four* ways to input data into Hive tables.

LOAD DATA examples

We have you start out by placing data into the data_types_table you created using Listing 13-7. Doing so illustrates the LOAD DATA command and will serve to cement some of the concepts from the last section. The syntax for the LOAD DATA command is shown in Listing 13-13.

Listing 13-13:   LOAD DATA Command Syntax

```
"LOAD DATA [LOCAL] INPATH 'path to file' [OVERWRITE] INTO
        TABLE 'table name' [PARTITION partition column1
        = value1, partition column2 = value2,...]
```

A few areas in Listing 13-13 need an explanation. First, the optional LOCAL keyword tells Hive to copy data from the input file on the local file system into the Hive data warehouse directory (in our case, on the local file system). Without the LOCAL keyword, the data is simply moved (not copied) into the warehouse directory. Also you should be aware that when running in distributed mode, if you omit the LOCAL keyword Hive assumes your data is already in the HDFS, and in this case moves the data from its current HDFS location into the HDFS warehouse directory. Second, the optional OVERWRITE keyword, as you might imagine, causes the system to overwrite data in the specified table if it already has data stored in it. Finally, the optional PARTITION list tells Hive to partition the storage of the table into different directories in the data warehouse directory structure. This powerful concept improves query performance in Hive, and we demonstrate its use later in this section. When you think about the magnitude of data that can be managed by Hive in the HDFS, partitioning makes a lot of sense. Rather than run a MapReduce job over the entire table to find the data you want to view or analyze, you can isolate a segment of the table and save a lot of system time with partitions.

Apache Hive uses the MapReduce technology within Hadoop to query and analyze tables — though, in some cases, MapReduce is *not* used. It turns out that you can set the configuration variable hive.exec.mode.local.auto in the `hive-site.xml file`. When the variable is set to `true`, Hive tries to execute queries on small data sets locally without MapReduce whenever possible, to speed execution.

Listing 13-14 shows the commands to use to load the `data_types_table` with data. Again, we've annotated the listing so that we can discuss each step.

Listing 13-14:   Loading `our_first_table` with Data

```
(A) $ cat data.txt
100,32000,2000000,9200000000000000000,0.15625,4.9406564584
        124654,
1.23E+3,2013-09-21 20:19:52.025,true,
test string,\0xFFFFDDDDEEEEAAAA,1|2|3|4,key^1024,
1|3.1459|test struct,2|test union
(B) hive (data_types_db)> LOAD DATA LOCAL INPATH
        '/home/biadmin/Hive/data.txt' INTO TABLE
        data_types_table;
Copying data from file:/home/biadmin/Hive/data.txt
Copying file: file:/home/biadmin/Hive/data.txt
Loading data to table data_types_db.data_types_table
Table data_types_db.data_types_table stats:
        [num_partitions: 0, num_files: 1, num_rows: 0,
        total_size: 185, raw_data_size: 0]
OK
Time taken: 0.287 seconds
(C) hive> SELECT * FROM data_types_table;
OK
100     32000   2000000 9200000000000000000         0.15625
        4.940656458412465
1230    2013-09-21 20:19:52.025         true    test string
\0xFFFFDDDDEEEEAAAA       [1,2,3,4]        {"key":1024}
{"first":1,"second":3.1459,"third":"test struct"}
(D) {2:"test union"}
Time taken: 0.201 seconds, Fetched: 1 row(s)
```

Step (A) is a listing (using the Unix `cat` command) of data you intend to load. This data file has only one record in it, but there's a value for each field in the table. Note the field and complex type delimiters. As we specified at table creation time (refer to Listing 13-7 or 13-9), fields are separated by a comma; collections (such as `STRUCT` and `UNIONTYPE`) are separated by the vertical bar or pipe character (|); and the `MAP` keys and values are separated by the caret character (^). Step (B) has the `LOAD DATA` command, and in Step (C) you're retrieving the record you just loaded in Step (B) so that you can view the data.

 The data retrieved using the `SELECT` command is as expected, but the last field — see line (D) — needs some attention. Note how the `UNIONTYPE` works. `UNIONTYPE`s in Hive can store different data types, but only one at a time. In the `data.txt` file you list in Step (A), you specify to use the third data type in the `our_union` field. (It's the third one because you start counting at zero, of course.) So you specify a string — in this case, `test union` — after the `2` in the data file.

The last example in this subsection sets up other examples later in this chapter. We have downloaded some historical airline flight data for the years 2007 and 2008 from the website `http://stat-computing.org/dataexpo/2009/the-data.html`. This data was compiled by the Research and Innovative Technology Administration, which coordinates with the U.S. Department of Transportation's Bureau of Transportation Statistics to provide data to statisticians and scientists. It's a classic use case for Apache Hive: We show you how to load this airline data into a Hive table, and then you get a chance to perform some analysis with HiveQL!

To put this airline data in perspective, the data for the year 2007 is approximately 671MB and the data for the year 2008 is 659MB. We don't want to overload the disk space on your virtual machine, so we downloaded only a few data files, though it appears that the files range between 100MB and 659MB in the case of the year 2008. If you were to download all 22 years' worth of data from `http://stat-computing.org/dataexpo/2009/the-data.html`, it would amount to well over 1 terabyte (TB) of information. This is a typical big data use case for Apache Hadoop and Hive running on a cluster of Linux servers. If you would attempt to analyze that much data on classic relational database systems, it would be costly and cumbersome at best.

So, after downloading the data and studying the data types listed on the website, we created two identical tables, named `FlightInfo2007` and `FlightInfo2008`, as you can see in steps (A) and (F) in Listing 13-15. Note that this data is posted on the aforementioned website as comma-separated text, so you'll use the classic text file format for your records, and we've specified comma separation for the record fields. Hive's LazySimpleSerDe does the rest of the job for you. Step (B) should also look familiar except that we didn't use the `LOCAL` keyword. That's because these files are large; you'll move the data into your Hive warehouse, not make another copy on your small and tired laptop disk. You'd likely want to do the same thing on a real cluster and not waste the storage.

Listing 13-15:   Flight Information Tables from 2007 and 2008

```
(A) CREATE TABLE IF NOT EXISTS FlightInfo2007 (
  Year SMALLINT, Month TINYINT, DayofMonth TINYINT,
          DayOfWeek TINYINT,
  DepTime SMALLINT, CRSDepTime SMALLINT, ArrTime SMALLINT,
          CRSArrTime SMALLINT,
  UniqueCarrier STRING, FlightNum STRING, TailNum STRING,
  ActualElapsedTime SMALLINT, CRSElapsedTime SMALLINT,
  AirTime SMALLINT, ArrDelay SMALLINT, DepDelay SMALLINT,
  Origin STRING, Dest STRING,Distance INT,
  TaxiIn SMALLINT, TaxiOut SMALLINT, Cancelled SMALLINT,
  CancellationCode STRING, Diverted SMALLINT,
  CarrierDelay SMALLINT, WeatherDelay SMALLINT,
  NASDelay SMALLINT, SecurityDelay SMALLINT,
          LateAircraftDelay SMALLINT)
COMMENT 'Flight InfoTable'
```

(continued)

Listing 13-15 *(continued)*

```
ROW FORMAT DELIMITED
FIELDS TERMINATED BY ','
LINES TERMINATED BY '\n'
STORED AS TEXTFILE
TBLPROPERTIES ('creator'='Bruce Brown', 'created_at'='Thu
        Sep 19 10:58:00 EDT 2013');


(B) hive (flightdata)> LOAD DATA INPATH '/home/biadmin/
        Hive/Data/2007.csv' INTO TABLE FlightInfo2007;
Loading data to table flightdata.flightinfo2007
Table flightdata.flightinfo2007 stats: [num_partitions:
        0, num_files: 2, num_rows: 0, total_size:
        1405756086, raw_data_size: 0]
OK
Time taken: 0.284 seconds;
(C) hive (flightdata)> SELECT * FROM FlightInfo2007 LIMIT
        2;
OK
NULL    NULL    NULL    NULL    NULL    NULL    NULL
        NULL    UniqueCarrier   FlightNum       TailNum
        NULL    NULLNULL    NULL    NULL    Origin
        Dest    NULL    NULL    NULL    NULL
        CancellationCode        NULL    NULL
        NULLNULL    NULL    NULL
2007    1       1       1       1232    1225    1341
        1340    WN      2891    N351    69      75
        54      1   7SMF    ONT     389     4       11
        0               0       0       0       0
        0       0
Time taken: 0.087 seconds, Fetched: 2 row(s)


(D) LOAD DATA INPATH '/home/biadmin/Hive/Data/2007.csv'
        OVERWRITE INTO TABLE FlightInfo2007;
(E) hive (flightdata)>  SELECT * FROM FlightInfo2007 LIMIT
        2;
OK
2007    1       1       1       1232    1225    1341
        1340    WN      2891    N351    69      75
        54      1   7SMF    ONT     389     4       11
        0               0       0       0       0
        0       0
2007    1       1       1       1918    1905    2043
        2035    WN      462     N370    85      90
        74      8   13      SMF     PDX     479     5
        6       0       0       0       0
        0       0       0
Time taken: 0.089 seconds, Fetched: 2 row(s)


(F) CREATE TABLE IF NOT EXISTS FlightInfo2008 LIKE
        FlightInfo2007;
(G) LOAD DATA INPATH '/home/biadmin/Hive/Data/2008.csv'
        INTO TABLE FlightInfo2008;
```

To test the LOAD DATA command and make sure everything works, you use the SELECT command as shown in the previous example, but this time you also use the LIMIT keyword [see step (C)] because this table is huge. Note that initially you have a bit of problem with the FlightInfo2007 table. Why are you seeing mostly all NULL values in the first record? The answer is that the 2007.csv file has a header on the first line giving the descriptions of the columns in the rest of the file. These descriptions match the website's explanation of the fields we used to define the data types. So the solution was simple: We downloaded another copy of the data, deleted the header line, and ran the command again — this time, using the OVERWRITE keyword. Now, in Step (E) you can see that the problem has been solved. In Step (F), the LIKE keyword instructs Hive to copy the existing FlightInfo2007 table definition when creating the FlightInfo2008 table. In Step (G) you're using the same technique as in Step (B).

The problem with NULL values seemed trivial enough, but this example points to an interesting aspect of Hive that we need to explain before we move on to the next Hive DML command.

In Listing 13-15, Hive could not (at first) match the first record with the data types you specified in your CREATE TABLE statement. So the system showed NULL values in place of the real data, and the command completed successfully. This behavior illustrates that Hive uses a Schema on Read verification approach as opposed to the Schema on Write verification approach, which you find in RDBMS technologies. This is one reason why Hive is so powerful for big data analytics — it lets you discover and explore your data in a relaxed fashion as opposed to a strict structured approach. A typical RDBMS system would have returned errors when the data didn't match. Hive didn't return an error when we tried to load data into the table that didn't match our schema — it simply showed NULL values, and then you figured out the bit about the data-types disconnect by inspecting the data and adjusted accordingly.

INSERT examples

Another Hive DML command to explore is the INSERT command. You basically have three INSERT variants; we show you two of them in Listing 13-16. To demonstrate this new DML command, we have you create a new table that will hold a subset of the data in the FlightInfo2008 table you created in the previous example. In Step (A), you create this new table and specify that the file format will be row columnar (Step (B)) instead of text. This format is more compact than text and often performs better, depending on your access patterns. (If you're accessing a small subset of columns instead of entire rows, try the RCFILE format.)

The default SerDe for RCFILE format is the ColumnarSerDe. You can verify this fact by running the DESCRIBE EXTENDED myFlightInfo HiveQL command from the command line interface.

Listing 13-16: Partitioned Version of 2008 Flight Information Table

```
(A) CREATE TABLE IF NOT EXISTS myFlightInfo (
  Year SMALLINT, DontQueryMonth TINYINT, DayofMonth
          TINYINT, DayOfWeek TINYINT,
  DepTime SMALLINT, ArrTime SMALLINT,
  UniqueCarrier STRING, FlightNum STRING,
  AirTime SMALLINT, ArrDelay SMALLINT, DepDelay SMALLINT,
  Origin STRING, Dest STRING, Cancelled SMALLINT,
  CancellationCode STRING)
COMMENT 'Flight InfoTable'
PARTITIONED BY(Month TINYINT)
ROW FORMAT DELIMITED
FIELDS TERMINATED BY ','
LINES TERMINATED BY '\n'
(B) STORED AS RCFILE
TBLPROPERTIES ('creator'='Bruce Brown', 'created_at'='Mon
          Sep  2 14:24:19 EDT 2013');

(C) INSERT OVERWRITE TABLE myflightinfo
  PARTITION (Month=1)
  SELECT Year, Month, DayofMonth, DayOfWeek, DepTime,
          ArrTime, UniqueCarrier,
          FlightNum, AirTime, ArrDelay, DepDelay, Origin,
          Dest, Cancelled,
          CancellationCode
  FROM FlightInfo2008 WHERE Month=1;

(D) FROM FlightInfo2008
INSERT INTO TABLE myflightinfo
  PARTITION (Month=2)
  SELECT Year, Month, DayofMonth, DayOfWeek, DepTime,
          ArrTime, UniqueCarrier, FlightNum,
  AirTime, ArrDelay, DepDelay, Origin, Dest, Cancelled,
          CancellationCode WHERE Month=2
... (Months 3 through 11 skipped for brevity)
INSERT INTO TABLE myflightinfo
  PARTITION (Month=12)
  SELECT Year, Month, DayofMonth, DayOfWeek, DepTime,
          ArrTime, UniqueCarrier, FlightNum,
  AirTime, ArrDelay, DepDelay, Origin, Dest, Cancelled,
          CancellationCode WHERE Month=12;

(E) hive (flightdata)> SHOW PARTITIONS myflightinfo;
OK
month=1
month=10
month=11
month=12
...
month=9
```

```
(F) $ ls
/home/biadmin/Hive/warehouse/flightdata.db/myflightinfo
month=1    month=11   month=2   month=4   month=6   month=8
month=10   month=12   month=3   month=5   month=7   month=9

(G) $HIVE_HOME/bin/hive --service rcfilecat
   /home/biadmin/Hive/warehouse/flightdata.db/myflightinfo/
        month=12/000000_0
...
2008     12        13      6        655      856      DL
         1638      85      0        -5       PBI      ATL
         0
2008     12        13      6        1251     1446     DL
         1639      89      9        11       IAD      ATL
         0
2008     12        13      6        1110     1413     DL
         1641      104     -5       7        SAT      ATL
         0
```

After creating the table, you use the INSERT OVERWRITE command [see Step (C)] to insert data via a SELECT statement from the FlightInfo2008 table. Note that you're partitioning your data using the PARTITION keyword based on the Month field. After you're finished, you'll have 12 table partitions, or actual directories, under the warehouse directory in the file system on your virtual machine, corresponding to the 12 months of the year. As we explain earlier, partitioning can dramatically improve your query performance if you want to query data in the myFlightInfo table for only a certain month. You can see the results of the PARTITION approach with the SHOW PARTITIONS command in Steps (E) and (F). Notice in Step (D) that you're using a variant of the INSERT command to insert data into multiple partitions at one time. We have only shown month 2 and 12 for brevity but months 3 through 11 would have the same syntax.

Partitions are quite useful to the Hive programmer. However, it's not uncommon to encounter a data set where partitioning could become unwieldy, especially if multiple partitions are specified [PARTITION BY(Country STRING, PersonName STRING), for example]. Twelve partitions are one thing — 7 billion partitions would be quite another! The solution to partition sprawl is *bucketing*. Bucketing in Hive works by allowing you to specify some reasonable number of buckets, and then the system attempts to evenly distribute the data into the number of buckets you specify. [That could look something like PARTITION BY(...) CLUSTERED BY(BucketingColumn) INTO x BUCKETS.] Additionally, this feature enables *table sampling* — a technique that allows Hive users to write queries on a sample of the data instead of the entire table. HiveQL table sampling can be very useful for big data analytics. (For more information on bucketing and table sampling see https://cwiki. apache.org/confluence/display/Hive/LanguageManual+Sampling.)

You can also use this FROM table1 INSERT INTO table2 SELECT ... format to insert into multiple tables at a time. We have you use INSERT instead of OVERWRITE here to show the option of inserting instead of overwriting. Hive allows only appends, not inserts, into tables, so the `INSERT` keyword simply instructs Hive to append the data to the table. Finally, note in Step (G) that you have to use a special Hive command service (`rcfilecat`) to view this table in your warehouse, because the `RCFILE` format is a binary format, unlike the previous `TEXTFILE` format examples.

We say at the beginning of this subsection that the `INSERT` DML command has *three* variants. (You've been dying to find out what the third variant is, right?) Well, the third one is the Dynamic Partition Inserts variant. In Listing 13-16, you partition the `myFlightInfo` table into 12 segments, 1 per month. If you had hundreds of partitions, this task would have become quite difficult, and it would have required scripting to get the job done. Instead, Hive supports a technique for dynamically creating partitions with the `INSERT OVERWRITE` statement. So, if you find yourself needing to leverage table partitioning with a large, and possibly variable, number of partitions, check out the Dynamic Partition Inserts feature in the Hive DML Language Manual at `https://cwiki.apache.org/confluence/display/Hive/ Tutorial - Tutorial-Dynamic-PartitionInsert`.

Create Table As Select (CTAS) examples

In the Hive DML example in this section, we illustrate the powerful technique in Hive known as *Create Table As Select,* or *CTAS*. Its constructs allow you to quickly derive Hive tables from other tables as you build powerful schemas for big data analysis.

Listing 13-17 shows you how CTAS works, and it sets the stage for other HiveQL examples later in this chapter.

Listing 13-17: An Example of Using CREATE TABLE . . . AS SELECT

```
(A) hive> CREATE TABLE myflightinfo2007 AS
    > SELECT Year, Month, DepTime, ArrTime, FlightNum,
         Origin, Dest FROM FlightInfo2007
    > WHERE (Month = 7 AND DayofMonth = 3) AND
         (Origin='JFK' AND Dest='ORD');
(B) hive> SELECT * FROM myFlightInfo2007;
OK
2007    7       700     834     5447    JFK     ORD
2007    7       1633    1812    5469    JFK     ORD
2007    7       1905    2100    5492    JFK     ORD
2007    7       1453    1624    4133    JFK     ORD
2007    7       1810    1956    4392    JFK     ORD
2007    7       643     759     903     JFK     ORD
2007    7       939     1108    907     JFK     ORD
2007    7       1313    1436    915     JFK     ORD
2007    7       1617    1755    917     JFK     ORD
2007    7       2002    2139    919     JFK     ORD
```

```
Time taken: 0.089 seconds, Fetched: 10 row(s)
hive> CREATE TABLE myFlightInfo2008 AS
    > SELECT Year, Month, DepTime, ArrTime, FlightNum,
          Origin, Dest FROM FlightInfo2008
    > WHERE (Month = 7 AND DayofMonth = 3) AND
          (Origin='JFK' AND Dest='ORD');
hive> SELECT * FROM myFlightInfo2008;
OK
2008      7        930      1103      5199      JFK      ORD
2008      7        705      849       5687      JFK      ORD
2008      7        1645     1914      5469      JFK      ORD
2008      7        1345     1514      4392      JFK      ORD
2008      7        1718     1907      1217      JFK      ORD
2008      7        757      929       1323      JFK      ORD
2008      7        928      1057      907       JFK      ORD
2008      7        1358     1532      915       JFK      ORD
2008      7        1646     1846      917       JFK      ORD
2008      7        2129     2341      919       JFK      ORD
Time taken: 0.186 seconds, Fetched: 10 row(s)
```

In Step A, you build two smaller tables derived from the `FlightInfo2007`
and `FlightInfo2008` by selecting a subset of fields from the larger tables
for a particular day (in this case, July 3), where the origin of the flight is
New York's JFK airport (JFK) and the destination is Chicago's O'Hare airport
(ORD). Then in Step B you simply dump the contents of these small tables so
that you can view the data.

Querying and Analyzing Data

Earlier sections in this chapter describe Hive data types, Hive's DDL, and
Hive's DML, but now we help you explore some HiveQL features for querying and analyzing data. Keep in mind, though, that it is beyond the scope of
this chapter to provide an exhaustive treatise on HiveQL as it stands today.
Moreover, the vibrant and active Apache Hive community continually *adds*
to an already extensive feature set, which makes exhaustive coverage even
more difficult. We concentrate on the high points here, knowing full well that
finishing this chapter will get you excited about the new potential of big data
analytics at your fingertips with Apache Hive. We begin by exploring table
joins in Hive.

For an exhaustive list of HiveQL features, consult the Hive Language Manual at
this page:

```
https://cwiki.apache.org/confluence/display/Hive/
          LanguageManual
```

Joining tables with Hive

You probably know already that experts in relational database modeling and design typically spend a lot of their time designing normalized databases, or *schemas*. Database *normalization* is a technique that guards against data loss, redundancy, and other anomalies as data is updated and retrieved. The experts follow a number of rules to arrive at a normalized database, but Rule 1 is that you must end up with a *group* of tables. (One large table storing all your data is not normal — pun intended.) There are exceptions, depending on the use case, but the law of many tables is generally followed closely, especially for databases that support transactions or analytic processing (business intelligence, for example). When you begin to query and analyze your data, tables are joined based on the defined relationships between them using SQL — which means that the disks are ultimately busy on your server when you start joining tables, and busy disks usually result in slower user response times. However, the good news is that RDBMSs and EDWs are tuned to make joins as fast as possible.

What does all this have to do with joins in Hive? Well, remember that the underlying operating system for Hive is (surprise!) Apache Hadoop: MapReduce is the engine for joining tables, and the Hadoop File System (HDFS) is the underlying storage. It's all good news for the user who wants to create, manage, and analyze large tables with Hive. The potential to unlock information that's hidden in massive data structures is exciting. However, joins with Hive usually don't perform as well as they do in the RDBMS/EDW world, so first-time users are often surprised by the "pokiness" of the system response. Remember that MapReduce and HDFS are optimized for through-put with big data analytics and that, in this world, *latencies* — user response times, in other words — are usually high. Hive is designed for batch-style analytic processing, not for fast online transaction processing. Users who want the best possible performance with SQL on Apache Hadoop have solutions available, and we look at those solutions in more detail in Chapter 14. For now, keep this dynamic in mind when you start joining tables with Hive. Also note that Hive architects usually denormalize their databases to some extent, so having fewer larger tables is commonplace. That's why complex data types such as STRUCTs and ARRAYs are provided. You can use these complex data types to pack a lot more data into a single table. Because Hive table reads and writes via HDFS usually involve very large blocks of data, the more data you can manage altogether in one table, the better the overall performance.

Disk and network access is a lot slower than memory access, so minimize HDFS reads and writes as much as possible.

With this background information in mind, you can tackle making joins with Hive. Fortunately, the Hive development community was realistic and understood that users would want and need to join tables with HiveQL.

This knowledge becomes especially important with EDW augmentation, as explained in Chapter 10. Use cases such as "queryable" archives often require joins for data analysis.

Earlier in this chapter, we show you how to use Hive's Create Table As Select (CTAS) technique for creating new tables from existing tables. Now we show you a Hive join example using our flight data tables. Listing 11-17 shows you how to create and display a myflightinfo2007 table and a myflightinfo2008 table from the larger FlightInfo2007 and FlightInfo2008 tables. The plan all along was to use the CTAS created myflightinfo2007 and myflightinfo2008 tables to illustrate how you can perform joins in Hive. Figure 13-8 shows the result of an inner join with the myflightinfo2007 and myflightinfo2008 tables using the SQuirreL SQL client.

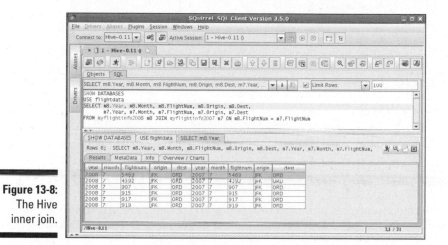

Figure 13-8:
The Hive inner join.

Hive supports *equi-joins,* a specific type of join that only uses equality comparisons in the join predicate. (ON m8.FlightNum = m7.FlightNum, from Figure 13-8 above, is one example of an equi-join.) Other comparators such as Less Than (<) are not supported. This restriction is only because of limitations on the underlying MapReduce engine. Also, you cannot use OR in the ON clause.

Figure 13-8 illustrates the earlier example of the inner join and two other Hive join types. Note that you can confirm the results of an inner join by reviewing the contents of the myflight2007 and myflight2008 tables in Listing 13-17. Figure 13-9 illustrates how an inner join works using a Venn diagram, in case you're not familiar with the technique. The basic idea here is that an inner join returns the records that match between two tables. So an inner join is a perfect analysis tool to determine which flights are the same from JFK (New York) to ORD (Chicago) in July of 2007 and July of 2008.

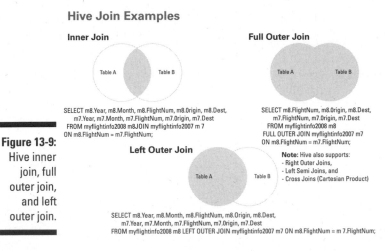

Hive Join Examples

Inner Join

Table A   Table B

SELECT m8.Year, m8.Month, m8.FlightNum, m8.Origin, m8.Dest,
m7.Year, m7.Month, m7.FlightNum, m7.Origin, m7.Dest
FROM myflightinfo2008 m8JOIN myflightinfo2007 m 7
ON m8.FlightNum = m7.FlightNum;

Full Outer Join

Table A   Table B

SELECT m8.FlightNum, m8.Origin, m8.Dest,
m7.FlightNum, m7.Origin, m7.Dest
FROM myflightinfo2008 m8
FULL OUTER JOIN myflightinfo2007 m7
ON m8.FlightNum = m7.FlightNum;

Left Outer Join

Table A   Table B

Note: Hive also supports:
- Right Outer Joins,
- Left Semi Joins, and
- Cross Joins (Cartesian Product)

Figure 13-9:
Hive inner
join, full
outer join,
and left
outer join.

SELECT m8.Year, m8.Month, m8.FlightNum, m8.Origin, m8.Dest,
m7.Year, m7.Month, m7.FlightNum, m7.Origin, m7.Dest
FROM myflightinfo2008 m8 LEFT OUTER JOIN myflightinfo2007 m7 ON m8.FlightNum = m 7.FlightNum;

Optimizing Hive joins is a hot topic in the Hive community. For more information on current optimization techniques, see the Join Optimization page on the
Hive wiki at

```
https://cwiki.apache.org/confluence/display/Hive/LanguageM
          anual+JoinOptimization
```

Improving your Hive queries with indexes

Creating an index is common practice with relational databases when you
want to speed access to a column or set of columns in your database.
Without an index, the database system has to read all rows in the table to
find the data you have selected. Indexes become even more essential when
the tables grow extremely large, and as you now undoubtedly know, Hive
thrives on large tables. As you would expect, Hive supports index creation
on tables, though its functionality is still somewhat immature as of this
writing. However, as we've said, the Hive community is active, and indexing
will eventually mature. Even with its current limitations, indexing offers an
approach to speed up Hive queries with little effort, so we show you a brief
example.

You can optimize Hive queries in at least five ways: First, with a little research,
you can often speed your joins by leveraging certain optimization techniques,
as described on the Hive wiki. (Check out `https://cwiki.apache.org/`
`confluence/display/Hive/LanguageManual+JoinOptimization`.)
Second, column-oriented storage options (see the "Defining table file formats"
section, earlier in the chapter) can be quite helpful. Remember that the ORC
file format is new as of Hive 0.11. Third, we demonstrate and discuss how to
partition tables in Listing 13-16. Fourth, the Hive community has provided

indexing, as illustrated in Listing 13-18. Finally, don't forget the `hive.exec.mode.local.auto` configuration variable we mention earlier, in the section "Seeing How the Hive Data Manipulation Language Works."

In Listing 13-18, we list the steps necessary to index the `FlightInfo2008` table. This extremely large table has millions of rows, so it makes a good candidate for an index or two.

Listing 13-18:   Creating an Index on the FlightInfo2008 Table

```
(A) CREATE INDEX f08_index ON TABLE flightinfo2008
        (Origin) AS 'COMPACT' WITH DEFERRED REBUILD;
(B) ALTER INDEX f08_index ON flightinfo2008 REBUILD;
(C) hive (flightdata)> SHOW INDEXES ON FlightInfo2008;
OK
f08index                    flightinfo2008          origin
        flightdata__flightinfo2008_f08index__  compact
Time taken: 0.079 seconds, Fetched: 1 row(s)
(D) hive (flightdata)> DESCRIBE
        flightdata__flightinfo2008_f08index__;
OK
origin                      string                      None
_bucketname                 string
_offsets                    array<bigint>
Time taken: 0.112 seconds, Fetched: 3 row(s)
(E) hive (flightdata)> SELECT Origin, COUNT(1) FROM
        flightinfo2008 WHERE Origin = 'SYR' GROUP BY
        Origin;
SYR     12032
Time taken: 17.34 seconds, Fetched: 1 row(s)
(F) hive (flightdata)> SELECT Origin, SIZE(`_offsets`)
        FROM flightdata__flightinfo2008_f08index__
        WHERE origin = 'SYR';
SYR     12032
Time taken: 8.347 seconds, Fetched: 1 row(s)
(G) hive (flightdata)> DESCRIBE
        flightdata__flightinfo2008_f08index__;
OK
origin                      string                      None
_bucketname                 string
_offsets                    array<bigint>
Time taken: 0.12 seconds, Fetched: 3 row(s)
```

Step (A) creates the index using the 'COMPACT' index handler on the `Origin` column. Hive also offers a bitmap index handler as of the 0.8 release, which is intended for creating indexes on columns with a few unique values. In Step (A) the keywords WITH DEFERRED REBUILD instructs Hive to first create an empty index; Step (B) is where you actually build the index with the ALTER INDEX ... REBUILD command. Deferred index builds can be very useful in workflows where one process creates the tables and indexes, another loads the data and builds the indexes and a final process performs data analysis. (For more on workflows — more specifically, Oozie workflows — check out Chapter 9. As of this writing, Hive doesn't provide automatic index maintenance, so you need to rebuild the index if you overwrite or append data to the table. Also, Hive indexes support table partitions, so a rebuild can be limited to a partition. (Refer to Listing 13-16 for more information on partitions.) Step (C) illustrates how you can list or show the indexes created against a particular table. Step (D) illustrates an important point regarding Hive indexes: Hive indexes are implemented as tables. This is why you need to first create the index table and then build it to populate the table. Therefore, you can use indexes in at least two ways:

- Count on the system to automatically use indexes that you create.

- Rewrite some queries to leverage the new index table (as we demonstrate in Listing 13-18).

The automatic use of indexes is progressing, but this aspect is a work in progress. Focusing on the second option, in Step (E) you write a query that seeks to determine how many flights left the Syracuse airport during 2008. To get this information, you leverage the COUNT aggregate function. You can see that Hive took 17.32 seconds on our virtual machine to report that 12,032 flights originated from Syracuse, New York. In Step (F), you leverage the new index table and use the SIZE function instead. Step (F) makes more sense after you study Step (D): Step (D) shows you what an index table looks like, where records each hold the column _bucketname, which is the location of the data in the Hive warehouse (/home/biadmin/Hive/warehouse, in this case), and an _offsets array, which is the index into the table (FlightInfo2008) in this case. So now the query in Step (F) makes sense. All Hive has to do is find the SYR origin (for Syracuse) in the flightdata__flightinfo2008_ f08index__ table and then count the rows in the _offsets' array to get the number of flights — a simple yet elegant way to double the performance (8.347 secs in Step (F) versus 17.34 in Step (E)) of the original query.

Windowing in HiveQL

The concept of *windowing,* introduced in the SQL:2003 standard, allows the SQL programmer to create a frame from the data against which aggregate and other window functions can operate. HiveQL now supports windowing per the SQL standard. Examples are quite helpful when explaining windowing and aggregate functions, so we start with an introductory example.

In our experience (and as other frequent flyers can attest), departure delays come with the territory when flying is your chosen mode of travel. It comes as no surprise, then, that the RITA-compiled flight data includes this information. One question we had when we first discovered this data set was, "What exactly is the average flight delay per day?" So we created a query in Listing 13-19 that produces the average departure delay per day in 2008.

Listing 13-19: Finding the Average Departure Delay per Day in 2008

```
(A) hive (flightdata)> CREATE VIEW avgdepdelay AS
            > SELECT DayOfWeek, AVG(DepDelay) FROM
        FlightInfo2008 GROUP BY DayOfWeek;
OK
Time taken: 0.121 seconds
(B) hive (flightdata)> SELECT * FROM avgdepdelay;
...
OK
1       10.269990244459473
2       8.97689712068735
3       8.289761053658728
4       9.772897177836702
5       12.158036387869656
6       8.645680904903614
7       11.568973392595312
Time taken: 18.6 seconds, Fetched: 7 row(s)
```

Before we explain the steps in this query, we have to say that TGIF, or "Thank God It's Friday," doesn't apply to everyone. It was no surprise to us that Friday — Day 5 under the results in Step (B) — had the highest number of delays.

Anyway, about that query in Step (A): We want to point out that Hive's Data Definition Language (DDL) also includes the CREATE VIEW statement, which can be quite useful. In Hive, views allow a query to be saved but data is not stored as with the Create Table as Select (CTAS) statement you learned about earlier in this chapter. When a view is referenced in HiveQL, Hive executes the query and then uses the results which could be part of a larger query. This can be very useful to simplify complex queries and break them down into logical components. Additionally, note the GROUP BY clause, which gathers all the days per week and allows the AVG aggregate function to provide a consolidated answer per day. This information is useful, of course, but what if we want to see some individual numbers per day? We consolidate the data with GROUP BY, and we have the answer we're looking for, though we've lost information as well. Solving this problem of information loss is where windowing becomes quite handy.

After we answered our question above about average flight delays per day, we came up with another question about the RITA 2008 flight data that Apache Hive can answer: "What is the first flight between Airport X and Y?" Suppose that in addition to this information, you want to know about subsequent flights, just in case you're not a "morning person." Well, this is a job for windowing in HiveQL! Listing 13-20 provides you with a query that answers these questions.

Listing 13-20:   Using Aggregate Window Functions on the Flight Data

```
(A) hive (flightdata)> SELECT f08.Month, f08.DayOfMonth,
        cr.description, f08.Origin, f08.Dest,
        f08.FlightNum, f08.DepTime, MIN(f08.DepTime)
OVER (PARTITION BY f08.DayOfMonth ORDER BY f08.DepTime)
FROM flightinfo2008 f08 JOIN Carriers cr ON
        f08.UniqueCarrier = cr.code
WHERE f08.Origin = 'JFK' AND f08.Dest = 'ORD' AND
        f08.Month = 1 AND f08.DepTime != 0;

...
OK
1    1  JetBlue Airways          JFK ORD 903    641 641
1    1  American Airlines Inc.   JFK ORD 1323   833 641
1    1  JetBlue Airways          JFK ORD 907    929 641
1    1  Comair Inc.              JFK ORD 5083   945 641
1    1  Comair Inc.              JFK ORD 5634   1215 641
1    1  JetBlue Airways          JFK ORD 915    1352 641
1    1  American Airlines Inc.   JFK ORD 1323   833 641
1    1  JetBlue Airways          JFK ORD 907    929 641
1    1  Comair Inc.              JFK ORD 5083   945 641
1    1  Comair Inc.              JFK ORD 5634   1215 641
1    1  JetBlue Airways          JFK ORD 915    1352 641
1    1  American Airlines Inc.   JFK ORD 1815   1610 641
1    1  JetBlue Airways          JFK ORD 917    1735 641
1    1  Comair Inc.              JFK ORD 5469   1749 641
1    1  Comair Inc.              JFK ORD 5492   2000 641
1    1  JetBlue Airways          JFK ORD 919    2102 641
1   31  JetBlue Airways          JFK ORD 919    48   48
1   31  JetBlue Airways          JFK ORD 903    635  48
1   31  Comair Inc.              JFK ORD 5447   650  48
1   31  American Airlines Inc.   JFK ORD 1323   840  48
1   31  JetBlue Airways          JFK ORD 907    921  48
1   31  JetBlue Airways          JFK ORD 917    1859 48
```

In Step (A), we've replaced the GROUP BY clause with the OVER clause where we specify the PARTITION or window over which we want the MIN aggregate function to operate. We've also included the ORDER BY clause so that we can see those subsequent flights after the first one. As you can see from the listing, on January 31, JetBlue has a nice, early flight at 12:48 a.m. — we'll opt for a later one, at 6:35 a.m. Early-riser issues aside, note that we have retained the information in the query output that would have been lost if we had chosen to use a GROUP BY clause again. This capability alone makes windowing a powerful feature, and there's more. Along with windowing in the Hive 0.11 release, the community provided some analytics functions that you can use in conjunction with windowing. Also at your disposal are these functions: RANK, ROW_NUMBER, DENSE_RANK, CUME_DIST, PERCENT_RANK, and NTILE. Finally, don't miss the use of JOIN in Listing 13-20: It's a real-life, practical example of an inner join in which we join the `FlightInfo2008` table with the `Carriers` table to get the airline name — rather than the cryptic code found in the `FlightInfo2008` table.

At the beginning of this chapter, we make the point that Hive is a key component of EDW augmentation. By importing, transforming, and analyzing the RITA flight data, we demonstrate how an EDW augmentation workflow might take shape. If data in your RDBMS or EDW can be enhanced by this flight data, Hive is the enabling technology to augment your existing IT system. Similarly, data from your RDBMS or EDW could have been exported to Apache Hive (perhaps using Apache Sqoop, as discussed in Chapter 13) and joined with this new flight data.

Other key HiveQL features

If this chapter is to be complete, we cannot leave a few other HiveQL features unmentioned. The following list summarizes them for you:

- **Security:** Apache Hive provides a security subsystem that can be quite helpful in preventing accidental data corruption or compromise among trusted members of workgroups. However, as of this writing, the Hive Language Manual clearly states that the Hive Security subsystem isn't designed to prevent nefarious users from compromising a Hive system. Hive security can be established for individual users, groups, and administrative roles. Hive provides privileges that can be granted or revoked to users, groups, or administrative roles. The Hive 0.10 release improved security in multi-user environments by providing authorization to the metastore, and future Hive releases will provide increasing integration with the Hadoop security framework. Kerberos is emerging as the technology of choice for securing Apache Hadoop.

- **Multi-User Locking:** Hive supports multi-user warehouse access when configured with Apache Zookeeper. Without this support, one user may read a table at the same time another user is deleting that table — which is, obviously, unacceptable. (For more information on Apache Zookeeper, see Chapter 12.) Multi-user access is enabled via configuration variables in the hive-site.xml file. Once configured, Hive implicitly acquires locks through Zookeeper for certain table operations. Users can also explicitly manage locks in the Hive CLI. Locks and associated configuration properties/variables are described in the Hive Language Manual.

- **Compression:** Data compression can not only save space on the HDFS but also improve performance by reducing the overall size of input/output operations. Additionally, compression between the Hadoop mappers and reducers can improve performance, because less data is passed between nodes in the cluster. Hive supports intermediate compression between the mappers and reducers as well as table output compression. Hive also understands how to ingest compressed data into the warehouse. Files compressed with Gzip or Bzip2 can be read by Hive's LOAD DATA command.

✔ **Functions:** HiveQL provides a rich set of built-in operators, built-in functions, built-in aggregate functions, and built-in table-generating functions. Several examples in this chapter use built-in operators as well as built-in aggregate functions (AVG, MIN, and COUNT, for example). To list all built-in functions for any particular Hive release, use the SHOW FUNCTIONS HiveQL command. You can also retrieve information about a built-in function by using the HiveQL commands DESCRIBE FUNCTION *function_name* and DESCRIBE FUNCTION EXTENDED *function_ name*. Using the EXTENDED keyword sometimes returns usage examples for the specified built-in function. Additionally, Hive allows users to create their own functions, called user-defined functions, or UDFs. Using Hive's Java-based UDF framework, you can create additional functions, including aggregates and table-generating functions. This feature is one of the reasons that Hive can function as an ETL tool.

Chapter 14

Integrating Hadoop with Relational Databases Using Sqoop

. . . .

. . . .

*P*erforming analytics on large, diverse data sets is a natural fit for Apache Hadoop. The whole point of the Hadoop File System (HDFS) is that it excels at providing a massively scalable, diverse data store that, when combined with the many analytic tools available on the Hadoop platform — from Map Reduce to Mahout and others — gives you a lean, mean, analytics machine when you hitch your data store wagon to Apache Hadoop.

This rosy picture presents a slight problem, however: It turns out that most of the world's structured data is already stored in relational database management systems (RDBMSs), and it's common practice to leverage structured query language (SQL, for short) for data transformation, processing, and analysis — and SQL is decidedly *not* a natural fit for Apache Hadoop. The Hadoop community knew what it was getting into, though, and planned to provide support for structured relational data — an SQL "fix," as it were — early on. Folks have been looking at combining and then analyzing field sensor data with the corresponding product data stored in a RDBMS or data warehouse, for example, a use case that places Apache Hive, with its SQL-like HiveQL, at its center.

It sounds like a great idea, but you may be wondering how, in this particular use case, you can get the data from the RDBMS onto the Apache Hadoop cluster, where Apache Hive can then do its magic. What's the "scoop" on that, you ask? (How's that for setting up a pun that refers to the chapter title?)

The answer, of course, is "*SQ*L to Had*oop*," or Sqoop, for short. Sqoop was first announced in 2009 by Aaron Kimball as a database import tool for Hadoop, and three years later (March 2012, to be exact), Sqoop became a top-level Apache project. The glory of Sqoop lies in the fact that it not only allows you to import relational data but also provides an export mechanism. The result is that Sqoop can provide an efficient mechanism for loading an RDBMS table by exporting data stored in HDFS, a use case perfectly suited for scenarios where you make use of Hadoop as an enterprise data warehouse (EDW) preprocessing engine. (See Chapter 11 for more on that scenario.)

Sqoop has grown a lot since its introduction in 2009. Along the way, Apache Sqoop committers have also added import support for Hive and HBase, making Sqoop a powerful addition to the Apache Hadoop ecosystem. In this chapter, you get the chance to explore the old and the new of Sqoop, from imports to exports to other, jazzier Sqoop tools. (You'll also come across a ton of hands-on examples.)

The Principles of Sqoop Design

When it comes to Sqoop, a picture is often worth a thousand words, so check out Figure 14-1, which gives you a bird's-eye view of the Sqoop architecture.

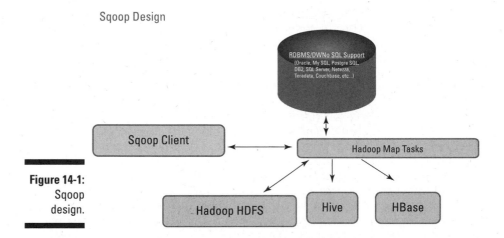

Sqoop Design

Figure 14-1:
Sqoop
design.

The idea behind Sqoop is that it leverages *map* tasks — tasks that perform the parallel import and export of relational database tables — right from within the Hadoop MapReduce framework. This is good news because the MapReduce framework provides fault tolerance for import and export jobs along with parallel processing! You'll appreciate the fault tolerance if there is a failure during a large table import or export because the MapReduce framework will recover without requiring you to start the process all over again. (For more information on the MapReduce framework, see Chapter 6.)

Sqoop can import data to Hive and HBase. Note, however, that the arrows to Hive and HBase point in only one direction in Figure 14-1. Data stored in any relational database with JDBC support can be directly imported into the Hive or HBase systems with Sqoop. Exports, however, are performed from data stored in HDFS. Therefore, if you need to export your Hive tables, you point Sqoop to HDFS directories that store your Hive tables. If you need to export HBase tables, you first have to export them to HDFS and then execute the Sqoop export command.

Scooping Up Data with Sqoop

Sqoop provides Hadoop with export and import capability to and from any RDBMS or data warehouse (DW) that supports the Java Database Connectivity (JDBC) application programming interface (API) suite. All major RDBMS and DW vendors generally provide JDBC-compliant drivers for their products. In addition, Sqoop releases are bundled with special connector technology for a variety of popular products. As of this writing, Sqoop version 1.4.4 provides special connectors for MySQL, PostgreSQL, Oracle, Microsoft SQL Server, DB2, and Netezza. These special connectors take advantage of specific features within the individual database systems in order to improve import/export performance and functionality. Additionally, third-party connectors are available that aren't bundled with Sqoop for other NoSQL data store and data warehouse providers (Couchbase and Teradata from Cloudera, for example). Sqoop also includes a generic JDBC connector that only supports the Java JDBC API.

Connectors and Drivers

Sqoop connectors generally go hand in hand with a JDBC driver. Sqoop does not bundle the JDBC drivers because they are usually proprietary and licensed by the RDBMS or DW vendor. So there are three possible scenarios for Sqoop, depending on the type of data management system (RDBMS, DW, or NoSQL) you are trying to interact with. Let's take a look at each one:

✔ **Your data management system is supported by one of the bundled Sqoop connectors listed above.** In this case, you need to acquire the JDBC driver from your data management system provider and install the `.jar` file associated with it in your `$SQOOP_HOME/lib` directory. (`$SQOOP_HOME` is an environment variable that refers to the directory pathname on your system where you install Apache Sqoop.) For the hands-on examples shown in this chapter, we installed the `mysql-connector-java-5.1.26-bin.jar` file from `http://dev.mysql.com/downloads/connector` in our `$SQOOP_HOME/lib` directory.

✔ **Sqoop does not include a connector for your database management system.** That means you need to download one from a 3rd party vendor, along with a JDBC driver if the connector requires one. (Couchbase and Teradata both do, for example.)

✔ **Your database management system does not provide a Sqoop connector but a JDBC driver is available.** In this case, you leverage Sqoop's generic JDBC connector and download and install your vendor's JDBC driver.

For an in-depth discussion of Sqoop connectors and drivers, see the following blog entry: `https://blogs.apache.org/sqoop/date/201309`. For the latest release, documentation, and connector information, check out `http://sqoop.apache.org`.

Importing Data with Sqoop

Ready to dive into importing data with Sqoop? Start by taking a look at Figure 14-2, which illustrates the steps in a typical Sqoop import operation from an RDBMS or a data warehouse system. Nothing too complicated here — just a typical Products data table from a (typical) fictional company being imported into a typical Apache Hadoop cluster from a typical data management system (DMS).

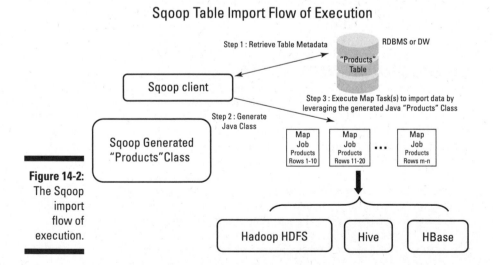

Figure 14-2: The Sqoop import flow of execution.

During Step 1, Sqoop uses the appropriate connector to retrieve the Products table metadata from the target DMS. (The metadata is used to map the data types from the Products table to data types in the Java language.) Step 2 then uses this metadata to generate and compile a Java class that will be used by one or more map tasks to import the actual rows from the Products table. Sqoop saves the generated Java class to temp space or to a directory you specify so that you can leverage it for the subsequent processing of your data records.

The Sqoop generated Java code that is saved for you is like the gift that keeps on giving! With this code, Sqoop imports records from the DMS and stores them to HDFS using one of three formats that you can pick: binary Avro data, binary sequence files, or delimited text files. Afterwards, this code is available to you for subsequent data processing. Sequence files are a natural choice if you're importing binary data types and you'll need the generated Java class to serialize and deserialize your data later on — perhaps for MapReduce processing or exporting. (More on exporting later — right now, we're focusing on imports.) Avro data — based on Apache's own serialization framework — is useful if you need to interact with other applications after the import to HDFS. If you choose to store your imported data in delimited text format, you may find the generated Java code valuable later on as you parse and perform data format conversions on your new data. Later in this chapter, you'll see that the generated code also helps you merge data sets after Sqoop import operations and the final example in this chapter illustrates how the generated Java code can help avoid ambiguity when processing delimited text data.

Finally, during Step 3, Sqoop divides the data records in the Products table across a number of map tasks (with the number of mappers optionally specified by the user) and imports the table data into HDFS, Hive, or HBase.

Importing data into HDFS

Figure 14-2 gives you the big-picture view of the Sqoop data import process. Time to look at the process in a bit more detail, with the help of a few hands-on examples.

Figure 14-3 helps you imagine a relational database used by a fictional service company that has been taking (you guessed it) Apache Hadoop service calls and now wants to move some of its data onto Hadoop to run Hive queries, leverage HBase scalability and performance, and run text analytics on its customer's problem descriptions.

We discuss the Service Order Database in Chapter 12 and explain how it might be converted to an HBase schema. Sqoop is the tool you'll want to use to import data from relational tables into HBase tables on Hadoop.

In Listing 14-1 we show the MySQL commands we used to build the Service Order Database you see in Figure 14-3. (We filled in a couple records in the diagram shown in Figure 14-3 to make things crystal clear.) We installed a MySQL RDBMS that we could import from and export to using Sqoop. Since these commands also show you the data we load into our Service Order Database, we'll be referring back to this listing several times in this chapter to confirm that our Sqoop examples work properly.

My SQL Normalized Service Order Database Schema

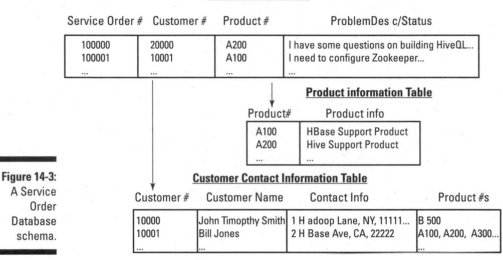

Service Orders Table

Service Order #	Customer #	Product #	ProblemDes c/Status
100000	20000	A200	I have some questions on building HiveQL...
100001	10001	A100	I need to configure Zookeeper...
...	...	...	...

Product information Table

Product#	Product info
A100	HBase Support Product
A200	Hive Support Product
...	...

Customer Contact Information Table

Customer #	Customer Name	Contact Info	Product #s
10000	John Timopthy Smith	1 H adoop Lane, NY, 11111...	B 500
10001	Bill Jones	2 H Base Ave, CA, 22222	A100, A200, A300...
...	...		...

Figure 14-3:
A Service Order Database schema.

Listing 14-1:   MySQL Commands to Build the Service Order Database

```
/* Create the Service Orders Database */

CREATE DATABASE serviceorderdb;
USE serviceorderdb;

/* Create the Product Information Table */

CREATE TABLE productinfo(
productnum CHAR (4) PRIMARY KEY,
productdesc VARCHAR(100)
);

/* Create the Customer Contact Information Table */

CREATE TABLE customercontactinfo(
customernum INT PRIMARY KEY,
customername VARCHAR(100),
contactinfo VARCHAR(100),
productnums SET('A100','A200','A300','B400','B500','C500','C600','D700')
);

/* Create the Service Orders Table */

CREATE TABLE serviceorders(
serviceordernum INT PRIMARY KEY,
customernum INT,
productnum CHAR(4),
status VARCHAR(100),
```

```
FOREIGN KEY (customernum) REFERENCES customercontactinfo(customernum),
FOREIGN KEY (productnum) REFERENCES productinfo(productnum)
);

/* Insert product data into the Product Information Table */

INSERT INTO productinfo VALUES ('A100', 'HBase Support Product');
INSERT INTO productinfo VALUES ('A200', 'Hive Support Product');
INSERT INTO productinfo VALUES ('A300', 'Sqoop Support Product');
INSERT INTO productinfo VALUES ('B400', 'Ambari Support Product');
INSERT INTO productinfo VALUES ('B500', 'HDFS Support Product');
INSERT INTO productinfo VALUES ('C500', 'Mahout Support Product');
INSERT INTO productinfo VALUES ('C600', 'Zookeeper Support Product');
INSERT INTO productinfo VALUES ('D700', 'Pig Support Product');

/* Insert customer data into the Customer Contact Information Table */

INSERT INTO customercontactinfo
VALUES (10000, 'John Timothy Smith', '1 Hadoop Lane, NY, 11111,
        John.Smith@xyz.com', 'B500');

INSERT INTO customercontactinfo
VALUES (10001, 'Bill Jones', '2 HBase Ave, CA, 22222',
        'A100,A200,A300,B400,B500,C500,C600,D700');

INSERT INTO customercontactinfo
VALUES (20000, 'Jane Ann Doe', '1 Expert HBase Ave, CA, 22222',
        'A100,A200,A300');

INSERT INTO customercontactinfo
VALUES (20001, 'Joe Developer', '1 Piglatin Ave, CO, 33333', 'D700');

INSERT INTO customercontactinfo
VALUES (30000, 'Data Scientist', '1 Statistics Lane, MA, 33333', 'A300,C500');

/* Enter service orders into the Service Orders Table */

INSERT INTO serviceorders
VALUES (100000, 20000, 'A200', 'I have some questions on building HiveQL
                queries? My Hadoop for Dummies book has not arrived yet!');

INSERT INTO serviceorders
VALUES (100001, 10001, 'A100', 'I need to understand how to configure Zookeeper
                for my HBase Cluster?');

INSERT INTO serviceorders
VALUES (200000, 20001, 'D700', 'I am writing some Piglatin and I have a few
                questions?');

INSERT INTO serviceorders
VALUES (200001, 30000, 'A300', 'How do I merge my data sets after Sqoop
                incremental imports?');
```

Listing 14-2 confirms that the MySQL Service Order Database has been created using the commands in Listing 14-1, and shows you the table names that we'll import from using Sqoop.

Listing 14-2: The MySQL show tables Command

```
mysql> show tables;
+------------------------+
| Tables_in_serviceorderdb |
+------------------------+
| customercontactinfo    |
| productinfo            |
| serviceorders          |
+------------------------+
3 rows in set (0.00 sec)
```

Now that you have seen the MySQL Service Order Database records that are just waiting to be exploited, it's time to turn your attention to Hadoop and run your first Sqoop command. For this example, we downloaded an Apache Hadoop distribution that provides us with Sqoop, and we already had in place an HDFS as well as Hive and HBase. (For more information on setting up your Apache Hadoop environment, see Chapter 3.)

You can find a thorough list of Apache Hadoop bundles at `http://wiki.apache.org/hadoop/Distributions` and Commercial Support.

Note, however, that we don't pull out the trusty `import` command right off the bat. Sqoop includes several handy tools along with `import` and `export`, including the `list-databases` command, which we use in Listing 14-3. Using that command, you can confirm that you have connectivity and visibility into the MySQL database.

Listing 14-3: The Sqoop list-databases Command

```
$ sqoop list-databases --connect jdbc:mysql://localhost/ \
                        --username root -P
Enter password:
13/08/15 17:21:00 INFO manager.MySQLManager: Preparing to
          use a MySQL streaming resultset.
information_schema
mysql
performance_schema
serviceorderdb
```

The `serviceorderdb` (bolded in Listing 14-3) is shown to be available, so now you can list the tables within `serviceorderdb` by using the Sqoop `list-tables` command, as shown in Listing 14-4. Notice that now we're adding the database that we want Sqoop to access in the `jdbc:mysql` URL.

Listing 14-4: The Sqoop list-tables Command

```
$ sqoop list-tables \
        --connect jdbc:mysql://localhost/serviceorderdb \
        --username root -P
Enter password:
13/08/15 17:22:01 INFO manager.MySQLManager: Preparing to
        use a MySQL streaming resultset.
customercontactinfo
productinfo
serviceorders
```

Listing 14-3 and Listing 14-4 should assure you that Sqoop now has connectivity and can access the three tables from Figure 14-3. That means you can execute your first Sqoop `import` command and target the `serviceorders` table with a clean conscience. Sqoop `import` commands have this format:

```
sqoop import (generic arguments) (import arguments)
```

With the generic arguments, you point to your MySQL database and provide the necessary login information, just as we did with the preceding `list-tables` tool. In the import arguments, you (the user) have the ability to specify what you want to import and how you want the import to be performed. In Listing 14-5, we specify the `serviceorders` table and request that one map task be used for the import using the `-m 1` CLA. (By default, Sqoop would use four map tasks, but that would be overkill for this small table and our virtual machine.) We have also specified the `--class-name` for the generated code and specified the `--bindir` where the compiled code and `.jar` file should be located. (Without these arguments, Sqoop would place the generated Java source file in your current working directory and the compiled `.class` file and `.jar file` in `/tmp/sqoop-<username>/compile`.) The class name simply derives from the table name unless you specify a name with the help of the `--class-name` command line argument (CLA). The `--target-dir` is the location in HDFS where you want the imported table to be placed.

Listing 14-5: The Sqoop import serviceorders Table Command

```
$ sqoop import \
  --connect jdbc:mysql://localhost/serviceorderdb  \
  --username root -P \
  --table serviceorders -m 1 \
  --class-name serviceorders \
  --target-dir /usr/biadmin/serviceorders-import \
  --bindir .
Enter password:
...
13/08/25 14:43:56 INFO mapreduce.ImportJobBase:
        Transferred 356 bytes in 21.0736 seconds
        (16.8932 bytes/sec)
13/08/25 14:43:56 INFO mapreduce.ImportJobBase: Retrieved
        4 records.
```

The command ran fine, so you should have the same `serviceorders` data that's shown in Listing 14-1 now stored in your HDFS as well as the generated Java files in your current working directory. Listing 14-6 shows how you can use the `hadoop fs -cat` command to verify this.

Listing 14-6:　Displaying the serviceorders Table Now Stored in HDFS and Listing the Generated Java Files

```
$ hadoop fs -cat /usr/biadmin/serviceorders-import/part-m-00000
100000,20000,A200,I have some questions on building HiveQL queries? My Hadoop
             for Dummies book has not arrived yet!
100001,10001,A100,I need to configure Zookeeper for my HBase Cluster?
200000,10001,D700,I am writing some Piglatin and I have a few questions?
200001,20000,A300,How do I merge my data sets after Sqoop incremental imports?

$ ls *.jar *.java *.class
serviceorders.class  serviceorders.jar  serviceorders.java
```

In the next two listings, we show you some additional options that can help you specify in greater detail the data you want to import. Normally, Sqoop imports the entire table or tables that you specify. However, you can control the number and order of columns using the `--columns <col1, col2, . . .>` command line argument. You can also provide your own `SELECT` statement after the `--query` argument. In Listing 14-7, you use the `--query` argument to specify that you want to import only the names and contact information for those customers who have open service orders. (The `WHERE $CONDITIONS` token is required by Sqoop to help the map tasks divide and conquer the import operation — at the end of this section, we explain more about how Sqoop divides an import.)

Listing 14-7:　The Sqoop import Command Using the --query CLA

```
sqoop import --connect jdbc:mysql://localhost/serviceorderdb \
 --username root -P -m 2 \
 --query 'SELECT customercontactinfo.customername, customercontactinfo.
             contactinfo FROM customercontactinfo JOIN
serviceorders ON customercontactinfo.customernum = serviceorders.customernum
             WHERE $CONDITIONS' \
 --split-by serviceorders.serviceordernum \
 --boundary-query "SELECT min(serviceorders.serviceordernum),
             max(serviceorders.serviceordernum) FROM serviceorders" \
 --target-dir /usr/biadmin/customers \
 --verbose
```

This Sqoop import is somewhat complex, so we want to take the time to explain it in detail and discuss how Sqoop divides up the import job. It helps to understand that, by default, Sqoop performs the following statement to decide how to divide the table rows across the map tasks for importing:

```
SQL SELECT MIN(primary key col), MAX(primary key col) FROM
       table
```

That's the default behavior in an import operation, such as the one in Listing 14-5. The exception in that listing, of course, is that the table is very small and we used just the one map task. If it were a very large table, you would want more map tasks, to get the job done faster. Now, we made Listing 14-7 more extravagant — it uses two map tasks. In this case, Sqoop requires the `--split-by` and `--boundary-query` command line arguments because the `--table` CLA has been replaced by our own query using the `--query` CLA. So we're helping Sqoop divide the work across the two map tasks we created by specifying our own boundaries for the import. In this case, we know that the `serviceorders` table has the increasing integer primary key named `serviceordernum`, which lets Sqoop divide up the work. The `--boundary-query` command line argument lets you get creative to help Sqoop meet your table import requirements, but we keep it simple in this example.

Listings 14-8 and 14-9 confirm that our two map tasks did their job. This time we have two files to view because we used two map tasks.

Listing 14-8:   Output from Map Task 1

```
$ hadoop fs -cat /usr/biadmin/customers/part-m-00000
Jane Ann Doe,1 Expert HBase Ave, CA, 22222
Bill Jones,2 HBase Ave, CA, 22222
```

Listing 14-9:   Output from Map Task 2

```
$ hadoop fs -cat /usr/biadmin/customers/part-m-00001
Joe Developer,1 Piglatin Ave, CO, 33333
Data Scientist,1 Statistics Lane, MA, 33333
```

You can also control which rows are imported using the `--where` argument to provide a WHERE clause, as shown in Listing 14-10.

Listing 14-10:   The Sqoop import Command using the --where CLA with Results

```
sqoop import \
        --connect jdbc:mysql://localhost/serviceorderdb \
        --username root -P -m 1 \
        --table customercontactinfo \
        --where 'customernum >= 20000 and customernum < 30000' \
        --target-dir /user/biadmin/customers-range
$ hadoop fs -cat /user/biadmin/customers-range/part-m-00000
20000,Jane Ann Doe,1 Expert HBase Ave, CA, 22222,A100,A200,A300
20001,Joe Developer,1 Piglatin Ave, CO, 33333,D700
```

In Listing 14-10, we're back to using the default behavior, as in Listing 14-5. But because Sqoop lets us specify a WHERE clause using the `--where` command line argument, we download only those customers who have IDs between 20000 and 29999.

Are you getting a sense of the power and flexibility that Sqoop brings to Apache Hadoop? Big data analytics become far more valuable when combined with existing enterprise data, and Sqoop greatly simplifies and streamlines the overall process! In the preceding example, the fictional service company can now leverage the data in the `serviceorders` table, which is now stored as a flat file in HDFS, as part of a larger Hadoop text analytics or statistical analysis application.

Importing data into Hive

For our next example, we import all of the Service Order Database directly from MySQL into Hive and run a HiveQL query against the newly imported database on Apache Hadoop. (For more information on Hive, see Chapter 13). Listing 14-11 shows you how it's done.

Listing 14-11:   Hive and Sqoop commands to import the Service Order Database into Apache Hive

```
hive> create database serviceorderdb;
OK
Time taken: 1.343 seconds
hive> use serviceorderdb;
OK
Time taken: 0.062 seconds

$ sqoop import --connect jdbc:mysql://localhost/serviceorderdb \
   --username root -P \
   --table productinfo \
   --hive-import \
   --hive-table serviceorderdb.productinfo -m 1
Enter password:
...
13/08/16 15:17:08 INFO hive.HiveImport: Hive import complete.
$ sqoop import --connect jdbc:mysql://localhost/serviceorderdb \
   --username root -P \
   --table customercontactinfo \
   --hive-import \
   --hive-table serviceorderdb.customercontactinfo -m 1
Enter password:
...
13/08/16 17:21:35 INFO hive.HiveImport: Hive import complete.
$ sqoop import --connect jdbc:mysql://localhost/serviceorderdb \
   --username root -P \
   --table serviceorders \
   --hive-import \
   --hive-table serviceorderdb.serviceorders -m 1
Enter password:
...
13/08/16 17:26:56 INFO hive.HiveImport: Hive import complete.
```

When the import operations are complete, you run the `show tables` command to list the newly imported tables (see Listing 14-12), and then run a Hive query (see Listing 14-13) to show which Apache Hadoop technologies have open service orders in the database.

Listing 14-12:   Confirming the Sqoop Import Operations in Apache Hive

```
hive> show tables;
OK
customercontactinfo
productinfo
serviceorders
Time taken: 0.074 seconds
```

Listing 14-13:   HiveQL Query to Determine Which Products Have Open Service Orders Against Them

```
hive> SELECT productdesc FROM productinfo
    > INNER JOIN serviceorders
    > ON productinfo.productnum = serviceorders.productnum;
...
OK
HBase Support Product
Hive Support Product
Sqoop Support Product
Pig Support Product
Time taken: 28.552 seconds
```

Based on the Service Order Database we created and populated back in Listing 14-1, you can confirm the results in Listing 14-13. We have four open service orders on the products in bold. The Sqoop Hive import operation worked, and now the service company can leverage Hive to query, analyze, and transform its service order structured data. Additionally, the company can now combine its relational data with other data types (perhaps unstructured) as part of any new Hadoop analytics applications. Many possibilities now exist with Apache Hadoop being part of the overall IT strategy!

Importing data into HBase

Chapter 12 takes a look at how you can transform a relational database schema into an HBase schema, when appropriate. In this subsection, we demonstrate how Sqoop can be used to make that transformation much easier. Of course, our main goal here is to demonstrate how Sqoop can import data from an RDBMS or data warehouse directly into HBase, but it's always better to see how a tool is used in context versus how it's used in the abstract. Figure 14-4 shows how the Service Order Database might look after being transformed into an HBase schema.

HBase Schema for the Service Order Database

Figure 14-4:
The Service Order database, translated into an HBase schema.

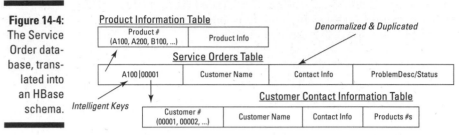

Because we talk a lot about the process and methodology of this transformation in Chapter 12, we hold off on explaining it here. (If you desperately need to know *this instant* how this process works, of course, take a look at Chapter 12.) For more information on the Denormalization, Duplication, and Intelligent Keys (DDI) methodology of translating relational database schemas into HBase schemas, pay particular attention to the section in Chapter 12 about transitioning from an RDBMS to HBase.

For this particular import example, we want to import the `customercontact info` table directly into an HBase table in preparation for building the HBase Service Order Database schema. (Refer to Figure 14-4.) To complete the HBase schema, you'd have to execute the same steps to import the `productinfo` table, and then the `serviceorders` table could be built with a Java MapReduce application.

Sqoop doesn't now permit you to import, all at once, a relational table directly into an HBase table having multiple column families. To work around this limitation, you create the HBase table first and then execute three Sqoop import operations to finish the task. Listing 14-14 shows the task of creating the table.

Listing 14-14:   HBase customercontactinfo Table Creation Command

```
hbase(main):017:0> create 'customercontactinfo', 'CustomerName',
hbase(main):018:0*          'ContactInfo', 'ProductNums'
0 row(s) in 1.0680 seconds
```

In Listing 14-15, for each Sqoop import command, note that we have bolded the target HBase column family specified by the `--column-family` CLA and the corresponding MySQL columns specified by the `–columns` CLA. The `customernum` primary key also becomes the HBase row key, as specified by the `--hbase-row-key` CLA.

Listing 14-15:   Sqoop Commands to Import the customercontactinfo Table Directly into a HBase Table

```
$ sqoop import \
    --connect jdbc:mysql://localhost/serviceorderdb \
    --username root -P \
    --table customercontactinfo \
    --columns "customernum,customername" \
    --hbase-table customercontactinfo \
    --column-family CustomerName \
    --hbase-row-key customernum -m 1
Enter password:
. . .
13/08/17 16:53:01 INFO mapreduce.ImportJobBase: Retrieved
          5 records.
$ sqoop import \
    --connect jdbc:mysql://localhost/serviceorderdb \
    --username root -P \
    --table customercontactinfo \
    --columns "customernum,contactinfo" \
    --hbase-table customercontactinfo \
    --column-family ContactInfo \
    --hbase-row-key customernum -m 1
Enter password:
. . .
13/08/17 17:00:59 INFO mapreduce.ImportJobBase: Retrieved
          5 records.
$ sqoop import \
    --connect jdbc:mysql://localhost/serviceorderdb \
    --username root -P \
    --table customercontactinfo \
    --columns "customernum,productnums" \
    --hbase-table customercontactinfo \
    --column-family ProductNums \
    --hbase-row-key customernum -m 1
Enter password:
. . .
13/08/17 17:05:54 INFO mapreduce.ImportJobBase: Retrieved
          5 records.
```

If you were to carry out an HBase scan of your new table (see Listing 14-16), you'd see that the import and translation from a relational database table on MySQL directly into HBase was a success. The customercontactinfo table in this example is rather small, but imagine the power you now have, using Sqoop and HBase, to quickly move relational tables that may be exceeding capacity on your RDBMS or data warehouse into HBase, where capacity is virtually unlimited and scalability is automatic.

Listing 14-16:   HBase Scan of the New customercontactinfo Table Confirming Success

```
hbase(main):033:0> scan 'customercontactinfo'
ROW          COLUMN+CELL
 10000       column=ContactInfo:contactinfo,
             timestamp=1376773256317, value=1 Hadoop Lane,
             NY, 11111, John.Smith@xyz.com
 10000       column=CustomerName:customername,
             timestamp=1376772776684, value=John Timothy
             Smith
 10000       column=ProductNums:productnums,
             timestamp=1376773551221, value=B500
 10001       column=ContactInfo:contactinfo,
             timestamp=1376773256317, value=2 HBase Ave, CA,
             22222
 10001       column=CustomerName:customername,
             timestamp=1376772776684, value=Bill Jones
 10001       column=ProductNums:productnums,
             timestamp=1376773551221,
             value=A100,A200,A300,B400,B500,C500,C600,D700
 20000       column=ContactInfo:contactinfo,
             timestamp=1376773256317, value=1 Expert HBase
             Ave, CA, 22222
 20000       column=CustomerName:customername,
             timestamp=1376772776684, value=Jane Ann Doe
 20000       column=ProductNums:productnums,
             timestamp=1376773551221, value=A100,A200,A300
 20001       column=ContactInfo:contactinfo,
             timestamp=1376773256317, value=1 Piglatin Ave,
             CO, 33333
 20001       column=CustomerName:customername,
             timestamp=1376772776684, value=Joe Developer
 20001       column=ProductNums:productnums,
             timestamp=1376773551221, value=D700
 30000       column=ContactInfo:contactinfo,
             timestamp=1376773256317, value=1 Statistics
             Lane, MA, 33333
 30000       column=CustomerName:customername,
             timestamp=1376772776684, value=Data Scientist
 30000       column=ProductNums:productnums,
             timestamp=1376773551221, value=C500
5 row(s) in 0.1120 seconds
```

Importing existing relational data via Sqoop into Hive and HBase tables can potentially enable a wide range of new and exciting data analysis workflows. If this feature is of interest to you, check out the Apache Sqoop documentation for additional Hive and HBase command line arguments and features.

Importing incrementally

If the tables you're planning to import into Hadoop are changing or growing (which means that you may be planning more than one import or perhaps continual imports), be sure to check out Sqoop's Incremental Import feature. Sqoop provides several options and tools to make incremental import operations flexible and straightforward.

Incremental import append mode

When you have a table that is receiving new rows and it has a column with a continually increasing value (like the `customernum` from our `customercontact info` table), you can leverage incremental append mode. Below we show how you can incrementally import all new customers from the fictional service company that have been appended to our MySQL `customercontactinfo` table since the last import operation.

First you need to know the number of the last customer in our MySQL `customercontactinfo` table. A quick review of Listing 14-1 shows that our last customer, Mr. Data Scientist, was given a customer number of 30000.

In the next step, you need to add three customers to our MySQL `customer contactinfo` table for the example to work properly. The SQL statements in Listing 14-17 will get the job done.

Listing 14-17:   Insert Commands in the MySQL customercontactinfo Table

```
INSERT INTO customercontactinfo VALUES (40000, 'Isaac
        Newton', '1 Gravity Lane, London, United
        Kingdom', 'C500');
INSERT INTO customercontactinfo VALUES (50000, 'Johann
        Kepler', '1 Astronomy Street, Württemberg,
        Germany', 'A100,B500,C500');
INSERT INTO customercontactinfo VALUES (60000, 'Louis
        Pasteur', '1 Bacteriology Ave, Dole, France',
        'A100,A200,A300,B500,C600');
```

At this point, you're ready to let Sqoop do the work and import all new customers with a customer number greater than 30000. Listing 14-18 provides the command you can use.

Listing 14-18:   Sqoop Incremental Import Command to Pick Up New Customers in Hive

```
sqoop import \
          --connect jdbc:mysql://localhost/serviceorderdb \
          --username root -P \
          --table customercontactinfo -m 1 \
          --incremental append \
          --check-column customernum \
          --last-value 30000
Enter password:
...
13/08/24 14:15:28 INFO tool.ImportTool:  --incremental
          append
13/08/24 14:15:28 INFO tool.ImportTool:  --check-column
          customernum
(A) 13/08/24 14:15:28 INFO tool.ImportTool:  --last-value
          60000
(B) 13/08/24 14:15:28 INFO tool.ImportTool: (Consider
          saving this with 'sqoop job --create')
```

Listing 14-19 confirms our success. You now have three new customers stored in your HDFS file.

Listing 14-19:   New Customers Now Stored in HDFS after Sqoop Incremental Import

```
$ hadoop fs -cat /user/biadmin/customercontactinfo/part-m-00000
40000,Isaac Newton,1 Gravity Lane, London, United Kingdom,C500
50000,Johann Kepler,1 Astronomy Street, W_rttemberg, Germany,A100,B500,C500
60000,Louis Pasteur,1 Bacteriology Ave, Dole, France,A100,A200,A300,B500,C600
```

Note the last two lines of output from Listing 14-18. The line labeled A lets you know that, of the customer records that were imported, the last new record had the customer ID 60000 (Louis Pasteur). This handy bookkeeping feature in Sqoop gets even better! Line B suggests that you save the value for the next incremental import and consider using the sqoop-job tool to make the task easier. The `sqoop job --create` command works hand in hand with incremental imports. Using the `sqoop-job` tool, you can create a job that you can run as often as you need to, and Sqoop's metastore keeps track of the vital information — like `last-value`, in this case. Listing 14-20 creates a Sqoop job that you can call every time you need to import new customers into your HDFS. (We call our job *load-new-customers* but you call it whatever makes sense for your application.)

Listing 14-20: The sqoop job --create Command and Subsequent sqoop job --list to Confirm Results

```
$ sqoop job --create load-new-customers -- \
        import \
        --connect jdbc:mysql://localhost/serviceorderdb \
        --username root -P \
        --table customercontactinfo -m 1 \
        --incremental append \
        --check-column customernum \
        --last-value 60000
Enter password:
$ sqoop job --list
Available jobs:
  load-new-customers
```

Additionally, you can leverage another Sqoop tool — sqoop-metastore — to create an HSQLDB instance that can be accessed by other users on your network; now your Sqoop meta data can be shared by others on your team!

HSQLDB, which stands for *HyperSQL DataBase*, is an SQL database written in Java. For more information on HSQLDB, go to http://hsqldb.org. For the metastore thing to work, you also need to add some information to your $SQOOP_HOME/conf/sqoop-site.xml file.

After running the sqoop-metastore command, your team can leverage it in the sqoop job --create command by adding a --meta-connect command line argument, as shown in this example:

```
sqoop job
  --create load-new-customers \
  --meta-connect jdbc.hsqldb:hsql://<servername>:<port>/
          sqoop \
  --import \
  --table xyz \
  ...
```

Incremental import lastmodified mode

In addition to incremental append mode, Sqoop provides last modified mode. You can use this mode to incrementally import updates from a table to HDFS. For example, to import to HDFS any changes in the customercontactinfo table that took place yesterday, you would have to modify the table to include a LastUpdate column that would hold the timestamp for each update. With a new LastUpdate column, you could create this Sqoop command:

```
sqoop import
        --connect jdbc:mysql://localhost/serviceorderdb \
        --username root -P \
        --table customerinfo -m 1 \
        --incremental lastmodified \
        --check-column LastUpdate \
        --last-value "2013-08-23 00:00:00"
```

Note that, as with the incremental append mode option, the `sqoop-job` tool can come in quite handy for saving the `last-value` timestamp for subsequent `incremental lastmodified` imports. Speaking of subsequent imports, what do you suppose happens when you run the same command again (or job, if you created one) on, say, the next day to pick up more potential `customercontactinfo` table changes? The answer is that you get another file under the directory `customercontactinfo` in your HDFS with the `customercontactinfo` table modifications. So how do you merge these files? You use the `sqoop-merge` command, of course, which is the subject of the next subsection.

The sqoop merge tool

The `sqoop merge` tool works hand in hand with the incremental import lastmodified mode. Each import creates a new file, so if you want to keep the table data together in one file, you use the merge tool. The `sqoop merge` tool combines a newer data set with an older data set by overwriting rows from the older data set with the rows from the new dataset when the primary keys match. The `sqoop merge` command shown in the following example illustrates how this would look when using new and old `customercontactinfo` incremental imports:

The generated Java class file from the previous import (specified with `--jar-file customercontactinfo.jar`) is required to parse the records for this merge example. If you don't keep it around, you'll need to use the `codegen` tool to recreate it.

```
sqoop merge
    --new-data \
        /user/biadmin/customercontactinfo/part-m-00001 \
    --onto \
        /user/biadmin/customercontactinfo/part-m-00000 \
    --target-dir /user/biadmin/merged-customers \
    --jar-file customercontactinfo.jar \
    --class-name customercontactinfo \
    --merge-key customernum
```

Benefiting from additional Sqoop import features

With the hands-on examples from the preceding section in mind, we'd like to describe some additional import features that you should know about. It's beyond the scope of this chapter to cover every Sqoop feature in detail, but Table 14-1 exposes you to its more significant features. Also note that the Sqoop community is always innovating and adding functionality to Sqoop, so you should watch the community documentation pages under `http://sqoop.apache.org/docs` for the latest features and new Sqoop command options.

Table 14-1	Miscellaneous Sqoop Import Options
Command Line Arguments	**Description**
Generic	
`--driver <class-name>` `--connection-manager <manager-name>`	Earlier in the chapter under the subsection entitled "Connectors and Drivers" we explain three approaches for using Sqoop depending on which data management system you are interfacing with. If you need to download and install your own connector, then you'll need to use the `--connection-manager` CLA and possibly the `--driver` CLA as well. If you find yourself needing to use the generic JDBC connector, then you have to specify that with the `--connection-manager` CLA and your vendor specific JDBC driver with the `--driver` CLA.
Import	
`--append`	You can append imported data to an existing dataset stored in HDFS. Without the `--append` CLA, if you try to import to an existing HDFS directory, the import fails. With the `--append` CLA, the import data is written to a new file in the same HDFS directory and is given a name that doesn't conflict with the existing file(s).
`--as-avrodatafile,` `--as-sequencefile,` `--as-textfile`	These three arguments let you specify the import data format when it's stored on HDFS. The default import format is `textfile`.
`--direct`	Some of the Sqoop-supported databases offer high-performance tools for data movement that exceed the performance of their respective JDBC drivers. As of this writing, both MySQL and PostregSQL provide these high-performance tools, and you can leverage them by using the `--direct` argument along with the table-split-size argument via `--direct-split-size <n>`. Beware that there may be certain limitations in direct mode (e.g. large objects may not be supported) so consult your database documentation.

(continued)

Table 14-1 *(continued)*

Command Line Arguments	Description
`--map-column-java <mapping>, --map-column-hive <mapping>`	Sqoop lets you explicitly specify the Java type mapping for imports into HDFS and Hive.
`--inline-lob-limit <size>`	As you might expect, Sqoop can import large objects (BLOBs and CLOBs, in RDBMS terms). After all, Apache Hadoop is all about big data! As long as the large object doesn't exceed the size of the `--inline-lob-limit <size>` CLA, Sqoop stores the large object in line with the rest of the data in HDFS. However, if the large object exceeds the aforementioned limit specified by the CLA, it's stored in the subdirectory named `_lobs`, off the main HDFS import directory.
`--compress, --compression-codec <c>`	By default, data isn't compressed, but you can leverage gzip by specifying the `--compress` argument or your own algorithm using the `--compression-codec` argument. All three of the supported file types (text, sequence, and Avro) can be compressed.

Sending Data Elsewhere with Sqoop

Sqoop export operations are quite similar to import operations, with a couple of notable exceptions. First, Sqoop cannot determine the correct data types for your relational tables. SQL data types are numerous and rich, so it makes far more sense for you to first decide how you want to map your Hadoop data into relational database types, and then complete the export. In other words, you need to create the target table in your RDBMS or data warehouse first to hold the data you want to export. Second, when you execute the Sqoop export command, you specify the HDFS directory where the export data is stored. You cannot specify a Hive or HBase table name for exports, as you can with imports.

Figure 14-5 illustrates the steps involved in a Sqoop export from HDFS to an RDBMS or data warehouse system.

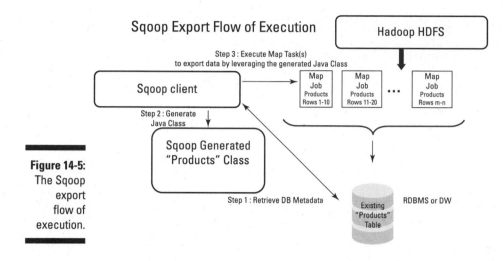

Sqoop Export Flow of Execution

Figure 14-5:
The Sqoop
export
flow of
execution.

As you can see, the Sqoop export flow of execution is similar to the import flow. Figure 14-5 focuses on the export of a potentially large Products file from HDFS into a similar Products data table in a data management system. Three map tasks are depicted to parallelize the process, but more or less could be specified by the user, based on the dataset size and the size of the Hadoop cluster. Carefully consider specifying the number of map tasks, in terms of both exports and imports. Too many map tasks can take *longer* if sufficient resources don't exist on your Hadoop cluster, and, similarly, too many map tasks can overwhelm the data management system as well.

Exporting data from HDFS

The following hands-on example demonstrates an export of a Hive table called `sev1_serviceorders`. A fictional service company has derived the table from the original `serviceorders` table that we show you how to import from the MySQL `serviceorderdb` earlier in this chapter. It was decided, after leveraging text analytics on the Apache Hadoop cluster against the database, that service orders for customer number 20000 should be treated with a severity level of 1 and be exported back to the MySQL database for report generation. (This example is contrived but still illustrative of a typical joint use case for Apache Hadoop and the RDBMS or data warehouse.)

Right off the bat, make sure that the MySQL `serviceorderdb` has an appropriate table to receive your Sqoop export. The data definition language to create the table is given in Listing 14-21.

Listing 14-21: MySQL Create Table Statement

```
CREATE TABLE sev1_serviceorders(
serviceordernum INT PRIMARY KEY,
customernum INT,
productnum CHAR(4),
status VARCHAR(100),
FOREIGN KEY (customernum) REFERENCES
        customercontactinfo(customernum),
FOREIGN KEY (productnum) REFERENCES
        productinfo(productnum)
);
```

The Hive `sev1_serviceorders` table can be created and displayed in several different ways, but for the sake of illustration, we've included a pair of possible HiveQL statements in Listings 14-22 and 14-23.

Listing 14-22: HiveQL Create Table Statement with INSERT Command to Load Data

```
hive> CREATE TABLE sev1_serviceorders(
    > serviceordernum INT,
    > customernum INT,
    > productnum STRING,
    > status STRING);
OK
Time taken: 0.7 seconds
hive> INSERT OVERWRITE TABLE sev1_serviceorders
    > SELECT * FROM serviceorders WHERE customernum =
        20000;
...
Total MapReduce CPU Time Spent: 1 seconds 30 msec
OK
Time taken: 26.836 seconds
```

Listing 14-23: HiveQL SELECT Command to Display the Contents of the New Table

```
hive> SELECT * FROM sev1_serviceorders;
OK
100000  20000  A200    I have some questions on building
        HiveQL queries? My Hadoop for Dummies book has
        not arrived yet!
Time taken: 0.167 seconds
```

Listing 14-23 confirms that everything is in place to perform the Sqoop export operation. Sqoop export commands are similar to import commands, as you can see in this example:

```
sqoop export (generic arguments) (export arguments)
```

In the export arguments, you specify in your HDFS the pathname to the Hive warehouse where the `sev1_serviceorders` table is stored. In addition, you specify the field delimiter that you want to use for your table, because Hive allows many different types of delimiters. Listing 14-24 shows a possible scenario, and Listing 14-25 shows the results.

Listing 14-24:   Sqoop export Command from HDFS to MySQL

```
$ sqoop export \
--connect jdbc:mysql://localhost/serviceorderdb \
--username root -P -m 1 \
--table sev1_serviceorders \
--export-dir /biginsights/hive/warehouse/serviceorderdb.db/sev1_serviceorders \
--input-fields-terminated-by '\0x0001'
Enter password:
...
13/08/18 19:08:27 INFO mapreduce.ExportJobBase: Exported 1 records.
```

Listing 14-25:   MySQL Export Results

```
mysql> select * from sev1_serviceorders;
| serviceordernum | customernum | productnum | status
|          100000 |       20000 | A200       | I have some questions on building
            HiveQL queries? My Hadoop for Dummies book has not arrived yet! |
1 row in set (0.00 sec)
```

Listing 14-25 confirms that the export was successful and the record you expected to be inserted into the `sev1_serviceorders` table in the MySQL database has in fact been inserted.

Just because we authors value thoroughness, we show you four distinct export approaches in this section: insert, update, update insert, and call procedures. The preceding example used the insert approach. In the following four sections, we explain each export approach (yes, even insert again) and their various options.

Sqoop exports using the Insert approach

In the hands-on export example in the previous section, the rows are exported from the Hive data warehouse (stored in HDFS) with the help of SQL INSERT statements in the MySQL RDBMS. The export operation was a small one, for the sake of illustration, but often, exports include very large tables with *millions* of rows. Sqoop handles large export use cases by way of batching techniques and by leveraging multiple map tasks to write the data in parallel. (As with imports, Sqoop uses four map tasks by default with exports.) The idea behind batching is to execute a group of SQL INSERT statements together instead of the serial approach of executing them one by one. The idea is straightforward, but the approach for batching differs from one database technology to another. The Sqoop designers knew this, so they made some good, educated guesses on batch default parameters and then gave us different options for adapting to, and tuning for, our database of choice.

This list describes two techniques that Sqoop users can leverage to batch export operations:

✔ **The** `--batch` **command line argument:** This argument allows Sqoop to batch together SQL `INSERT` statements using the JDBC PreparedStatement interface. So the Sqoop client creates a batch of the following statements using the JDBC APIs:

```
INSERT INTO table VALUES (col1,col2,...);
INSERT INTO table VALUES (col1,col2,...);
INSERT INTO table VALUES (col1,col2,...)
```

In theory, this technique should result in better export throughput because Sqoop's map task writers avoid sending individual `INSERT` statements and instead batch them together.

✔ **The** `-D <property=value>` **argument:** If you were to issue the `sqoop help export` command, you'd see a command line argument that begins with `-D` to allow you to set properties for Sqoop that would otherwise have to be set in the `$SQOOP_HOME/conf/sqoop-site.xml` file. If you leverage the `-D <property=value>` argument, you can set the `sqoop.export.records.per.statement` property to a value that determines the number of records per `INSERT` statement. For example, setting the aforementioned property to 3 would generate the `INSERT` statement

```
INSERT INTO "table" VALUES (x,y,z,...), (x,y,z,...),
    (x,y,z,...);
```

You can also set the `sqoop.export.statements.per.transaction` property to a value that specifies the number of `INSERT` statements to be executed before you commit the transaction.

Which option should you use? Well, it depends on your chosen database technology. The `--batch` command line argument may work fine, but it depends on how the JDBC driver was implemented. As of this writing, the default behavior for Sqoop 1.4.4 is to leverage the `-D <property=value>` argument, with records per statement set to 100 and statements per transaction set to 100. Therefore, every 10,000 rows, Sqoop commits your batch `INSERT` operations. By causing a commit every 10,000 rows, Sqoop avoids out-of-memory errors. We don't mean that the `-D <property=value>` argument works with every database technology — it just happens to be what the Sqoop designers chose, based on certain assumptions. Consult your vendor, or review the database documentation before executing batch Sqoop export commands to see which options are supported.

Sqoop exports using the Update and Update Insert approach

With insert mode, records exported by Sqoop are appended to the end of the target table. Sqoop also provides an update mode that you can use by providing the `--update-key <column(s)>` command line argument. This action causes Sqoop to generate a SQL `UPDATE` statement to run on the RDBMS or data warehouse. Assume that you want to update a three-column table with data stored in the HDFS file `/user/my-hdfs-file`. The file contains this data:

```
100, 1000, 2000
```

The following abbreviated Sqoop export command generates the corresponding SQL `UPDATE` statement on your database system:

```
$ sqoop export (Generic Arguments)
  --table target-relational-table \
  --update-key column1
  --export-dir /user/my-hdfs-file
  ...

Generates => UPDATE target-relational-table SET
                 column2=1000,column3=2000
            WHERE column1=100;
```

With the preceding export command, if the `target-relational-table` on your RDBMS or data warehouse system has no record with the matching value in `column1`, nothing is changed in `target-relational-table`. However, you may also include another argument that inserts or appends your data to `target-table` if no matching records are found. Think of it this way: If exists UPDATE else INSERT. This technique is often referred to as *upsert* in the database vernacular or as `MERGE` in other implementations. The argument for upsert mode is `--update-mode <mode>`, where `updateonly` is the default and `allowinsert` activates upsert mode. Check your database documentation or consult with your vender to determine whether upsert mode is supported with Apache Sqoop.

Sqoop exports using call stored procedures

Sqoop can also export HDFS data by calling a stored procedure in your RDBMS or data warehouse using the `--call <stored procedure>` command line argument. The following abbreviated Sqoop export command illustrates this approach:

```
sqoop export (Generic Arguments)
  --call my-stored-procedure \
  --export-dir /user/my-hdfs-export-data
```

In this example, Sqoop calls the `my-stored-procedure` for every record in the `/user/my-hdfs-export-data` file. Many use cases can leverage this feature. A classic example is that you already have existing stored procedures that you use to import data into your RDBMS or data warehouse.

A *stored procedure* is a subroutine that's stored in the RDBMS or data warehouse. It can centralize common logic that would otherwise have to exist at the application level.

Sqoop exports and transactions

The beauty of Sqoop is that it can export massive data sets to an RDBMS or data warehouse by batching SQL statements and leveraging parallel map writer tasks. However, the export operation is not *atomic* — it isn't an all-or-nothing entity, in other words. Individual writer tasks can fail, leaving the Sqoop export operation in a partially completed state. If this happens, your table data is corrupt and you're unlikely to be a "happy Hadooper." Sqoop solves this problem with the help of staging tables.

The idea here is that you can first export data to a staging table and after the export successfully completes, move your staging table to the final table in one atomic transaction. Use the command line argument `--staging-table <table name>` to specify your staging table, and use `--clear-staging-table` to clear the staging table before each subsequent export.

Staging tables aren't supported when using the `--direct` option, update mode, update insert mode, or called procedures. Staging tables are only available with the insert approach discussed above and demonstrated in Listing 14-25.

Looking at Your Sqoop Input and Output Formatting Options

In the earlier subsection "Importing Data with Sqoop," we talk about Sqoop's code generation feature. A bit later in the chapter — at Listing 14-5 or thereabouts — we also leverage code generation command-line arguments to demonstrate how you can control the code generation process and results. (Then you can use the `.jar` file for subsequent applications where you need to process the data now stored in HDFS.) Finally, in Listing 14-24, we use an `--input-fields-terminated-by '\0x0001'` command line argument to instruct the Sqoop export tool how to read and parse records managed by Hive before exporting to MySQL. Hive uses control-A characters ('\0x0001' in Listing 14-24) rather than the default comma for field termination. In this section, we help you take a closer look at input parsing CLAs as well as output line formatting CLAs. When you choose to import or export delimited text, you often need these CLAs.

Table 14-2 lists the input parsing CLAs which begin with --input, and the output line formatting CLAs. You'll probably notice that these CLAs are just opposites of each other.

Table 14-2	Sqoop Output Line Formatting and Input Parsing CLAs
Command Line Argument	**What It Does**
`--enclosed-by <char>` `--input-enclosed-by <char>`	Specifies a field-enclosing character (double quotes, for example).
`--optionally-enclosed-by <char>` `--input-optionally-enclosed-by <char>`	Specifies that if the data includes the `enclosed-by <char>`, say double quotes ("), then the double quotes should be written; otherwise, double quotes are optional — don't write them. So for example, if Sqoop imports a string field enclosed in double quotes then it will be written to HDFS with double quotes. Otherwise, other fields would not be written to HDFS with double quotes.
`--escaped-by <char>` `--input-escaped-by <char>`	Specifies an escape character to avoid ambiguity when parsing or writing records to HDFS. As an example, you might make the `--escaped-by` character a backslash (\) which would allow you to import a string with double quotes inside the string. When Sqoop writes the field to HDFS, the double quotes within the string would be preceded with a backslash. In a similar way, if you use the generated Java code to parse a string with quotes inside the string, specifying a backslash (\) with the `--input-escaped-by` CLA would save you from losing data because Sqoop would see the backslash, skip over the quotes and continue looking for the enclosing quotes.

(continued)

Table 14-2 *(continued)*

Command Line Argument	What It Does
`--fields-terminated-by <char>` `--input-fields-terminated-by <char>`	Specifies the field-termination character (a comma, for example).
`--lines-terminated-by <char>` `--input-lines-terminated-by <char>`	Specifies the record- or line-termination character (a new-line character for example).
`--mysql-delimeters <char>`	For output line formatting only, this CLA indicates that the default MySQL delimiters should be used for outputting records to HDFS. MySQL's default delimiter set is the following: fields: , lines: \n escaped by: \ optionally-enclosed-by: '

If you accidentally delete Java files generated by `sqoop-import` or `sqoop-export`, you can use the `sqoop-codegen` tool later to reproduce the files. The Sqoop codegen tool accepts the same CLAs in Table 14-2. You can also use `sqoop-codegen` independently and specify the jar file and class name for your `sqoop-import` or `sqoop-export` commands.

Getting down to brass tacks: An example of output line-formatting and input-parsing

To ensure that this whole output line formatting / input parsing feature in Sqoop is clear, we close this discussion with an example using our old standby, the Service Order Database. Imagine a call center operator from our fictional service company taking calls from customers and inputting their comments into the MySQL `serviceorderdb` that was used in earlier examples. You might imagine an operator entering commas in the problem description, in an attempt to keep the prose as clear as possible for the engineer, who would later try to solve the issue for the customer. However, unbeknownst to the call center operator, commas are the default field-termination characters for Sqoop — so later, when the IT staff decides to import part or all of the `serviceorderdb` into Hadoop for analysis, we have a problem. It could happen like this: the call center operator takes a service call from a customer and the MySQL system inserts the following record into the `serviceorderdb`.

```
INSERT INTO serviceorders VALUES (100000, 20000, 'A200',
        'I have some questions, on building HiveQL
        queries? My Hadoop for Dummies book has not
        arrived yet!');
```

Later on, the IT staff imports the `serviceorders` table into Apache Hadoop using this familiar command:

```
sqoop import \
  --connect jdbc:mysql://localhost/serviceorderdb \
  --username root -P \
  --table serviceorders -m 1
```

At this point, everything is good; even though a comma appears in the problem description, it's imported into HDFS verbatim. However, suppose that the IT staff decides to export the data from Hadoop back into a MySQL table later on, using this command:

```
sqoop export \
  --connect jdbc:mysql://localhost/serviceorderdb \
  --username root -P \
  --export-dir /user/biadmin/serviceorders \
  --table serviceorders -m 1
```

After the export operation, the MySQL database administrator looks at the new table and sees the following records:

```
mysql> select * from serviceorders;
...
| serviceordernum | customernum | productnum | status
|          100000 |       20000 | A200       | I have some questions
                  |
|          100001 |       10001 | A100       | I need to understand how to
          configure Zookeeper for my HBase Cluster? |
...
```

The Sqoop export command has interpreted the operator's comma as a field delimiter, and some vital data was lost. We're in danger of losing an important customer because we can't address the problem without an embarrassing return phone call to solve the data loss problem! It sounds bad, so what's the solution? The solution is output line formatting and input parsing CLAs. Two commands (one `import` and one `export` — see Listing 14-26) would solve the problem.

Listing 14-26: **An Output Line Formatting and Input Parsing Example**

```
sqoop import \
   --connect jdbc:mysql://localhost/serviceorderdb \
   --username root -P -m 1 \
   --table serviceorders \
   --target-dir /user/biadmin/serviceorders-test \
   --escaped-by \\ \
   --input-escaped-by \\ \
   --class-name serviceorderstest \
   --bindir /home/biadmin/serviceorders-test
sqoop export \
   --connect jdbc:mysql://localhost/serviceorderdb \
   --username root -P -m 1 \
   --table serviceorders \
   --export-dir /user/biadmin/serviceorders-test \
   --class-name serviceorderstest \
   --jar-file /home/biadmin/serviceorders-test/serviceorderstest.jar
```

Because this topic is important, we walk you through each step. First, in the import, we're specifying an output line formatting escape character(\). This character causes the generated code (which we're naming service-orderstest) to place a backslash (because of the --escaped by \ CLA) before the operator's comma in the HDFS records file. Then when the serviceorders records are exported from HDFS back to the MySQL serviceorders table (or another table like it), we'll reuse the generated code, which we saved in the /home/biadmin/serviceorders-test directory with the --bindir CLA. This generated code has an input parse method that knows how to read the problem description, so whenever it sees the backslash and comma (because of the --input-escaped-by \ CLA in the import command), it continues reading and exporting the whole problem description until it finds the final field-enclosing comma. Now, when the MySQL database administrator from the service company issues the SELECT statement, he or she sees the whole problem description.

The Linux shell uses the backslash (\) as a line continuation character so you can just keep on typing with a whole new line. (This is a pretty important little technique with Sqoop and its long command structures.) That's why we have three backslashes on the lines in Listing 14-26 where we are specifying the backslash as an escape character. We're escaping our *escape character* and continuing our line.

If you had chosen to import binary data from a data management system (DMS) with Sqoop, and store that data in HDFS using a sequence file (with the --as-sequencefile CLA), then you should save your generated Java class (like we did in Listing 14-26) so you can point to it (using the --class-name and --jar-file CLAs) if you need to export the data back to the DMS.

Sqoop 2.0 Preview

With all the success surrounding Sqoop 1.x upon its graduation from the Apache incubator, Sqoop has momentum! So, as you might expect, Sqoop 2.0 is in the works with exciting new features on the way. If you haven't already, we suggest checking out `http://sqoop.apache.org` for the full story. As of this writing, you can see that Sqoop 1.99.3 is downloadable, complete with documentation. We'd bet that you're wondering (like we are) how many 1.99.x releases will be available before the big 2.0 hits `http://sqoop.apache.org`. Well, our crystal ball only works part-time so the answer is "not yet."

We can still dream, right? And while we're dreaming, we can still provide you with a preview of Sqoop 2.0 features. However, you know the drill: The situation can change leading up to the 2.0 release, so we keep our description at a relatively high level of generality.

Figure 14-6 illustrates (documented) design plans for Sqoop 2.0.

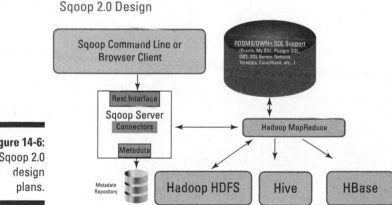

Figure 14-6: Sqoop 2.0 design plans.

As you can see, the big change in the works is that Sqoop 2.0 will have a separate server, which is good news for a number of reasons. First, you won't have to do so much work. The Sqoop connector and JDBC driver will be installed once by the system administrator for your cluster instead of once per Sqoop client. If you happen to be the system administrator, we extend our condolences. You still have to do the work, but maybe you'll like the next benefit: Sqoop 2.0 will be more secure! With a Sqoop server as part of the architecture, sensitive operations such as connecting to the database servers only have to happen on the Sqoop server and you'll have role-based access control. Additionally, Sqoop clients can leverage Sqoop from anywhere on the network (thanks to the new rest interface), and they will enjoy a new graphical user interface (GUI). We think you'll agree that the command line options are necessary and powerful for scripting purposes, but we all like a cool GUI from time to time. Sqoop requires many command line options, which can be error-prone without a GUI to guide you.

We'll leave this preview as is for now because we don't want to discuss features that might change. We would bet that you've noticed MapReduce (instead of just map tasks) proudly displayed in Figure 14-6. We've inserted it on purpose, but we'll wait to add our two cents until after we hear the exact details on how reducers are leveraged when the 2.0 announcement hits the community page. Until then, enjoy Sqoop 1.x and start experimenting with 1.99.x.

You can read more about the Sqoop 2 goals and architecture on this web site: `https://cwiki.apache.org/confluence/display/SQOOP/Sqoop+2`

Chapter 15

The Holy Grail: Native SQL Access to Hadoop Data

In This Chapter

▶ Seeing why SQL is important for Hadoop

▶ Looking at SQL access and the open source Hadoop community

▶ Evaluating proprietary SQL solutions

The NoSQL movement that has been happening over the past few years has taught two important lessons: a) Alternatives to relational databases can be a great help in solving a variety of problems and b) SQL isn't going anywhere. In fact, the NoSQL movement is now being rebranded as *NewSQL*, as in, "Here's a new technology where you can use SQL!" Even though we've seen a tremendous amount of innovation in the information management field — technologies are now available that can store graphs, documents, and key/value pairs at a massive scale — the IT market is still demanding SQL support for all of it. Hadoop is no exception, and a number of companies are investing heavily to drive open source projects and proprietary solutions for SQL access to Hadoop data.

SQL's Importance for Hadoop

There are compelling reasons that SQL has proven to be resilient. The IT industry has had 40 years of experience with SQL, since it was first developed by IBM in the early 1970s. With the increase in the adoption of relational databases in the 1980s, SQL has since become a standard skill for most IT professionals. You can easily see why SQL has been so successful: It's relatively easy to learn, and SQL queries are quite readable. This ease can be traced back to a core design point in SQL — the fact that it's a *declarative* language, as opposed to an *imperative* language. For a language to be declarative means that your queries deal only with the nature of the data being requested — ideally, there should be nothing in your query that determines *how* the processing should be executed. In other words, all you indicate in

SQL is what information you want back from the system — not how to get it. In contrast, with an imperative language (C, for example, or Java, or Python) your code consists of instructions where you define the actions you need the system to execute.

In addition to the (easily leveraged) skills of your SQL-friendly IT professionals, decades' worth of database applications have also been built with SQL interfaces. As we discuss in Chapter 11, when talking about how Hadoop can complement the data warehouse, it's clear that organizations will store structured data in Hadoop. And as a result, they'll run some of their existing application logic against Hadoop. No one wants to pay for applications to be rewritten, so a SQL interface is highly desirable.

With the development of SQL interfaces to Hadoop data, an interesting trend is that commercial business analytics and data management tools are almost all jumping on the Hadoop bandwagon, including business intelligence reporting; statistical packages; Extract, Transform, and Load frameworks (ETL); and a variety of other tools. In most cases, the interface to the Hadoop data is Hive (see Chapter 13) or one of the other solutions described in this chapter.

Looking at What SQL Access Actually Means

When we use the term *SQL access,* we do so knowing that we're relying on a few basic assumptions:

- ✓ **Language standards:** The most important standard, of course, entails the language itself. Many "SQL-like" solutions exist, though they usually don't measure up in certain fundamental ways — ways that would prevent even typical SQL statements from working. The American National Standards Institute (ANSI) established SQL as an official technical standard, and the IT industry accepts the ANSI SQL-92 standard as representing the benchmark for basic SQL compliance. ANSI has released a number of progressively more advanced versions over the years as database technologies have evolved.

- ✓ **Drivers:** Another key component in a SQL access solution is the *driver* — the interface for applications to connect and exchange data with the data store. Without a driver, there's no SQL interface for any client applications or tools to connect to for the submission of SQL queries. As such, any SQL on Hadoop solution has to have JDBC and ODBC drivers at the very least, because they're the most commonly used database interface technologies.

✔ **Real-time access:** Until Hadoop 2, MapReduce-based execution was the only available option for analytics against data stored in Hadoop. For relatively simple queries involving a full scan of data in a table, Hadoop was quite fast as compared to a traditional relational database. Keep in mind that this is a batch analysis use case, where *fast* can mean hours, depending on how much data is involved. But when it came to more complex queries, involving subsets of data, Hadoop did not do well. MapReduce is a batch processing framework, so achieving high performance for real-time queries before Hadoop 2 was architecturally impossible. One early motivator for YARN, the new resource management and scheduling system on the block, was this need to support other processing frameworks to enable real-time workloads, such as interactive SQL queries. Indeed, a proper SQL solution should not leave people waiting for reasonable queries. (For more on YARN, see Chapter 7.)

✔ **Mutable data:** A common question in many discussions around SQL support on Hadoop is "Can we use INSERT, UPDATE, and DELETE statements, as we would be able to do in a typical relational database?" For now, the answer is no, which reflects the nature of HDFS — it's focused on large, immutable files. At the time of this writing, technologies such as Hive offer read-only access to these files. Regardless, work is ongoing in the Hive Apache project to enable INSERT, UPDATE, and DELETE statements.

SQL Access and Apache Hive

At the time of this writing, Apache Hive is indisputably the most widespread data query interface in the Hadoop community. (We cover Hive in depth in Chapter 13, describing its structure and how to use it.)

Originally, the design goals for Hive were not for full SQL compatibility and high performance, but were to provide an easy, somewhat familiar interface for developers needing to issue batch queries against Hadoop. This rather piecemeal approach no longer works, so the demand grows for real SQL support and good performance. Hortonworks responded to this demand by creating the Stinger project, where it invested its developer resources in improving Hive to be faster, to scale at a petabyte level, and to be more compliant to SQL standards. This work was to be delivered in three phases.

In Phases 1 and 2, you saw a number of optimizations for how queries were processed as well as added support for traditional SQL data types; the addition of the ORCFile format for more efficient processing and storage; and integration with YARN for better performance. In Phase 3, the truly significant evolutions take place, which decouple Hive from MapReduce. Specifically, it involves the release of Apache Tez (described in Chapter 7), which is an alternative processing model for Hadoop, designed for interactive workloads.

Massively parallel processing databases

To provide a better understanding of the SQL-on-Hadoop alternatives to Hive in this chapter, we thought it would be helpful to provide a primer on massively parallel processing (MPP) databases first.

As we explain in Chapter 13, Apache Hive is layered on top of the Hadoop Distributed File System (HDFS) and the MapReduce system and presents an SQL-like programming interface to your data (HiveQL, to be precise). This combination of Hadoop technologies deployed on a cluster is similar to MPP databases that have existed for a while in the IT marketplace. MPP databases usually provide an SQL interface and a relational database management system (RDBMS) running on a cluster of servers networked together by a high-speed interconnect. The figure shows the components of an RDBMS that are typically included in the SQL-on-Hadoop solutions described in this chapter.

Relational data systems have evolved considerably to a point where best practices have emerged among most offerings in terms of an optimal query execution infrastructure. The figure above shows this in terms of the flow of a query as it's processed by an RDBMS engine. First, the query text is parsed and understood. Then the syntax tree for the query is compiled into a logical execution plan, which is then optimized to form the final physical execution plan, which is then executed by the runtime. For many of the SQL-on-Hadoop solutions, we're seeing similar components being deployed in Hadoop.

MPP clusters are usually referred to as having a Shared-Nothing architecture, because each system has its own CPU, memory and disk. However, through the database software and high-speed interconnects, the system functions as a whole and can scale as new servers are added to the cluster. The overall system is explicitly tuned to provide fast, interactive query response. MPP databases are often more flexible, scalable, and cost effective than the traditional RDBMS, hosted on a large multiprocessor server.

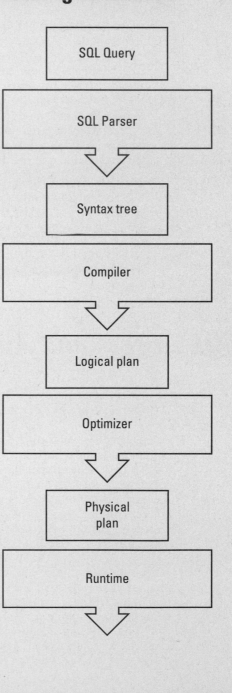

In addition to the Stinger project, Hortonworks is spearheading an ambitious initiative to enable Hive to support editing data at the row level — in other words, enabling INSERT, UPDATE, and DELETE statements against Hive data with full compliance with the ACID properties for database systems: Atomicity, Consistency, Isolation levels, and Durability. (For more on the ACID properties, see Chapter 11.)

Solutions Inspired by Google Dremel

For most people, the term *Dremel* brings to mind a handy high-speed, low-torque tool that works well for a variety of jobs around the house. But did you know that Google created a Dremel? Rather than produce *another* handheld mechanical tool, though, Google chose a fast software tool intended for interactive analysis of big data. As with other Google technologies that inspired parts of the Hadoop ecosystem, such as MapReduce (see Chapter 6), Google File System (HDFS, see Chapter 4), and BigTable (see HBase, Chapter 12), Google developed Dremel for use internally and then published a paper describing the purpose and design of the technology. (In other words, Dremel is not something you can download and use on your Hadoop cluster.)

You can find Google's Dremel whitepaper at this site:

```
http://research.google.com/pubs/pub36632.html
```

Google uses Dremel for a variety of jobs, including analyzing web-crawled documents, detecting e-mail spam, working through application crash reports, and more. Google's BigQuery service actually uses Dremel.

As we discuss in Chapter 1, Google designed MapReduce technology for batch processing over massive sets of data. As their needs evolved, so did their technology, and Google decided to create Dremel to improve performance for interactive queries against big data sets. The MapReduce approach provides scalability and query fault tolerance, but it's fundamentally a batch-based system, so response times for smaller queries (queries involving only a small part of an entire data set, for instance) are often not what users expect. So Google developed a query execution technology designed for interactive queries, which runs on intermediate servers on top of the Google File System (GFS). (Remember, GFS was the inspiration for Apache HDFS, which is Hadoop's file system.)

Similar to Hive, Dremel uses an SQL-like language (familiar to most programmers) and employs a columnar data layout. Dremel provides fast, interactive query response while preserving the scalability and fault tolerance found in Apache Hive. In the Dremel whitepaper, Google explains how it can perform aggregation queries within seconds over tables with a trillion rows — not bad at all.

So Google has its Dremel technology, which it uses internally, but then there are all the technologies "inspired by" Dremel (kind of like all those perfumes "inspired by" Drakkar Noir). We introduce you now to two "inspired by" products — Apache Drill and Cloudera Impala. The pattern here is similar in both cases:

Apache Drill

As of this writing, Drill is a candidate project in the Apache incubator. We don't mean that Apache Drill is especially sickly, though. The Apache Software Foundation (ASF) candidate technologies all begin as incubator projects before becoming official ASF technologies. You can read about the Apache Incubator at

```
http://incubator.apache.org
```

You can read about Drill at

```
http://incubator.apache.org/drill
```

Inspired by Google's Dremel technology, the stated performance goal for Drill is to enable SQL queries against a petabyte or more of data distributed across 10,000-plus servers. Figure 15-1 illustrates the architecture of Apache Drill.

Figure 15-1: Apache Drill architecture.

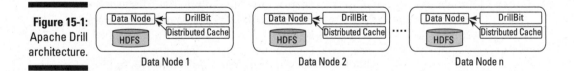

Data Node 1   Data Node 2   Data Node n

In Figure 15-1, we see that the key to the Drill architecture are the DrillBit servers deployed on each data node. Note that each server includes a query parser, compiler, optimizer, and runtime, but there is a master DrillBit server nominated by Zookeeper servers, which oversees the execution of the queries and looks after the task of pulling together the interim result sets into a single set of output.

Like Dremel, Drill can coexist with, and complement, MapReduce, but MapReduce isn't used to fulfill queries, as with Apache Hive. Instead, execution engines called *Drillbits* have been developed by members of the Drill community. This community aims to provide low-latency queries for applications such as real-time business intelligence dashboards, fraud detection, and other time-sensitive use cases. Drill supports nested data types such as Avro,

JSON, and Google protocol buffers. These nested data types allow for very large denormalized tables. The Drill development team is also working on providing extensive SQL support by targeting SQL2003 compliance. Finally, note that the Drill team is providing HBase support so that users will be able to query HBase tables with SQL.

Cloudera Impala

Cloudera is a leading Apache Hadoop software and services provider in the big data market. Like Apache Drill, Cloudera's Impala technology seeks to improve interactive query response time for Hadoop users. As we discuss in Chapter 13, Apache Hive has provided a familiar and powerful query mechanism for Hadoop users, but query response times are often unacceptable due to Hive's reliance on MapReduce. Cloudera's answer to this problem is Impala. Cloudera has developed an MPP query engine, written in C++, to replace the MapReduce layer leveraged by Apache Hive. Unlike Dremel and Drill, Cloudera decided that a native C++ MPP engine — instead of a Java engine — was the answer for fast, interactive Hadoop queries.

Note that Impala uses HiveQL as a programming interface, and Impala's Query Exec Engines are co-located with HDFS data nodes, in keeping with the Hadoop approach of co-locating data with processing tasks. Impala can also use HBase as a data store. In this sense, Impala is an extension to Apache Hadoop, providing a very high-performance alternative to the Hive-on-top-of-MapReduce model.

In Chapter 13, we present several Hive file formats: TEXTFILE, SEQUENCEFILE, RCFILE, and ORC. Cloudera and Twitter led the development of the new Hadoop file format PARQUET, which can be used with Impala and is available as open source on GitHub. The Parquet file format provides a robust columnar medium for storing data in Hadoop. It supports highly efficient compression and encoding, and is effective for storing nested data structures.

You can find Cloudera's Impala technology, which also was inspired by Google's Dremel invention, at https://github.com/cloudera/impala.

IBM Big SQL

IBM has a long history of working with SQL and database technology, as the introduction to this chapter makes clear. In keeping with this history, IBM's solution for SQL on Hadoop leverages components from its relational database technologies that are ported to run on Hadoop.

If you're at all familiar with IBM's product naming for its Big Data products and features, you can easily guess what they've named their SQL on Hadoop solution: Big SQL. The goal of Big SQL is to provide a SQL interface on Hadoop that gives users as much as possible of what they're used to with SQL interfaces for relational databases. This means extensive query syntax support, fast performance that doesn't require users having to monkey with their queries, and the ability to control data security.

Figure 15-2 shows a partial deployment of BigInsights, IBM's Hadoop distribution running Big SQL.

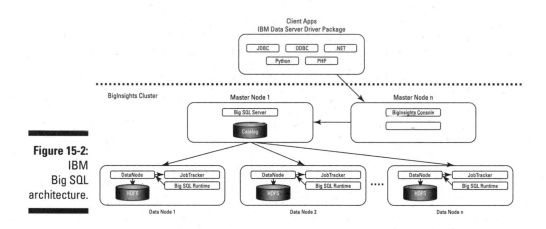

Figure 15-2:
IBM
Big SQL
architecture.

In Figure 15-2 you can see a subset of the master nodes and data nodes behind the BigInsights firewall. One of the master nodes is running the Big SQL server, which includes IBM's SQL compiler and optimizer. Also included on this master node is a catalog, where metadata and statistics about any cataloged data in HDFS is stored for use by the compiler/optimizer. Subsections of queries are sent to the applicable data nodes where requested data is stored, and there the Big SQL Runtime (which is IBM's SQL runtime) executes the workload. Rather than run mapper and reducer processes and persist files with intermediate result sets, Big SQL uses continuously running daemons that pass messages between each other. It's important to note that the data being queried is stored and managed by Hadoop. Big SQL supports standard Hadoop file formats — for example, RCFile and Parquet.

Big SQL provides the same extensive SQL support as the IBM relational database products — for example, ANSI SQL-2011, and compatibility for IBM's SQL Procedural Language (SQL/PL). (At the time of writing, IBM was working on providing support for Oracle's SQL dialect and their PL/SQL procedural language.) Along with the standard IBM SQL engine come a number of other capabilities, most notably IBM's row- and column-based security (also known as Fine-Grained Access Control, or FGAC), where only specific users can be authorized to see certain sets of data rows or columns.

Big SQL comes with the standard IBM Data Server Client, which includes a driver package (refer to Figure 15-2). Traditional database applications can connect to the BigInsights Hadoop cluster and securely exchange encrypted data over SSL.

Pivotal HAWQ

In 2010, EMC and VMware, market leaders in delivering IT as a service via cloud computing, acquired Greenplum Corporation, the folks who had successfully brought the Greenplum MPP Data Warehouse (DW) product to market. Later in 2012, Pivotal Labs, a leading provider of Agile software development services, was also acquired. Through this federation of companies, the Pivotal HD Enterprise platform was announced in early 2013. This platform, which is integrated with Apache Hadoop, includes the Pivotal HAWQ (Hadoop With Query) product — the former Greenplum MPP DW product. Though the Pivotal HD Enterprise platform also includes other components and technologies (VMware's GemFire, for example), we want to draw your attention to the Pivotal HAWQ product, Pivotal's approach to low-latency interactive SQL queries on Hadoop. Pivotal has integrated the Greenplum MPP Shared-Nothing DW with Apache Hadoop to enable big data analytics. The Pivotal HAWQ MPP DW stores its data in the Apache HDFS.

Pivotal HAWQ provides ANSI SQL support and enables SQL queries of HBase tables. HAWQ also includes its own set of catalog services instead of using the Hive metastore. The Pivotal HAWQ approach is to provide a highly optimized and fast Hadoop SQL query mechanism on top of Apache Hadoop.

Hadapt

Late in the year 2010, Hadapt was formed as a start-up by two Yale University students and an assistant professor of computer science. Professor Daniel Abadi and Kamil Bajda-Pawlikowski, a PhD student from Yale's computer science department, had been working on the research project HadoopDB. After this paper was published, Justin Borgman, a student from the Yale School of Management, became interested in the work. He would later team up with Professor Abadi and Kamil Bajda-Pawlikowski to form Hadapt.

The Hadapt strategy is to join Apache Hadoop with a Shared-Nothing MPP database to create an adaptive analytics platform. This approach provides a standard SQL interface on Hadoop and enables analytics across unstructured, semistructured, and structured data on the same cluster.

Like Apache Hive and other technologies, Hadapt provides a familiar JDBC/ODBC interface for submitting SQL or MapReduce jobs to the cluster. Hadapt provides a cost-based query optimizer, which can decide between a combination of MapReduce jobs and MPP database jobs to fulfill a query, or the job can be handled by the MPP database for fast interactive response. By joining an Apache Hadoop cluster with an MPP database cluster to create a hybrid system, Hadapt solves the query response time and partial SQL support (via HiveQL) found in Apache Hive.

The SQL Access Big Picture

SQL access to Hadoop data is a burning (and ongoing) concern. Many vendors are offering solutions — some are adding value to the Hadoop ecosystem by writing their own high-performance MPP engine to replace the higher-latency MapReduce system, and others are working hard to improve the performance of MapReduce by rewriting parts of the Hadoop system with native code (using the C and or C++ languages, for example) instead of with Java. Some have decided that integrating Shared-Nothing MPP database systems and Hadoop on the same platform is the way to go. History has shown that in technological battles such as this one, only one or two victors will emerge, leaving many solutions obsolete. The positive perspective in this case is that regardless of the specific winning technology, the interface will at least be SQL.

Part IV
Administering and Configuring Hadoop

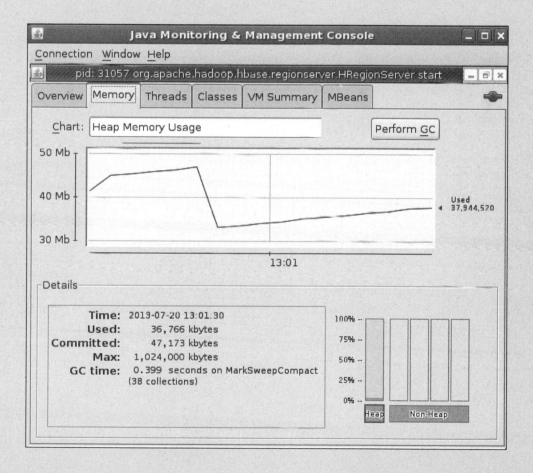

Check out the article "Processing graphs in Hadoop" (and more) online at
www.dummies.com/extras/hadoop.

In this part . . .

✔ Look at the Hadoop Deployment Big Picture

✔ Explore Hadoop administrative commands

✔ Plan for when things go wrong.

✔ See the importance of security in a Hadoop environment

✔ Check out the article "Processing graphs in Hadoop" (and more) online at www.dummies.com/extras/hadoop.

Chapter 16

Deploying Hadoop

At its core, Hadoop is a system for storing and processing data at a massive scale using a cluster of many individual compute nodes. In this chapter, we describe the tasks involved in building a Hadoop cluster, all the way from the hardware components in the compute nodes to different cluster configuration patterns, to how to appropriately size clusters. In at least one way, Hadoop is no different from many other IT systems: If you don't design your cluster to match your business requirements, you get bad results.

Working with Hadoop Cluster Components

While you're getting your feet wet with Hadoop, you're likely to limit yourself to using a pseudo-distributed cluster running in a virtual machine on a personal computer. Though this environment is a good one for testing and learning, it's obviously inappropriate for production-level performance and scalability. In this section, we talk about what's involved in advancing to the next step. More specifically, we describe what a distributed cluster looks like, where multiple nodes are dedicated to data storage and processing.

Distributed Hadoop clusters normally follow the model shown in Figure 16-1. Redundancy is critical in avoiding single points of failure, so you see two switches and three master nodes. (We explain the latter number later in this chapter, in the section "Master nodes.") You also see two edge nodes for client applications and connectivity to resources outside the cluster, and a sufficient number of slave nodes to store your data sets. You see variations on this model when using multiple racks or processing techniques that need additional master nodes (HBase with its region servers, for example). We get into the specifics in later sections.

| 10GbE Switch |
| 10GbE Switch |
| |
| Master Node |
| Master Node |
| Master Node |
| |
| Edge Node |
| |
| Slave Node |
| Slave Node |
| Slave Node |
| Slave Node |
| Slave Node |
| Slave Node |
| Slave Node |

Figure 16-1: Typical components in a Hadoop cluster.

Rack considerations

A core principle of Hadoop is scaling out with additional slave nodes to meet increasing data-storage and -processing demands. In a scale-out model, you must carefully consider cluster design because dozens, and even hundreds, of slave nodes will ultimately need to be racked, powered, networked, and cooled.

Server form factors

One of the first choices that IT architects will face when designing a Hadoop cluster is which of the following two form factors to use for Hadoop nodes:

- ✔ **Blade server:** Designed for maximum density, you can cram as many of these babies into one rack as possible. Blade servers fit into blade enclosures, which have many standard server components, like dedicated storage, networking, power, and cooling. These components are shared among the blade servers, which means that each individual blade server can be much smaller.

  Blade servers are an appealing choice on the surface because you could take a standard rack and deploy between 40 and 50 of these blade servers. The problem with using blades for Hadoop deployments is that they rely on certain shared components, which isn't in line with Hadoop's shared-nothing architecture, where each of the slave nodes are self-contained and have their own dedicated resources. More importantly, blades have little room for locally attached storage, often having no more than two or three drive bays. This is a non-starter for Hadoop, since slave nodes need much more dedicated storage capacity.

- ✔ **Rack server:** Complete servers with no shared components and room for hardware expansion, rack servers are the true choice for Hadoop because they're nicely self-contained. A rack server that's appropriately configured for being a Hadoop slave node typically occupies two RU, so you can fit 20 of them in a standard rack.

Cost of ownership

When choosing and designing a slave node, your most important considerations are typically the initial procurement costs and the storage volume. However, the cost of ownership is also important. It's a fine balancing act, however, because choices affecting procurement cost, power consumption, cooling, hardware performance, and density are often in opposition. In the name of helping you make good choices, we offer some (quite specific) advice:

- ✔ **Reserve redundant power supplies for the master nodes.** Having redundant power supplies for slave nodes is overkill — a power supply failure in a slave node wouldn't greatly affect the cluster. However, having redundant power supplies on all slave nodes would increase power consumption and generate more heat.

- ✔ **Choose middle-of-the-road clock speeds for** slave **node CPUs.** CPUs with higher clock speeds not only cost more but also use more power and generate far more heat.

✔ **Choose rack servers that are designed for Hadoop.** With the rising popularity of Hadoop, all major hardware vendors now offer rack servers that are ideal slave nodes, with 12 to 20 drive bays for locally attached storage. Rack servers designed to work as Hadoop slave nodes are typically too big to fit into a form factor of one RU, but taking up two RUs can result in wasted space. For the more efficient use of space, certain hardware vendors have released rack servers that cram multiple slave nodes into a single chassis. As an example, in this compressed form, a standard rack can have as many as 27 slave nodes (even with network switches), where each slave node has room for 15 disk drives for HDFS. The upshot of this arrangement is much higher density and better use of space in the data center.

Master nodes

The master nodes host the various storage and processing management services, described in this list, for the entire Hadoop cluster:

✔ **NameNode:** Manages HDFS storage. To ensure high availability, you have both an active NameNode and a standby NameNode. Each runs on its own, dedicated master node.

✔ **Checkpoint node (or backup node):** Provides *checkpointing* services for the NameNode. This involves reading the NameNode's edit log for changes to files in HDFS (new, deleted, and appended files) since the last checkpoint, and applying them to the NameNode's master file that maps files to data blocks. In addition, the Backup Node keeps a copy of the file system namespace in memory and keeps it in sync with the state of the NameNode. For high availability deployments, do not use a checkpoint node or backup node — use a Standby NameNode instead. In addition to being an active standby for the NameNode, the Standby NameNode maintains the checkpointing services and keeps an up-to-date copy of the file system namespace in memory.

✔ **JournalNode:** Receives edit log modifications indicating changes to files in HDFS from the NameNode. At least three JournalNode services (and it's always an odd number) must be running in a cluster, and they're lightweight enough that they can be colocated with other services on the master nodes.

✔ **Resource Manager:** Oversees the scheduling of application tasks and management of the Hadoop cluster's resources. This service is the heart of YARN.

✔ **JobTracker:** For Hadoop 1 servers, handles cluster resource management and scheduling. With YARN, the JobTracker is obsolete and isn't used. We mention it because a number of Hadoop deployments still haven't migrated to Hadoop 2 and YARN.

✔ **HMaster:** Monitors the HBase region servers and handles all metadata changes. To ensure high availability, be sure to use a second HMaster instance. The HMaster service is lightweight enough to be colocated with other services on the master nodes. In Hadoop 1, instances of the HMaster service run on master nodes. In Hadoop 2, with Hoya (HBase on Yarn), HMaster instances run in containers on slave nodes.

✔ **Zookeeper:** Coordinates distributed components and provides mechanisms to keep them in sync. Zookeeper is used to detect the failure of the NameNode and elect a new NameNode. It's also used with HBase to manage the states of the HMaster and the RegionServers. As with the JournalNode, you need at least three instances of Zookeeper nodes (and always an odd number), and they're lightweight enough to be colocated with other services on the master nodes.

Figure 16-2 shows an example of how Hadoop 2 services can be deployed.

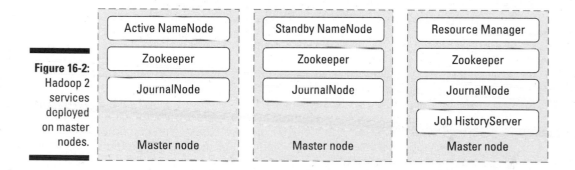

Figure 16-2:
Hadoop 2 services deployed on master nodes.

Here we've got three master nodes (with the same hardware), where the key services Active NameNode, Standby NameNode, and Resource Manager each have their own server. There are JournalNode and Zookeeper services running on each server as well, but as we mentioned earlier, these are lightweight and won't be a source of resource contention with the NameNode and Resource Manager services.

Figure 16-3 shows what master nodes look like for Hadoop 1 deployments.

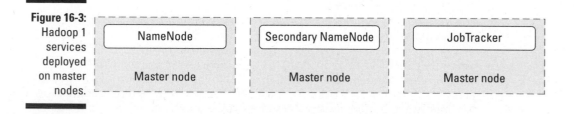

Figure 16-3:
Hadoop 1 services deployed on master nodes.

The principles are the same for Hadoop 1, where you need a dedicated master node for the NameNode, Secondary NameNode, and JobTracker services.

If you plan to use HBase with Hoya in Hadoop 2, you don't need any additional services. For Hadoop 1 deployments using HBase, see Figure 16-4 for the deployment of services on the Hadoop cluster's master nodes.

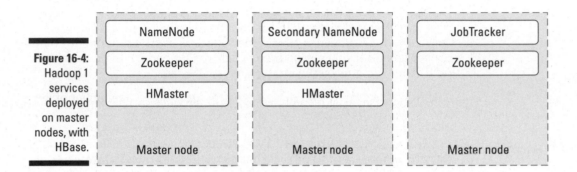

Figure 16-4: Hadoop 1 services deployed on master nodes, with HBase.

NameNode	Secondary NameNode	JobTracker
Zookeeper	Zookeeper	Zookeeper
HMaster	HMaster	
Master node	Master node	Master node

There are two differences when comparing these master servers to the Hadoop 1 master servers without HBase support: here we need two HMaster services (one to coordinate HBase, and one to act as a standby) and Zookeeper services on all three master nodes to handle failover. If you intend to use your Hadoop 1 cluster only for HBase, you can do without the JobTracker service, since HBase does not depend on the Hadoop 1 MapReduce infrastructure.

When people talk about hardware for Hadoop, they generally emphasize the use of *commodity* components — the inexpensive ones, in other words. We don't recommend taking that route for master nodes. Because you have to plunk down for only a few master nodes (typically, three or four), you aren't hit by multiplying costs if, for example, you decide to use expensive hard disk drives. Keep in mind that, without master nodes, there is no Hadoop cluster. Master nodes serve a mission-critical function, and even though you need redundancy, you should design them with high availability and resiliency in mind.

Recommended storage

For Hadoop master nodes, regardless of the number of slave nodes or uses of the cluster, the storage characteristics are consistent. Use four 900GB SAS drives, along with a RAID HDD controller configured for RAID 1+0. SAS drives are more expensive than SATA drives, and have lower storage capacity, but they are faster and much more reliable. Deploying your SAS drives as a RAID array ensures that the Hadoop management services have a redundant store for their mission-critical data. This gives you enough stable, fast, and redundant storage to support the management of your Hadoop cluster.

Recommended processors

At the time of this writing, most reference architectures recommend using motherboards with two CPU sockets, each with six or eight cores. The Intel Ivy Bridge architecture is commonly used.

Recommended memory

Memory requirements vary considerably depending on the scale of a Hadoop cluster. Memory is a critical factor for Hadoop master nodes because the active and standby NameNode servers rely heavily on RAM to manage HDFS. As such, we recommend the use of error-correcting memory (ECC) for Hadoop master nodes. Typically, master nodes need between 64GB and 128GB of RAM.

The NameNode memory requirement is a direct function of the number of file blocks stored in HDFS. As a rule, the NameNode uses roughly 1GB of RAM per million HDFS blocks. (Remember that files are broken down into individual blocks and replicated so that you have three copies of each block.)

The memory demands of Resource Manager, HMaster, Zookeeper, and JournalNode servers are considerably less than for the NameNode server. However, it's good practice to size the master nodes in a consistent fashion so that they're interchangeable in case of hardware failure.

Recommended networking

Fast communication is vital for the services on master nodes, so we recommend using a pair of bonded 10GbE connections. (In case networking jargon is new to you, GbE stands for GigaBit Ethernet.) This bonded pair provides redundancy, but also doubles throughput to 20GbE. For smaller clusters (for instance, less than 50 nodes) you could get away with using 1 GbE connectors.

Slave nodes

In a Hadoop universe, slave nodes are where Hadoop data is stored and where data processing takes place. The following services enable slave nodes to store and process data:

- **NodeManager:** Coordinates the resources for an individual slave node and reports back to the Resource Manager.

- **ApplicationMaster:** Tracks the progress of all the tasks running on the Hadoop cluster for a specific application. For each client application, the Resource Manager deploys an instance of the ApplicationMaster service in a container on a slave node. (Remember that any node running the NodeManager service is visible to the Resource Manager.)

✔ **Container:** A collection of all the resources needed to run individual tasks for an application. When an application is running on the cluster, the Resource Manager schedules the tasks for the application to run as container services on the cluster's slave nodes.

✔ **TaskTracker:** Manages the individual map and reduce tasks executing on a slave node for Hadoop 1 clusters. In Hadoop 2, this service is obsolete and has been replaced by YARN services.

✔ **DataNode:** An HDFS service that enables the NameNode to store blocks on the slave node.

✔ **RegionServer:** Stores data for the HBase system. In Hadoop 2, HBase uses Hoya, which enables RegionServer instances to be run in containers.

Figure 16-5 shows the services deployed on Hadoop 2 slave nodes.

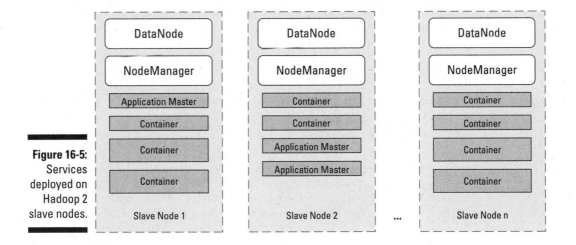

Figure 16-5: Services deployed on Hadoop 2 slave nodes.

Here, each slave node is always running a DataNode instance (which enables HDFS to store and retrieve data blocks on the slave node) and a NodeManager instance (which enables the Resource Manager to assign application tasks to the slave node for processing). The container processes are individual tasks for applications that are running on the cluster. Each running application has a dedicated ApplicationMaster task, which also runs in a container, and tracks the execution of all the tasks executing on the cluster until the application is finished.

With HBase on Hadoop 2, the container model is still followed, as we can see in Figure 16-6.

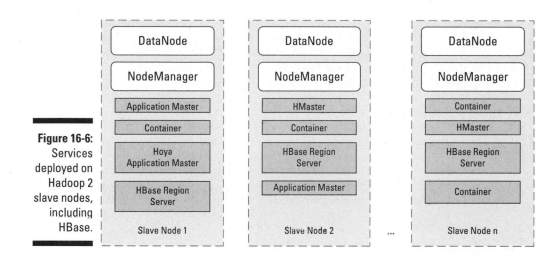

Figure 16-6:
Services
deployed on
Hadoop 2
slave nodes,
including
HBase.

HBase on Hadoop 2 is initiated by the Hoya Application Master, which requests containers for the HMaster services. (You need multiple HMaster services for redundancy.) The Hoya Application Master also requests resources for RegionServers, which likewise run in special containers.

Figure 16-7 shows the services deployed on Hadoop 1 slave nodes.

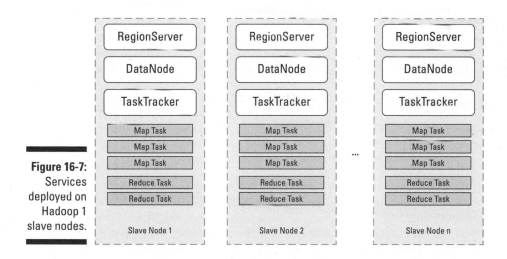

Figure 16-7:
Services
deployed on
Hadoop 1
slave nodes.

For Hadoop 1, each slave node is always running a DataNode instance (which enables HDFS to store and retrieve data blocks on the slave node) and a TaskTracker instance (which enables the JobTracker to assign map and reduce tasks to the slave node for processing). Slave nodes have a fixed number of map slots and reduce slots for the execution of map and reduce tasks respectively. If your cluster is running HBase, a number of your slave nodes will need to run a RegionServer service. The more data you store in HBase, the more RegionServer instances you'll need.

The hardware criteria for slave nodes are rather different from those for master nodes (refer to the "Master nodes" section earlier in this chapter); in fact, the criteria don't match those found in traditional hardware reference architectures for data servers. Much of the buzz surrounding Hadoop is due to the use of commodity hardware in the design criteria of Hadoop clusters, but keep in mind that *commodity* hardware does not refer to consumer-grade hardware. Hadoop slave nodes still require enterprise-grade hardware, but at the lower end of the cost spectrum, especially for storage.

Recommended storage

Enterprise storage is normally configured as a RAID array, but with Hadoop, the optimal configuration is the almost comically simple JBOD — Just a Bunch Of Disks. That's right — JBOD is just a bunch of disks that are directly (and independently) connected with the slave node's motherboard. For Hadoop slave nodes, you need two sets of hard disk drives: one set for the operating system and the other set for HDFS. Two 500GB SATA drives are sufficient for the operating system. Most hardware manufacturers have released rack servers specially designed for Hadoop, which enable individual slave nodes to house an additional 12 to20 drives for dedicated HDFS storage. Be sure to choose large form-factor (LFF) drives (3½ inches) for HDFS storage, because they have a higher capacity and are less expensive. At the time of this writing, 3TB SATA LFF drives are the most practical and cost-effective choice, though 4TB SATA drives will likely become a common choice.

Keep in mind the following information about Hadoop slave node storage:

✔ Twelve 3TB drives provide 36 terabytes of raw storage for your Hadoop cluster, which enables you to store 12 terabytes of data in HDFS, given the default replication factor of 3.

✔ For efficient and cost-effective performance, ensure a 1:1 ratio of CPU cores to drives dedicated to HDFS.

✔ Though the drives used for slave nodes are in the more economical commodity class, it's practical to connect them with a faster and more stable controller. Because many Hadoop workloads are I/O bound, we recommend using a SAS 6 gigabytes-per-second controller.

Never use an operating system drive for HDFS, because it compromises performance.

Recommended processors

At the time of this writing, dual-socket servers that have Intel Ivy Bridge processors that are clocked between 2 and 2.5 GHz represent the best balance of performance and cost for slave nodes. And, as we mentioned in the guidelines for storage earlier in the "Recommended storage" section, the number of drives you choose should be consistent with the number of CPU cores present — we recommend you should maintain a 1:1 ratio. If you're using 12 drives for HDFS, for example, you use two 6-core CPUs, and if you're using 16 drives, you use two 8-core CPUs. This configuration is practical for many applications, but if you're going to run processor-intensive workloads and you need fast performance, you can maintain a higher ratio of CPU cores to HDFS drives, for example 3 CPU cores for every two drives. As with any performance optimization exercise, at some point you will hit a bottleneck. For example, if you increase the ratio of CPU cores to HDFS drives too much, you will find your applications spending most of their time waiting for disk read or write operations.

Recommended memory

For most workloads, considering the nature of the processor and disk specifications given in the previous two sections, 48GB of RAM is sufficient for slave nodes. For maximum performance, however, you must fully populate the RAM channels for the slave node processors. For example, a dual-core server with three RAM channels per processor will have 48GB of RAM divided between six 8GB memory modules (DIMMs).

If you're not up on RAM channels, here's a quick primer. Most modern motherboard chipsets now use multi-channel memory. This enables the CPU to access its memory in parallel, which increases the data transfer speed by as many times as there are channels. For example, data transfers between the memory and CPU on servers with triple-channel memory architecture will be three times as fast as servers with single-channel memory architecture. The catch here is that for multi-channel memory to work well, each slot for the memory channel must be populated with an identical memory module.

For Hadoop clusters where you know that the workload will be memory intensive (for example, HBase deployments), we recommend doubling the number of DIMMs, for a total of 96GB of RAM per slave node (as per the preceding example, which is twelve 8GB DIMMs).

Recommended networking

For slave nodes, we recommend a pair of bonded network connections, to provide redundancy *and* to double throughput. The deciding factor here is speed. If your cluster's slave nodes have 48GB or more dedicated to HDFS, we recommend 10GbE connections to be able to handle the data transfer demands that arise from dense storage. Otherwise, we recommend 1GbE connections.

A key concept in good cluster design is the separation of duties between master nodes and slave nodes. Their purposes are radically different, and their design patterns reflect this. For production clusters, do not give in to the temptation to add DataNode and NodeManager (or TaskTracker, for Hadoop 1) servers to your master nodes. Keep separate elements separate, in other words.

Edge nodes

Edge nodes are the interface between the Hadoop cluster and the outside network. For this reason, they're sometimes referred to as *gateway* nodes. Most commonly, edge nodes are used to run client applications and cluster administration tools. They're also often used as staging areas for data being transferred into the Hadoop cluster. As such, Oozie, Pig, Sqoop, and management tools such as Hue and Ambari run well there. Figure 16-8 shows the processes you can run on Edge nodes.

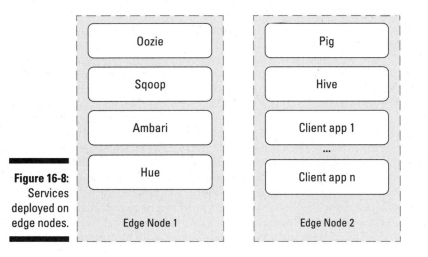

Figure 16-8:
Services deployed on edge nodes.

Edge nodes are often overlooked in Hadoop hardware architecture discussions. This situation is unfortunate because edge nodes serve an important purpose in a Hadoop cluster, and they have hardware requirements that are different from master nodes and slave nodes. In general, it's a good idea to minimize deployments of administration tools on master nodes and slave nodes to ensure that critical Hadoop services like the NameNode have as little competition for resources as possible.

You should avoid placing a data transfer utility like Sqoop on anything but an edge node, as the high data transfer volumes could risk the ability of Hadoop services on the same node to communicate. The messages Hadoop services exchange are their lifeblood, so high latency means the whole node could be cut off from the cluster.

Figure 16-8 shows two edge nodes, but for many Hadoop clusters a single edge node would suffice. Additional edge nodes are most commonly needed when the volume of data being transferred in or out of the cluster is too much for a single server to handle.

Recommended storage

For edge nodes in a Hadoop cluster, use enterprise class storage. For edge nodes focused on administration tools and running client applications, we recommend using four 900GB SAS drives, along with a RAID HDD controller configured for RAID 1+0.

Edge nodes oriented to ingesting data obviously need much more storage space, so you can add drives to the edge node. In this case, use LFF SAS drives because much higher capacities are available, as compared to smaller form-factor SAS drives.

Recommended processors

A general-purpose edge node would be well served by a processor configuration similar to one used for slave nodes — specifically, a dual-socket server with Ivy Bridge processors clocked at between 2 and 2.5GHz.

Recommended memory

For most workloads we see on edge nodes, 48GB of RAM is sufficient.

Recommended networking

To enable communication between the outside network and the Hadoop cluster, edge nodes need to be multi-homed into the private subnet of the Hadoop cluster as well as into the corporate network.

A multi-homed computer is one that has dedicated connections to multiple networks. This is a practical illustration of why edge nodes are perfectly suited for interaction with the world outside the Hadoop cluster. Keeping your Hadoop cluster in its own private subnet is an excellent practice, so these edge nodes serve as a controlled window inside the cluster.

For edge nodes that serve the purpose of running client applications or administration tools, we recommend two pairs of bonded 1GbE network connections: one pair to connect to the Hadoop cluster and another pair for the outside network.

Edge nodes oriented to handling high inbound and outbound data transfer rates will need two (or more) pairs of bonded 10GbE network connectors: one pair to connect to the Hadoop cluster and another pair for the outside network or specific data ingest sources.

Networking

As with any distributed system, networking can make or break a Hadoop cluster: Don't "go cheap." A great deal of chatter takes place between the master nodes and slave nodes in a Hadoop cluster that is essential in keeping the cluster running, so we definitely recommend enterprise-class switches.

For each rack in your cluster, you need two top-of-rack (ToR) switches, for both redundancy and performance. We recommend using 10GbE for ToR switches.

ToR switches are network switches that connect all the computers in a rack together. You normally see them at the very top of a rack, which is why people say "top-of-rack." An alternative networking approach is to use end-of-row (EoR) switches but, we don't see this very often. The ToR approach is simpler from a networking perspective for growing clusters. For example, adding slave nodes and additional racks is far easier with ToR switches than EoR.

When you have more than three racks, you need at least two core switches (again, primarily for redundancy, but also for performance). These core switches handle massive amounts of traffic, so 40GbE is a necessity.

If you're building or expanding a cluster to span multiple racks, we strongly recommend engaging networking experts who are familiar with Hadoop, your future growth plans, and your workload. Bad networking can severely hamper performance, but it can also make future growth painful and expensive.

Hadoop Cluster Configurations

Many of the decisions you need to make in terms of the composition of racks and networking are dependent on the scale of your Hadoop cluster. It has three main permutations, as discussed in the following three sections.

Small

A single-rack deployment is an ideal starting point for a Hadoop cluster, as shown in Figure 16-9.

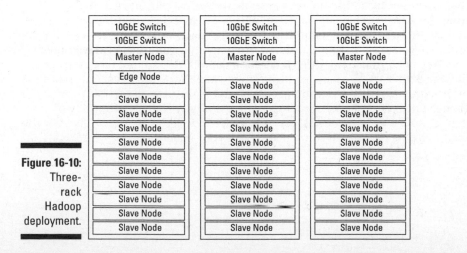

10GbE Switch
10GbE Switch
Master Node
Master Node
Master Node
Edge Node
Slave Node
Slave Node
Slave Node
Slave Node
Slave Node
Slave Node
Slave Node

Figure 16-9:
Single-rack
Hadoop
deployment.

Here, the cluster is fairly self-contained, but because It still has relatively few slave nodes, the true benefits of Hadoop's resiliency aren't yet apparent.

Medium

A medium-size cluster has multiple racks, where the three master nodes are distributed across the racks, as shown in Figure 16-10.

10GbE Switch	10GbE Switch	10GbE Switch
10GbE Switch	10GbE Switch	10GbE Switch
Master Node	Master Node	Master Node
Edge Node	Slave Node	Slave Node
Slave Node	Slave Node	Slave Node
Slave Node	Slave Node	Slave Node
Slave Node	Slave Node	Slave Node
Slave Node	Slave Node	Slave Node
Slave Node	Slave Node	Slave Node
Slave Node	Slave Node	Slave Node
Slave Node	Slave Node	Slave Node
Slave Node	Slave Node	Slave Node
Slave Node	Slave Node	Slave Node
Slave Node	Slave Node	Slave Node

Figure 16-10:
Three-
rack
Hadoop
deployment.

Hadoop's resiliency is starting to become apparent: Even if an entire rack were to fail (for example, both ToR switches in a single rack), the cluster would still function, albeit at a lower level of performance. A slave node failure would barely be noticeable.

Large

In larger clusters with many racks, like the example shown in Figure 16-11, the networking architecture required is pretty sophisticated.

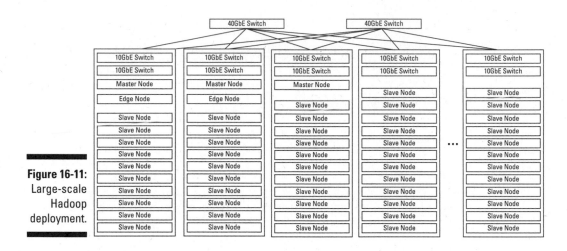

Figure 16-11:
Large-scale
Hadoop
deployment.

Regardless of how many racks Hadoop clusters expand to, the slave nodes from any rack need to be able to efficiently "talk" to any master node.

As the number of slave nodes increases to the point where you have more than three racks, additional racks are composed only of slave nodes, aside from the ToR switches. If you're using HBase heavily on your cluster, you may add master nodes to host additional HMaster and Zookeeper services. If you graduate to a truly massive scale, where you have hundreds of slave nodes, you may need to use the HDFS federation capabilities so that large portions of your data sets are managed by different NameNode services. (For more information on HDFS federation, see Chapter 4.) For every additional Active NameNode, you will need a corresponding Standby NameNode and two master nodes to host these servers. With HDFS federation, the sky is truly the limit in terms of how far you can scale out your clusters.

Alternate Deployment Form Factors

Though Hadoop works best when it's installed on a physical computer, where the processing has direct access to dedicated storage and networking, Hadoop has alternative deployments. And though they are less efficient than the dedicated hardware we describe earlier in this chapter, in certain cases alternatives are worthwhile options.

Virtualized servers

A major trend in IT centers over the past decade is virtualization, where a large server can host several "virtual machines" which look and act like single machines. In place of dedicated hardware, an organization's entire set of applications and repositories is deployed on virtualized hardware. This approach has many advantages: The centralization of IT simplifies maintenance, IT investment is maximized because of fewer unused CPU cycles, and the overall hardware footprint is lower, resulting in a lower total cost of ownership.

Organizations in which IT deployments are entirely virtualized sometimes mandate that every new application follow this model. Though Hadoop can be deployed in this manner, essentially as a virtual cluster (with virtual master nodes and virtual slave nodes), performance suffers, partially because for most virtualized environments, storage is SAN-based and isn't locally attached. Because Hadoop is designed to work best when all available CPU cores are able to have fast access to independently spinning disks, a bottleneck is created as all the map and reduce tasks start processing data via the limited networking between the CPUs and the SAN. Since the degree of isolation between virtualized server resources is limited (virtual servers share resources with each other), Hadoop workloads can also be affected by other activity. When your virtual server's performance is affected by another server's workload, that's actually known in IT circles as a "noisy neighbor" problem!

Virtualized environments can be quite useful, though, in some cases. For example, if your organization needs to complete a one-time exploratory analysis of a large data set, you can easily create a temporary cluster in your virtualized environment. This method is often a faster way to gain internal approval than to endure the bureaucratic hassles of procuring new dedicated hardware.

As we experiment with Hadoop, we often run it on our laptop machines via a virtual machine (VM). Hadoop is extremely slow in this kind of environment, but if you're using small data sets, it's a valuable learning and testing tool.

Cloud deployments

Variations of virtualized environments are cloud computing providers such as Amazon, Rackspace, and IBM SoftLayer. Most major public cloud providers now have MapReduce or Hadoop offerings available for use. Again, their performance is inferior to deploying your cluster on dedicated hardware, but it's improving. Cloud providers are making Hadoop-optimized environments available where slave nodes have locally attached storage and dedicated networking. Also, hypervisors are becoming far more efficient, with reduced overhead and latency.

Don't consider a cloud solution for long-term applications, because the cost of renting cloud computing resources is significantly higher than that of owning and maintaining a comparable system. With a cloud provider, you're paying for convenience and for being able to offload the overhead of provisioning hardware. However, the cloud is an ideal platform for testing, education, and one-time data processing tasks. We use public cloud offerings often for proof-of-concept exercises in Hadoop, and we're able to easily conjure up a made-to-order cluster in a matter of minutes.

Aside from performance and cost considerations, you have regulatory considerations with public cloud deployments. If you have sensitive data, which must be stored either in-house or in-country, a public cloud deployment isn't an option. In cases like this, where you need the convenience of a cloud-based deployment, a private cloud is a good option, if it's available.

Sizing Your Hadoop Cluster

Sizing any data processing system is as much a science as it is an art. With Hadoop, you consider the same information as you would with a relational database, for example. Most significantly, you need to know how much data you have, estimate its expected growth rates, and establish a retention policy (how long to keep the data). The answers to these questions serve as your starting point, which is independent of any technology-related requirements.

After you determine how much data you need to store, you can start factoring in Hadoop-specific considerations. Suppose that you have a telecom company and you've established that you need 750 terabytes (TB) of storage space for its call detail record (CDR) log files. You retain these records to obey government regulations, but you can also analyze them to see churn patterns and monitor network health, for example. To determine how much storage space you need and, as a result, how many racks and slave nodes you need, you carry out your calculations with these factors in mind:

✔ **Replication:** The default replication factor for data in HDFS is 3. The 500 terabytes of CDR data for the telecom company in the example then turns into 1500 terabytes.

✔ **Swap space:** Any analysis or processing of the data by MapReduce needs an additional 25 percent of space to store any interim and final result sets. (The telecom company now needs 1875 terabytes of storage space.)

✔ **Compression:** The telecom company stores the CDRs in a compressed form, where the average compression ratio is expected to be 3:1. We now need 625 terabytes.

✔ **Number of slave nodes:** Assuming that each slave node has twelve 3TB drives dedicated to HDFS, each slave node has 36 terabytes of raw HDFS storage available, so the company needs 18 slave nodes.

✔ **Number of racks:** Because each slave node uses 2RU and the company in the example needs three master nodes (1RU apiece) and two ToR switches (1RU apiece), you need a total of 41RU. It's 1RU less than the total capacity of a standard rack, so a single rack is sufficient for this deployment. Regardless, no room remains for growth in this cluster, so it's prudent to buy a second rack (and two additional ToR switches) and divide the slave nodes between the two racks.

✔ **Testing:** Maintaining a test cluster that's a smaller scale representation of the production cluster is a standard practice. It doesn't have to be huge, but you want at least five data nodes so that you get an accurate representation of Hadoop's behavior. As with any test environment, it should be isolated on a different network from the production cluster.

✔ **Backup and disaster recovery:** Like any production system, the telecom company will also need to consider backup and disaster recovery requirements. This company could go as far as to create a mirror cluster to ensure they have a hot standby for their entire system. This is obviously the most expensive option, but is appropriate for environments where constant uptime is critical. At the least expensive end of the spectrum (beyond not backing up the data at all), the telecom company could regularly backup all data (including the data itself, applications, configuration files, and metadata) being stored in their production cluster to tape. With tape, the data is not immediately accessible, but it will enable a disaster recovery effort in the case that the entire production Hadoop cluster fails.

As with your own personal computer, when the main hard disk drive fills with space, the system slows down considerably. Hadoop is no exception. Also, a hard drive performs better when it's less than 85 to 90 percent full. With this information in mind, if performance is important to you, you should bump up the swap-space factor from 25 to 33 percent.

Chapter 17

Administering Your Hadoop Cluster

. . . .

In This Chapter

▶ Seeing why having a well-running Hadoop cluster is good for you

▶ Exploring administration commands

▶ Improving performance and setting benchmarks

▶ Planning for when things go wrong

▶ Working with Apache Hadoop's Capacity Scheduler

▶ Dealing with security issues

▶ Adding resources to your administrator toolset

. . . .

You'll want to keep your Hadoop cluster running smoothly and at a high level of performance. For that to happen, you need to master the mysteries of Hadoop administration. Part of this process involves careful planning to ensure that you deploy and configure appropriate hardware for your Hadoop cluster, the use of judicious benchmarking to evaluate performance, and a good understanding of the anticipated workloads.

Complicating matters a bit is the fact that not only is most of the Hadoop ecosystem quite compartmentalized, but each component also has its own administrative issues. We deal with these issues in various sections throughout this book, where appropriate. This chapter (Chapter 17) introduces you to more general administrative concepts.

Achieving Balance: A Big Factor in Cluster Health

A cluster is said to be *balanced* if no under- or overutilized slave nodes are in the cluster. In this context, a *utilization level* is defined in terms of the percentage of space that's used. A Hadoop cluster can become imbalanced whenever a major change occurs — say, when a slave node is added to the cluster. An imbalanced cluster can lead to bandwidth problems and reduced *read parallelism* (where many applications can read data independently, instead of having to wait their turn), and a Hadoop administrator should be prepared to redistribute data blocks when cluster imbalance occurs.

The goal, then, is to spread data as uniformly as possible across the slave nodes in the cluster. As much as this idea seems to make obvious sense, it isn't always achievable. When a slave node is added to an existing cluster, the NameNode must choose which existing slave nodes are to receive some of the new data blocks. One goal is to place different replicas of a particular block across server racks to minimize the loss of an entire rack. Another goal is to reduce network I/O by placing one replica on the same rack as the node that's writing to a file.

Despite your best-laid plans, various competing factors might cause new data to be placed across the slave nodes in a non-uniform manner. Luckily, one tool can analyze block placement and rebalance data across the slave nodes for you: the Hadoop `balancer` command, which gets a nice mention in the following section, in Table 17-1.

Mastering the Hadoop Administration Commands

Any Hadoop administrator worth his salt must master a comprehensive set of commands for cluster administration. Table 17-1 summarizes the most important commands. Know them, and you will advance a long way along the path to Hadoop wisdom. Table 17-2 summarizes the Hadoop `dfsadmin` command options.

Table 17-1	Administration Commands		
Command	*What It Does*	*Syntax*	*Example*
balancer	Runs the cluster-balancing utility. The specified threshold value, which represents a percentage of disk capacity, is used to overwrite the default threshold value (10 percent). To stop the rebalancing process, press Ctrl+C.	`hadoop balancer [-threshold <threshold>]`	`hadoop balancer -threshold 20`
daemonlog	Gets or sets the log level for each daemon. Connects to `http://host:port/logLevel?log=name` and prints or sets the log	`hadoop daemonlog -getlevel <host:port> <name>; hadoop daemonlog`	`hadoop daemonlog -getlevel 10.250.1. 15:50030`

Command	What It Does	Syntax	Example

	level of the daemon that's running at *host*: *port*. Hadoop daemons generate log files that help you determine what's happening on the system, and you can use the daemonlog command to temporarily change the log level of a Hadoop component when you're debugging the system. The change becomes effective when the daemon restarts.	`-setlevel`
		`<host:port>`
		`<name> <level>`
			`org.apache.`
			`hadoop.`
			`mapred.`
			`JobTracker;`
			`hadoop`
			`daemonlog -`
			`setlevel`
			`10.250.1.`
			`15:50030`
			`org.apache.`
			`hadoop.`
			`mapred.`
			`JobTracker`
			`DEBUG`

datanode	Runs the HDFS DataNode service, which coordinates storage on each slave node. If you specify -rollback, the DataNode is rolled back to the previous version. Stop the DataNode and distribute the previous Hadoop version before using this option.	`hadoop datanode`
		`[-rollback]`
			`hadoop datanode`
			`-`
			`rollback`

dfsadmin	Runs a number of Hadoop Distributed File System (HDFS) administrative operations. Use the -help option to see a list of all supported options. The generic options are a common set of options supported by several commands. (For detailed information about generic options, visit http:// hadoop.apache.org/ docs/r2.0.5-alpha/ hadoop-project-dist/hadoop-common/ CommandsManual. html. For detailed information about the individual dfsadmin command options, see Table 17-2.)	`hadoop dfsadmin` `[GENERIC_OPTIONS]` `[-report]` `[-safemode` `enter	leave` `| get	wait]` `[-refreshNodes]` `[-finalizeUpgrade]` `[-upgradeProgress` `status	details |` `force] [-metasave` `filename]` `[-setQuota <quota>` `<dirname>. . .` `<dirname>]` `[-clrQuota` `<dirname>. . .` `<dirname>]` `[-restoreFailed` `Storage` `true|false|check]` `[-help [cmd]]`	

(continued)

Table 17-1 *(continued)*

Command	What It Does	Syntax	Example
mradmin	Runs a number of MapReduce administrative operations. Use the `-help` option to see a list of all supported options. Again, the generic options are a common set of options that are supported by several commands. (For detailed information about these options, visit `http://hadoop.apache.org/docs/r2.0.5-alpha/hadoop-project-dist/hadoop-common/CommandsManual.html`.) If you specify `-refreshServiceAcl`, `mradmin` reloads the service-level authorization policy file (JobTracker reloads the authorization policy file); `-refreshQueues` reloads the queue access control lists (ACLs) and state (JobTracker reloads the `mapred-queues.xml` file); `-refreshNodes` refreshes the hosts information at the JobTracker; `-refreshUserToGroupsMappings` refreshes user-to-groups mappings; `-refreshSuperUserGroupsConfiguration` refreshes superuser proxy groups mappings; and `-help [cmd]` displays help for the given command or for all commands if none is specified.	`hadoop mradmin [ GENERIC_OPTIONS ] [-refreshServiceAcl] [-refreshQueues] [-refreshNodes] [-refreshUserToGroupsMappings] [-refreshSuperUserGroupsConfiguration] [-help [cmd]]`	`hadoop mradmin -help -refreshNodes`

Command	What It Does	Syntax	Example
`jobtracker`	Runs the MapReduce JobTracker node, which coordinates the data processing system for Hadoop. If you specify `-dumpConfiguration`, the configuration that's used by the JobTracker and the queue configuration in JSON format are written to standard output.	`hadoop jobtracker [-dump Configuration]`	`hadoop jobtracker -dump Configuration`
`namenode`	Runs the NameNode, which coordinates the storage for the whole Hadoop cluster. If you specify `-format`, the NameNode is started, formatted, and then stopped; with `-upgrade`, the NameNode starts with the upgrade option after a new Hadoop version is distributed; with `-rollback`, the NameNode is rolled back to the previous version (remember to stop the cluster and distribute the previous Hadoop version before using this option); with `-finalize`, the previous state of the file system is removed, the most recent upgrade becomes permanent, rollback is no longer available, and the NameNode is stopped; finally, with `-importCheckpoint`, an image is loaded from the checkpoint directory (as specified by the `fs.checkpoint.dir` property) and saved into the current directory.	`hadoop namenode [-format] | [-upgrade] | [-rollback] | [-finalize] | [-import Checkpoint]`	`hadoop namenode -finalize`

(continued)

Table 17-1 *(continued)*

Command	What It Does	Syntax	Example
secondary namenode	Runs the secondary NameNode. If you specify `-checkpoint`, a checkpoint on the secondary NameNode is performed if the size of the EditLog (a transaction log that records every change that occurs to the file system metadata) is greater than or equal to `fs.checkpoint.size`; if you specify `-force`, a checkpoint is performed regardless of the EditLog size; specify `-geteditsize` and the EditLog size is printed.	`hadoop secondary namenode [-checkpoint [force]] | [-geteditsize]`	`hadoop secondary namenode -geteditsize`
tasktracker	Runs a MapReduce TaskTracker node.	`hadoop tasktracker`	`hadoop tasktracker`

Table 17-2   The Hadoop `dfsadmin` Command

Option	What It Does
`-report`	Reports basic file system information and statistics.
`-safemode enter | leave | get | wait`	Manages *safe* mode, a NameNode state in which changes to the name space are not accepted and blocks can be neither replicated nor deleted.
	The NameNode is in safe mode during startup so that it doesn't prematurely start replicating blocks even though there are already enough replicas in the cluster.

Option	What It Does
-refreshNodes	Forces the NameNode to reread its configuration, including the dfs.hosts.exclude file. The NameNode decommissions nodes after their blocks have been replicated onto machines that will remain active.
-finalizeUpgrade	Completes the HDFS upgrade process. DataNodes and the NameNode delete working directories from the previous version in order to keep things nice and neat.
-upgradeProgress status | details | force	Requests the standard or detailed current status of the distributed upgrade, or forces the upgrade to proceed.
-metasave filename	Saves the NameNode's primary data structures to *filename* in a directory that's specified by the hadoop.log.dir property. File *filename,* which is overwritten if it already exists, contains one line for each of these items: a) DataNodes that are exchanging heartbeats (electronic "signs of life") with the NameNode; b) blocks that are waiting to be replicated; c) blocks that are being replicated; and d) blocks that are waiting to be deleted.
-setQuota <quota> <dirname>... <dirname>	Sets an upper limit on the number of names in the directory tree. You can set this limit (a long integer) for one or more directories simultaneously.
clrQuota <dirname>... <dirname>	Clears the upper limit on the number of names in the directory tree. You can clear this limit for one or more directories simultaneously.
-restoreFailedStorage true | false | check	Turns on or off the automatic attempts to restore failed storage replicas. If a failed storage location becomes available again, the system attempts to restore edits and the fsimage during a checkpoint. The check option returns the current setting.
-help [cmd]	Displays help information for the given command or for all commands if none is specified.

Understanding Factors for Performance

Many factors affect the performance of a Hadoop cluster, including the hardware configuration of machines in the cluster, the software configuration, and how well the map and reduce tasks are tuned for the particular jobs they perform when processing your workloads. This section takes a look at each one of these factors in turn.

Hardware

As you might expect, because each node in a Hadoop cluster is used to store (DataNode) *and* process (TaskTracker) data, the hardware should be configured with both roles in mind. Always use the fastest machines you can afford, with processing speed a function of the number of cores available. Also, remember that having lots of RAM minimizes the number of times that data must be read from disk. RAM requirements for the NameNode increase in proportion to the total number of data blocks in the cluster, and extra RAM on the NameNode accommodates the future growth of the cluster. Disk speed affects the degree of throughput that can be achieved, and the number of disks per node affects the cluster's ability to "scale up," which in this case means the ability to add storage to individual nodes in the system.

MapReduce

Tuning the number of map tasks and reduce tasks for a particular job in your workload is another way that you can optimize performance, because each task has a significant level of overhead that can represent a significant cost for you when the length of time spent on task execution ends up being relatively short.

If your jobs involve larger data sets, increasing the block size reduces the number of tasks, which also has a positive impact on performance.

When planning to maximize the performance of your Hadoop cluster, you often have to make a trade-off between the overhead of data movement and your IO (input/output) costs. If your nodes have local storage disks, it might make sense to move MapReduce processing to those nodes so that input/output is minimized. If, on the other hand, the data isn't available locally, you have to move it to the nodes where processing will occur. This situation can result in network congestion and eroded performance when data volumes are very large. Although data replication can address this issue by producing a local copy of the data at each processing node, creating, distributing, and storing replicas in a large cluster can be quite costly.

Benchmarking

After you have defined the types of workloads to run on your system, you can begin to benchmark those workloads to identify input/output and data processing bottlenecks.

So, what exactly is benchmarking? Many types of benchmarking are out there, but when the term is applied to a Hadoop cluster, what's usually meant is a process whereby you compare the cluster's performance either to previously measured values or to published best-of-breed values. Performance benchmarking involves the monitoring of specific indicators (for example, throughput, response time) under controlled conditions. Benchmarking is typically an ongoing process that's designed to promote continuous improvement.

When you have set up a new cluster, benchmarking is a good way to determine whether the cluster was set up correctly. See whether you get the expected results. Your expectations might be driven by published results from other clusters that were configured in a similar way. You can also tune the cluster by comparing monitored results with benchmark values.

To produce the best results, run benchmarks when your cluster isn't being used by others.

It just so happens that the Hadoop distribution includes a number of benchmarks you can use. Examples include TestDFSIO, NNBench, and MRBench (in hadoop-*test*.jar) and TeraSort (in hadoop-*examples*.jar). If you're curious about what these benchmarks can offer, check out this list:

- ✓ **TestDFSIO:** The TestDFSIO benchmark is useful for testing the I/O performance of the HDFS. This benchmark uses a MapReduce job to read and write files in separate map tasks, whose output is used for collecting statistics that are accumulated in the reduce tasks to produce a summary result. The benchmark data is then appended to a local file named TestDFSIO_results.log and written to standard output.

- ✓ **NNBench:** The NNBench benchmark is useful for load-testing the NameNode. This benchmark simulates a high volume of file manipulation requests against the HDFS to "stress-test" the NameNode's ability to manage the HDFS.

- ✓ **MRBench:** The MRBench benchmark loops small jobs to determine whether they're running efficiently. It's used to test the MapReduce layer.

- ✓ **TeraSort:** The TeraSort benchmark sorts a fixed amount of data as quickly as possible. This benchmark tests both the HDFS and MapReduce layers of your Hadoop cluster and is useful for comparing the performance of your cluster with other clusters. You can use the TeraSort benchmark to fine-tune your Hadoop configuration after running the TestDFSIO benchmark.

To get a list of the benchmarks that come with Hadoop, run the JAR file with no arguments:

```
% hadoop jar $HADOOP_INSTALL/hadoop-*-test.jar
```

To retrieve usage information for a specific benchmark, run the benchmark with no arguments. For example:

```
% hadoop jar $HADOOP_INSTALL/hadoop-*-test.jar TestDFSIO
```

When tuning the cluster, be sure to include jobs that are similar to the workloads you'll run most often. The standard benchmarks that come with Hadoop are fine in general, but tune the cluster for your specific workloads. And remember to test the same set of jobs and data every time so that you can meaningfully compare runs.

Tolerating Faults and Data Reliability

The glory of Apache Hadoop is that, in a Hadoop cluster, data is distributed across a number of balanced machines, and replication is used to ensure both data reliability and fault tolerance.

By default, each block is replicated to three slave nodes. The *replication factor* is configurable. Block replication is maintained by the system automatically. The NameNode is responsible for detecting failed slave nodes or unavailable replicas and ensures that usable replicas are copied to other nodes.

The DataNode service on each slave node sends heartbeats (indicating their good health) to the NameNode by using the same port number that was defined for the NameNode daemon (typically, TCP 9000 or TCP 8020). A *heartbeat* is a periodic signal in the form of a TCP handshake, which is the procedure that takes place between two TCP/IP nodes to establish a connection. As you might expect, regular heartbeats from a DataNode tell the NameNode that the DataNode is alive and well. By default, the heartbeat interval is three seconds, and if the NameNode doesn't receive a heartbeat from a particular DataNode within ten minutes, the DataNode is presumed to be "dead," and its blocks are scheduled for replication on other nodes.

Keep the heartbeat frequency high, even on big clusters. NameNodes can handle thousands of heartbeats per second without difficulty, and the granularity of the information that is provided in this way is essential to maintaining good cluster health.

Every tenth heartbeat from a particular DataNode is a *block report,* by which the DataNode identifies its blocks to the NameNode. This information is used by the NameNode to determine whether the correct number of block replicas exists. If a DataNode is dead, its data is of course unavailable, but the NameNode is aware of which replicas died along with the node and can replicate those blocks to other slave nodes.

You expect your Hadoop cluster to be always available. One way to make it happen is to configure the HDFS High Availability (HA) feature, using a shared NFS directory.

Prior to the Hadoop 2.x series, the NameNode was a *single point of failure* in an HDFS cluster — in other words, if the machine on which the single NameNode was configured became unavailable, the entire cluster would be unavailable until the NameNode could be restarted. This was bad news, especially in the case of unplanned outages, which could result in significant downtime if the cluster administrator weren't available to restart the NameNode.

The solution to this problem is addressed by the HDFS High Availability feature. The idea is to run two NameNodes in the same cluster — one active NameNode and one hot standby NameNode. If the active NameNode crashes or needs to be stopped for planned maintenance, it can be quickly *failed over* to the hot standby NameNode, which now becomes the active NameNode. The key is to keep the standby node synchronized with the active node; this action is now accomplished by having both nodes access a shared NFS directory. All namespace changes on the active node are logged in the shared directory. The standby node picks up those changes from the directory and applies them to its own namespace. In this way, the standby NameNode acts as a current backup of the active NameNode. The standby node also has current block location information, because DataNode heartbeats are routinely sent to both active and standby NameNodes.

To ensure that only one NameNode is the "active" node at any given time, configure a *fencing process* for the shared storage directory; then, during a failover, if it appears that the failed NameNode still carries the active state, the configured fencing process prevents that node from accessing the shared directory and permits the newly active node (the former standby node) to complete the failover.

The machines that will serve as the active and standby NameNodes in your High Availability cluster should have equivalent hardware. The shared NFS storage directory, which must be accessible to both active and standby NameNodes, is usually located on a separate machine and can be mounted on each NameNode machine. To prevent this directory from becoming a single point of failure, configure multiple network paths to the storage directory, and ensure that there's redundancy in the storage itself. Use a dedicated network-attached storage (NAS) appliance to contain the shared storage directory.

Putting Apache Hadoop's Capacity Scheduler to Good Use

Although it might seem that Hadoop is an inherently limitless resource, there are limits to its capacity, and cluster resources must be managed appropriately to avoid performance issues. You don't have to be an organization such as Yahoo! or Facebook, which control some of the largest Hadoop clusters in the world, to appreciate the need for capacity management.

Apache Hadoop's Capacity Scheduler was designed to address — you guessed it — capacity management. The Capacity Scheduler, a pluggable scheduler and console for Hadoop, uses *job queues* to facilitate the organized sharing of Hadoop clusters. It guarantees minimum capacity levels for all queues and makes unused capacity available to overloaded queues, which leads to optimized cluster utilization.

The Capacity Scheduler provides a set of limits to ensure that a single application cannot consume a disproportionate amount of cluster resources, thereby promoting fairness and stability.

You can assign jobs to specific queues and, as an administrator, define each queue's *maximum capacity* — a limit on the amount of resources a queue can claim beyond its guaranteed capacity.

Each queue enforces additional restrictions, including a limit on

- ✔ The resources that a specific user can access if multiple users are accessing the queue at the same time
- ✔ The number of accepted or active jobs per queue or per user
- ✔ The number of pending tasks per queue or per user

Moreover, *hierarchical queues* ensure that resources are shared among an organization's subqueues before another organization's queues are allowed to access unused resources.

From a security perspective, each queue has access control lists (ACLs) that control which users are authorized to submit applications to specific queues. Moreover, users cannot view or change the applications of other users.

As an administrator, you can change queue definitions, properties, and ACLs at run time, but you cannot delete queues. You can, however, stop a queue at run time to block the submission of new applications while existing applications are running. Because existing applications continue to run, the queue is able to run its course. Administrators can also start any stopped queues.

To take advantage of the Capacity Scheduler, you have to configure your ResourceManager (see Chapter 7) to use it. To do so, set the `yarn.resourcemanager.scheduler.class` property in the `conf/yarn-site.xml` file to

```
org.apache.hadoop.yarn.server.resourcemanager.scheduler.
        capacity.CapacityScheduler
```

The configuration file for the Capacity Scheduler is `conf/capacity-scheduler.xml`. You can edit this file to define new queues or to modify existing ones. After editing the configuration file, run `yarn rmadmin -refreshQueues`, as shown here:

```
$ vi $HADOOP_CONF_DIR/capacity-scheduler.xml
$ $HADOOP_YARN_HOME/bin/yarn rmadmin -refreshQueues
```

The Capacity Scheduler has the predefined queue named `root`. All other queues are defined as children of the `root` queue.

It's easy to define new queues: Simply configure the `yarn.scheduler.capacity.root.queues` property with a list of child queue names, separated by commas. For example, to add two child queues (q1 and q2), you'd do this:

```
<property>
  <name>yarn.scheduler.capacity.root.queues</name>
  <value>q1,q2</value>
  <description>The child queues under root.
  </description>
</property>
```

The queue hierarchy is denoted by a path notation (starting with `root`) in which each queue is separated by a dot: `yarn.scheduler.capacity.queue-path.queues`. For example:

```
<property>
  <name>yarn.scheduler.capacity.root.q1.queues</name>
  <value>q1a1,q1a2</value>
  <description>The child queues under q1.
  </description>
</property>
```

For more information about the Capacity Scheduler, visit

```
http://hadoop.apache.org/docs/current/hadoop-yarn/hadoop-
        yarn-site/CapacityScheduler.html
```

Setting Security: The Kerberos Protocol

When we speak about security in a Hadoop context, we are referring to an *authentication* method to ensure that users of the Hadoop cluster are who they say they are. File system permissions, which enforce *authorization,* are designed to control the file operations (such as read or write) that a specific user or group can perform. For various reasons, including the importance of protecting sensitive data from users who don't have a business need to access such data, shared clusters, including Hadoop clusters, must have effective authentication mechanisms in place.

Secure authentication of Hadoop clusters has been available through the Kerberos protocol since Hadoop 2. Kerberos is a mature, open source computer network authentication protocol that enables nodes to securely verify their identity to one another. Kerberos does not manage file or directory permissions.

The Kerberos protocol is implemented as a series of negotiations between a client, the authentication server (AS), and the service server (SS). This is what happens, in a nutshell: When a user logs on, the client authenticates itself to the AS, which sends the username to a key distribution center (KDC). The KDC then issues a time-stamped ticket-granting ticket (TGT), which is encrypted and returned to the client.

When the client wants to communicate with another node, it sends the TGT to a ticket-granting server (TGS), which verifies that the TGT is valid. The TGS then issues a ticket and session keys, which are returned to the client. The client, in turn, sends the ticket and a service request to the service server (SS), which, in the case of a Hadoop cluster, might be the NameNode or the JobTracker.

A TGT expires after a certain period (ten hours, by default) but can be renewed for as long as a week. You can provide a single sign-on to Hadoop by automating the authentication process at operating system login.

To use Kerberos authentication with Hadoop, you must install and configure a key distribution center. Enable Kerberos authentication by setting the `hadoop.security.authentication` property in `core-site.xml` to `kerberos`. Enable service-level authorization by setting the `hadoop.security.authorization` property in the same file to `true`. You should also configure access control lists (ACLs) in the `hadoop-policy.xml` configuration file to specify which users and groups have permission to connect to the various Hadoop services, such as NameNode communication.

Expanding Your Toolset Options

You are not alone. Lots of very smart people have come up with a bunch of tools and interfaces that you can use to make administering a Hadoop cluster easier. Two of the more prominent tools are Hue and Ambari, which we highlight in the upcoming sections.

Hue

Hue is a browser-based graphical user interface to Apache Hadoop. Folks just call it Hue these days, but the name originates as an acronym for Hadoop User Experience.

Hue was initially developed as an open source project by Cloudera. Although Hue comes bundled with Cloudera (and with many Hadoop distributions to boot), it's also available from GitHub as open source code. With Hue, you can browse the HDFS (by using FileBrowser); create and manage user accounts; monitor your cluster; submit and view MapReduce or YARN jobs (by using JobSub and JobBrowser); enable a user interface (named Beeswax) to Hive; use an HBase browser; access query editors for Hive, Pig, Cloudera Impala, and Sqoop 2; and much more.

Table 17-3 summarizes the various components that make up the Hue offering.

Table 17-3	The Components of Hue, a Graphical User Interface to Apache Hadoop
Component	*What You Can Do with It*
File Browser	Upload, browse, and manipulate files and directories in the Hadoop Distributed File System (HDFS).
HBase Browser	Quickly access very large tables, create new tables, add data, or modify existing data.
Cloudera Search	Search for data that's stored in the HDFS or HBase. SQL and programming skills aren't required, because Cloudera Search provides a simple, full-text interface for searching.
Job Designer	Create and submit MapReduce, YARN, or Java jobs to your Hadoop cluster.

(continued)

Table 17-3 *(continued)*

Component	What You Can Do with It
Job Browser	Monitor the MapReduce or YARN jobs that are running on your Hadoop cluster. Jobs appear in a list, and you can link to a list of tasks for a specific job. You can view task details or logs to troubleshoot failed jobs.
Metastore Manager	Manage the databases, tables, and partitions of the Hive metastore, which is shared by Beeswax and Cloudera Impala. You can use the Metastore Manager to create or drop a database; create, browse, or drop tables; or import data into tables. (For more on Apache Hive, see Chapter 13.)
Beeswax Hive User Interface	Run and manage queries on Apache Hive, a distributed data warehouse for data that's stored in the HDFS. You can download query results in a Microsoft Office Excel worksheet or a text file.
Sqoop 2	Efficiently move large amounts of data between relational databases and the HDFS.
Cloudera Impala	Issue low-latency SQL queries against data that's stored in the HDFS or HBase without the need for data movement or transformation. This massively parallel processing query engine runs natively on Apache Hadoop.
Pig Editor	Edit your Pig scripts with autocompletion and syntax highlighting. (For more on Pig and Pig scripting, see Chapter 8.)
Oozie Editor and Dashboard	Define Oozie workflow and coordinator applications, run workflow and coordinator jobs, and view the status of those jobs. (For more on Oozie, see Chapter 10.)
Zookeeper User Interface	Browse the Znode hierarchy of your Zookeeper cluster, and add, edit, or delete Znodes. (For more on Zookeeper, see Chapter 12.)
User Admin	Add, delete, and manage Hue users or groups (if you're the administrator); add users or groups individually or import them from an LDAP directory. Granted permissions determine which Hue applications, or application features, users or groups can access.

Hue also comes with a software development kit (SDK) that enables you to reuse Hue libraries and build applications on top of Hadoop.

Hue is designed to enhance the Hadoop user experience by facilitating real-time interaction with data and helping you to get results faster. It's intended to be used by a variety of users and is offered in several languages, including Spanish, French, German, Portuguese, Brazilian Portuguese, Japanese, simplified Chinese, and Korean.

For information about getting started with Hue, including development prerequisites, visit one of these sites:

```
https://github.com/cloudera/hue
http://cloudera.github.io/hue/docs-2.0.1/manual.html
```

Ambari

Apache Ambari is a tool for provisioning, configuring, managing, and monitoring Apache Hadoop clusters. With Ambari, you can deploy and operate a complete Hadoop stack by using a browser-based management interface.

Apache Ambari is still undergoing *incubation* at the Apache Software Foundation (ASF); incubation is required of all newly accepted projects until their infrastructure is deemed consistent with other successful ASF projects.

The Apache Ambari project is designed to simplify Hadoop management by providing a set of simple GUI tools. It now supports the following Hadoop components: the HDFS, MapReduce, Hive, HCatalog, HBase, ZooKeeper, Oozie, Pig, and Sqoop.

Ambari makes it easy for system administrators to perform the tasks described in this list:

- ✔ Provision a Hadoop cluster:

    - *Ambari provides an easy-to-use wizard to help you install Hadoop services.*

    - *Ambari handles the configuration of Hadoop services for your cluster.*

- ✔ Manage a Hadoop cluster:

    - *Ambari provides central management for starting, stopping, and reconfiguring Hadoop services across your entire cluster.*

- ✔ Monitor a Hadoop cluster:

    - *Ambari provides a dashboard for monitoring the health and status of your Hadoop cluster.*

- *Ambari leverages Ganglia for metrics collection. Ganglia, a BSD-licensed open source project, is a scalable distributed monitoring system for high-performance computing systems such as clusters. For information about Ganglia monitoring, visit* `http://ganglia.sourceforge.net`.

- *Ambari leverages Nagios for system alerting and sends e-mails when your attention is needed, such as when a node fails. Nagios, an open source application, offers monitoring and alerting services for servers, switches, applications, and services. For information about Nagios monitoring, visit* `www.nagios.org`.

Ambari also helps application developers and system integrators integrate Hadoop provisioning, management, and monitoring capabilities into their own applications by using Ambari's Representational State Transfer (REST) APIs. (REST is an architectural style for client/server communication over HTTP.)

Ambari now supports the 64-bit version of these operating systems:

✔ RHEL (Redhat Enterprise Linux) 5 and 6

✔ CentOS 5 and 6

✔ OEL (Oracle Enterprise Linux) 5 and 6

✔ SLES (SuSE Linux Enterprise Server) 11

For more information about the Apache Ambari, visit one of these sites:

```
http://incubator.apache.org/ambari
http://hortonworks.com/hadoop/ambari
```

Hadoop User Experience (Hue)

Hadoop User Experience (Hue, for short) is a browser-based graphical user interface to Apache Hadoop. You can use Hue to

✔ Browse the HDFS

✔ Create and manage user accounts

✔ Monitor the cluster

✔ Submit and view MapReduce or YARN jobs (by using JobSub and JobBrowser)

✔ Enable Beeswax, an aptly named user interface for Apache Hive, which is Hadoop's data warehouse infrastructure with SQL-like features

✔ Use an HBase browser

✔ Access query editors for (the aforementioned) Hive, Pig, Cloudera Impala (a query engine with SQL capabilities) and Sqoop 2

Hue was developed as an open source project by — and is available from — Cloudera (www.cloudera.com/). The current version of Hue is 2.3.0.

Table 17-4 summarizes the various components that come packaged with Hue.

Table 17-4	Hue Components
Component	*What You Can Do with It*
File Browser	Upload, browse, and manipulate files and directories in the Hadoop distributed file system (HDFS).
HBase Browser	Quickly access very large tables, create new tables, add data, or modify existing data.
Cloudera Search	Search for data that's stored in the HDFS or HBase. SQL and programming skills aren't required, because Cloudera Search provides a simple, full-text interface for searching.
Job Designer	Create and submit MapReduce, YARN, or Java jobs to your Hadoop cluster.
Job Browser	Monitor the MapReduce or YARN jobs that are running on your Hadoop cluster. Jobs appear in a list, and you can link to a list of tasks for a specific job. You can view task details or logs to troubleshoot failed jobs.
Metastore Manager	Manage the databases, tables, and partitions of the Hive metastore that are shared by Beeswax and Cloudera Impala. You can use the Metastore Manager to create or drop a database; create, browse, or drop tables; and import data into tables.
Beeswax Hive User Interface	Run and manage queries on Apache Hive. You can download query results in a worksheet or text file in Microsoft Office Excel. (For more on Hive, see Chapter 13.)
Sqoop 2	Efficiently move large amounts of data between relational databases and the HDFS.
Cloudera Impala	Issue low-latency SQL queries against data stored in the HDFS or in HBase without the need for data movement or transformation. (This massively parallel processing query engine runs natively on Apache Hadoop.)
Pig Editor	Edit Pig scripts with autocompletion and syntax highlighting. (For much more on Pig, see Chapter 8.)
Oozie Editor and Dashboard	Define Oozie workflow and coordinator applications, run workflow and coordinator jobs, and view the status of those jobs. (For more on Oozie, check out Chapter 10.)

(continued)

Table 17-4 *(continued)*

Component	What You Can Do with It
Zookeeper User Interface	Browse the Znode hierarchy of the Zookeeper cluster, and add, edit, or delete Znodes. (You can find lots more on Zookeeper in Chapter 13.)
User Admin	Add, delete, and manage Hue users or groups (if you're the administrator). You can add users or groups individually or import them from an LDAP directory, such as a corporate e-mail directory. Granted permissions determine which Hue applications or application features can be accessed by users or groups.

Hue also comes supplied with an SDK (System Development Kit) that enables you to reuse Hue libraries and build applications on top of Hadoop.

Hue is designed to enhance the Hadoop user experience by facilitating real-time interaction with data and by helping you get results faster. Intended to be used by a variety of users, Hue is offered in several languages, including Spanish, French, German, Portuguese, Brazilian Portuguese, Japanese, simplified Chinese, and Korean.

For information about getting started with Hue, including development prerequisites, visit one of these sites:

```
https://github.com/cloudera/hue
http://cloudera.github.io/hue/docs-2.0.1/manual.html
```

The Hadoop shell

The *Hadoop shell* is a family of commands that you can run from your operating system's command line. The shell has two sets of commands: one for file manipulation (similar in purpose and syntax to Linux commands that many of us know and love) and one for Hadoop administration. For a detailed description of the file management commands available in the Hadoop shell, see the section in Chapter 5 about managing files with the Hadoop file system commands. For details on the administration commands in the Hadoop shell, see the "Mastering the Hadoop Administration Commands" section, earlier in this chapter.

Basic Hadoop Configuration Details

In Hadoop 0.19.x or earlier, you had to modify only one configuration file, `hadoop-site.xml`, in order to lay the groundwork for your Hadoop project. In Hadoop 0.21 and later, however, you have a bit more work coming your way. More specifically, you need to configure three separate XML files, all found in the `HADOOP_HOME/conf` directory:

- `core-site.xml`
- `hdfs-site.xml`
- `mapred-site.xml`

Your Hadoop configuration is driven by two distinct types of configuration files:

- **Default (read-only):** Files here include `src/core/core-default.xml`, `src/hdfs/hdfs-default.xml`, and `src/mapred/mapred-default.xml`.

- **Site-specific configuration:** Files here include `conf/core-site.xml`, `conf/hdfs-site.xml`, and `conf/mapred-site.xml`.

These files are also known as resources. A *resource* contains a set of name/value pairs as XML data. Each resource is identified by either a string value or a path. If you specify a string value, the classpath is searched for a file whose name matches that value. If you specify a path, the local file system is searched directly. The default resources (XML files), which are read-only, reside inside the `hadoop-common` and `hadoop-hdfs` JAR files. These files, which are read from the JAR files directly, should never be modified.

The site-specific resources are loaded from the classpath, and their values are used to override the corresponding values in the matching default resource. If you've surmised that the previous statement implies that the default resource is loaded first, followed by the site-specific resource, you're right! For example:

- `core-default.xml`: Contains read-only default values for your Hadoop configuration and is read in first.

- `core-site.xml`: Contains site-specific configuration values for your Hadoop deployment and is read in second; contains only those values that need to be changed from the default.

The following code example shows a configuration specification from a `core-site.xml` file:

```
<property>
  <name>hadoop.tmp.dir</name>
  <value>/home/hadoop/hadoop-0.20.2/hdfs-tmp</value>
  <description>A base for other temporary
         directories.</description>
</property>
```

Note that each `<property>` element (`<name>`, `<value>`, and `<description>` in this example) defines a specific configuration name/value pair. The file can contain any number of these `<property>` elements, which are enclosed by one `<configuration>` element, as in this example:

```
<configuration>
...
<property>
  <name>...</name>
  <value>...</value>
  <description>...</description>
</property
...
</configuration>
```

The `<description>` element is optional but can be quite useful for tracking details about the property it describes.

Your applications can specify additional resources, and they're also loaded in the order in which they're specified, *after* the system-defined resources have been loaded.

Configuration parameter values can be declared as `final` so that user applications can't change them later, as shown in the following example (from a sample `hdfs-site.xml` file):

```
<property>
    <name>dfs.hosts.include</name>
    <value>/etc/hadoop/conf/hosts.include</value>
    <final>true</final>
</property>
```

After a value is declared to be `final`, no subsequently loaded resource can alter that value.

Finally, the following code example shows a configuration specification from a `mapred-site.xml` file:

```
<property>
  <name>mapred.local.dir</name>
  <value>/home/hadoop/hadoop-0.20.2/mapred-tmp</value>
  <description>Comma-separated list of paths on the local
           file system where temporary MapReduce data is
           written.</description>
</property>
```

A ton of parameter names and values are associated with the resources in the following list. To see a list of a resource's parameter names and values, check out its URL:

✔ `core-default.xml`: `http://hadoop.apache.org/docs/current/hadoop-project-dist/hadoop-common/core-default.xml`

✔ `hdfs-default.xml`: `http://hadoop.apache.org/docs/current/hadoop-project-dist/hadoop-hdfs/hdfs-default.xml`

✔ `mapred-default.xml`: `http://hadoop.apache.org/docs/current/hadoop-mapreduce-client/hadoop-mapreduce-client-core/mapred-default.xml`

Part V
The Part of Tens

Enjoy an additional Hadoop Part of Tens chapter online at `www.dummies.com/extras/hadoop`.

In this part . . .

- Check out the Ten Hadoop Resources Worthy of a Bookmark.
- Find out Ten Reasons to Adopt Hadoop.
- Enjoy an additional Hadoop Part of Tens chapter online at www.dummies.com/extras/hadoop.

Chapter 18

Ten Hadoop Resources Worthy of a Bookmark

In This Chapter

▶ Learning Hadoop — for free

▶ Finding the Hadoop information you need — fast

▶ Setting up a lifelong learning plan for Hadoop

*F*rom its roots in the early 2000s as an Internet search engine indexer, Hadoop has evolved to become a large-scale, general-purpose computing platform. Indeed, competence in Hadoop is one of the hottest skills you can list on a résumé in today's IT job market. If we can tell you one thing from our collective century-plus years of IT experience across multiple jobs and technology domains, it's that you should *never* reach the finish line of your learning roadmap.

Hadoop continues to evolve in a fascinating manner — especially when you consider all the Apache subprojects (and associated projects) that work within the Hadoop ecosystem. You're off to a great start with this book, though this fast-paced environment will continue to change. For example, many new processing frameworks for YARN are being developed that will introduce a wide variety of data processing options to Hadoop. We believe that the Hive project will explode with innovation, especially when you add YARN (see Chapter 7) and Tez (see Chapter 7 again) to the mix. The point? If you want to stay on top of Hadoop, you have to invest in it with a lifelong learning plan.

We highlight the free areas of Hadoop training in keeping with its open source spirit. You'll see that most vendors have found that they can make money delivering top-notch Hadoop training, so they often have both options: for-fee and for-free.

In this chapter, we describe what we think are ten terrific Hadoop resources that are worthy of creating a bookmark in your browser. These resources not only pick up from where we leave off in this book but also help you create a lifelong learning plan for Hadoop. From virtual universities, to 'zines and websites and more, you can continue learning in order to stay on the leading edge of the Hadoop curve, or simply to ensure that you have a solid understanding of the technology.

Central Nervous System: Apache.org

The Apache Software Foundation (ASF) is the central community for open source software projects. (**Note:** The group's charter stipulates that Apache software must be used for public good — so we're assuming that you'll use Hadoop for tasks other than finding better ways to increase the cost of gas.) Not just any project can be an Apache project — many consensus-driven processes convert a piece of software from its initial designs and beta code (its *incubator* status) to full-fledged, generally available software. You can find more about ASF at `http://apache.org`.

The ASF isn't just where projects like Hadoop are managed — it's where they "live and breathe." Today, there are hundreds of Apache projects. With this in mind, you should bookmark the Apache Hadoop page (`http://projects.apache.org/projects/hadoop.html`) as one of your main-stay learning resources. This site is important because you can access the source code there. You can also open or view Hadoop-related defects or bugs; view the license; access mailing lists for the community; download a versioned Hadoop feature, component, or branch (not just those marked stable); and more.

At this point, you've entered the Valhalla of Hadoop links — the Apache.org site is über-Hadoop Land, and is the home of Hadoop's development. You can think of the site as Hadoop's central nervous system. We make no guarantee that everything there is easy to consume, but its information is generally valuable — and straight from the source of Hadoop's developers.

Tweet This

Twitter isn't the place to learn Hadoop per se — after all, you can't easily master MapReduce programming in lessons that span only 140 characters. Be that as it may, quite a number of big data gurus are on Twitter, and they express opinions and point to resources that can make you a smarter Hadoop user.

A number of top-influencer lists in the Twitter landscape cover Hadoop and big data, and that's the best way to find these Hadoop personalities and add them to your Twitter lists. Here are a couple notable lists where you can find the most distinguished personalities covering Hadoop and big data on Twitter — including some of the authors of this book:

- **#BigData100 (Big Data Republic):** `tinyurl.com/ouk6lb8`
- **Top 200 Big Data Influencers (Onalytica):** `tinyurl.com/oq6677s`

Hortonworks University

Hortonworks University (`hortonworks.com/hadoop-training`) provides Hadoop training and certifications. The site offers Hadoop courses built for either administrator or developer practitioners with the option of a rigorous certification program. Hortonworks employs some of the deepest and most noted Hadoop experts in the world, so you're assured of quality expertise behind the courseware.

Hortonworks University has for-free and for-fee training. We focus on the free stuff in this chapter, so we think that the place you'll head to is the Hortonworks Sandbox (`hortonworks.com/products/Hortonworks-sandbox`) and its Resources page (`hortonworks.com/resources`). If you're looking for fee-based training, you can find it there as well.

The Hortonworks Sandbox gives you a portable Hadoop environment with an accompanying set of tutorials that cover a wide arrange of features from the latest HDP distribution. (This distribution is also used extensively in for-fee training).

The aforementioned Resources pages provide a wide array of document-based tutorials, videos, presentations, demos, and more. It also provides a decent roadmap to get started, aptly named "Getting Started with Hadoop" (`hortonworks.com/get-started`).

Cloudera University

Cloudera University (`university.cloudera.com`) is similar in its business model and charter to Hortonworks University, providing a number of learning avenues that run the gamut from traditional text to video. Cloudera is a prominent fixture in the Hadoop world. (Doug Cutting, the "father" of Hadoop is its chief architect.) The site offers an extensive set of courses, and more, which are based on the Cloudera Distribution for Hadoop (CDH).

Some courses are offered for a fee with in-classroom instruction, but one option lets you take certain courses for free in an online video series — for example, Cloudera Essentials for Apache Hadoop, at `university.cloudera.com/onlineresources.html`. When we took the course, we would have liked to have seen more-engaging materials in the courseware, but the instructors are engaging, considering that you're watching a recorded video (plus, nobody gets mad at you for chewing gum while in class).

We think that the Introduction to Data Science class at Cloudera University is pretty cool. Next to the *big data* label, *data science* is likely one of the most overused, or most misunderstood, labels — but people in that profession are commanding even higher salaries than Hadoop experts are. Cloudera even has a certification program (the Cloudera Certified Professional: Data Scientist), which we found to be a unique and terrific idea.

Cloudera University includes a number of modules in its e-learning catalog (`university.cloudera.com/onlineresources/elearning.html`). Because Cloudera is focused on Hadoop as well as on its own set of Hadoop add-ons, the site offers training in the full spectrum of features that Cloudera brings to the table. For example, in Figure 18-1 you can see an example of the course An Introduction to Impala. (Impala, if you're curious, is the Cloudera alternative to Hive; we cover Impala in Chapter 15.)

To get started with CDH and create an environment to complement your knowledge of Hadoop (or any Cloudera technology, for that matter), you can find packaged code and virtual images at `cloudera.com/content/support/en/downloads.html`.

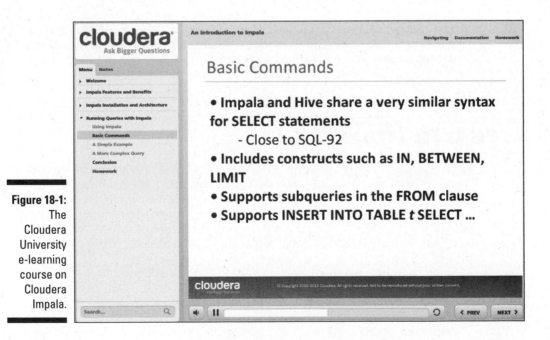

Figure 18-1:
The Cloudera University e-learning course on Cloudera Impala.

BigDataUniversity.com

BigDataUniversity.com (the case doesn't matter when you enter the URL in your browser) is a fantastic resource for learning about — you guessed it — big data. Of course, big data isn't just Hadoop, so you'll find more than Hadoop resources at this site. This university has over 100,000 students enrolled and learning about Hadoop and big data every day.

You'll notice right off the bat that this isn't a typical IBM resource. For example, you won't fill out dozens of fields and answer all kinds of questions that make you feel like you're getting set up for a cold call. We like to think of BigDataUniversity.com as free, in-your-place and at-your-pace Hadoop training. The word *free* is the key here: Unlike the other two universities we detail in this chapter, there isn't a fee-based component anywhere on the site.

The university moniker for this site isn't an accident — it has quite an extensive list of courseware that expands beyond Hadoop (bigdatauniversity. com/courses). From a Hadoop perspective, you won't just find courses on "Hadoop Fundamentals," but also "Hadoop and the Amazon Cloud," "Hadoop Reporting and Analytics" and more — including some database stuff. That's why we really like this resource – it gives off a Swiss Army knife vibe that gives you a place to expand your Hadoop knowledge even further into the big data domain.

Courses at BigDataUniversity.com are composed of traditional reading materials, mixed with multimedia, and code examples. An example of the Hadoop Fundamentals I course is shown in Figure 18-2.

From the navigation panel on the left, you can see multiple lessons and even a teaching assistant that can provide technical assistance if you get stuck. When you're done with a course, you can take a test. If you pass — you get a certificate!

Another nice feature of this site is that you can leverage the IBM Smart Cloud and create your own Hadoop cluster for free.

If you'd rather host your Hadoop platform locally, you can use IBM InfoSphere BigInsights, IBM's own Hadoop distribution. A Quick Start Edition (available at www.ibm.com/developerworks/downloads/im/ biginsightsquick) comes with its own set of tutorials, which showcase not only Hadoop but also certain IBM enhancements. (The BigInsights Quick Start Edition includes the Text Analytics Toolkit, for example, which includes an Eclipse-based text analytics development environment with an accompanying SQL-like declarative language that runs on Hadoop, and other platforms.) You can use any Hadoop distribution for the courseware on BigDataUniversity.com.

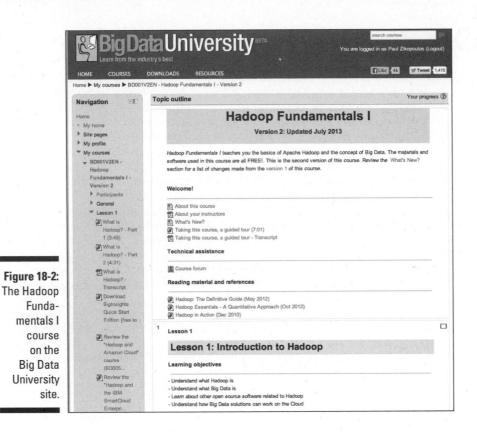

Figure 18-2:
The Hadoop Fundamentals I course on the Big Data University site.

planet Big Data Blog Aggregator

We love it when the name of a site tells you exactly what it does — like planet Big Data Blog Aggregator (www.planetbigdata.com): It's an aggregator of blogs about big data, Hadoop, and other related topics on the planet (well, on Planet Earth anyway).

Both big names and no-names show up on the site, but that's helpful: Though there's undoubtedly commitment to Hadoop by Cloudera, Hortonworks, IBM, and others, it's often refreshing and valuable to get exposure to the thoughts and opinions of grass roots, non-affiliated practitioners by communities not tied to a specific vendor in your learning roadmap.

Are you a big data blogger? Get your blog included in the planet Big Data Blog Aggregator list by e-mailing planetbigdata@gmail.com.

Quora's Apache Hadoop Forum

The Quora Apache Hadoop forum (`www.quora.com/Apache-Hadoop`) is the cornerstone for anyone looking to find out more about Hadoop, or about big data in general, for that matter.

As in any forum, the range of questions and answers you can find at this site is dizzying, but they all lead you to what you're looking for: knowledge. The site has linkages to Hadoop and to its individual components — for example, it has specific forums for MapReduce, HDFS, Pig, HBase, and more. The site also has associated Hadoop forums; for example, Cloudera and Hortonworks have specific discussion groups for their distributions — a testament to how popular this forum is.

Of course, as you transform yourself into a Hadoop demigod, you can answer questions that are posted to the forum and develop your Hadoop influence. (A lot of the active participants in this forum are on the Twitter lists we identify earlier in this chapter.)

The IBM Big Data Hub

The IBM Big Data Hub (`www.ibmbigdatahub.com`) is an excellent place to learn about Hadoop and its ecosystem. Despite being owned and operated by IBM, this site's content isn't always linked with IBM products.

The IBM Big Data Hub provides any visitor with enough knowledge to quench anyone's thirst for big data. You'll find all sorts of blogs, videos, analysts' articles, use cases, infographics, presentations, and more. It's truly a treasure trove of big data resources. This site also aggregates videos from the IBM Big Data and Analytics page at YouTube (`youtube.com/user/ibmbigdata`), which leads you into even more top-notch resources. For example, it has videos such as "What Is Big Data?" and "What Is Hadoop?" that feature some of the authors of this book.

Conferences Not to Be Missed

There are many Hadoop conferences, and even more big data conferences. We're recommending the Hadoop Summit (`hadoopsummit.org`) and Strata Hadoop World (`strataconf.com`) as the quintessential conferences not to be missed. Typically, a distribution vendor co-sponsors these conferences. For example, Yahoo! and Hortonworks sponsor the Hadoop Summit, and Cloudera is the co-sponsor of Strata Hadoop World.

Both Strata Hadoop World and the Hadoop Summit are *the* gathering places of the brightest Hadoop minds in the business; these conferences attract a wide array of Hadoop-interested professionals, including decision makers, architects, developers, analysts, and more.

The Strata Hadoop World name didn't come by accident; two formerly separate and independent conferences (Strata and Hadoop World) have now joined forces to become one of the world's largest gatherings of the Apache Hadoop community. A look at the curriculum makes obvious its focus on all aspects of Hadoop — from sessions devoted to hands-on practitioners to sessions devoted to business use cases.

The Hadoop Summit can be considered a competitor to Strata Hadoop World (though if you're lucky, your bosses will pay for you to go to both). The summit features the same themes and, likely, a lot of the same presenters. One aspect that we find appealing is that the conference tracks are chosen by the community at large as opposed to a conference committee. In the June 2013 Hadoop Summit that took place in San Jose, over 6,000 community members cast over 15,000 votes to create the seven tracks that became the pillars of the conference.

If your appetite leans more in the direction of big data, we think that the yearly IBM Insight Conference (www.ibm.com/software/data/2013-conference) is a must-attend event. It not only features deep, hands-on Hadoop labs and sessions but also runs the gamut of big data topics, including stream computing, governance, the interaction of Hadoop and relational databases, and more.

The Google Papers That Started It All

What is now known as Hadoop has its genesis in a number of papers written by Google employees who were focused on the problem of indexing the Web. While the Apache Nutch project (an open source technology for crawling the Web) was turning its focus on scaling outward in order to index higher volumes of web data, Google published a paper, "The Google File System" (October 2003: research.google.com/archive/gfs.html), which greatly influenced Doug Cutting and his Nutch co-founder, Mike Cafarella. Shortly after, Google released its paper "MapReduce: Simplified Data Processing on Large Clusters" (December 2004: research.google.com/archive/mapreduce.html).

Together, the concept of a distributed file system and a large-scale parallel processing framework were taken by Cutting and Cafarella to develop Apache Hadoop. Of course, Cutting commercialized this work while at Yahoo!, and the rest, as they say, is history.

Here's a great question for a game of Trivial Pursuit for IT geeks: Whatever happened to Mike Cafarella, who cofounded Hadoop with Doug Cutting?" The answer? He's an associate professor at the University of Michigan, and he's working on the Hadoop-complementary project RecordBreaker. Some call him the "Pete Best of big data." (Pete Best was the original drummer for The Beatles.)

A host of other Google papers have influenced the Hadoop ecosystem as well. For example, Google's paper "Bigtable: A Distributed Storage System for Structured Data (November 2006: `research.google.com/archive/bigtable.html`) is the inspiration behind HBase, among other NoSQL technologies.

Though these papers represent the original ideas behind Hadoop, and parts of its ecosystem, as a tribute to where it all began, we've included Google Research (`research.google.com`) and its collection of groundbreaking research papers in our list. Even today, reading these papers gives you a strong appreciation of where Hadoop came from and, potentially, some ideas of where it might evolve.

The Bonus Resource: What Did We Ever Do B.G.?

Considering the impact that Google has had on Hadoop, we thought it prudent to toss in one more related resource to keep in mind if you're on the hunt for Hadoop information: Google. (It's fair to lump YouTube into Google because not only does Google own it, but it has also become one of the top three Internet search sites.) From watching how to bake a pie to solving a problem on your computer to learning about Hadoop, after you type what you're looking for, there's a great chance that you'll find it. All this, of course, makes us wonder: What did we ever do B.G. (before Google)?

Chapter 19

Ten Reasons to Adopt Hadoop

In This Chapter

▶ The price is right

▶ The (open source) community is there

▶ Companies love Hadoop — they really do

▶ Scalability isn't a problem

▶ Hadoop plays nicely with traditional tools

▶ Hadoop has broad tastes in data types

▶ Hadoop can face (almost) any analytical challenge

▶ Full data sets are the norm (no sampling)

▶ Hardware's ability to deal with Hadoop improves every day

▶ Flexible workloads? No problem!

*H*adoop is a powerful and flexible platform for large-scale data analysis. This statement alone is a compelling reason to consider using Hadoop for your analytics projects, especially for solutions involving the use cases we describe in Chapter 2. To help further tip the scales, this chapter lists ten compelling reasons to deploy Hadoop as part of your big data solution.

Though we're excited about Hadoop and we want to promote its adoption, in some cases other software solutions are more appropriate. For example, replacing an online transaction processing database system with Hadoop is almost never a good idea. Architecture decisions come down to requirements, which may include performance thresholds, fine-grained access control, data column masking, or a host of other data governance-related considerations. If your project's criteria align with the characteristics and capabilities of Hadoop that we describe throughout this book, the reasons in this chapter apply to you!

Hadoop Is Relatively Inexpensive

At the time we wrote this book, the cost per terabyte to implement a Hadoop cluster was cheaper than the per-terabyte cost to set up a tape backup system. Granted, a Hadoop system costs more to operate, because the disk drives holding the data are all online and powered, unlike tape drives. But this interesting metric still shows the tremendous potential value of an investment in Hadoop.

The primary reason Hadoop is inexpensive is its reliance on commodity hardware. Traditional solutions in enterprise data management depend on expensive resources to ensure high availability and fast performance. Storage is an excellent example, because the typical relational data warehouse uses expensive SAS disk drives arranged in RAID arrays. By contrast, Hadoop was designed to run with inexpensive SATA drives, where availability is provided by replicating individual data blocks three times. The assumption that all hardware fails is a core principle for Hadoop, so it was designed to run on less expensive hardware.

You may look at this section's heading and say, "Of course Hadoop is inexpensive. Open source software is free!" Well, if you're a hobbyist programmer, then yes, you may download and play with Hadoop for free. But if you're an enterprise that's deploying Hadoop in places where it's delivering business value, you can't get by with a hobbyist mentality; you need an enterprise-ready software license and a support contract to boot. The bottom line is that although a respectable Hadoop distribution will cost you license and support fees, these expenses for Hadoop are far lower than for large relational database technologies.

On the three-legged stool of IT solution costs, we've covered only the hardware and software legs. One other critical ingredient is services, or *skills*. When Hadoop was younger, fewer people had Hadoop skills, so folks were seeing major shortages of trained personnel. Also, Hadoop was a more difficult platform to use a few years ago, which made the skills shortage even more acute. The open source community has made progress in improving Hadoop's usability — most significantly with Hive. People with SQL skills — a large contingent of IT professionals — can now query data using a SQL dialect that's becoming increasingly compatible with SQL-92, which reduces the dependency on, for example, MapReduce skills.

Hadoop Has an Active Open Source Community

Whenever an organization invests in a software package, a key consideration is the long-term relevance of the software it bought. No business wants to purchase software licenses and build specific skills around technologies that will be either obsolete or irrelevant in the coming months and years.

In that regard, you don't need to worry about Hadoop. The Apache Hadoop project is on the path of long-term adoption and relevance. Its key projects have dozens of *committers* (see below) and hundreds of developers contributing code. Though a few of these people are academics or hobbyists, the majority of them are paid by enterprise software companies to help grow the Hadoop platform.

Since the Hadoop community projects are part of the Apache Software Foundation (ASF), here's a bit of background. The ASF provides the key ingredients for a community to manage the development and release of a software project. For example, the ASF features a governance structure to ensure an open and democratic approach to evolving the project; an issue tracking framework to manage bugs and new feature development; and a software license that encourages easy adoption and future innovation.

Anyone can be a contributor for an Apache project. In fact, projects with large numbers of developers representing diverse interests contributing code are considered the healthiest. To ensure code integrity and that development is being done according to the project's democratically agreed upon direction, it's only the project's committers that have write access to the project's code repository. A *committer* is a special role that the Project Management Committee (PMC) votes to assign to contributors who have shown both deep expertise and personal investment. The PMC itself is made up of committers who are effectively the stewards of the Apache project, voting on its overall direction, major features, and releases.

In addition to the large numbers of individual people contributing to Hadoop projects, a significant number of software companies are actively investing top development talent in growing the Apache Hadoop ecosystem, including larger IT companies such as IBM, Intel, Microsoft, and Yahoo! but also a multitude of smaller and younger companies — most notably, Cloudera, Hortonworks, Facebook, and MapR.

Along with the number of committers, contributors, and companies funding open source development work, the number of recently filed bug reports is an excellent indicator of technology uptake. All reasonably sophisticated software will inevitably have bugs, so in general the more people using the software, the more bugs will surface. Apache projects make bug reporting highly visible via the JIRA interface. If you search on the Internet for *Hadoop JIRA,* you'll quickly see dozens of bug reports opened for the Hadoop ecosystem project and others.

Hadoop Is Being Widely Adopted in Every Industry

As with the adoption of relational database technology from the 1980s and onward, Hadoop solutions are springing up in every industry. Looking at the generic use cases we describe in Chapter 2, you can easily imagine most of them having a specific application for a business in any industry.

From what we're seeing firsthand as we work with clients on building Hadoop solutions, most businesses with large-scale information management challenges are seriously exploring Hadoop. Broad consensus from media stories and analyst reports now indicate that almost every Fortune 500 company has embarked on a Hadoop project.

Hadoop Can Easily Scale Out As Your Data Grows

Rising data volumes are a widespread big data challenge now faced by organizations. In highly competitive environments where analytics is increasingly becoming the deciding factor in determining winners and losers, being able to analyze those increasing volumes of data is becoming a high priority. Even now, most traditional data processing tools, such as databases and statistical packages, require larger scale hardware (more memory, disk, and CPU cores) to handle the increasing data volumes. This scale-up approach is limiting and cost-ineffective, given the need for expensive components.

In contrast to the scale-up model, where faster and higher capacity hardware is added to a single server, Hadoop is designed to *scale out* with ease by adding data nodes. These data nodes, representing increased cluster storage capacity and processing power, can easily be added on the fly to an active cluster. There are some software solutions using a scale-out model, but they often have complex dependencies and require application logic to change when resources are added or subtracted. Hadoop applications have no dependencies on the layout of racks or data nodes and require no changes as the numbers of active nodes change.

Traditional Tools Are Integrating with Hadoop

With increased adoption, businesses are coming to depend on Hadoop and are using it to store and analyze critical data. With this trend comes an appetite for the same kinds of data management tools that people are accustomed to having for their traditional data sources, such as a relational database. Here are some of the more important application categories where we're seeing integration with Hadoop:

- **Business analysis tools:** Analysts can build reports against data stored in HDFS and cataloged using Hive. (Cognos, Microstrategy, and Tableau support this tack, for example.)

- **Statistical analysis packages:** Statisticians can apply their models on large data sets stored in HDFS and have that processing be pushed down to the Hadoop cluster to be run on the data nodes, where the data is stored. (For example, both SAS and SPSS have enabled limited push-down to MapReduce, as we discussed in Chapter 9.)

- **Data integration tools:** Data architects can enable high-speed data exchange between Hadoop and relational databases, and varying degrees of being able to push down transformation logic to the Hadoop cluster. (For example, both IBM DataStage and Informatica have parallel connectors to Hadoop enabling high speed data transfer and varying degrees of ability to have custom data transformation algorithms execute on the data nodes.)

Hadoop Can Store Data in Any Format

One feature of Hadoop reflects a key NoSQL principle: Store data first, and apply any schemas after it is queried. (For more on the ideas behind NoSQL, check out Chapter 11.) One major benefit that accrues to Hadoop from acting in accordance with this principle is that you can literally store any kind of data in Hadoop: completely unstructured, binary formats, semistructured log files, or relational data. But along with this flexibility comes a curse: After you store data, you eventually want to analyze it — and analyzing messy data can be difficult and time consuming. The good news here is that increasing numbers of tools can mitigate the analysis challenges commonly seen in large, messy data sets.

Hadoop Is Designed to Run Complex Analytics

You can not only store just about anything in Hadoop but also run just about any kind of algorithm against that data. The machine learning models and libraries included in Apache Mahout are prime examples, and they can be used for a variety of sophisticated problems, including classifying elements based on a large set of training data.

Hadoop Can Process a Full Data Set (As Opposed to Sampling)

For fraud-analysis types of use cases (see Chapter 2), industry data from multiple sources indicates that less than 3 percent of all returns and claims are audited. Granted, in many circumstances, such as election polling, analyzing small sample sets of data is useful and sufficient. But when 97 percent of returns and claims are unaudited, even with good sampling rules, many fraudulent returns still occur. By being able to run fraud analysis against the entire corpus of data, you now get to decide whether to sample.

Hardware Is Being Optimized for Hadoop

One of the more interesting Hadoop-related news items we've recently read is that Intel is now a player in the Hadoop distribution market. This new strategy raised many eyebrows: "What's a hardware manufacturer doing selling software?" This move by Intel was a shrewd one because its distribution work shows the seriousness and commitment behind its open source integration efforts. With Hadoop, Intel sees a tremendous opportunity to sell more hardware. After all, Hadoop clusters can feature hundreds of nodes, all requiring processors, motherboards, RAM, and hard disk drives. Intel has been investing heavily in understanding Hadoop so that it can build Intel-specific hardware optimizations that its Hadoop contributors can integrate into open source Hadoop projects. Other major hardware vendors (such as IBM, Dell, and HP) are also actively bringing Hadoop-friendly offerings to market.

Hadoop Can Increasingly Handle Flexible Workloads (No Longer Just Batch)

During the four-year lead-up to the release of Hadoop 2, a great deal of attention was directed at solving the problem of having a single point of failure (SPOF) with the HDFS NameNode (see Chapter 4). Though this particular success was no doubt an important improvement, since it did much to enable enterprise stability, we would argue that YARN is a far more significant development (see Chapter 7). Until Hadoop 2, the only processing that could be done on a Hadoop cluster was restricted to the MapReduce framework. This was acceptable for the log analytics use cases that Hadoop was originally built for, but with increased adoption came the real need for increased flexibility.

By decoupling resource management and scheduling responsibilities and implementing them in a generic framework, YARN can provision and manage a wider variety of processing models. At the time Hadoop 2 was released, MapReduce was still the only production-ready framework available. But active projects exist for in-memory processing, streaming data analysis, graph analysis, and much more.

The following statement is, for us, the perfect closing note for this book: We're about to see Hadoop become a truly multipurpose, flexible data processing engine. Where it once could support only batch workloads, it can now support real-time queries, and even a completely different processing approach by analyzing streaming data while it's still in motion.

Index